Pierced

Also by Jerry Scott and Jim Borgman

Zits: Sketchbook 1
Growth Spurt: Zits Sketchbook 2
Don't Roll Your Eyes at Me, Young Man!: Zits Sketchbook 3
Are We an "Us"?: Zits Sketchbook 4
Zits Unzipped: Zits Sketchbook 5
Busted!: Zits Sketchbook 6
Road Trip: Zits Sketchbook 7
Teenage Tales: Zits Sketchbook No. 8
Thrashed: Zits Sketchbook No. 9
Pimp My Lunch: Zits Sketchbook No. 10
Are We Out of the Driveway Yet? Zits Sketchbook No. 11
Rude, Crude, and Tattooed: Zits Sketchbook No. 12

Treasuries
Humongous Zits
Big Honkin' Zits
Zits: Supersized
Random Zits
Crack of Noon
Alternative Zits
Jeremy and Mom

Pierced

A ZITS® CLOSE-UP
BY JERRY SCOTT
AND JIM BORGMAN

**Andrews McMeel
Publishing, LLC**

Kansas City

Zits® is syndicated internationally by King Features Syndicate, Inc. For information, write King Features Syndicate, Inc., 300 West Fifty-Seventh Street, New York, New York 10019.

08 09 10 11 12 BAM 10 9 8 7 6 5 4 3 2 1

ISBN-13: 978-0-7407-7741-7
ISBN-10: 0-7407-7741-6

Library of Congress Control Number: 2008926289

Zits® may be viewed online at
www.kingfeatures.com.

www.andrewsmcmeel.com

ATTENTION: SCHOOLS AND BUSINESSES

Andrews McMeel books are available at quantity discounts with bulk purchase for educational, business, or sales promotional use. For information, please write to: Special Sales Department, Andrews McMeel Publishing, LLC, 1130 Walnut Street, Kansas City, Missouri 64106.

I drive way too fast to worry about cholesterol.
—Steven Wright

Introduction

The *Zits* years can be harrowing—ask any parent who has ever had to resod the neighbor's lawn after his or her teenager blew up the sprinkler system with a cherry bomb. In *Zits*, we try to capture some of the grit and terror of the teenage years without significantly adding to the stress levels of our already angst-filled and white-knuckled readers.

Pierce, a transfer student with a pet rat and a past that maybe we don't want to know about, began life in *Zits* as the vaguely dangerous drummer for Jeremy's band, Goat Cheese Pizza. He's one of those people that "stuff just happens to." His mother has had him GPS'd.

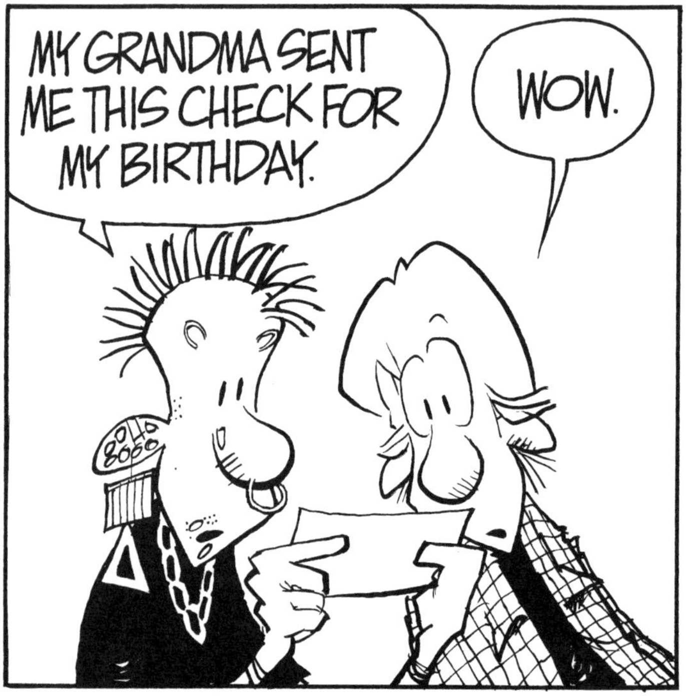
MY GRANDMA SENT ME THIS CHECK FOR MY BIRTHDAY.
WOW.

Pierce was created out of the need to have a more dangerous and reckless character on the *Zits* stage, representing all of the what-were-you-thinking nitwits of the teenage species. He is partially inspired by a kid we knew named Dan, as good-hearted a guy as you'll ever meet, who nonetheless once accidentally set his neighbor's deck on fire at 2:00 A.M. It's a long story. They all are.

As cartoonists, we can have Pierce do things our readers might be uneasy seeing Jeremy do, like throwing a party when his parents are out of town ("Who knew that seven hundred drunken teenagers would be so rowdy?") or getting the Sistine Chapel ceiling tattooed on the roof of his mouth. As Jeremy's friends go, Hector is his anchor; Pierce is his roman candle.

Scientists will tell you that Pierce is living testimony to the delayed development of the prefrontal lobe. That's the part of the brain that connects action to consequence, and it is oh-so-slowly meandering toward maturity during the teenage years.

Over time we have learned that Pierce is a kid with almost limitless empathy for misfit animals, who will take on a second summer job to buy his Madagascar hissing cockroach anger management therapy. He worries that his pet centipede has restless leg syndrome. Pierce's instinct for kindness is rivaled only by his appetite for risk. Turns out he isn't so much dangerous as foolhardy and fun loving, once you get behind his armored exterior. It's a fine line, but parents cling to such distinctions.

And beneath that face of silver lies a heart of gold.

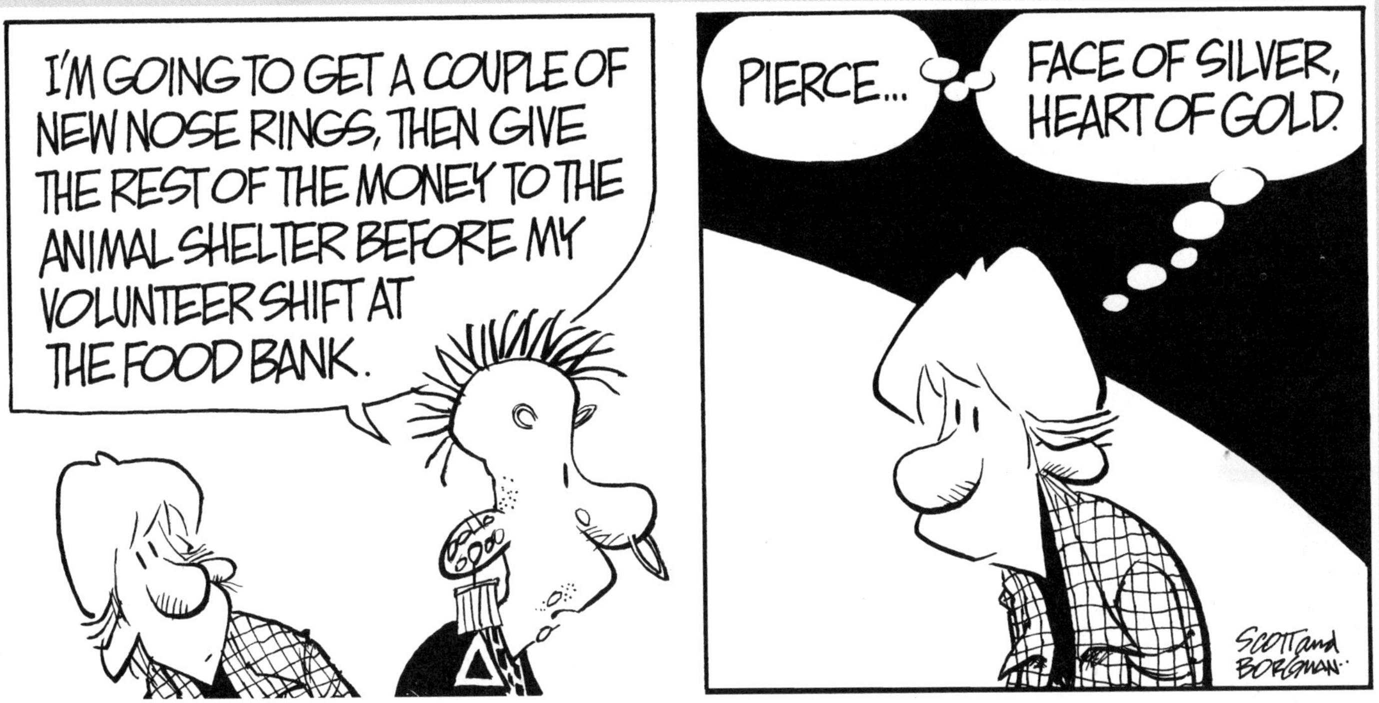
I'M GOING TO GET A COUPLE OF NEW NOSE RINGS, THEN GIVE THE REST OF THE MONEY TO THE ANIMAL SHELTER BEFORE MY VOLUNTEER SHIFT AT THE FOOD BANK.
PIERCE...
FACE OF SILVER, HEART OF GOLD.
SCOTT and BORGMAN

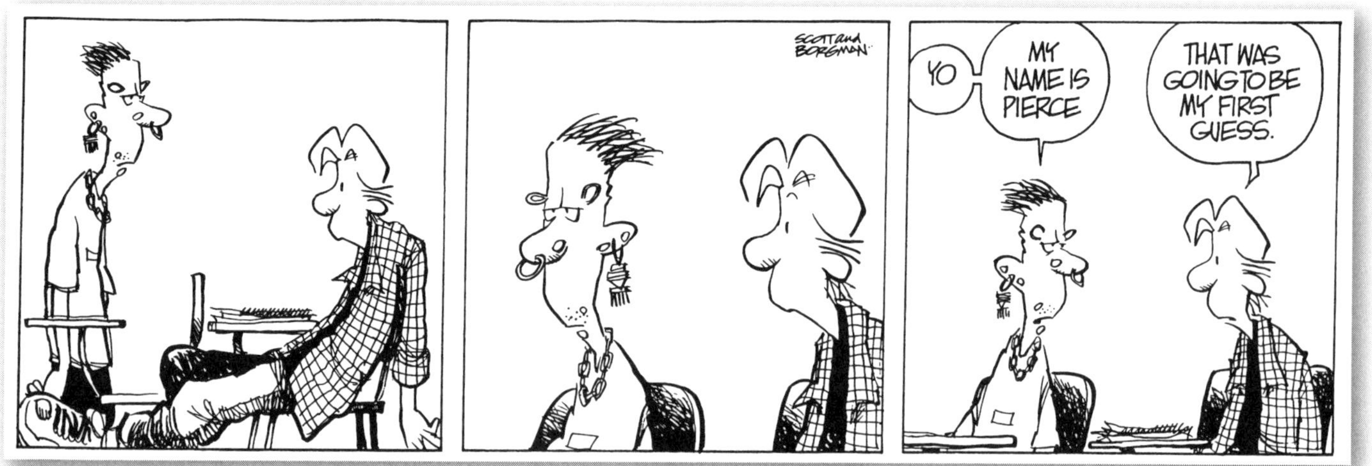
SCOTT and BORGMAN
YO
MY NAME IS PIERCE
THAT WAS GOING TO BE MY FIRST GUESS.

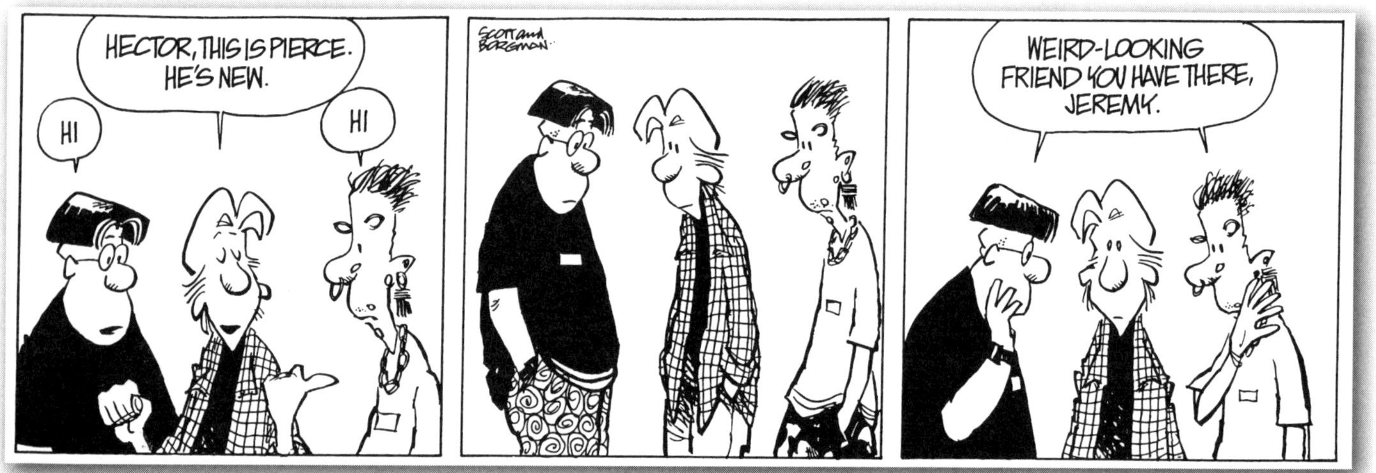
HI
HECTOR, THIS IS PIERCE. HE'S NEW.
HI
SCOTT and BORGMAN
WEIRD-LOOKING FRIEND YOU HAVE THERE, JEREMY.

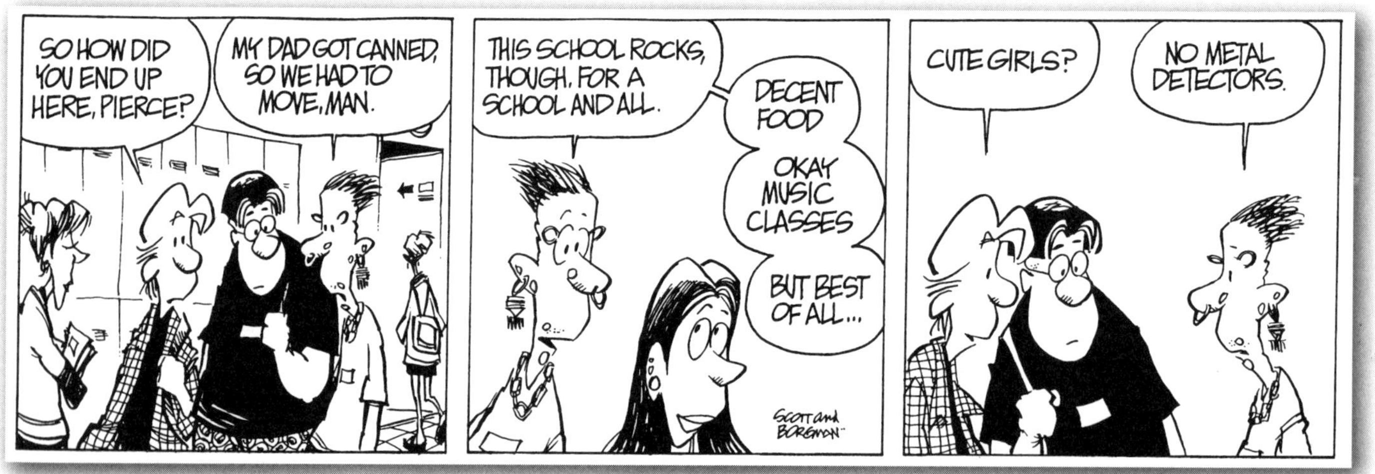
SO HOW DID YOU END UP HERE, PIERCE?
MY DAD GOT CANNED, SO WE HAD TO MOVE, MAN.
THIS SCHOOL ROCKS, THOUGH. FOR A SCHOOL AND ALL.
DECENT FOOD
OKAY MUSIC CLASSES
BUT BEST OF ALL...
SCOTT and BORGMAN
CUTE GIRLS?
NO METAL DETECTORS.

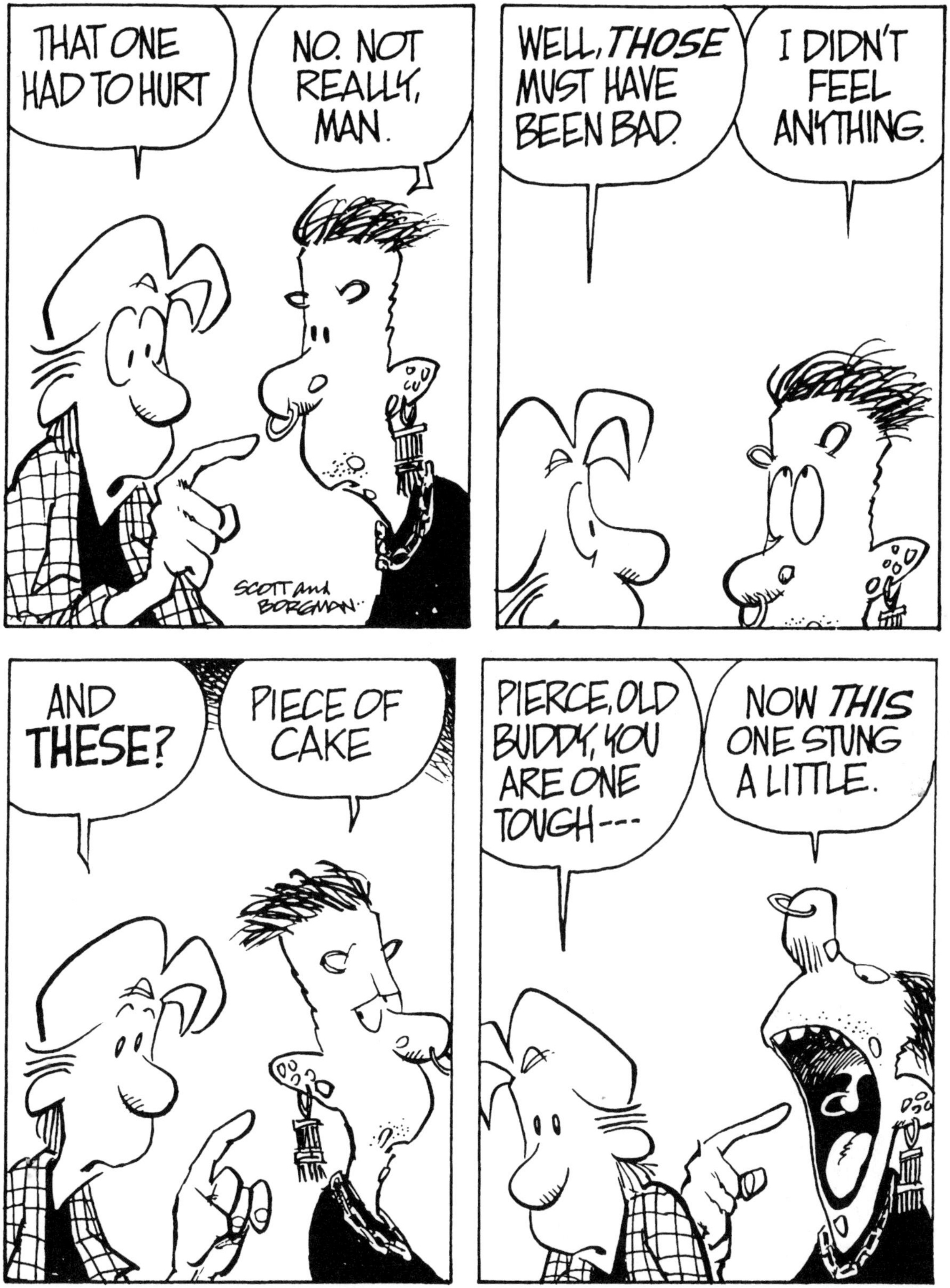
THAT ONE HAD TO HURT
NO. NOT REALLY, MAN.
SCOTT and BORGMAN
WELL, THOSE MUST HAVE BEEN BAD.
I DIDN'T FEEL ANYTHING.
AND THESE?
PIECE OF CAKE
PIERCE, OLD BUDDY, YOU ARE ONE TOUGH---
NOW THIS ONE STUNG A LITTLE.

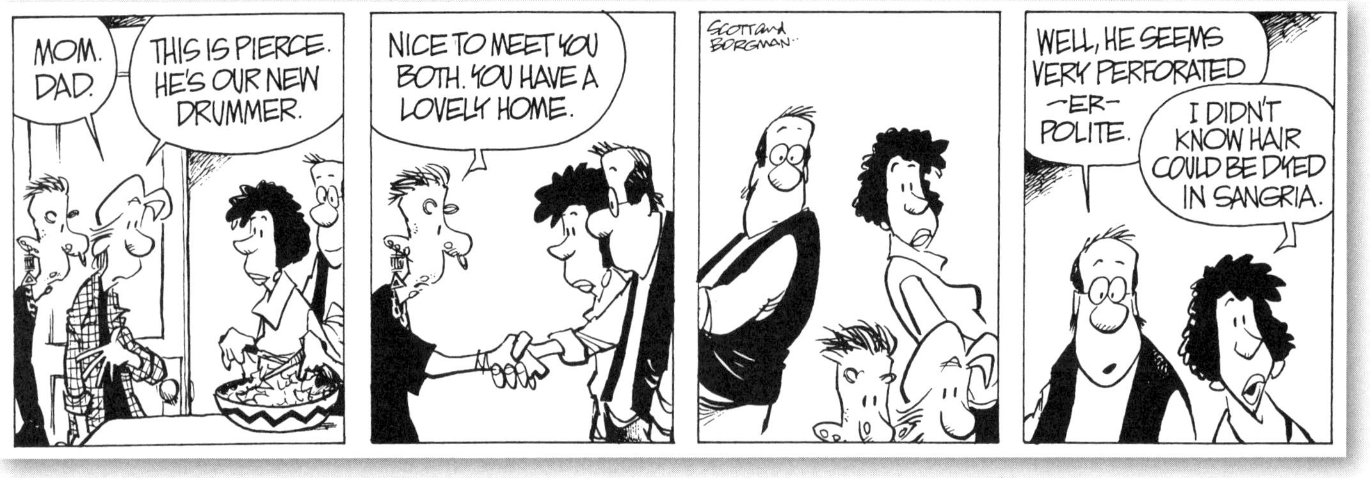
MOM. DAD.
THIS IS PIERCE. HE'S OUR NEW DRUMMER.
NICE TO MEET YOU BOTH. YOU HAVE A LOVELY HOME.
SCOTT and BORGMAN
WELL, HE SEEMS VERY PERFORATED —ER— POLITE.
I DIDN'T KNOW HAIR COULD BE DYED IN SANGRIA.

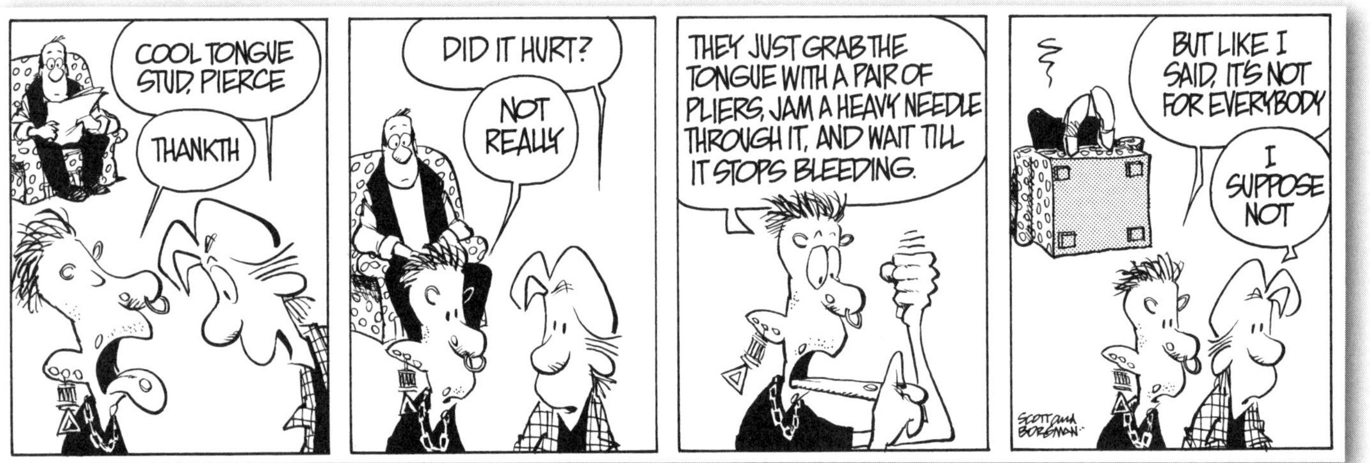
COOL TONGUE STUD, PIERCE
THANKTH
DID IT HURT?
NOT REALLY
THEY JUST GRAB THE TONGUE WITH A PAIR OF PLIERS, JAM A HEAVY NEEDLE THROUGH IT, AND WAIT TILL IT STOPS BLEEDING.
BUT LIKE I SAID, IT'S NOT FOR EVERYBODY
I SUPPOSE NOT
SCOTT and BORGMAN

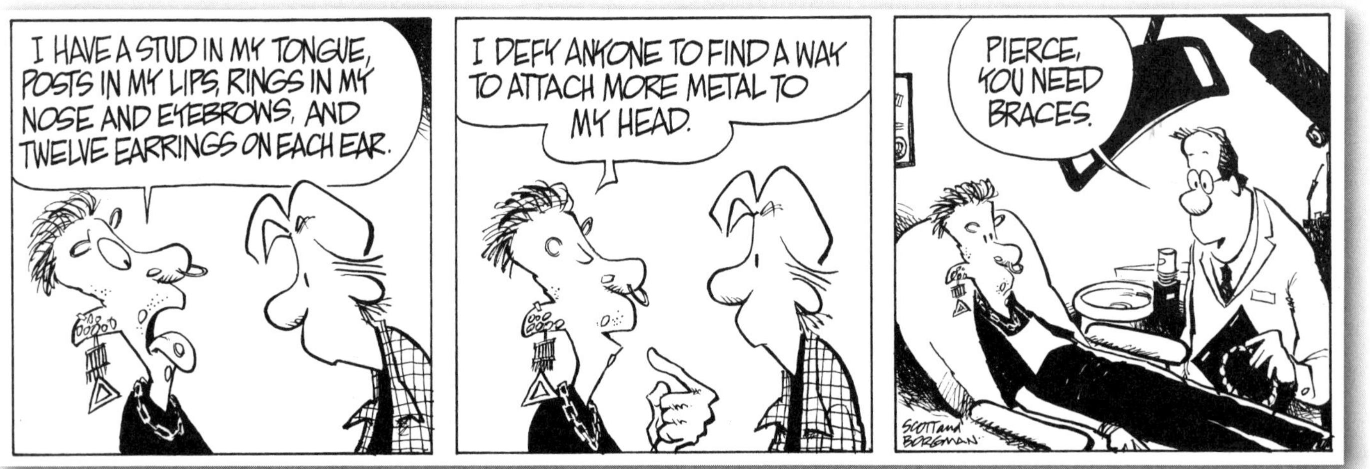
I HAVE A STUD IN MY TONGUE, POSTS IN MY LIPS, RINGS IN MY NOSE AND EYEBROWS, AND TWELVE EARRINGS ON EACH EAR.
I DEFY ANYONE TO FIND A WAY TO ATTACH MORE METAL TO MY HEAD.
PIERCE, YOU NEED BRACES.
SCOTT and BORGMAN

Zits
by JERRY SCOTT and JIM BORGMAN

GREAT. MY PHONE BATTERY IS DEAD!
DUDE.
DO YOU WANT TO CALL FROM MY HOUSE, PIERCE?
YEAH. OKAY.
IT'S TOO BAD THAT TECHNOLOGY IS STILL SO LIMITED.
I KNOW.
THERE SHOULD BE SOME KIND OF SYSTEM IN PLACE THAT WOULDN'T REQUIRE PEOPLE TO CARRY PHONES AROUND WHEREVER THEY GO.
YEAH!
LIKE COMMUNICATION CENTERS PLACED IN AREAS WHERE PEOPLE CONGREGATE.
AND THERE WOULD BE INDIVIDUAL GLASS ENCLOSURES WHERE YOU COULD MAKE A CALL IN PRIVACY.
LIKE A PHONE BOOTH?
SCOTT and BORGMAN
CATCHY TERM
I CAN'T BELIEVE NOBODY'S EVER THOUGHT OF IT BEFORE.
PROGRESS MOVES SO SLOWLY.

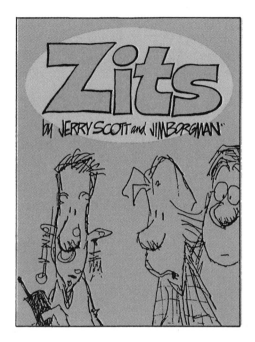

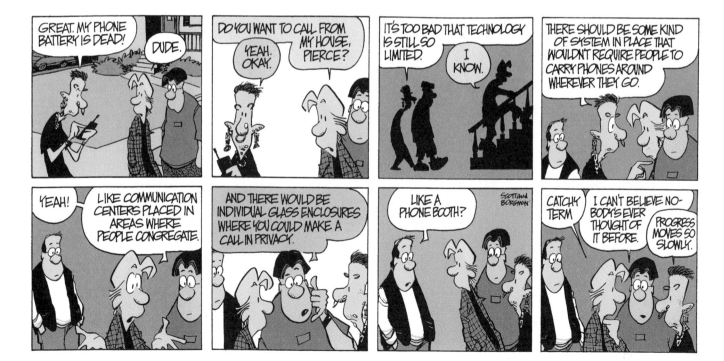

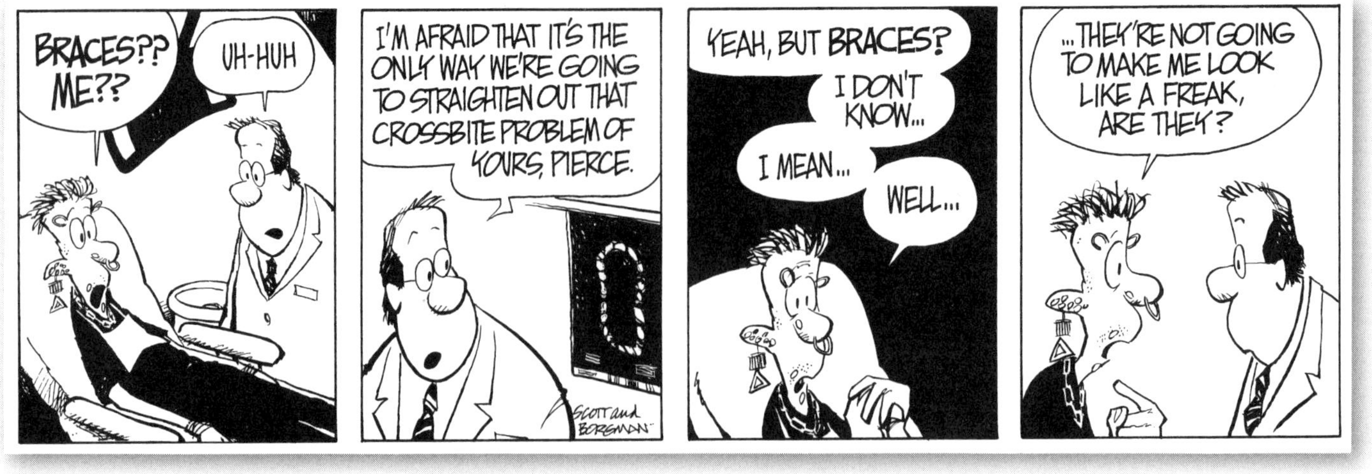
BRACES?? ME??
UH-HUH
I'M AFRAID THAT IT'S THE ONLY WAY WE'RE GOING TO STRAIGHTEN OUT THAT CROSSBITE PROBLEM OF YOURS, PIERCE.
SCOTT and BORGMAN
YEAH, BUT BRACES?
I DON'T KNOW...
I MEAN...
WELL...
...THEY'RE NOT GOING TO MAKE ME LOOK LIKE A FREAK, ARE THEY?

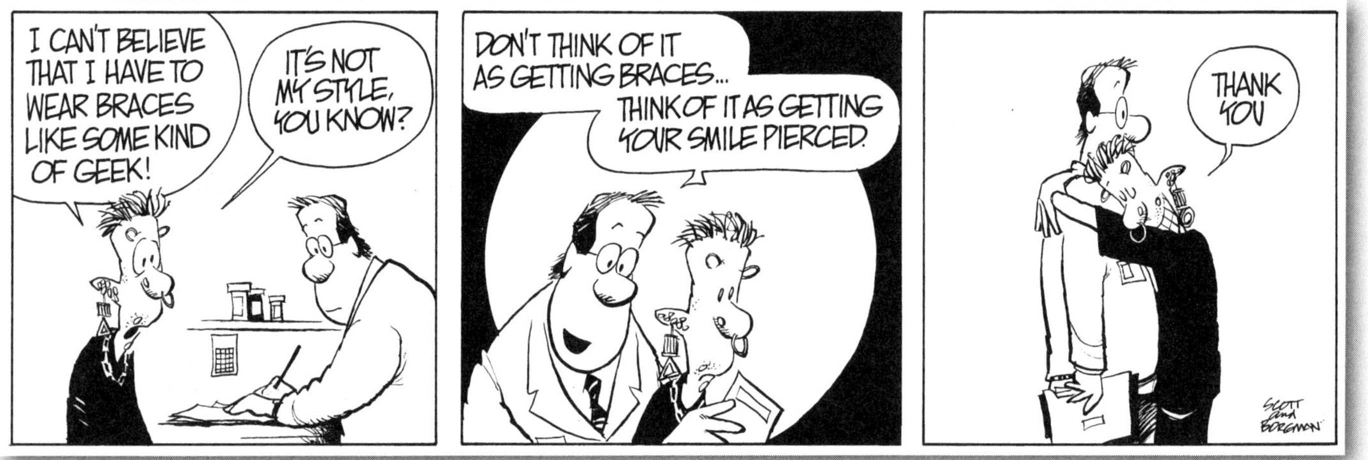
I CAN'T BELIEVE THAT I HAVE TO WEAR BRACES LIKE SOME KIND OF GEEK!
IT'S NOT MY STYLE, YOU KNOW?
DON'T THINK OF IT AS GETTING BRACES...
THINK OF IT AS GETTING YOUR SMILE PIERCED.
THANK YOU
SCOTT and BORGMAN

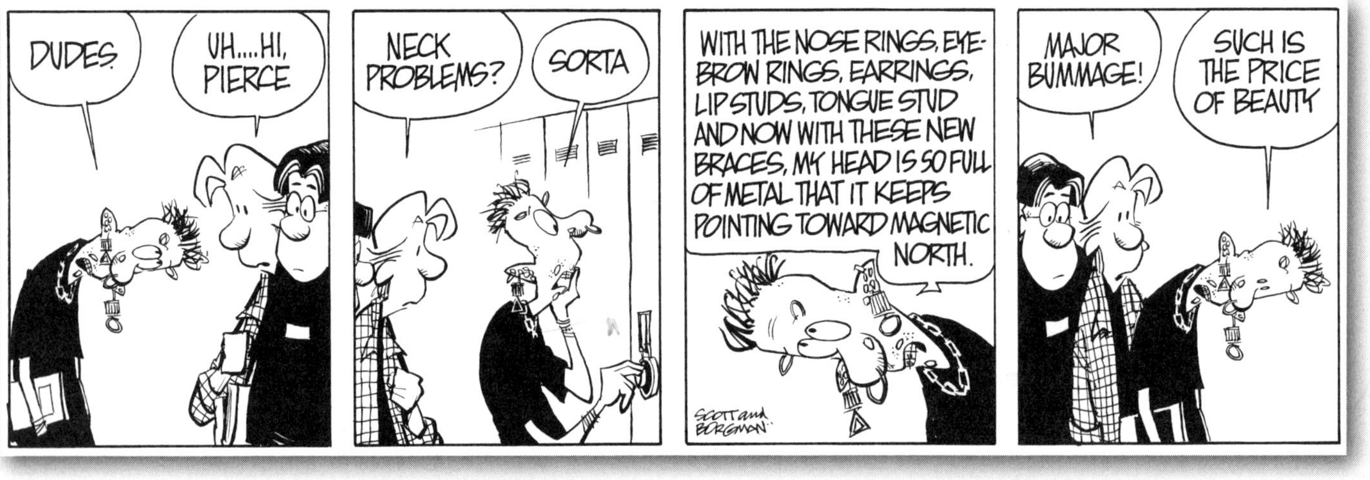
DUDES
UH....HI, PIERCE
NECK PROBLEMS?
SORTA
WITH THE NOSE RINGS, EYE-BROW RINGS, EARRINGS, LIP STUDS, TONGUE STUD AND NOW WITH THESE NEW BRACES, MY HEAD IS SO FULL OF METAL THAT IT KEEPS POINTING TOWARD MAGNETIC NORTH.
SCOTT and BORGMAN
MAJOR BUMMAGE!
SUCH IS THE PRICE OF BEAUTY

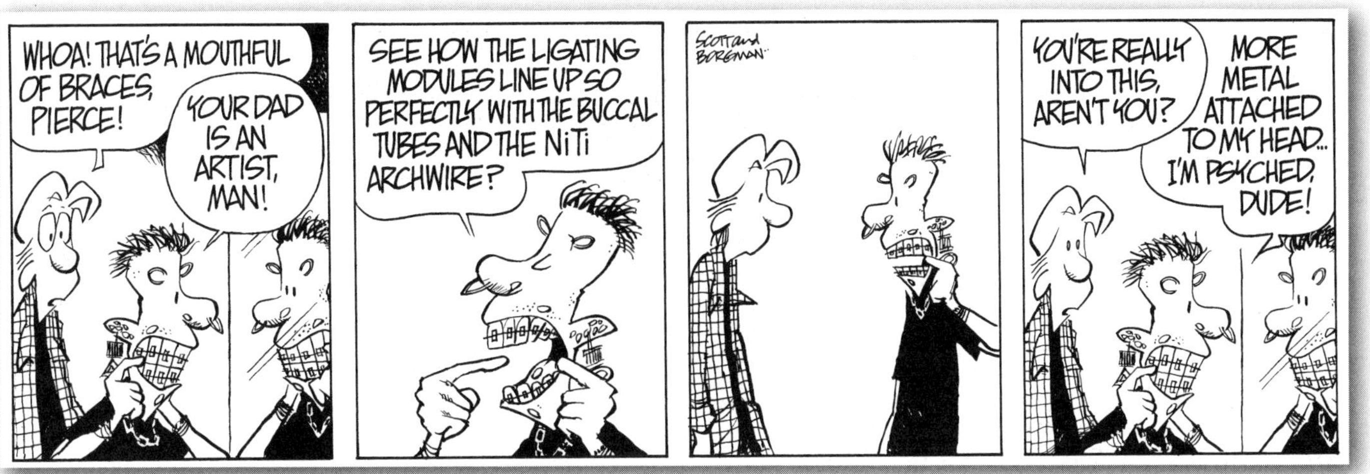
WHOA! THAT'S A MOUTHFUL OF BRACES, PIERCE!
YOUR DAD IS AN ARTIST, MAN!
SEE HOW THE LIGATING MODULES LINE UP SO PERFECTLY WITH THE BUCCAL TUBES AND THE NiTi ARCHWIRE?
SCOTT and BORGMAN
YOU'RE REALLY INTO THIS, AREN'T YOU?
MORE METAL ATTACHED TO MY HEAD... I'M PSYCHED, DUDE!

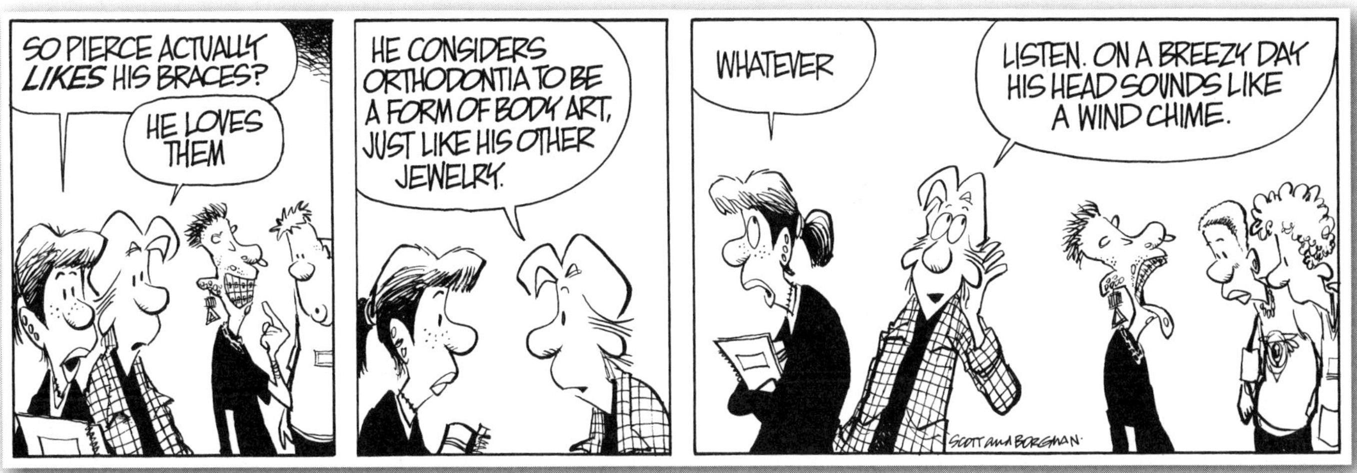
SO PIERCE ACTUALLY *LIKES* HIS BRACES?
HE LOVES THEM
HE CONSIDERS ORTHODONTIA TO BE A FORM OF BODY ART, JUST LIKE HIS OTHER JEWELRY.
WHATEVER
LISTEN. ON A BREEZY DAY HIS HEAD SOUNDS LIKE A WIND CHIME.
SCOTT and BORGMAN

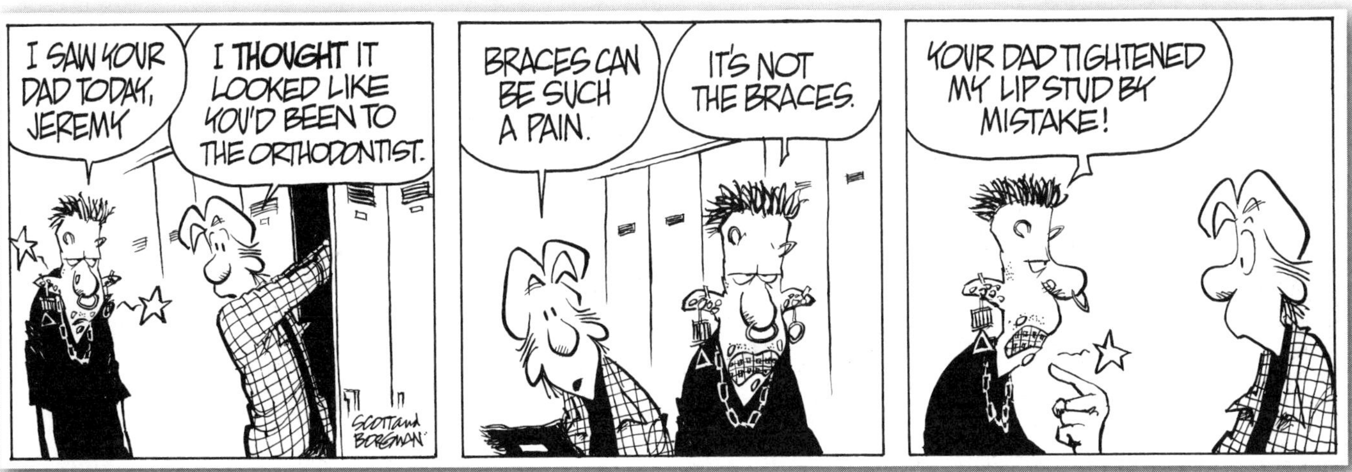
I SAW YOUR DAD TODAY, JEREMY
I **THOUGHT** IT LOOKED LIKE YOU'D BEEN TO THE ORTHODONTIST.
SCOTT and BORGMAN
BRACES CAN BE SUCH A PAIN.
IT'S NOT THE BRACES.
YOUR DAD TIGHTENED MY LIP STUD BY MISTAKE!

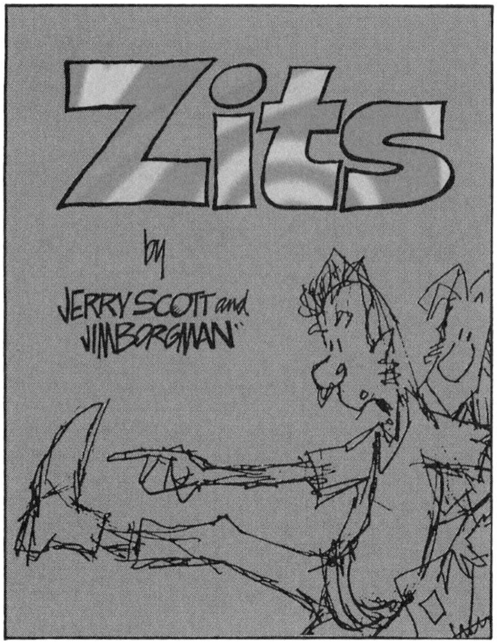
Zits
by
JERRY SCOTT and JIM BORGMAN

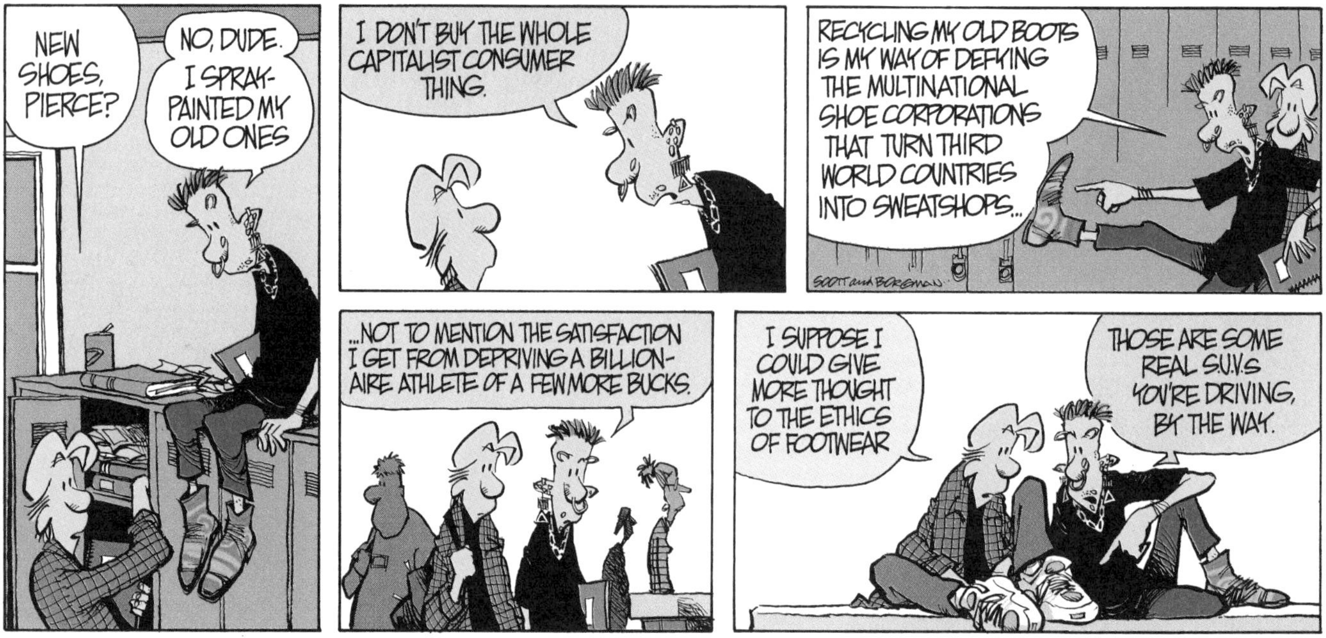
NEW SHOES, PIERCE?
NO, DUDE. I SPRAY-PAINTED MY OLD ONES
I DON'T BUY THE WHOLE CAPITALIST CONSUMER THING.
RECYCLING MY OLD BOOTS IS MY WAY OF DEFYING THE MULTINATIONAL SHOE CORPORATIONS THAT TURN THIRD WORLD COUNTRIES INTO SWEATSHOPS...
SCOTT and BORGMAN
...NOT TO MENTION THE SATISFACTION I GET FROM DEPRIVING A BILLION-AIRE ATHLETE OF A FEW MORE BUCKS.
I SUPPOSE I COULD GIVE MORE THOUGHT TO THE ETHICS OF FOOTWEAR
THOSE ARE SOME REAL S.U.V.s YOU'RE DRIVING, BY THE WAY.

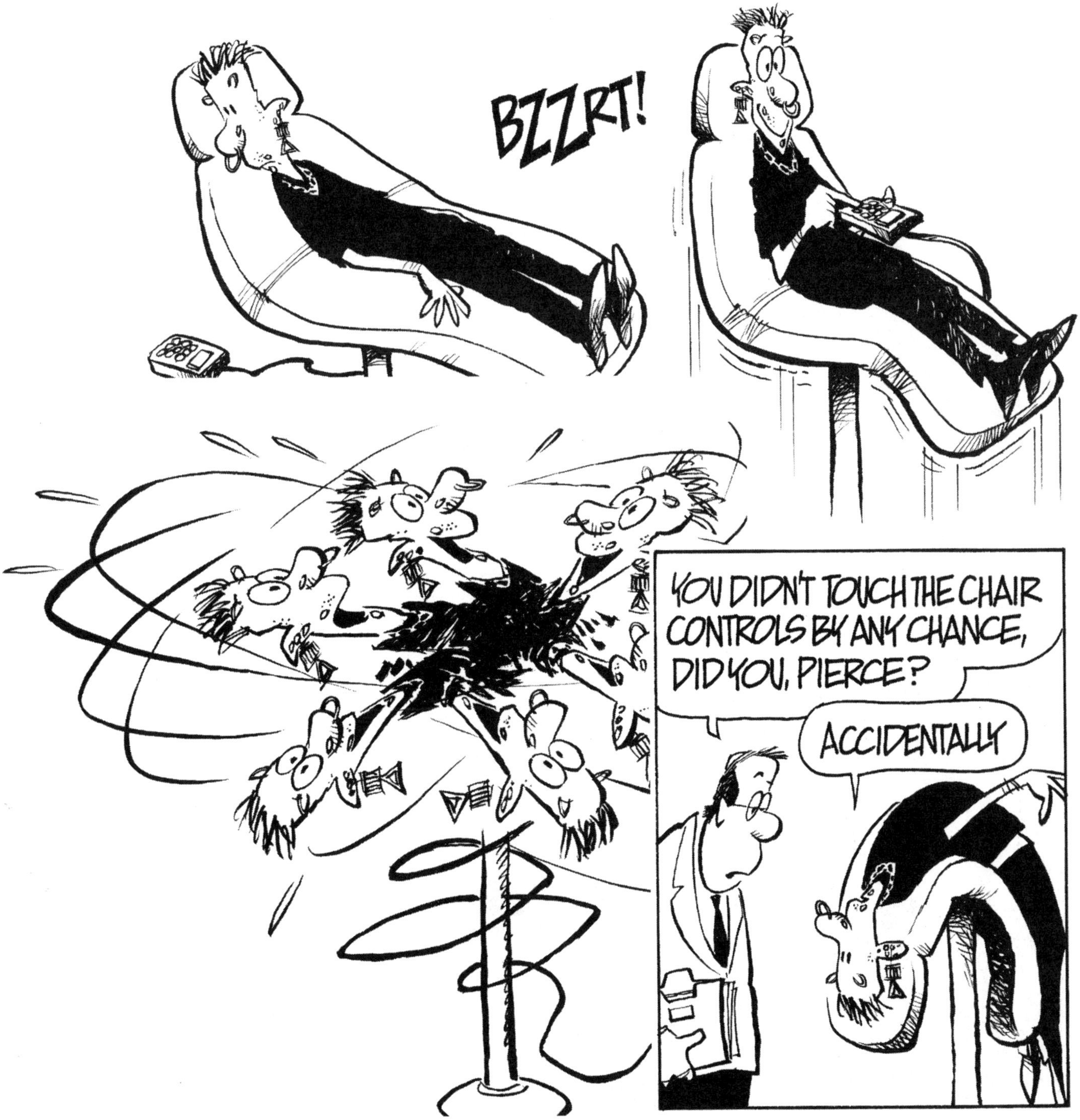
BZZRT!
YOU DIDN'T TOUCH THE CHAIR CONTROLS BY ANY CHANCE, DID YOU, PIERCE?
ACCIDENTALLY

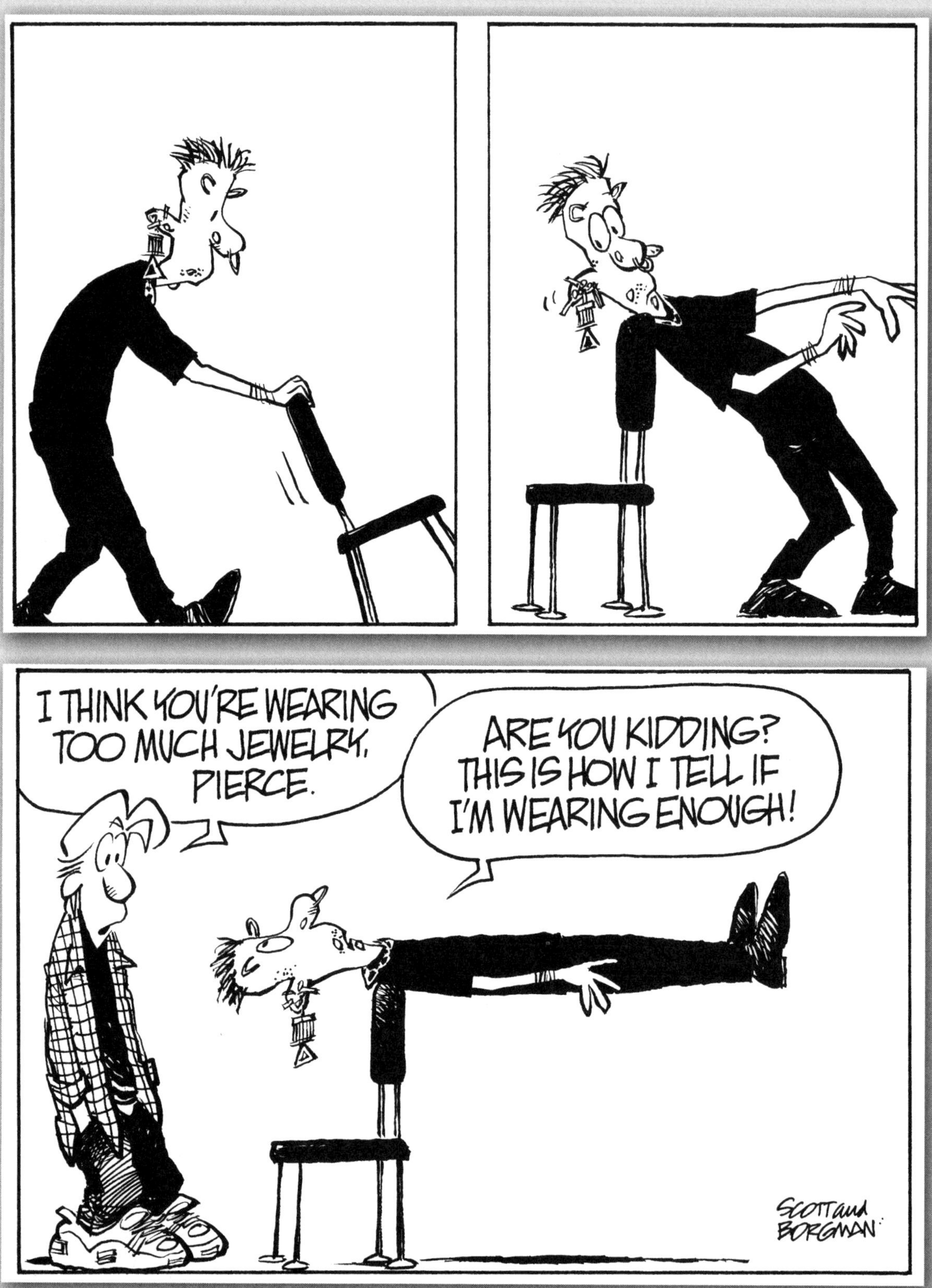
I THINK YOU'RE WEARING TOO MUCH JEWELRY, PIERCE.
ARE YOU KIDDING? THIS IS HOW I TELL IF I'M WEARING ENOUGH!
SCOTT and BORGMAN

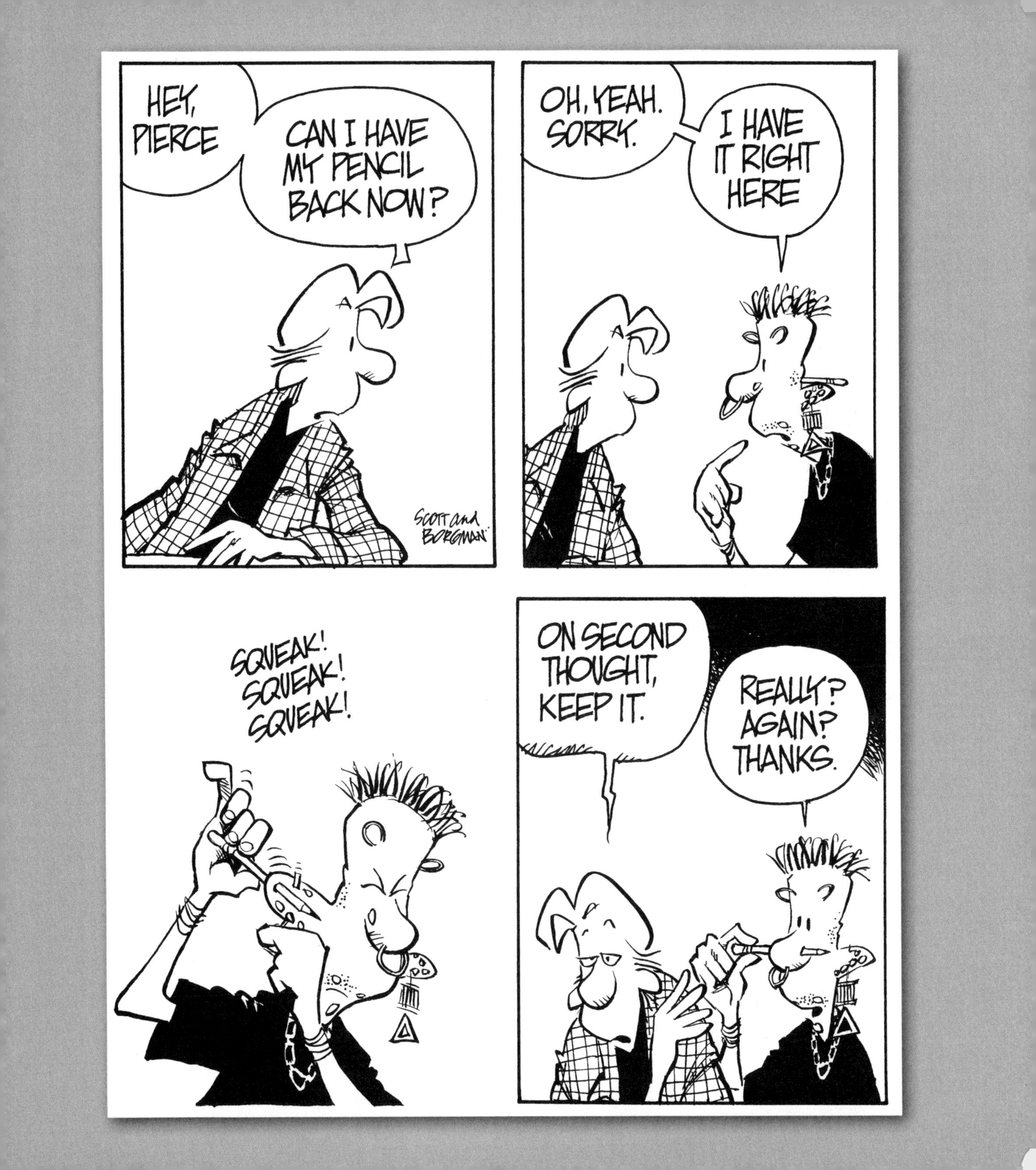
HEY, PIERCE
CAN I HAVE MY PENCIL BACK NOW?
SCOTT and BORGMAN
OH, YEAH. SORRY.
I HAVE IT RIGHT HERE
SQUEAK! SQUEAK! SQUEAK!
ON SECOND THOUGHT, KEEP IT.
REALLY? AGAIN? THANKS.

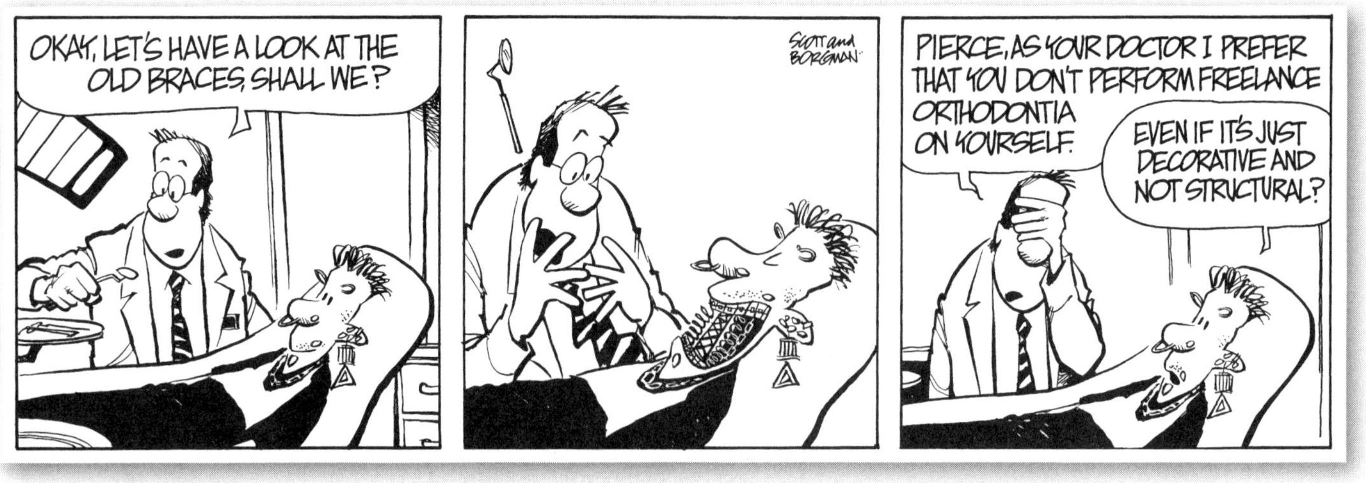
OKAY, LET'S HAVE A LOOK AT THE OLD BRACES, SHALL WE?
SCOTT and BORGMAN
PIERCE, AS YOUR DOCTOR I PREFER THAT YOU DON'T PERFORM FREELANCE ORTHODONTIA ON YOURSELF.
EVEN IF IT'S JUST DECORATIVE AND NOT STRUCTURAL?

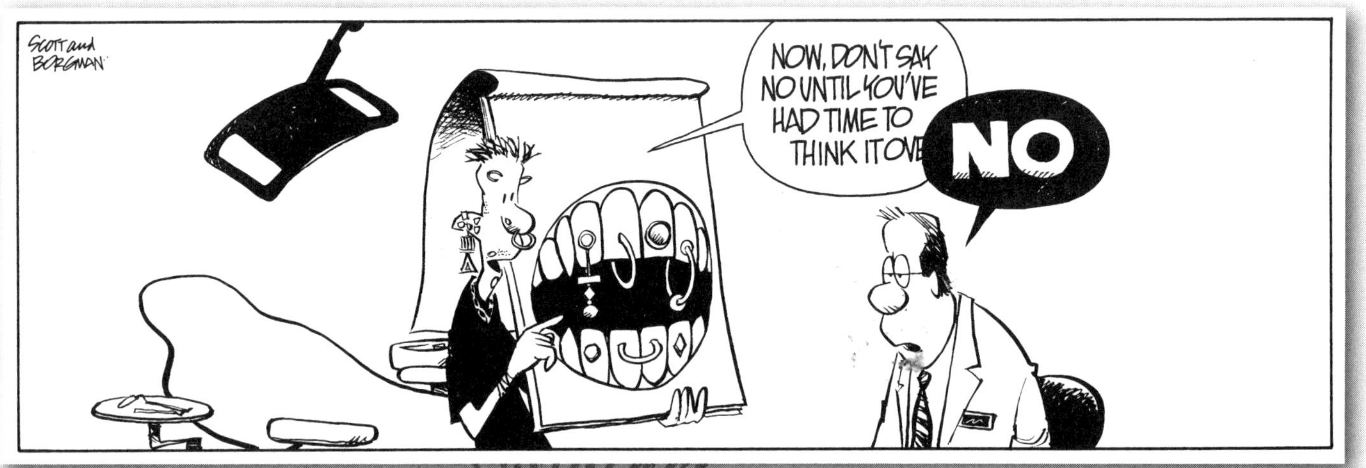
SCOTT and BORGMAN
NOW, DON'T SAY NO UNTIL YOU'VE HAD TIME TO THINK IT OVE
NO

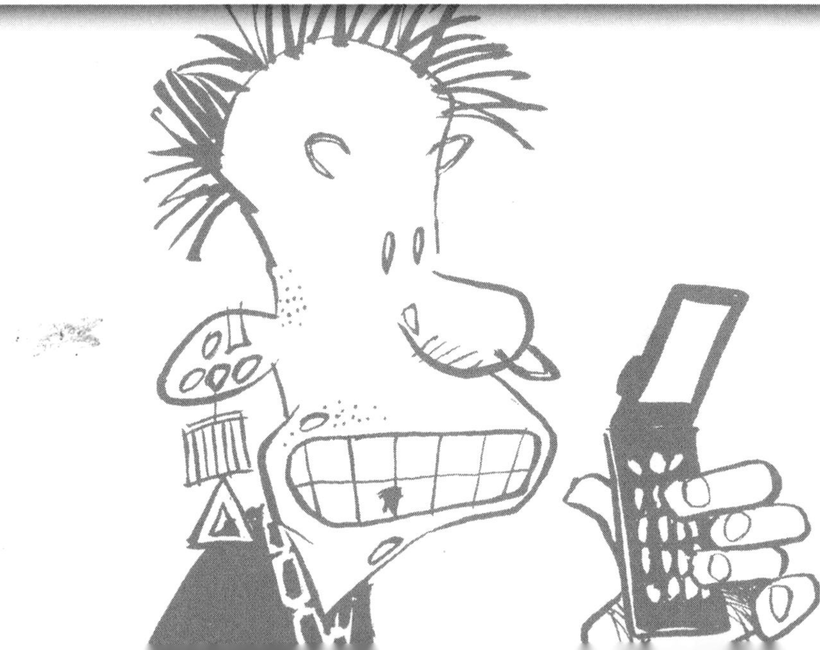

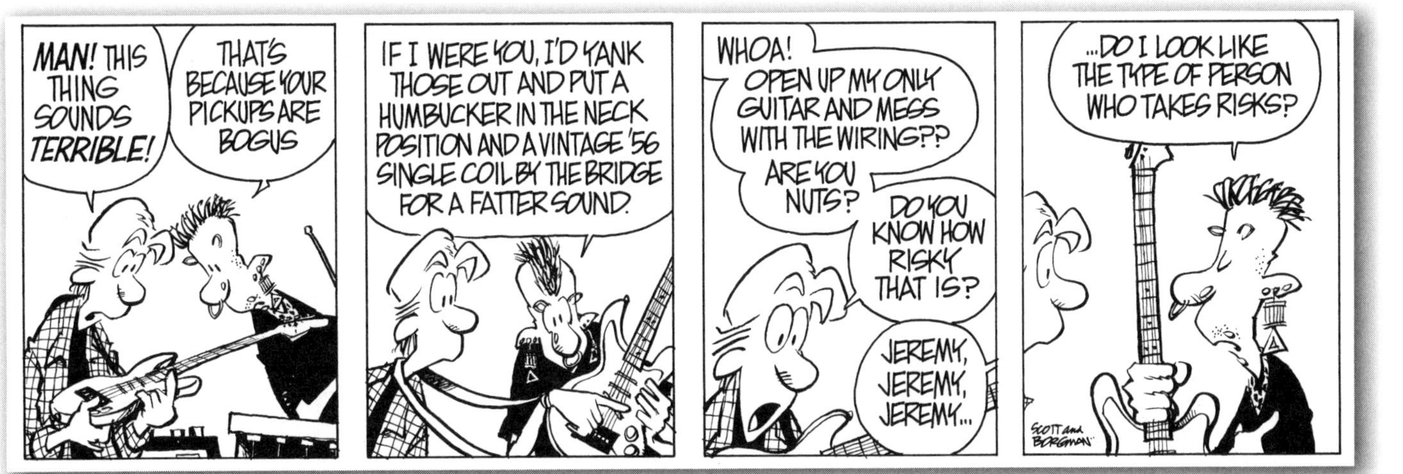
MAN! THIS THING SOUNDS TERRIBLE!
THAT'S BECAUSE YOUR PICKUPS ARE BOGUS
IF I WERE YOU, I'D YANK THOSE OUT AND PUT A HUMBUCKER IN THE NECK POSITION AND A VINTAGE '56 SINGLE COIL BY THE BRIDGE FOR A FATTER SOUND.
WHOA!
OPEN UP MY ONLY GUITAR AND MESS WITH THE WIRING??
ARE YOU NUTS?
DO YOU KNOW HOW RISKY THAT IS?
JEREMY, JEREMY, JEREMY...
...DO I LOOK LIKE THE TYPE OF PERSON WHO TAKES RISKS?
SCOTT and BORGMAN

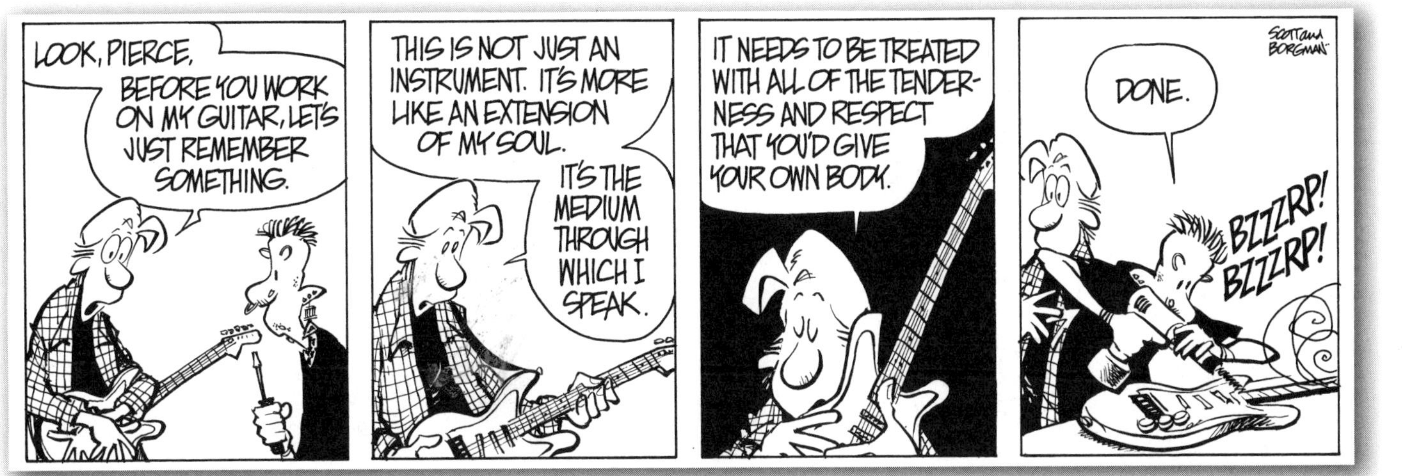
LOOK, PIERCE,
BEFORE YOU WORK ON MY GUITAR, LET'S JUST REMEMBER SOMETHING.
THIS IS NOT JUST AN INSTRUMENT. IT'S MORE LIKE AN EXTENSION OF MY SOUL.
IT'S THE MEDIUM THROUGH WHICH I SPEAK.
IT NEEDS TO BE TREATED WITH ALL OF THE TENDERNESS AND RESPECT THAT YOU'D GIVE YOUR OWN BODY.
SCOTT and BORGMAN
DONE.
BZZZRP! BZZZRP!

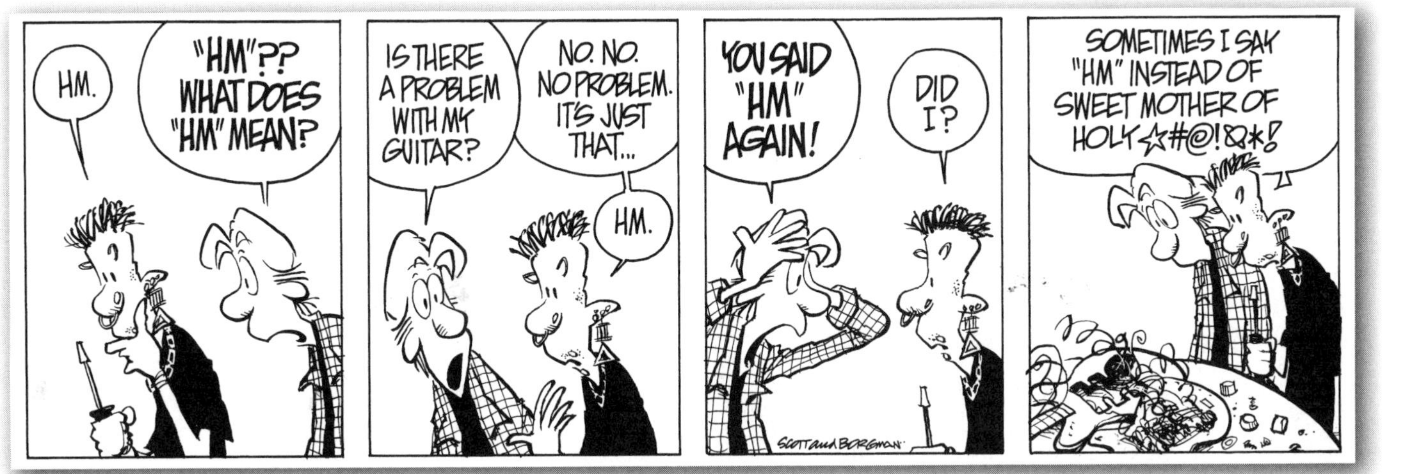
HM.
"HM"?? WHAT DOES "HM" MEAN?
IS THERE A PROBLEM WITH MY GUITAR?
NO. NO. NO PROBLEM. IT'S JUST THAT...
HM.
YOU SAID "HM" AGAIN!
DID I?
SCOTT and BORGMAN
SOMETIMES I SAY "HM" INSTEAD OF SWEET MOTHER OF HOLY☆#@!&*!

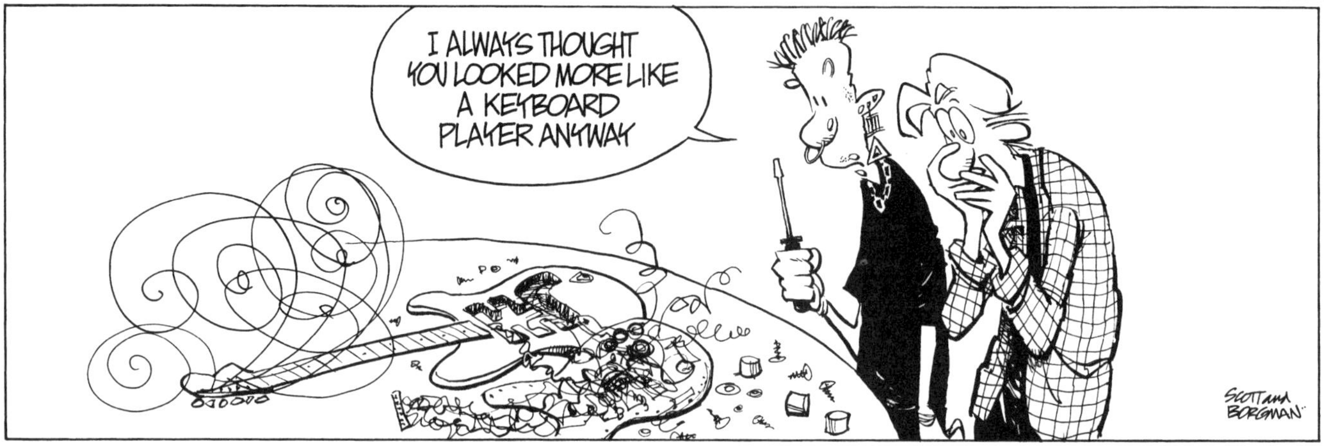
I ALWAYS THOUGHT YOU LOOKED MORE LIKE A KEYBOARD PLAYER ANYWAY
SCOTT AND BORGMAN

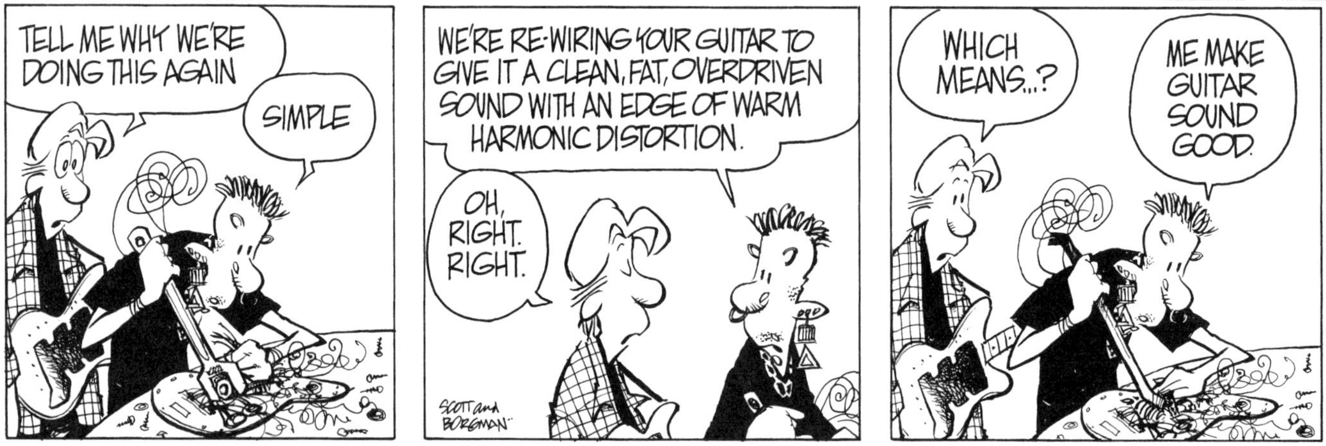
TELL ME WHY WE'RE DOING THIS AGAIN
SIMPLE
SCOTT AND BORGMAN
WE'RE RE-WIRING YOUR GUITAR TO GIVE IT A CLEAN, FAT, OVERDRIVEN SOUND WITH AN EDGE OF WARM HARMONIC DISTORTION.
OH, RIGHT. RIGHT.
WHICH MEANS...?
ME MAKE GUITAR SOUND GOOD.

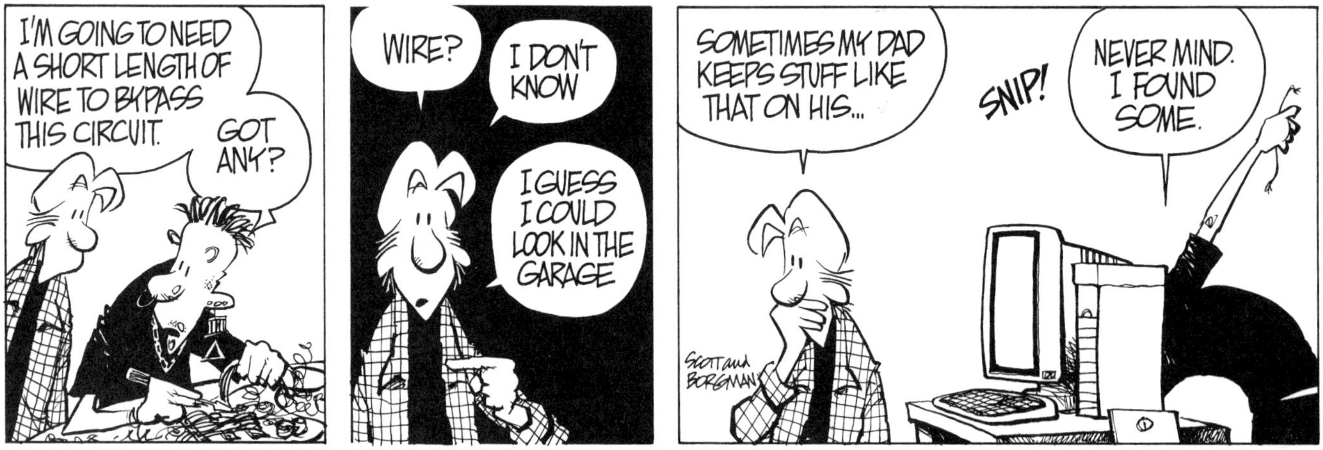
I'M GOING TO NEED A SHORT LENGTH OF WIRE TO BYPASS THIS CIRCUIT.
GOT ANY?
WIRE?
I DON'T KNOW
I GUESS I COULD LOOK IN THE GARAGE
SOMETIMES MY DAD KEEPS STUFF LIKE THAT ON HIS...
SNIP!
NEVER MIND. I FOUND SOME.
SCOTT AND BORGMAN

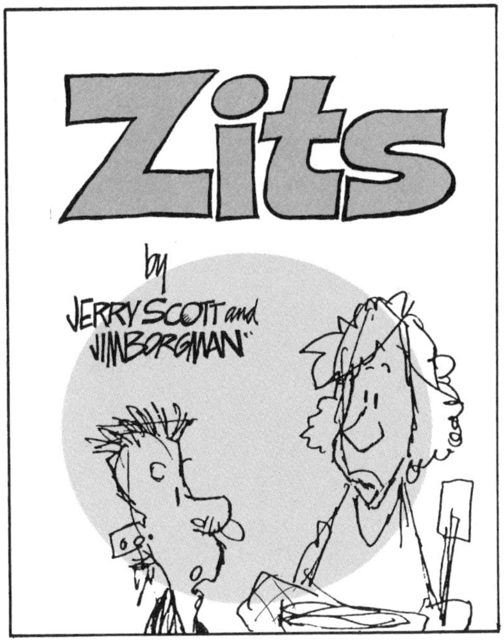
Zits
by
JERRY SCOTT and
JIM BORGMAN

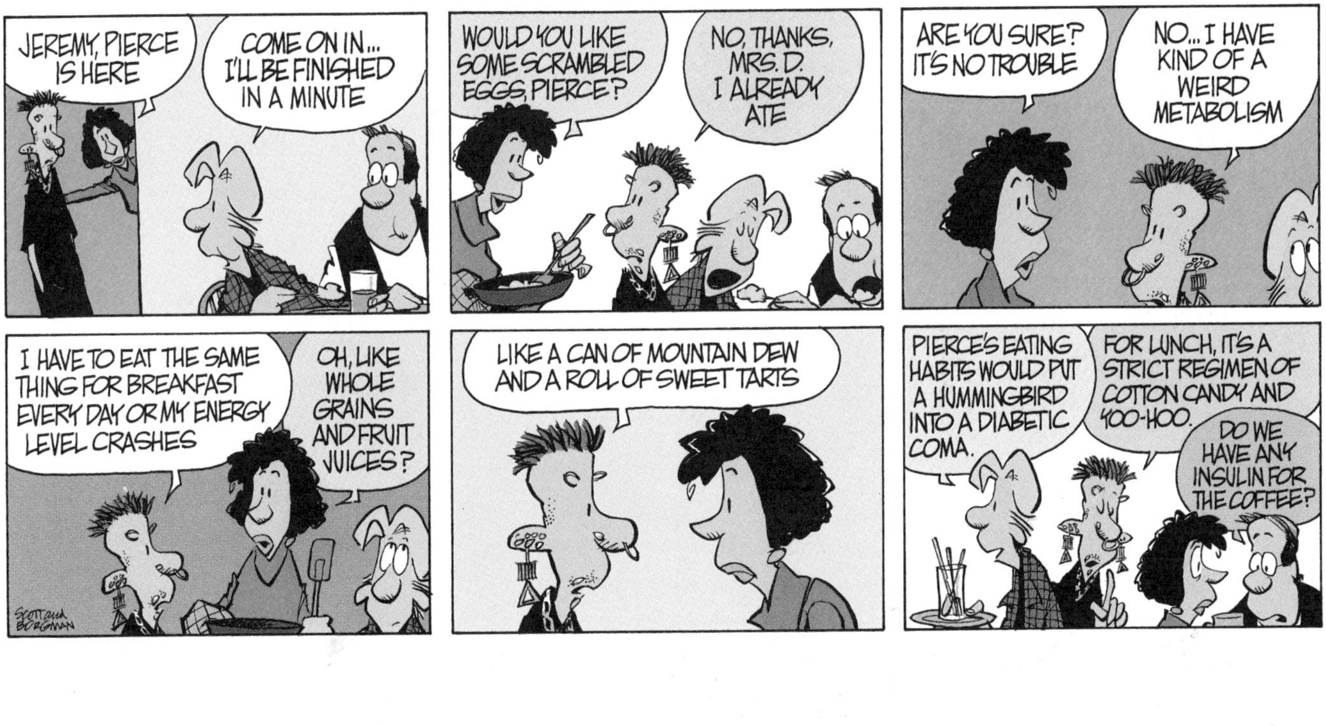
JEREMY, PIERCE IS HERE
COME ON IN... I'LL BE FINISHED IN A MINUTE
WOULD YOU LIKE SOME SCRAMBLED EGGS, PIERCE?
NO, THANKS, MRS. D. I ALREADY ATE
ARE YOU SURE? IT'S NO TROUBLE
NO... I HAVE KIND OF A WEIRD METABOLISM
I HAVE TO EAT THE SAME THING FOR BREAKFAST EVERY DAY OR MY ENERGY LEVEL CRASHES
OH, LIKE WHOLE GRAINS AND FRUIT JUICES?
LIKE A CAN OF MOUNTAIN DEW AND A ROLL OF SWEET TARTS
PIERCE'S EATING HABITS WOULD PUT A HUMMINGBIRD INTO A DIABETIC COMA.
FOR LUNCH, IT'S A STRICT REGIMEN OF COTTON CANDY AND YOO-HOO.
DO WE HAVE ANY INSULIN FOR THE COFFEE?

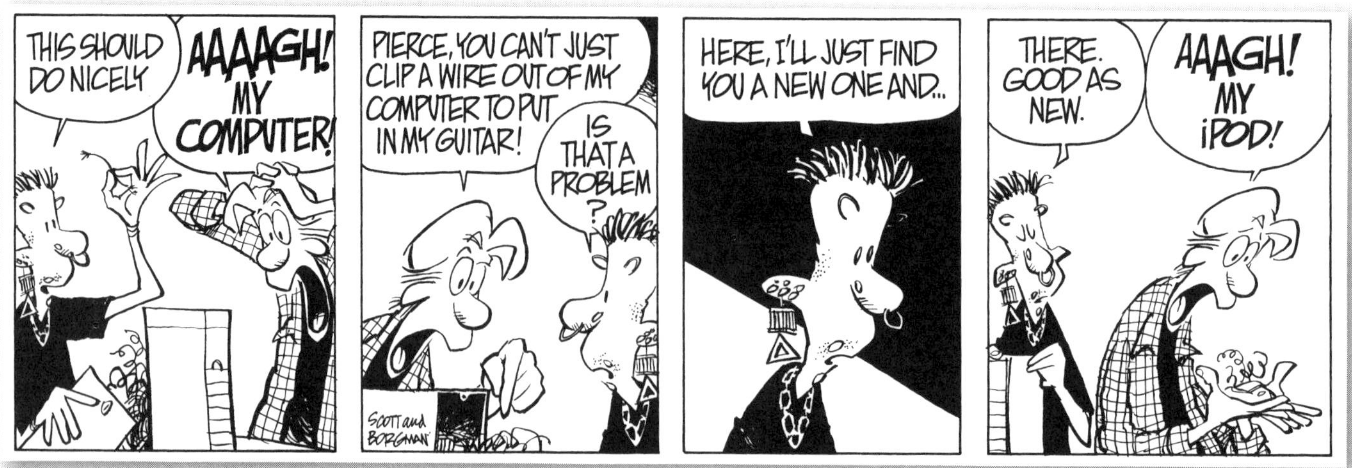
THIS SHOULD DO NICELY
AAAAGH! MY COMPUTER!
PIERCE, YOU CAN'T JUST CLIP A WIRE OUT OF MY COMPUTER TO PUT IN MY GUITAR!
IS THAT A PROBLEM?
SCOTT and BORGMAN
HERE, I'LL JUST FIND YOU A NEW ONE AND...
THERE. GOOD AS NEW.
AAAGH! MY iPOD!

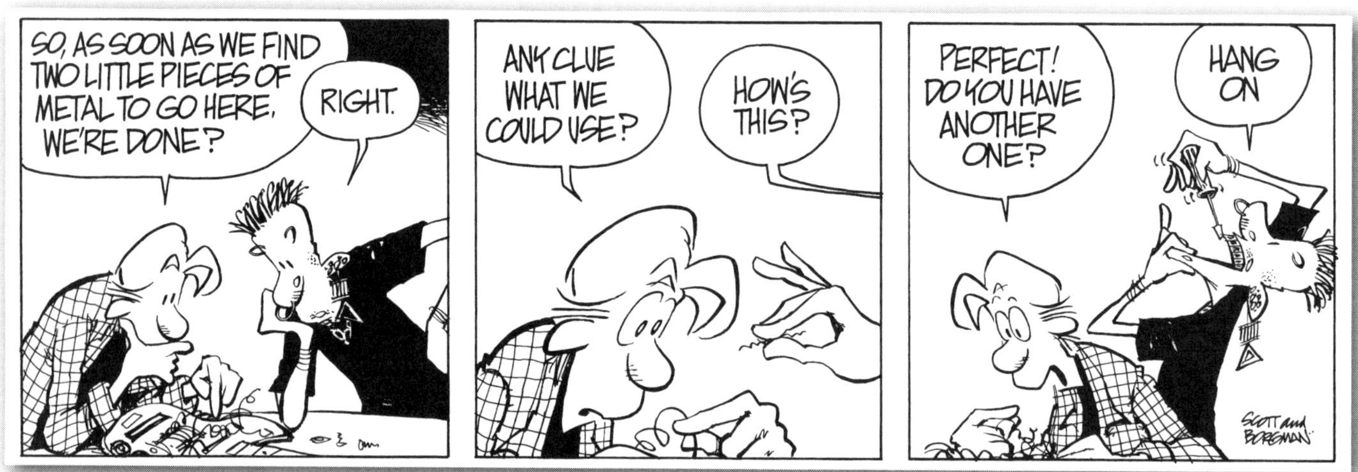
SO, AS SOON AS WE FIND TWO LITTLE PIECES OF METAL TO GO HERE, WE'RE DONE?
RIGHT.
ANY CLUE WHAT WE COULD USE?
HOW'S THIS?
PERFECT! DO YOU HAVE ANOTHER ONE?
HANG ON
SCOTT and BORGMAN

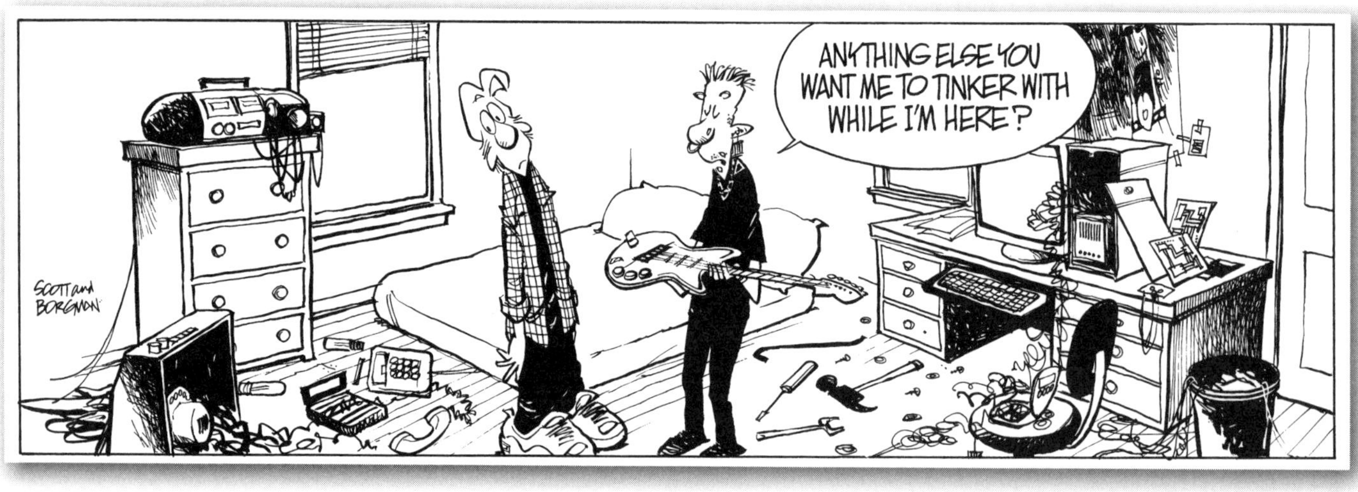
SCOTT and BORGMAN
ANYTHING ELSE YOU WANT ME TO TINKER WITH WHILE I'M HERE?

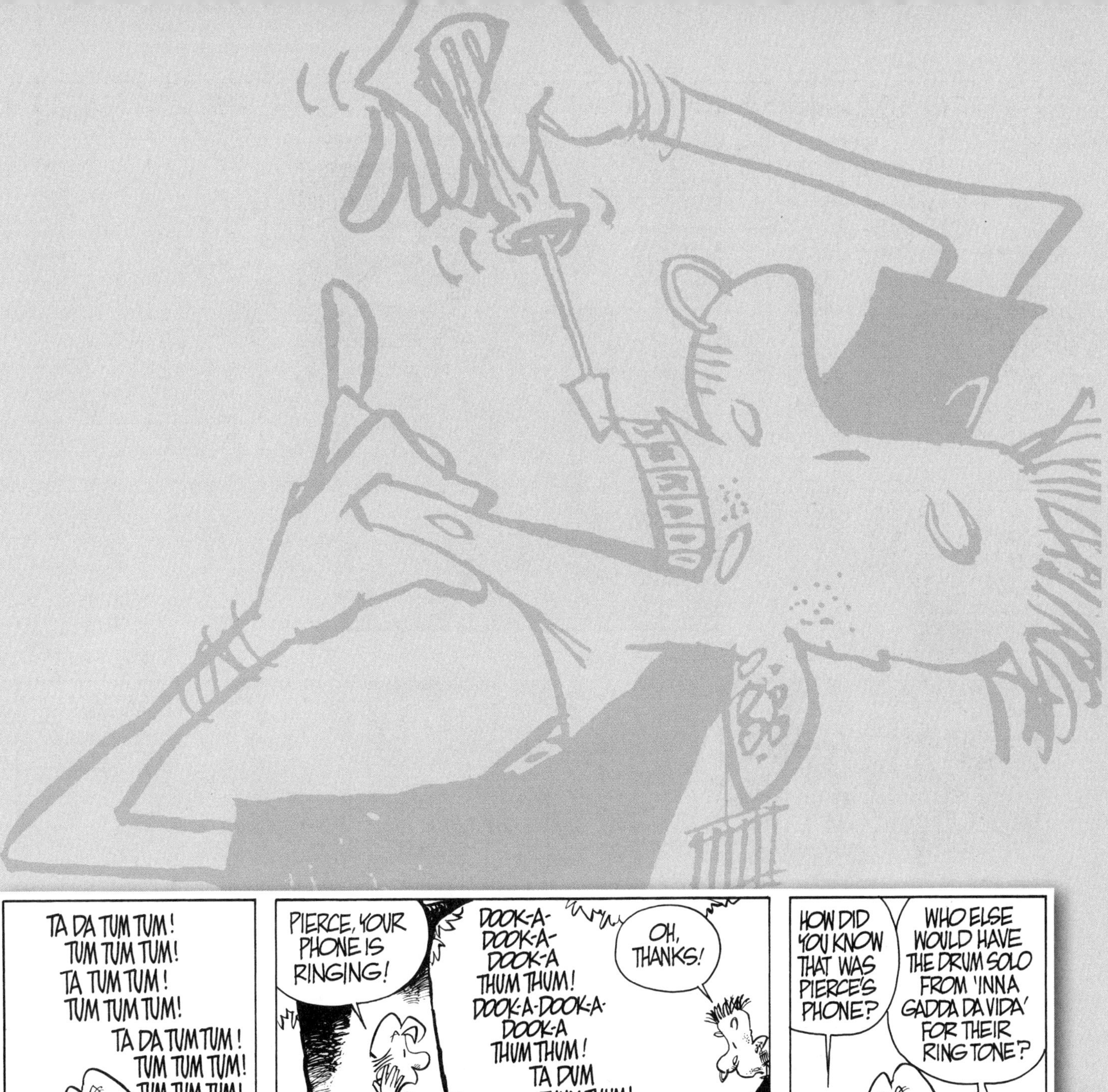

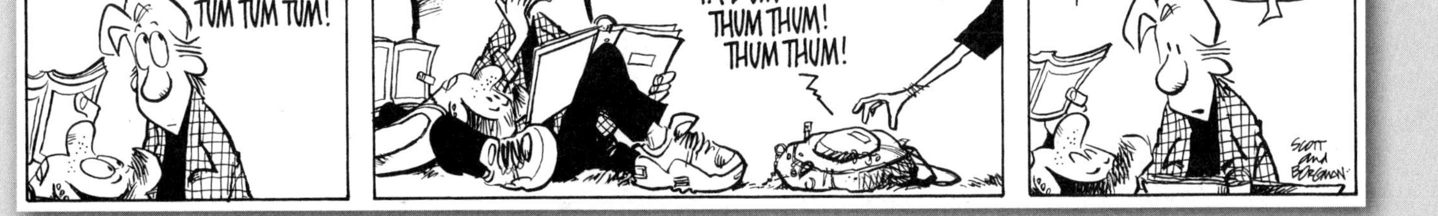
TA DA TUM TUM! TUM TUM TUM! TA TUM TUM! TUM TUM TUM! TA DA TUM TUM! TUM TUM TUM! TUM TUM TUM!
PIERCE, YOUR PHONE IS RINGING!
DOOK-A-DOOK-A-DOOK-A THUM THUM! DOOK-A-DOOK-A-DOOK-A THUM THUM! TA DUM THUM THUM! THUM THUM!
OH, THANKS!
HOW DID YOU KNOW THAT WAS PIERCE'S PHONE?
WHO ELSE WOULD HAVE THE DRUM SOLO FROM 'INNA GADDA DA VIDA' FOR THEIR RING TONE?
SCOTT and BORGMAN

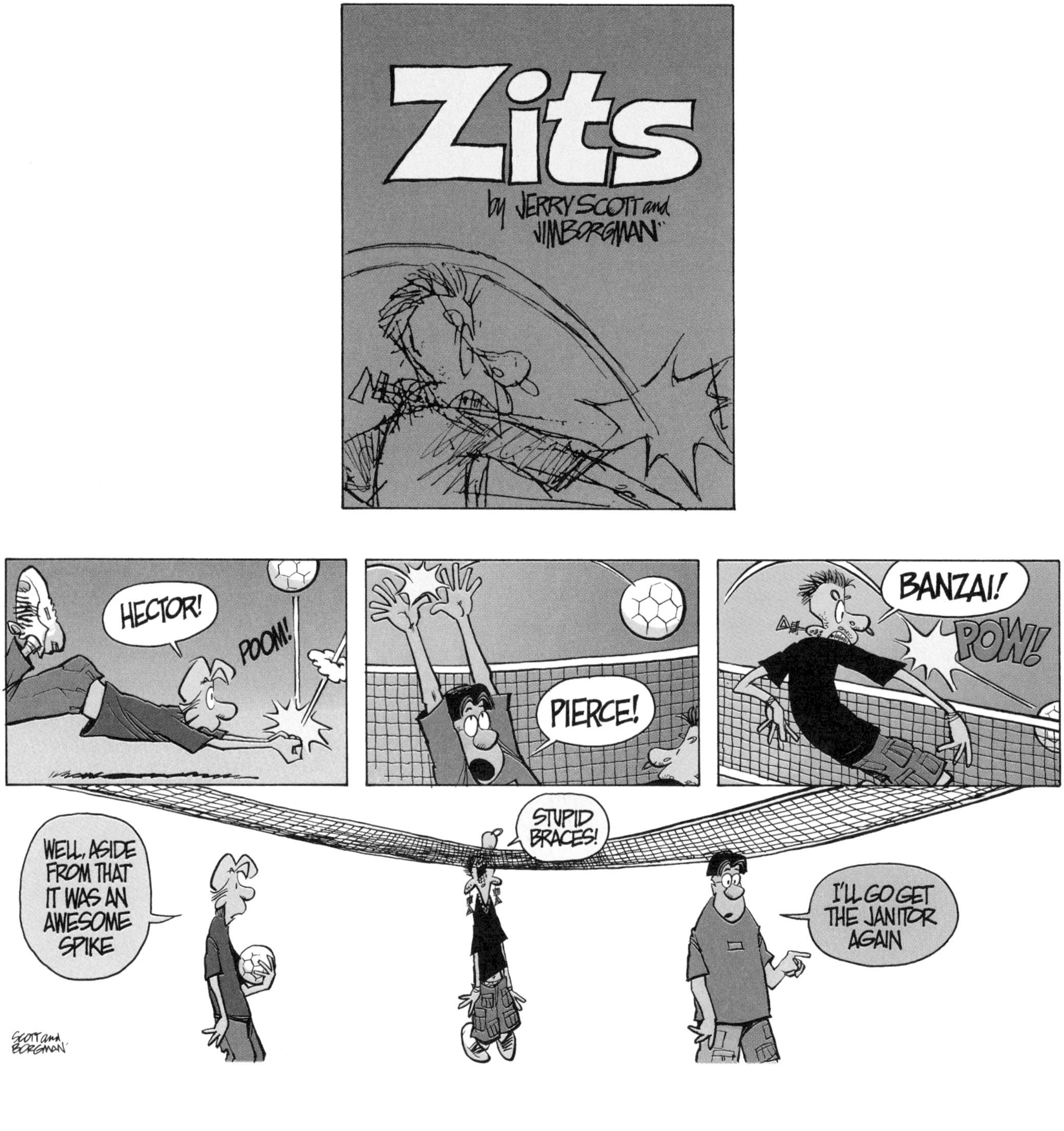
Zits
by JERRY SCOTT and JIM BORGMAN
HECTOR!
POOM!
PIERCE!
BANZAI!
POW!
WELL, ASIDE FROM THAT IT WAS AN AWESOME SPIKE
STUPID BRACES!
I'LL GO GET THE JANITOR AGAIN
SCOTT and BORGMAN

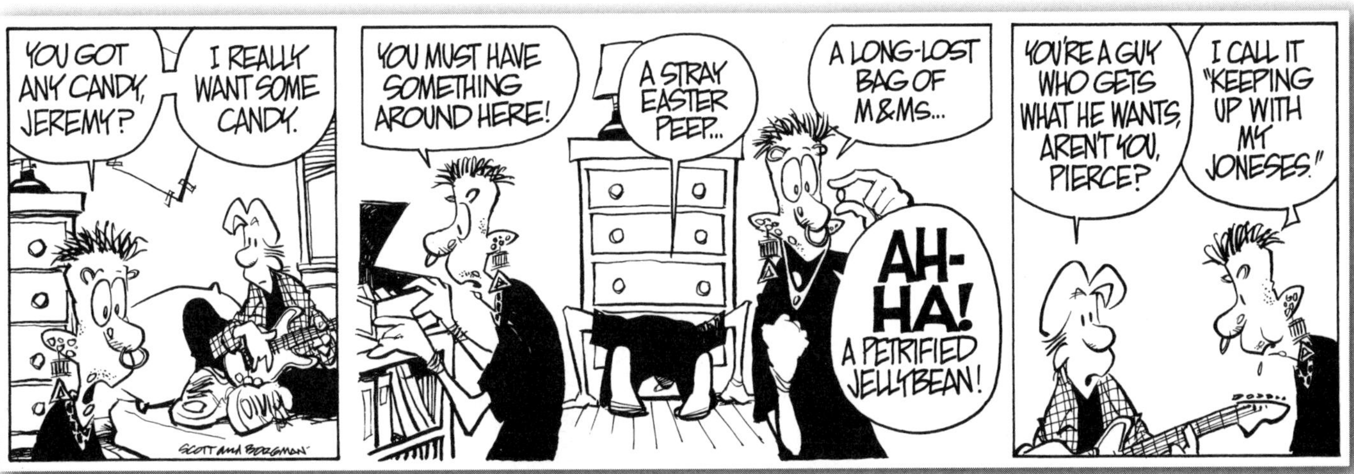
YOU GOT ANY CANDY, JEREMY?
I REALLY WANT SOME CANDY.
SCOTT AND BORGMAN
YOU MUST HAVE SOMETHING AROUND HERE!
A STRAY EASTER PEEP...
A LONG-LOST BAG OF M&MS...
AH-HA! A PETRIFIED JELLYBEAN!
YOU'RE A GUY WHO GETS WHAT HE WANTS, AREN'T YOU, PIERCE?
I CALL IT "KEEPING UP WITH MY JONESES."

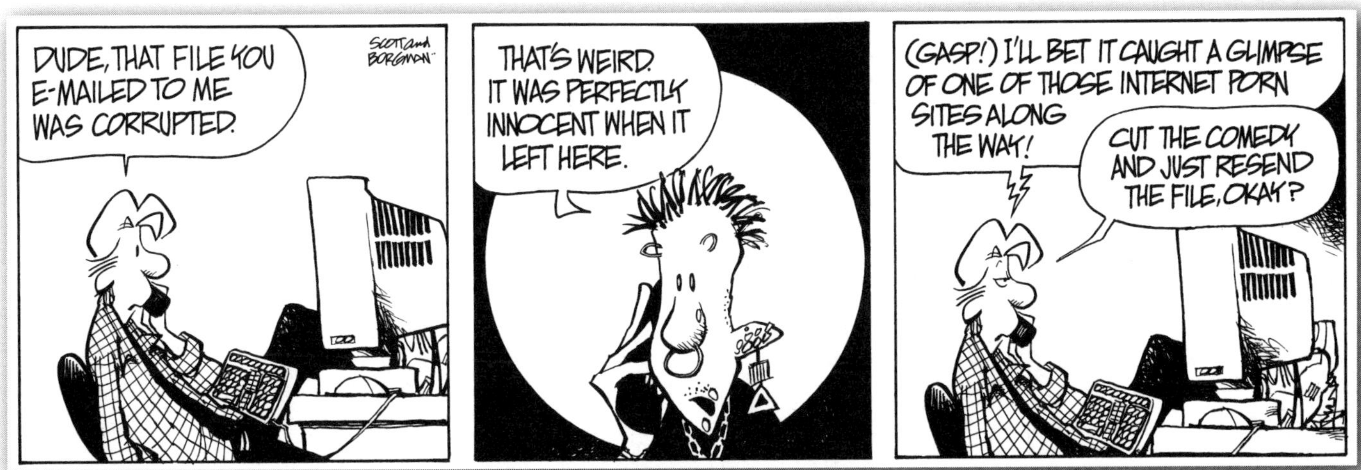
DUDE, THAT FILE YOU E-MAILED TO ME WAS CORRUPTED.
SCOTT AND BORGMAN
THAT'S WEIRD. IT WAS PERFECTLY INNOCENT WHEN IT LEFT HERE.
(GASP!) I'LL BET IT CAUGHT A GLIMPSE OF ONE OF THOSE INTERNET PORN SITES ALONG THE WAY!
CUT THE COMEDY AND JUST RESEND THE FILE, OKAY?

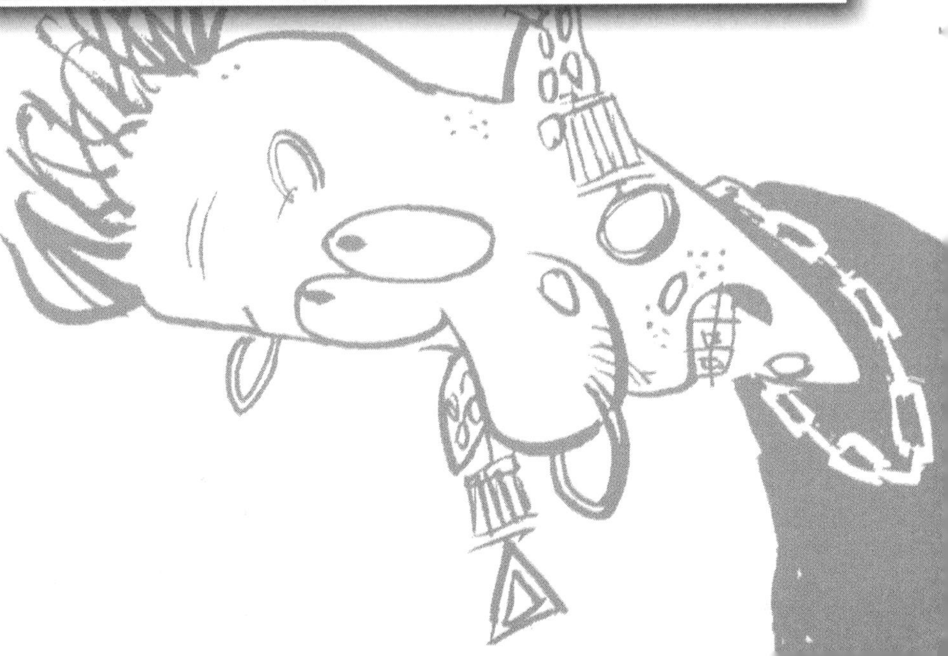

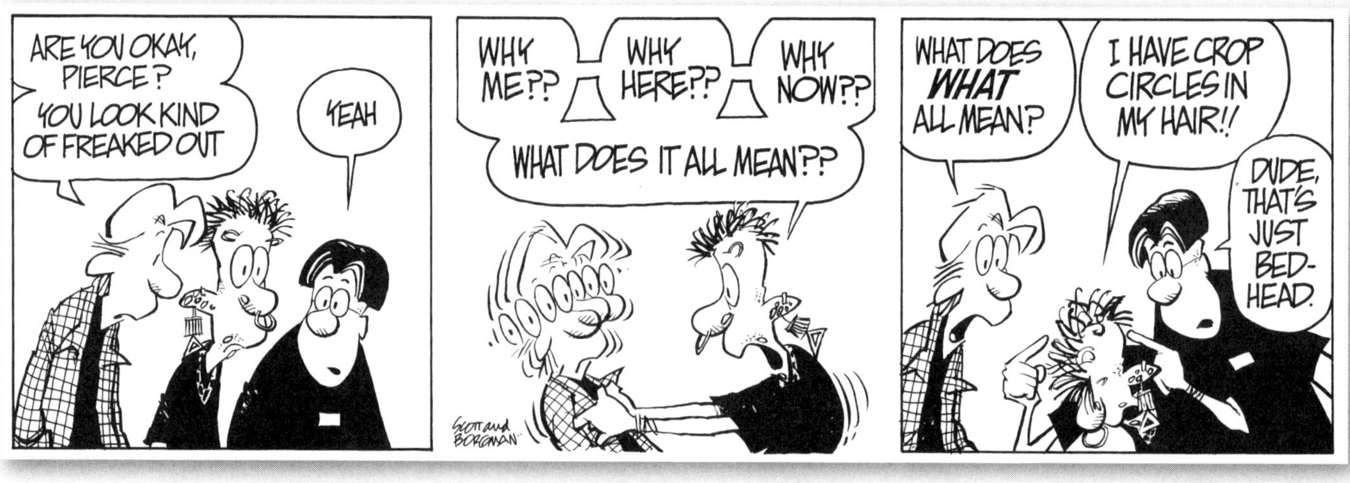
ARE YOU OKAY, PIERCE?
YOU LOOK KIND OF FREAKED OUT
YEAH
WHY ME??
WHY HERE??
WHY NOW??
WHAT DOES IT ALL MEAN??
WHAT DOES *WHAT* ALL MEAN?
I HAVE CROP CIRCLES IN MY HAIR!!
DUDE, THAT'S JUST BED-HEAD.
SCOTT and BORGMAN

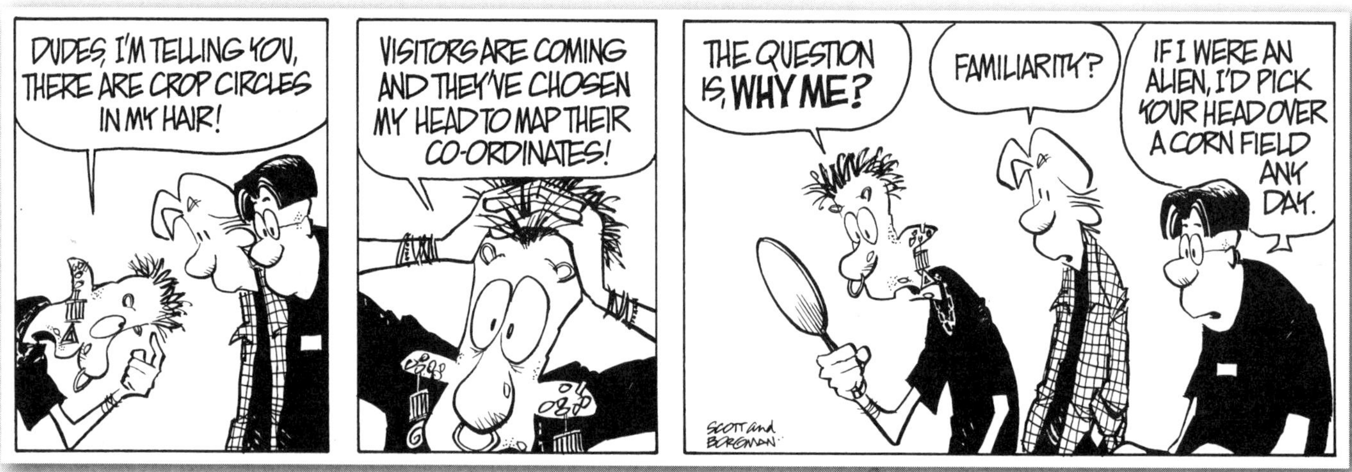
DUDES, I'M TELLING YOU, THERE ARE CROP CIRCLES IN MY HAIR!
VISITORS ARE COMING AND THEY'VE CHOSEN MY HEAD TO MAP THEIR CO-ORDINATES!
THE QUESTION IS, **WHY ME?**
FAMILIARITY?
IF I WERE AN ALIEN, I'D PICK YOUR HEAD OVER A CORN FIELD ANY DAY.
SCOTT and BORGMAN

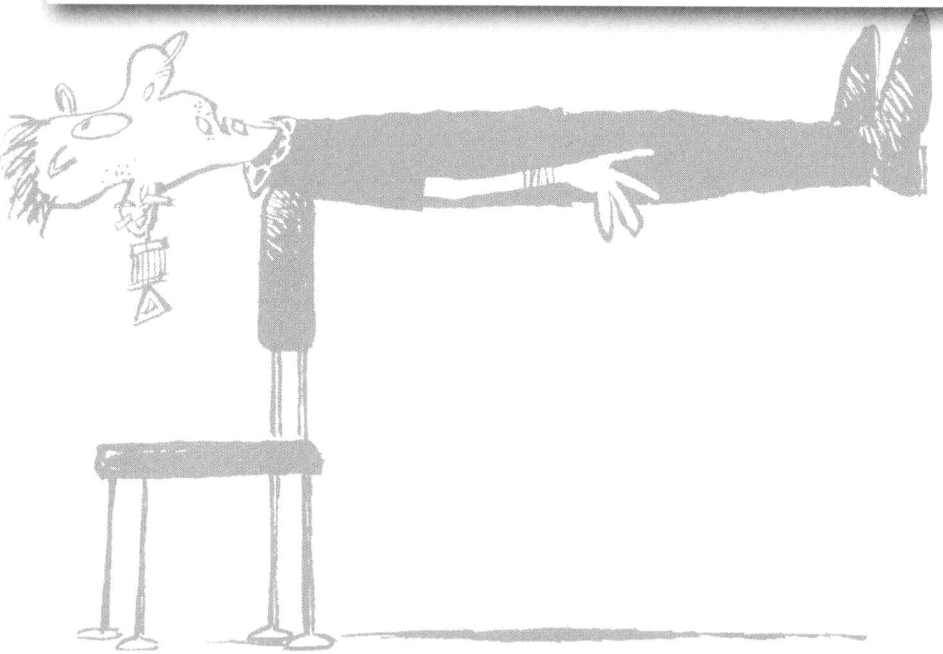

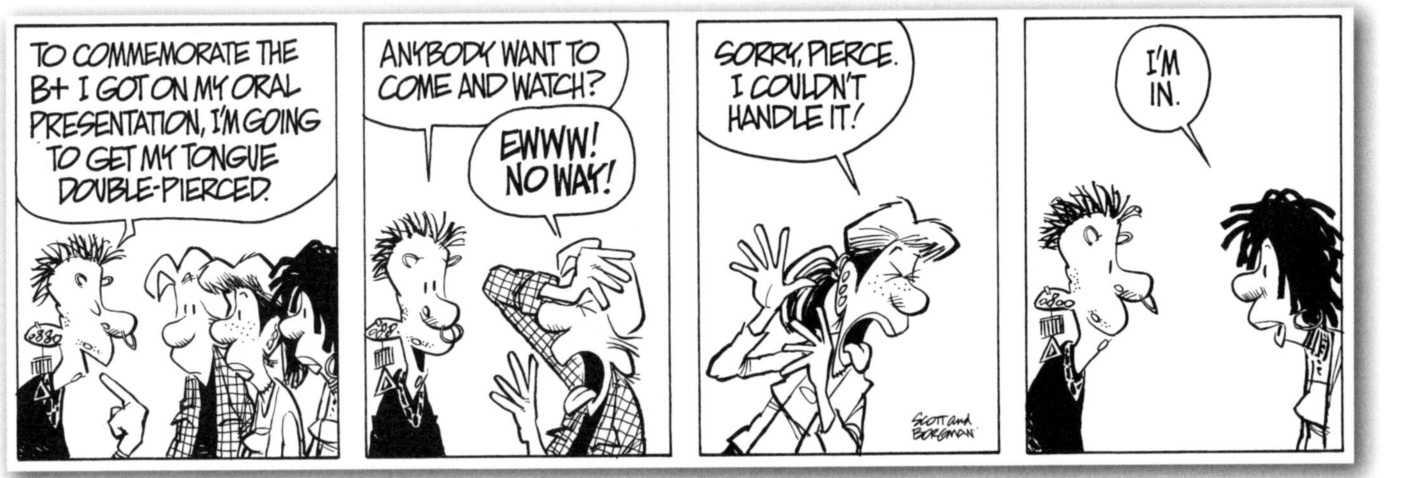
TO COMMEMORATE THE B+ I GOT ON MY ORAL PRESENTATION, I'M GOING TO GET MY TONGUE DOUBLE-PIERCED.
ANYBODY WANT TO COME AND WATCH?
EWWW! NO WAY!
SORRY, PIERCE. I COULDN'T HANDLE IT!
SCOTT and BORGMAN
I'M IN.

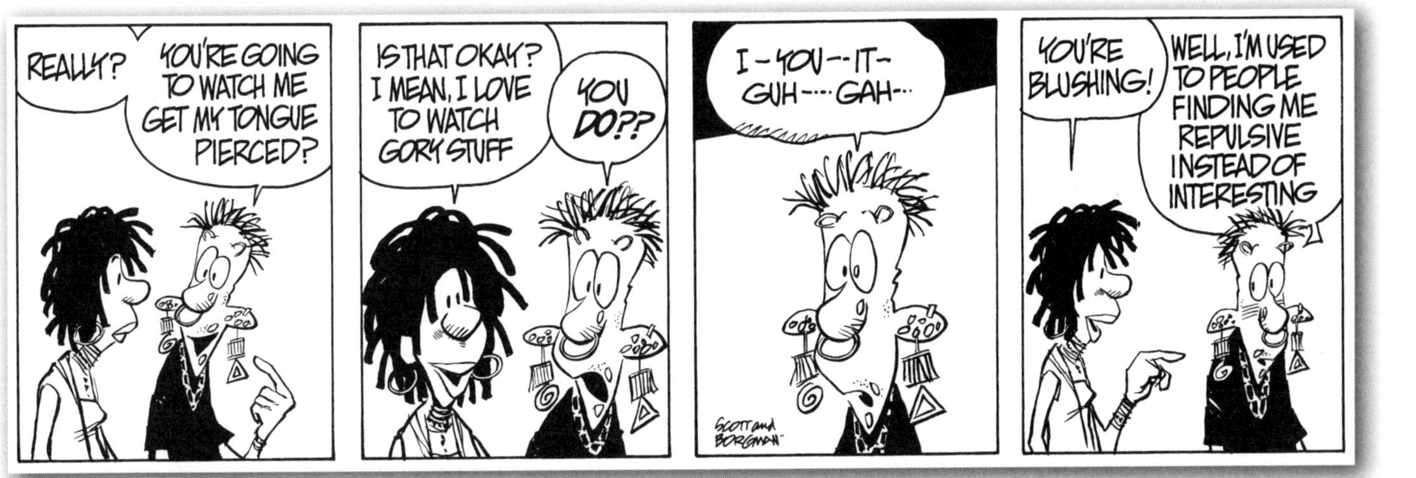
REALLY?
YOU'RE GOING TO WATCH ME GET MY TONGUE PIERCED?
IS THAT OKAY? I MEAN, I LOVE TO WATCH GORY STUFF
YOU DO??
I - YOU -- IT- GUH ---- GAH---
SCOTT and BORGMAN
YOU'RE BLUSHING!
WELL, I'M USED TO PEOPLE FINDING ME REPULSIVE INSTEAD OF INTERESTING

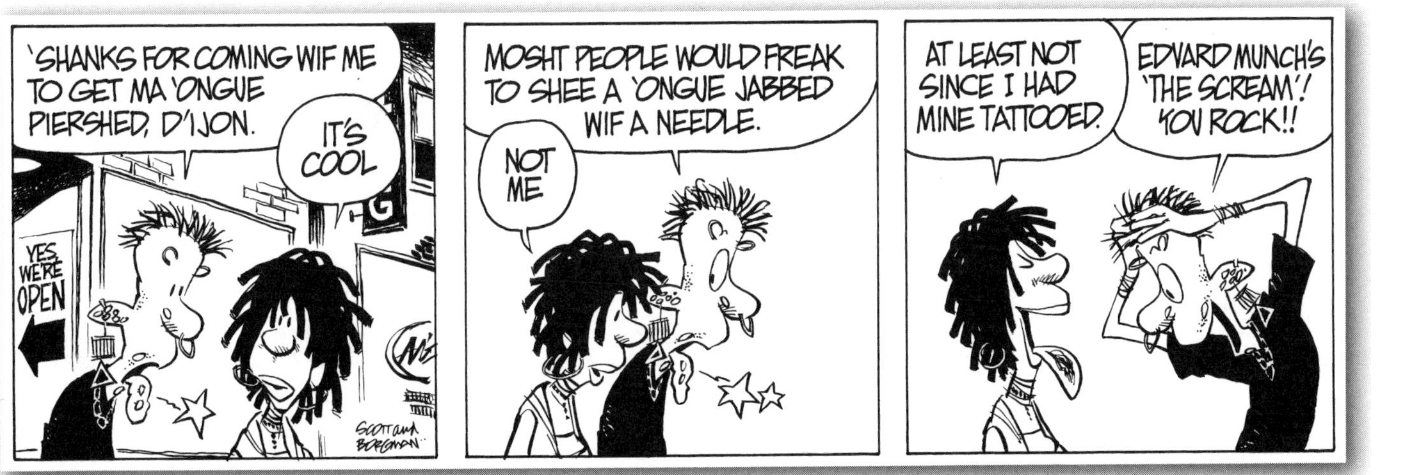
'SHANKS FOR COMING WIF ME TO GET MA 'ONGUE PIERSHED, D'IJON.
IT'S COOL
YES, WE'RE OPEN
G
SCOTT and BORGMAN
MOSHT PEOPLE WOULD FREAK TO SHEE A 'ONGUE JABBED WIF A NEEDLE.
NOT ME
AT LEAST NOT SINCE I HAD MINE TATTOOED.
EDVARD MUNCH'S 'THE SCREAM'! YOU ROCK!!

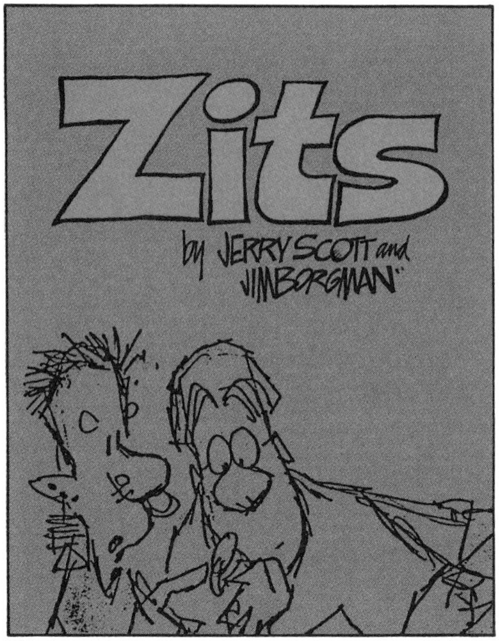
Zits
by JERRY SCOTT and JIM BORGMAN

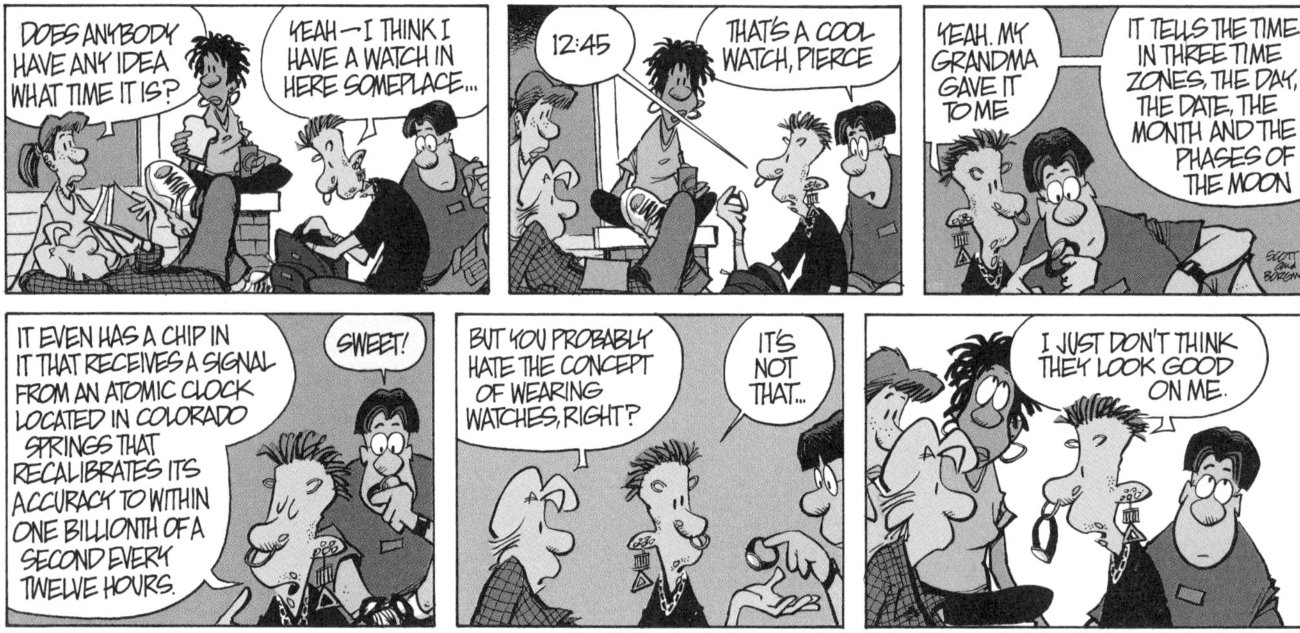
DOES ANYBODY HAVE ANY IDEA WHAT TIME IT IS?
YEAH—I THINK I HAVE A WATCH IN HERE SOMEPLACE...
12:45
THAT'S A COOL WATCH, PIERCE
YEAH. MY GRANDMA GAVE IT TO ME
IT TELLS THE TIME IN THREE TIME ZONES, THE DAY, THE DATE, THE MONTH AND THE PHASES OF THE MOON
SCOTT and BORGMAN
IT EVEN HAS A CHIP IN IT THAT RECEIVES A SIGNAL FROM AN ATOMIC CLOCK LOCATED IN COLORADO SPRINGS THAT RECALIBRATES ITS ACCURACY TO WITHIN ONE BILLIONTH OF A SECOND EVERY TWELVE HOURS.
SWEET!
BUT YOU PROBABLY HATE THE CONCEPT OF WEARING WATCHES, RIGHT?
IT'S NOT THAT...
I JUST DON'T THINK THEY LOOK GOOD ON ME.

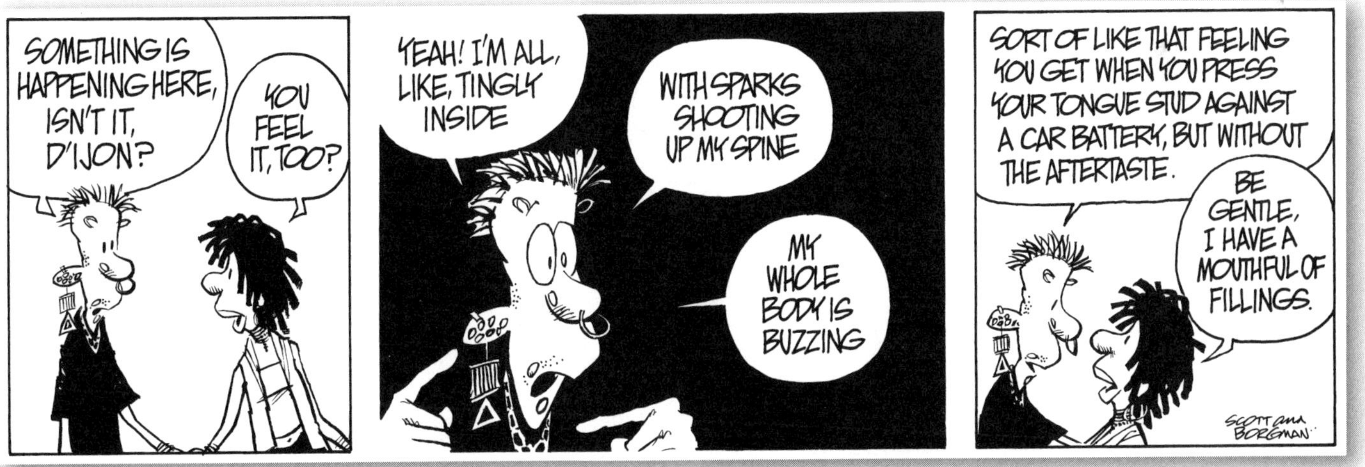
SOMETHING IS HAPPENING HERE, ISN'T IT, D'IJON?
YOU FEEL IT, TOO?
YEAH! I'M ALL, LIKE, TINGLY INSIDE
WITH SPARKS SHOOTING UP MY SPINE
MY WHOLE BODY IS BUZZING
SORT OF LIKE THAT FEELING YOU GET WHEN YOU PRESS YOUR TONGUE STUD AGAINST A CAR BATTERY, BUT WITHOUT THE AFTERTASTE.
BE GENTLE, I HAVE A MOUTHFUL OF FILLINGS.
SCOTT and BORGMAN

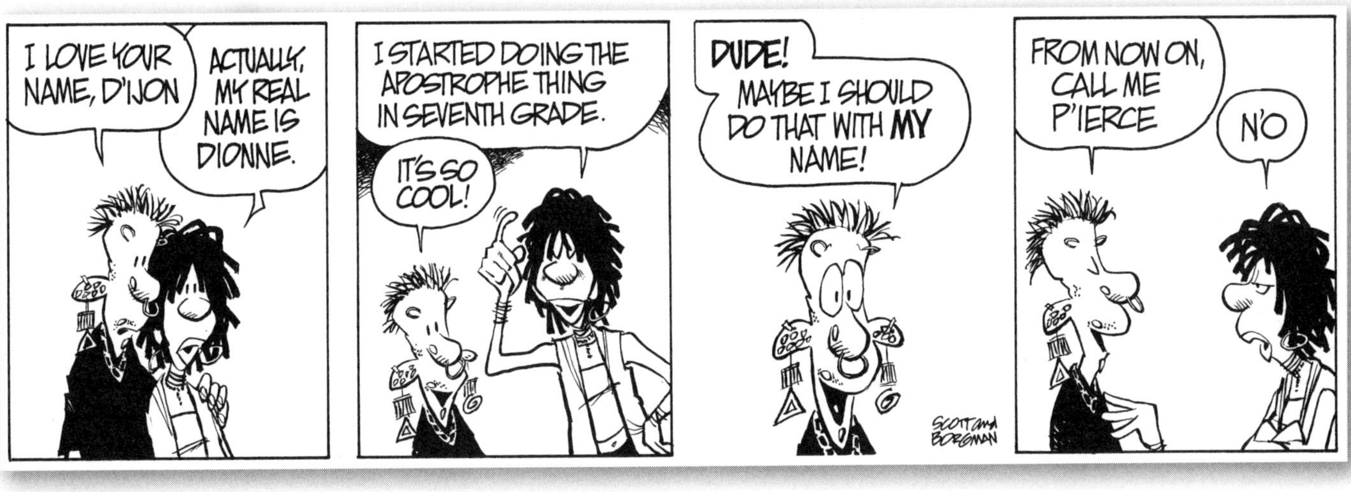
I LOVE YOUR NAME, D'IJON
ACTUALLY, MY REAL NAME IS DIONNE.
I STARTED DOING THE APOSTROPHE THING IN SEVENTH GRADE.
IT'S SO COOL!
DUDE! MAYBE I SHOULD DO THAT WITH MY NAME!
SCOTT and BORGMAN
FROM NOW ON, CALL ME P'IERCE
N'O

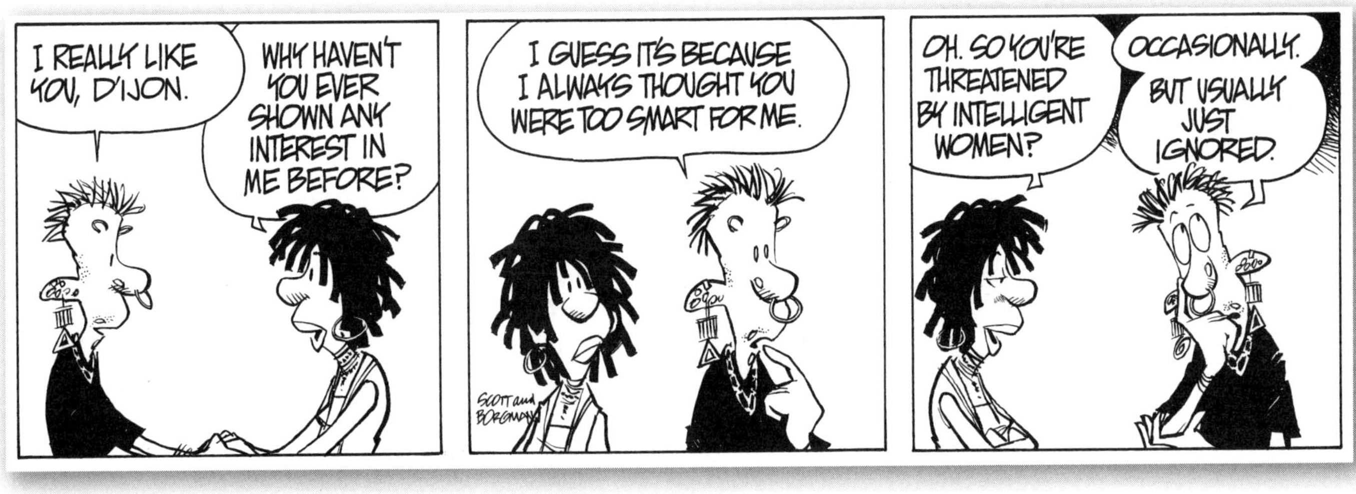
I REALLY LIKE YOU, D'IJON.
WHY HAVEN'T YOU EVER SHOWN ANY INTEREST IN ME BEFORE?
I GUESS IT'S BECAUSE I ALWAYS THOUGHT YOU WERE TOO SMART FOR ME.
SCOTT and BORGMAN
OH. SO YOU'RE THREATENED BY INTELLIGENT WOMEN?
OCCASIONALLY. BUT USUALLY JUST IGNORED.

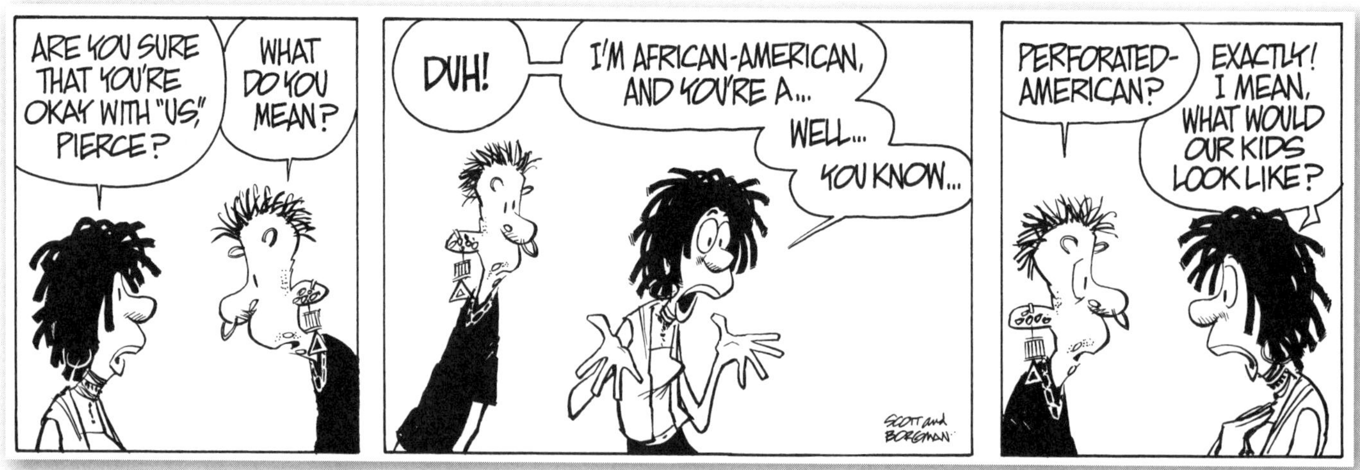
ARE YOU SURE THAT YOU'RE OKAY WITH "US," PIERCE?
WHAT DO YOU MEAN?
DUH!
I'M AFRICAN-AMERICAN, AND YOU'RE A...
WELL...
YOU KNOW...
SCOTT and BORGMAN
PERFORATED-AMERICAN?
EXACTLY! I MEAN, WHAT WOULD OUR KIDS LOOK LIKE?

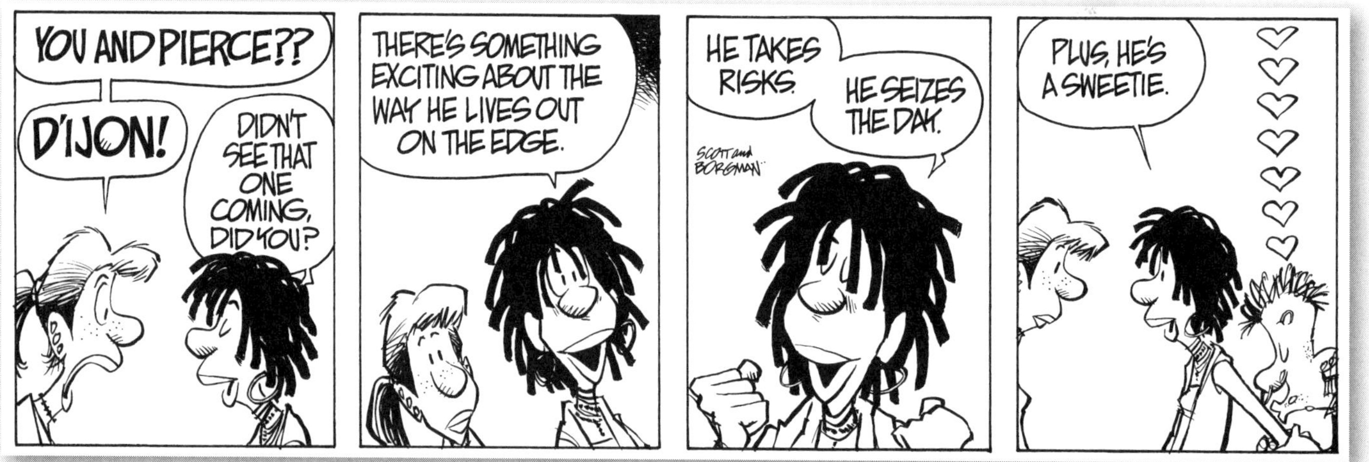
YOU AND PIERCE??
D'IJON!
DIDN'T SEE THAT ONE COMING, DID YOU?
THERE'S SOMETHING EXCITING ABOUT THE WAY HE LIVES OUT ON THE EDGE.
HE TAKES RISKS.
HE SEIZES THE DAY.
SCOTT and BORGMAN
PLUS, HE'S A SWEETIE.

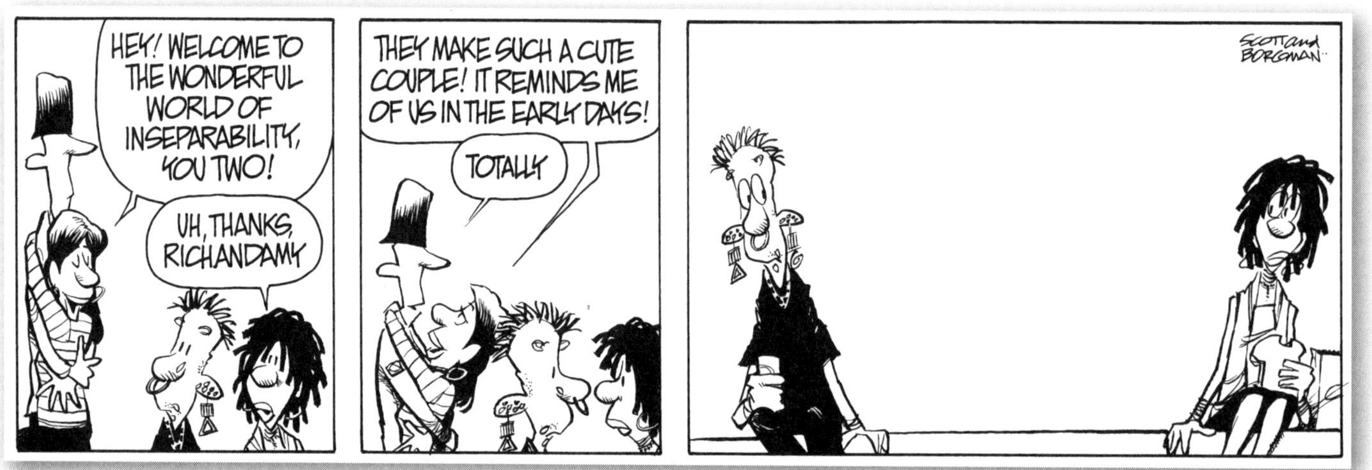
HEY! WELCOME TO THE WONDERFUL WORLD OF INSEPARABILITY, YOU TWO!
UH, THANKS, RICHANDAMY
THEY MAKE SUCH A CUTE COUPLE! IT REMINDS ME OF US IN THE EARLY DAYS!
TOTALLY
SCOTT and BORGMAN

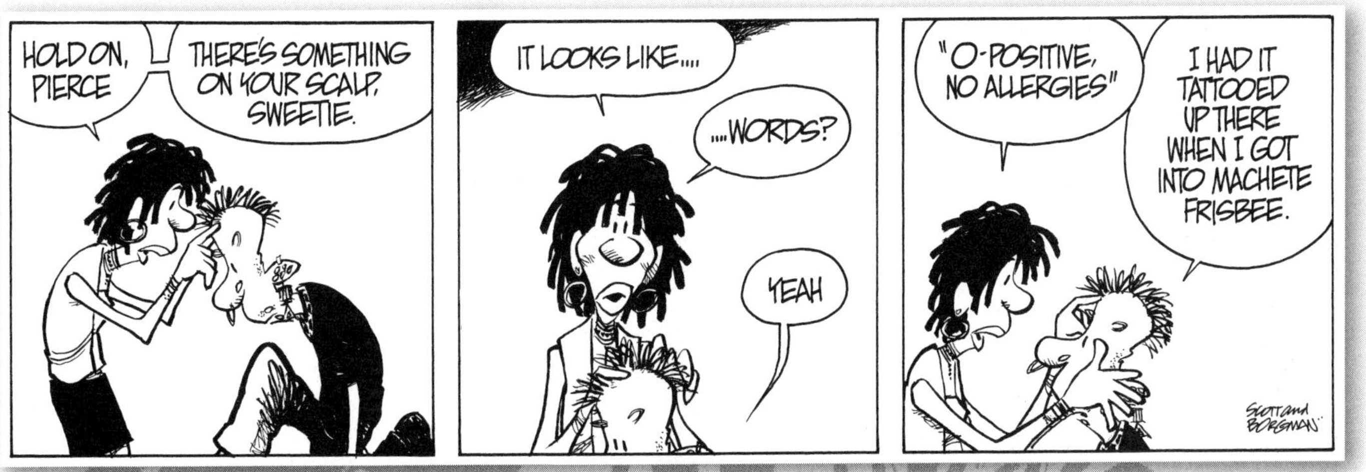
HOLD ON, PIERCE
THERE'S SOMETHING ON YOUR SCALP, SWEETIE.
IT LOOKS LIKE....
....WORDS?
YEAH
"O-POSITIVE, NO ALLERGIES"
I HAD IT TATTOOED UP THERE WHEN I GOT INTO MACHETE FRISBEE.
SCOTT and BORGMAN

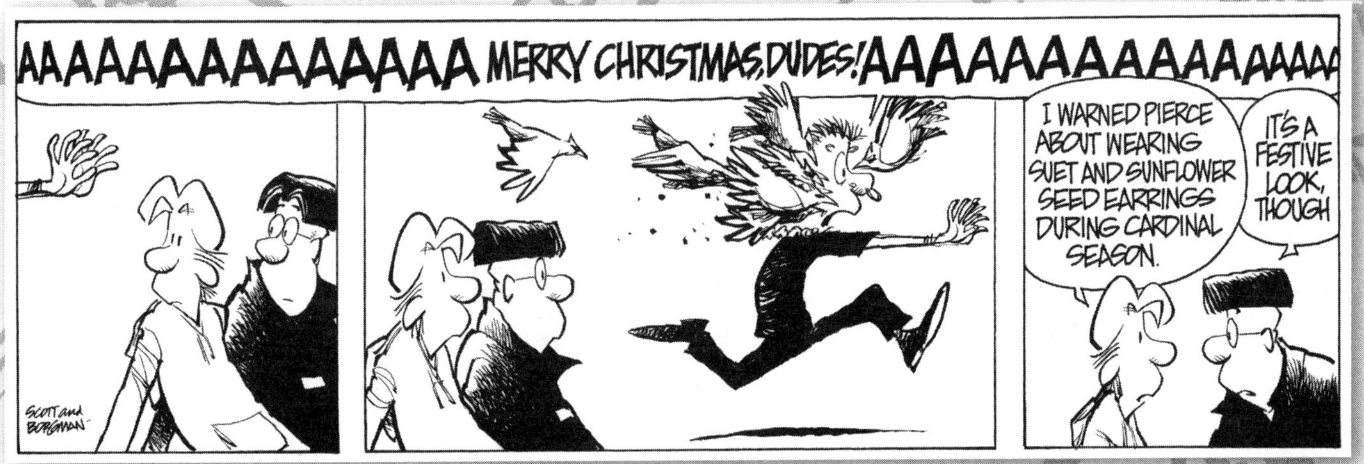
AAAAAAAAAAAAAA MERRY CHRISTMAS, DUDES! AAAAAAAAAAAAAAAA
SCOTT and BORGMAN
I WARNED PIERCE ABOUT WEARING SUET AND SUNFLOWER SEED EARRINGS DURING CARDINAL SEASON.
IT'S A FESTIVE LOOK, THOUGH

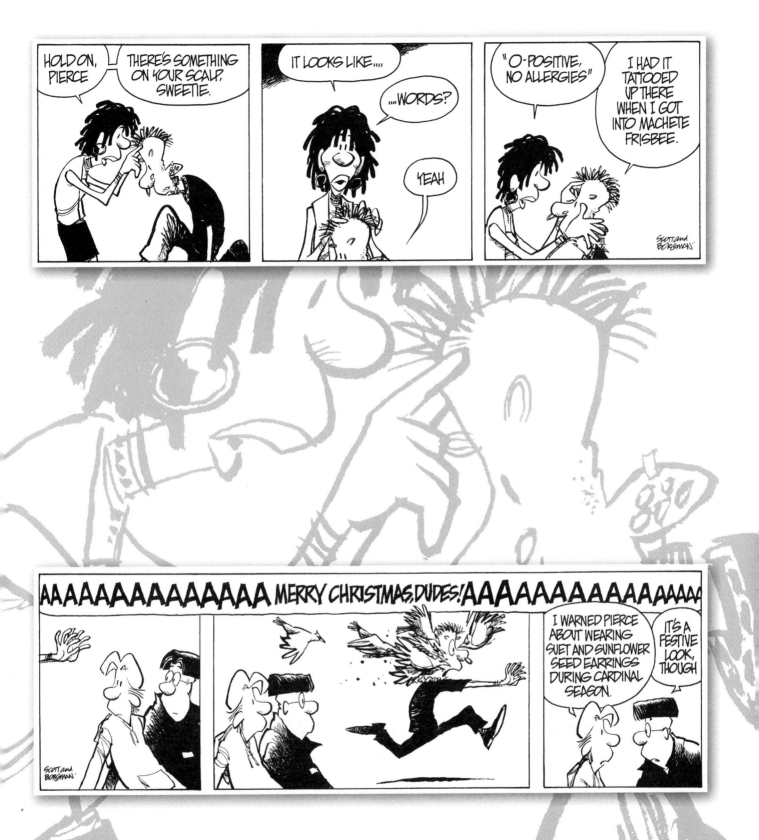

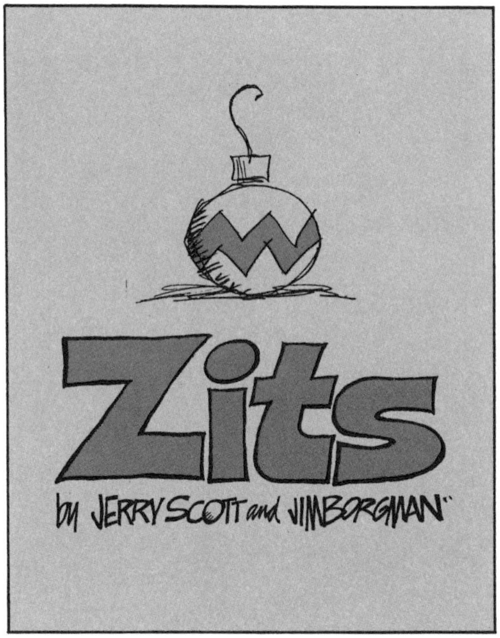
Zits
by JERRY SCOTT and JIM BORGMAN

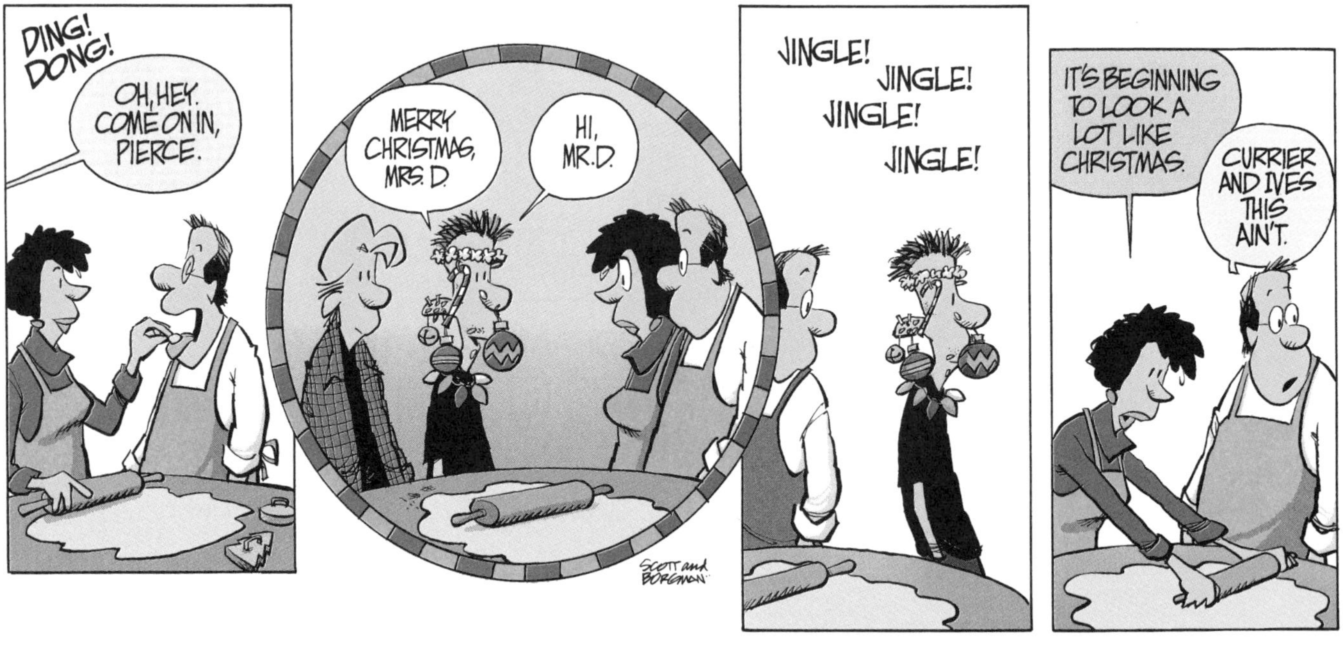
DING! DONG!
OH, HEY. COME ON IN, PIERCE.
MERRY CHRISTMAS, MRS. D.
HI, MR. D.
SCOTT and BORGMAN
JINGLE!
JINGLE!
JINGLE!
JINGLE!
IT'S BEGINNING TO LOOK A LOT LIKE CHRISTMAS.
CURRIER AND IVES THIS AIN'T.

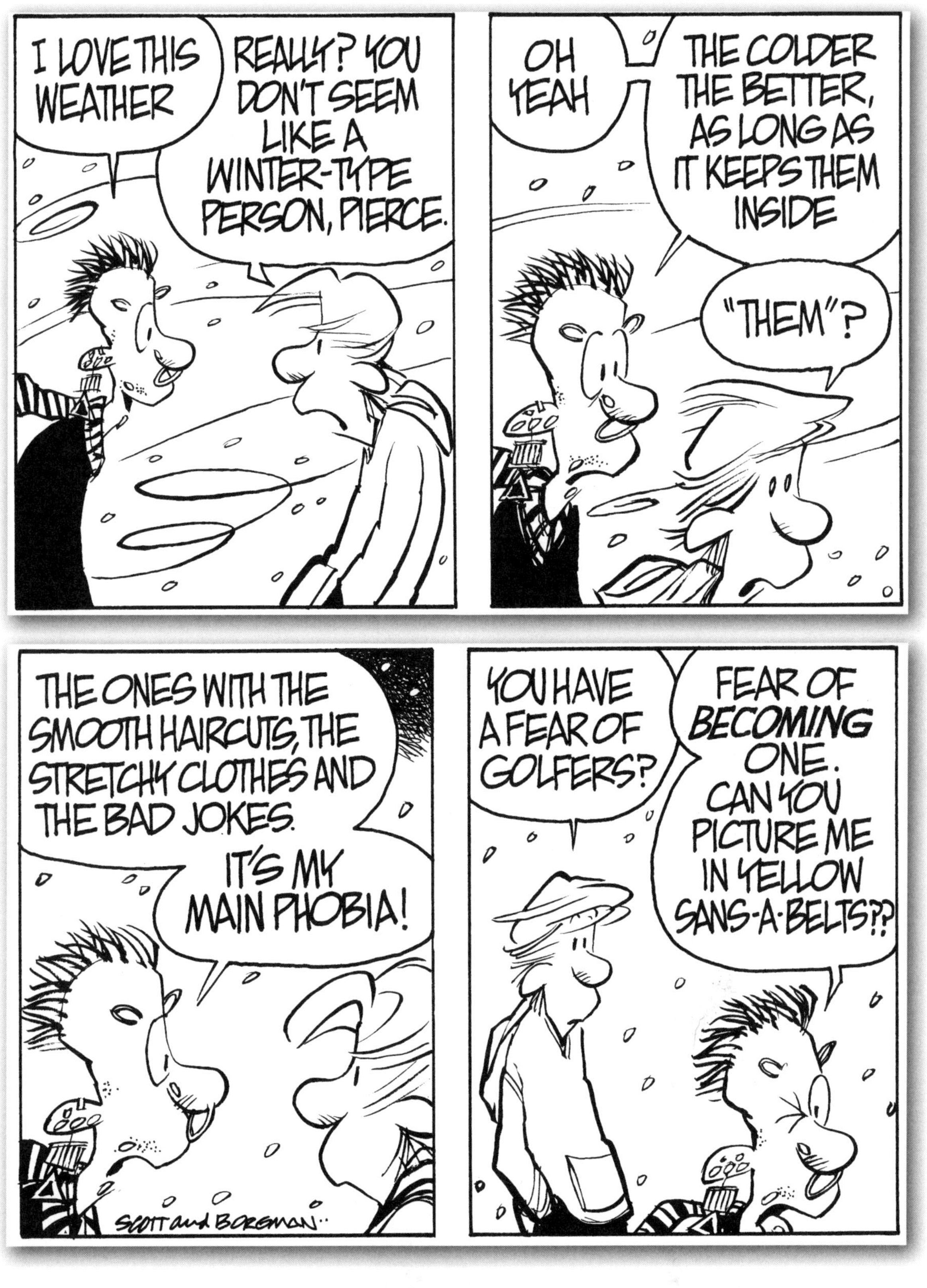
I LOVE THIS WEATHER
REALLY? YOU DON'T SEEM LIKE A WINTER-TYPE PERSON, PIERCE.
OH YEAH
THE COLDER THE BETTER, AS LONG AS IT KEEPS THEM INSIDE
"THEM"?
THE ONES WITH THE SMOOTH HAIRCUTS, THE STRETCHY CLOTHES AND THE BAD JOKES.
IT'S MY MAIN PHOBIA!
SCOTT and BORGMAN
YOU HAVE A FEAR OF GOLFERS?
FEAR OF *BECOMING* ONE. CAN YOU PICTURE ME IN YELLOW SANS-A-BELTS??

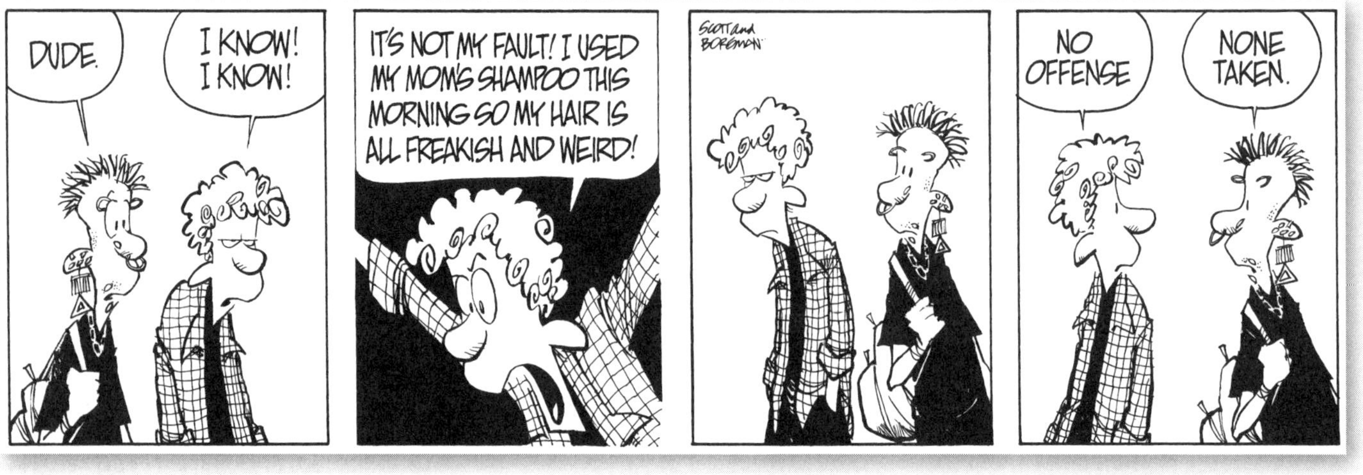
DUDE.
I KNOW! I KNOW!
IT'S NOT MY FAULT! I USED MY MOM'S SHAMPOO THIS MORNING SO MY HAIR IS ALL FREAKISH AND WEIRD!
SCOTT and BORGMAN
NO OFFENSE
NONE TAKEN.

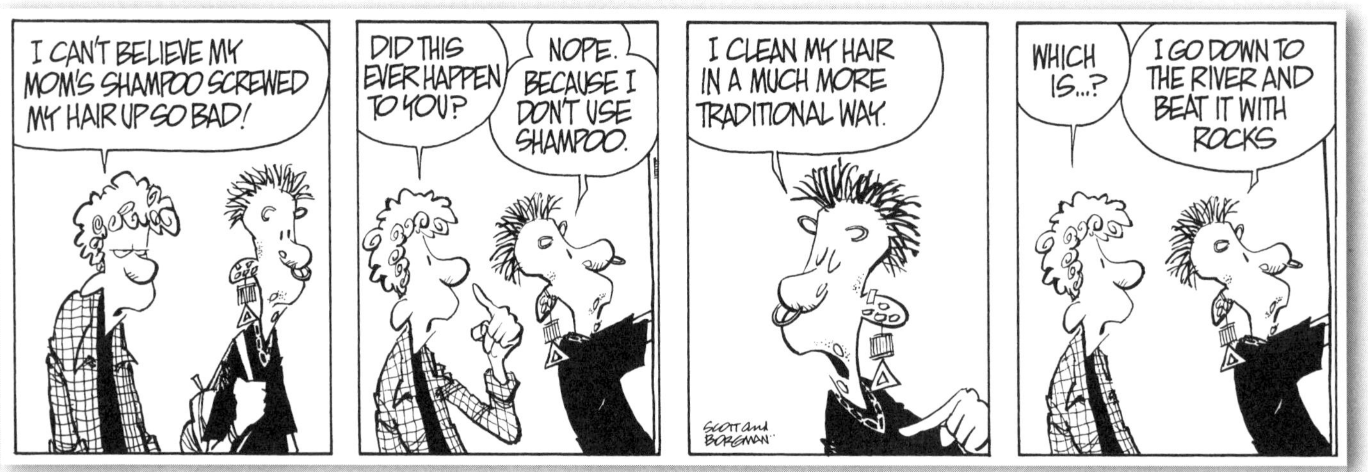
I CAN'T BELIEVE MY MOM'S SHAMPOO SCREWED MY HAIR UP SO BAD!
DID THIS EVER HAPPEN TO YOU?
NOPE. BECAUSE I DON'T USE SHAMPOO.
I CLEAN MY HAIR IN A MUCH MORE TRADITIONAL WAY.
SCOTT and BORGMAN
WHICH IS...?
I GO DOWN TO THE RIVER AND BEAT IT WITH ROCKS

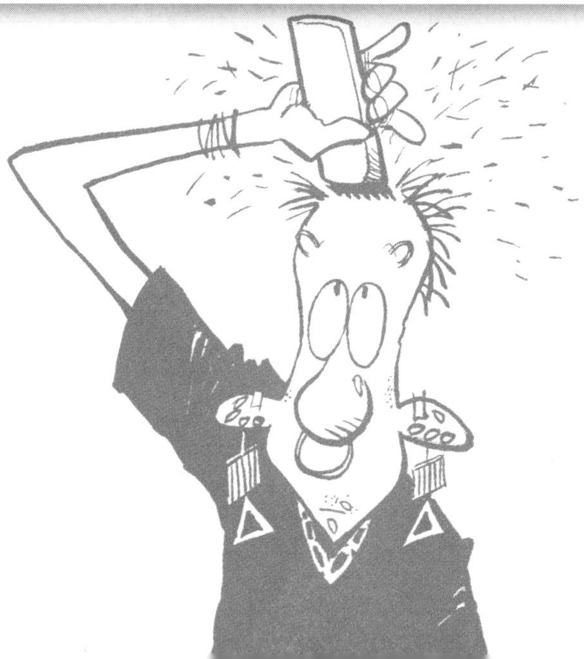

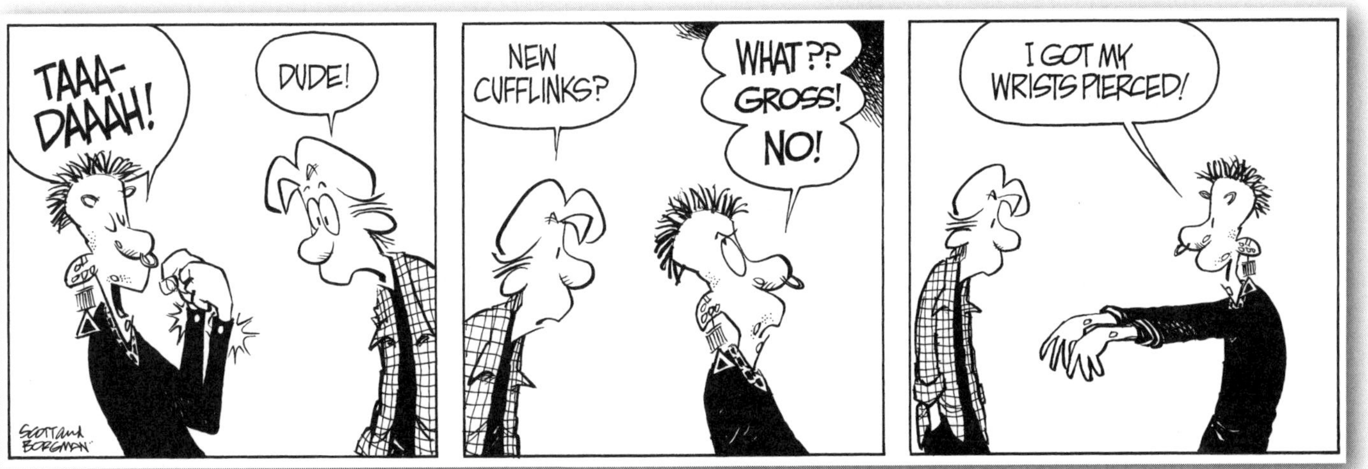
TAAA-DAAAH!
DUDE!
NEW CUFFLINKS?
WHAT?? GROSS!
NO!
I GOT MY WRISTS PIERCED!
SCOTT and BORGMAN

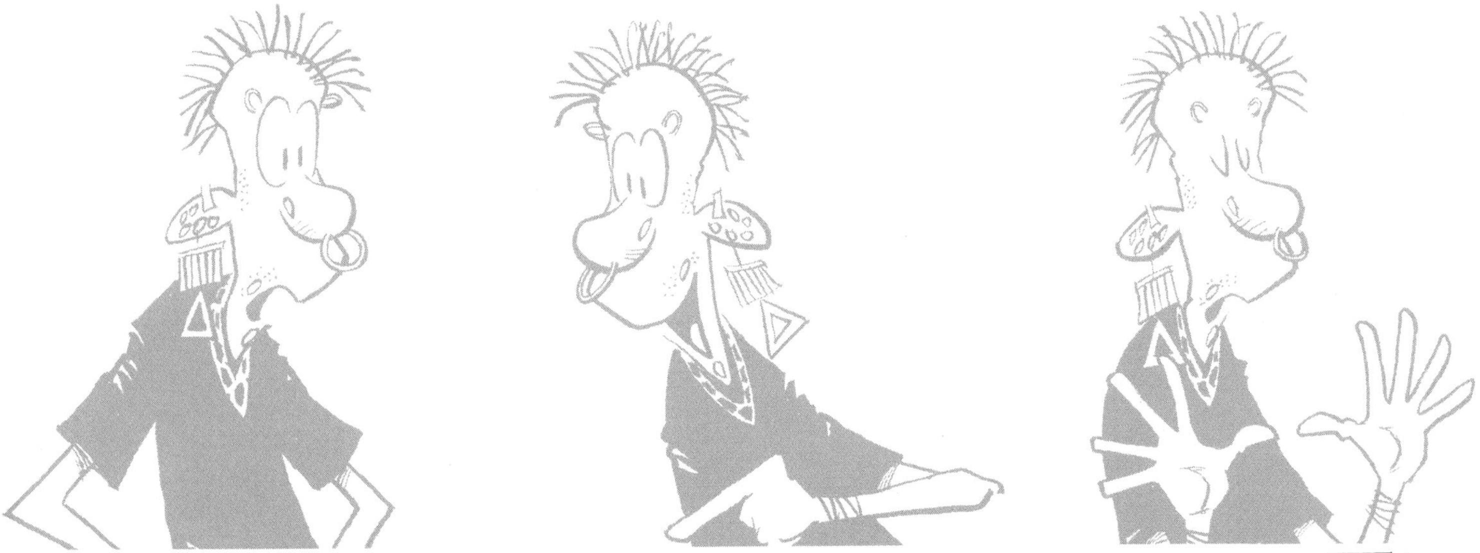

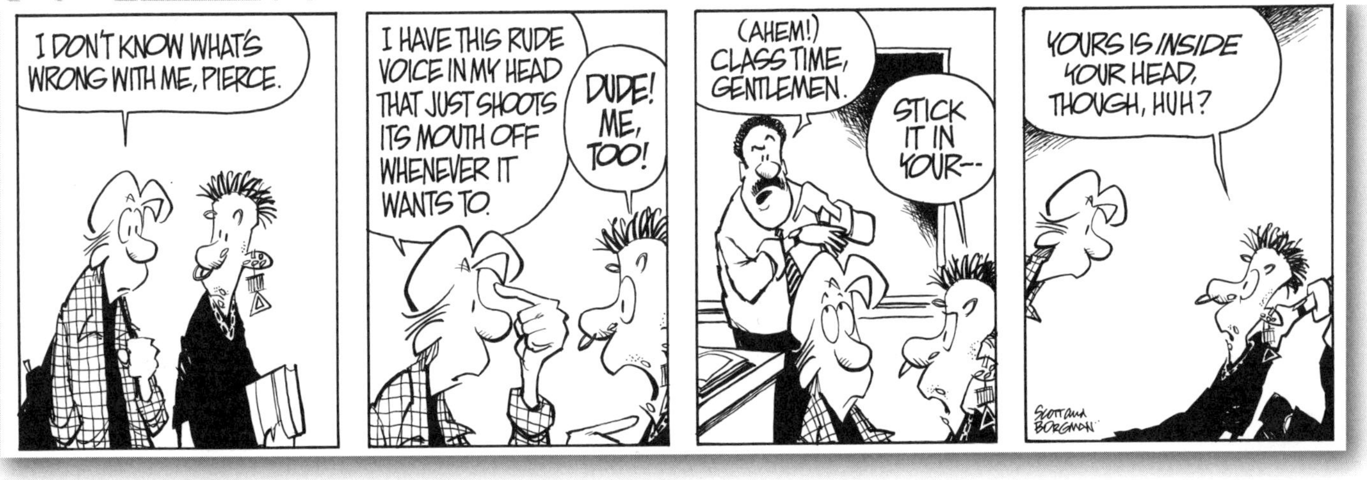
I DON'T KNOW WHAT'S WRONG WITH ME, PIERCE.
I HAVE THIS RUDE VOICE IN MY HEAD THAT JUST SHOOTS ITS MOUTH OFF WHENEVER IT WANTS TO.
DUDE! ME, TOO!
(AHEM!) CLASS TIME, GENTLEMEN.
STICK IT IN YOUR--
YOURS IS INSIDE YOUR HEAD, THOUGH, HUH?
SCOTT and BORGMAN

Zits
by
JERRY SCOTT and
JIM BORGMAN

SCOTT and BORGMAN
OOPS! GOTTA GO!
WE JUST PASSED YOU THREE MINUTES AGO, PIERCE! HOW CAN YOU BE FINISHED WITH LUNCH ALREADY?
SIMPLE
I CONSUME FROM 12:47 TO 12:50 AND I CHEW FROM 12:50 TO 1:30.
SO THAT'S THE NOISE I HEAR DURING ALGEBRA!

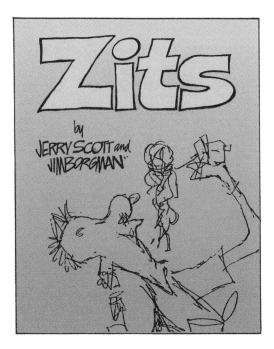

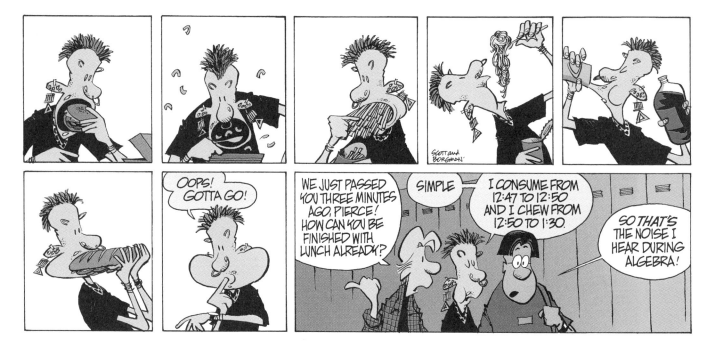

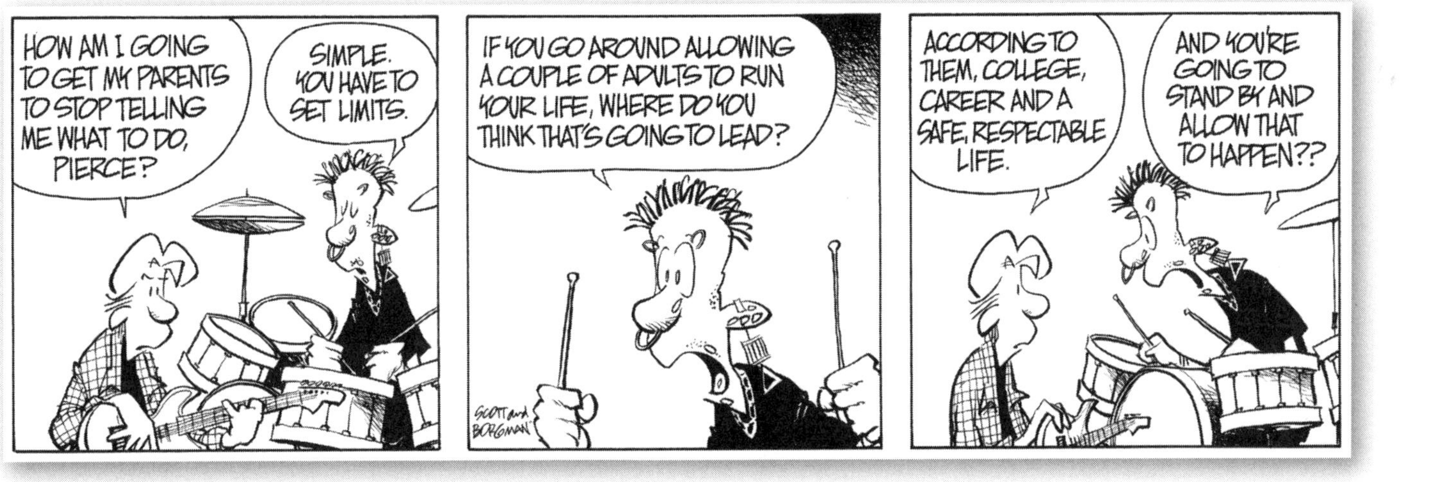
HOW AM I GOING TO GET MY PARENTS TO STOP TELLING ME WHAT TO DO, PIERCE?
SIMPLE. YOU HAVE TO SET LIMITS.
IF YOU GO AROUND ALLOWING A COUPLE OF ADULTS TO RUN YOUR LIFE, WHERE DO YOU THINK THAT'S GOING TO LEAD?
SCOTT and BORGMAN
ACCORDING TO THEM, COLLEGE, CAREER AND A SAFE, RESPECTABLE LIFE.
AND YOU'RE GOING TO STAND BY AND ALLOW THAT TO HAPPEN??

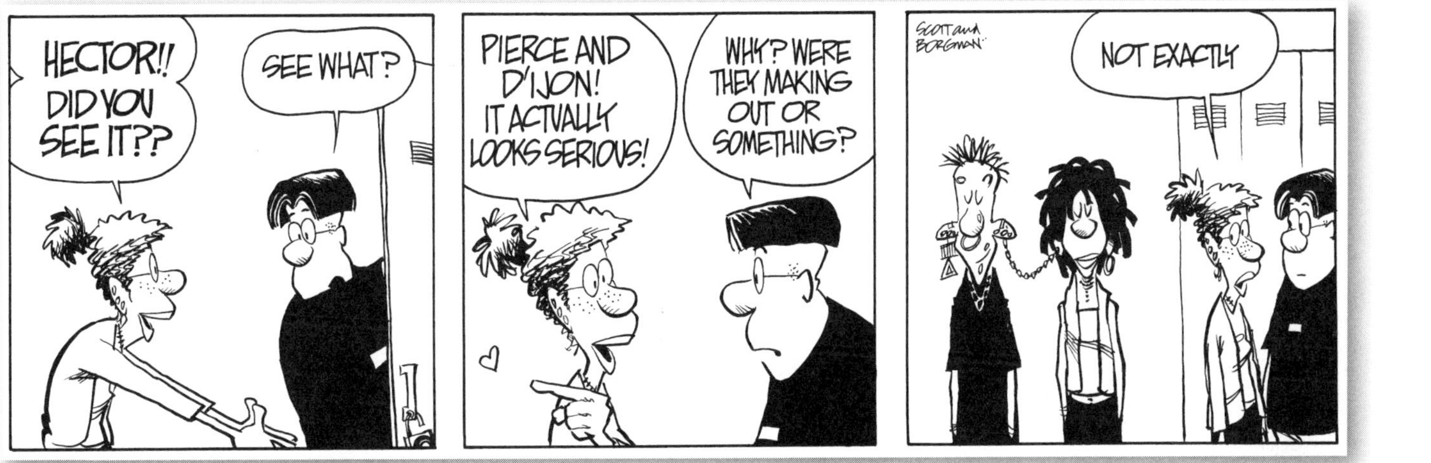
HECTOR!! DID YOU SEE IT??
SEE WHAT?
PIERCE AND D'IJON! IT ACTUALLY LOOKS SERIOUS!
WHY? WERE THEY MAKING OUT OR SOMETHING?
SCOTT and BORGMAN
NOT EXACTLY

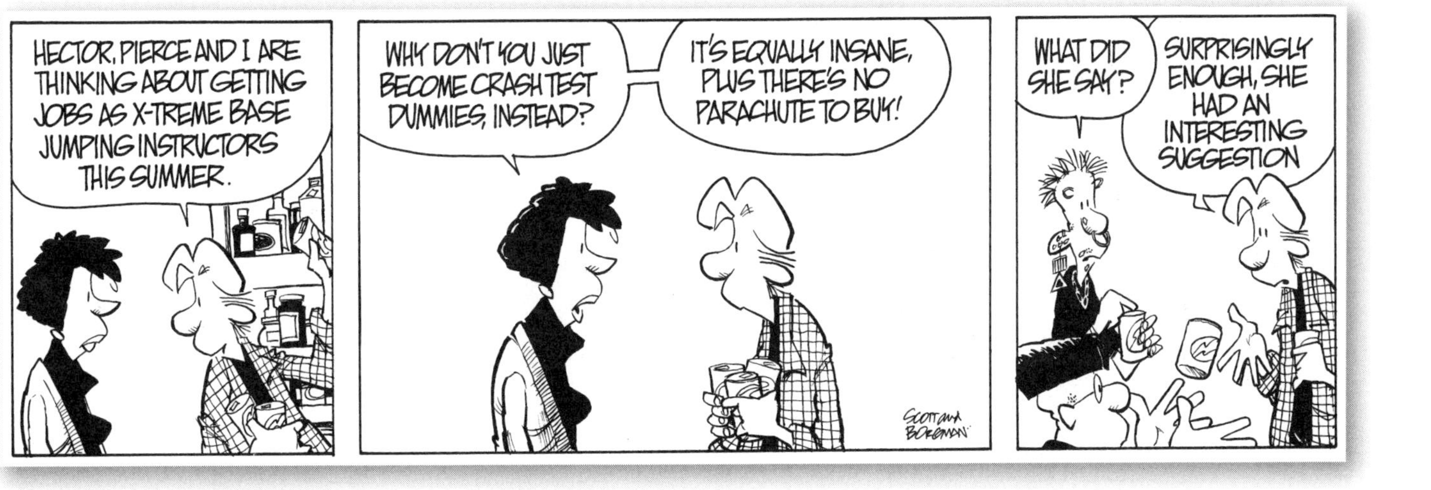
HECTOR, PIERCE AND I ARE THINKING ABOUT GETTING JOBS AS X-TREME BASE JUMPING INSTRUCTORS THIS SUMMER.
WHY DON'T YOU JUST BECOME CRASH TEST DUMMIES, INSTEAD?
IT'S EQUALLY INSANE, PLUS THERE'S NO PARACHUTE TO BUY!
SCOTT and BORGMAN
WHAT DID SHE SAY?
SURPRISINGLY ENOUGH, SHE HAD AN INTERESTING SUGGESTION

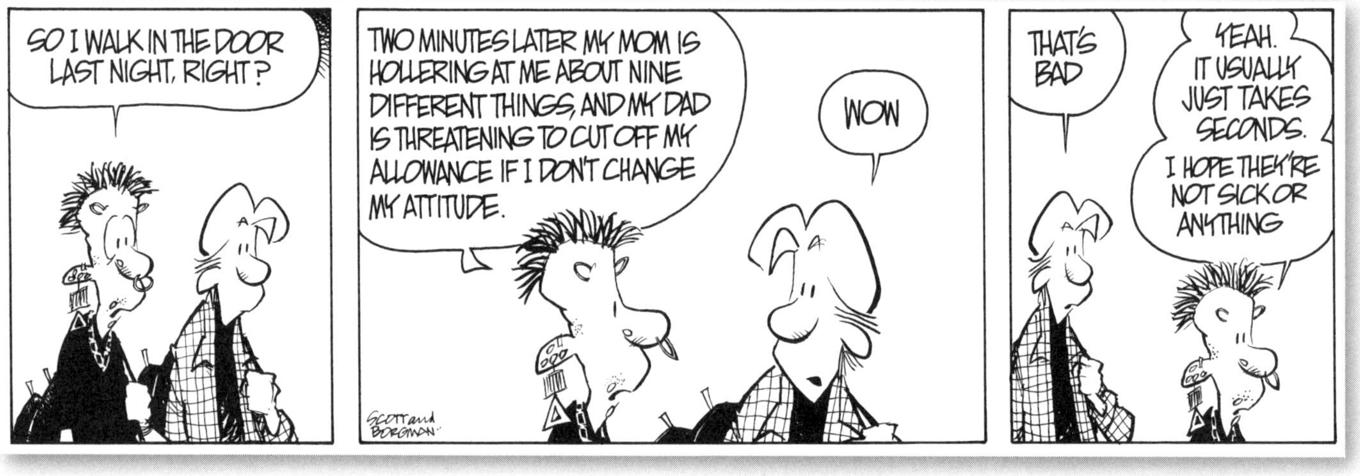
SO I WALK IN THE DOOR LAST NIGHT, RIGHT?
TWO MINUTES LATER MY MOM IS HOLLERING AT ME ABOUT NINE DIFFERENT THINGS, AND MY DAD IS THREATENING TO CUT OFF MY ALLOWANCE IF I DON'T CHANGE MY ATTITUDE.
WOW
THAT'S BAD
YEAH. IT USUALLY JUST TAKES SECONDS.
I HOPE THEY'RE NOT SICK OR ANYTHING
SCOTT and BORGMAN

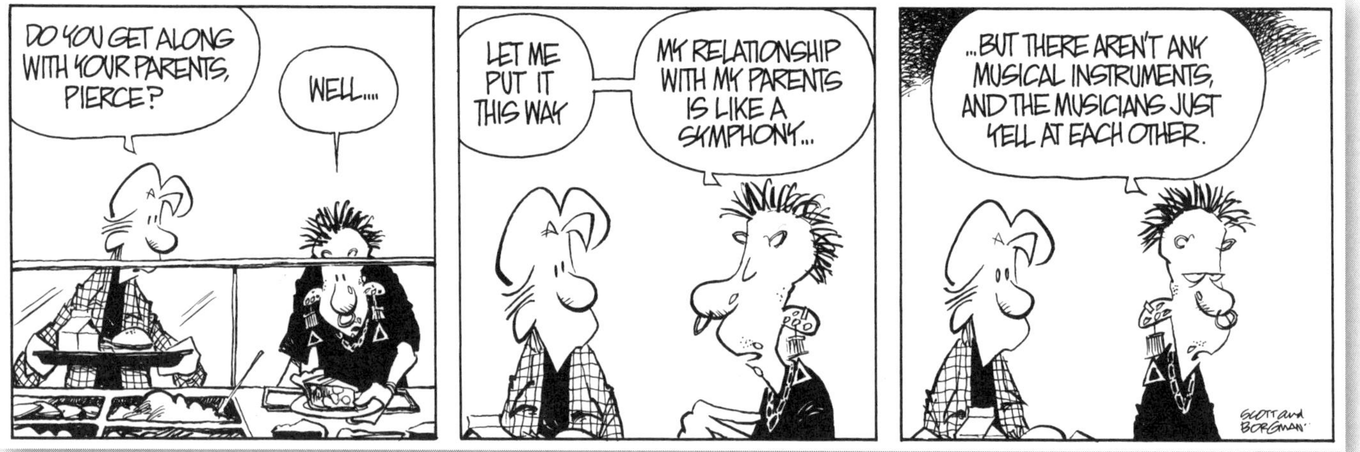
DO YOU GET ALONG WITH YOUR PARENTS, PIERCE?
WELL....
LET ME PUT IT THIS WAY
MY RELATIONSHIP WITH MY PARENTS IS LIKE A SYMPHONY...
...BUT THERE AREN'T ANY MUSICAL INSTRUMENTS, AND THE MUSICIANS JUST YELL AT EACH OTHER.
SCOTT and BORGMAN

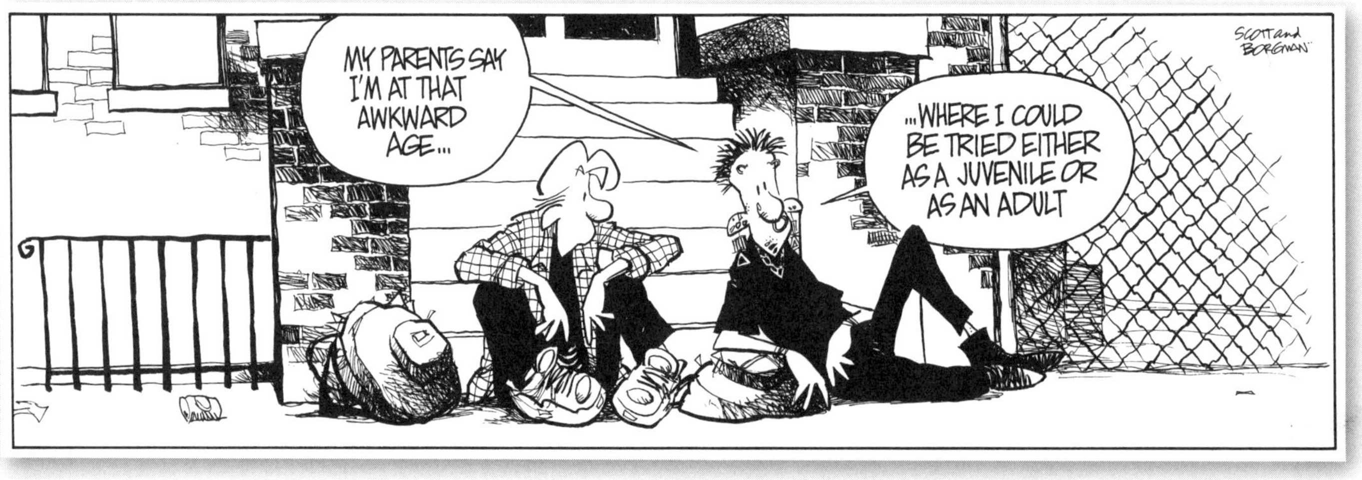
SCOTT and BORGMAN
MY PARENTS SAY I'M AT THAT AWKWARD AGE...
...WHERE I COULD BE TRIED EITHER AS A JUVENILE OR AS AN ADULT

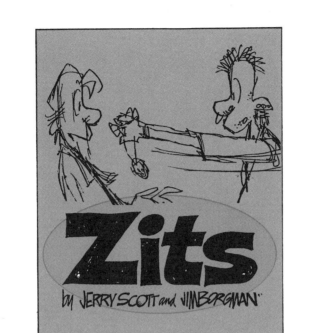

Zits

by JERRY SCOTT and JIM BORGMAN

DID YOU GET IT?

WAS THERE EVER ANY DOUBT?

I REALLY APPRECIATE YOU HELPING ME OUT, PIERCE. I DON'T KNOW ANYTHING ABOUT BUYING JEWELRY.

THAT'S WHY YOU COME TO AN EXPERT.

NOW, I GAVE THIS A LOT OF THOUGHT, AND BASED ON THE TENDER NATURE OF YOUR AND SARA'S RELATIONSHIP....

I CHOSE THIS STUNNING NECKLACE!

A PAIR OF JEWELED SKULLS WITH INTERTWINED SNAKES IN THE EYE SOCKETS, FRAMED BY A BARBED WIRE HEART.

I NORMALLY WOULDN'T RECOMMEND SOMETHING THIS SENTIMENTAL, BUT, HEY → IT'S VALENTINE'S DAY, RIGHT?

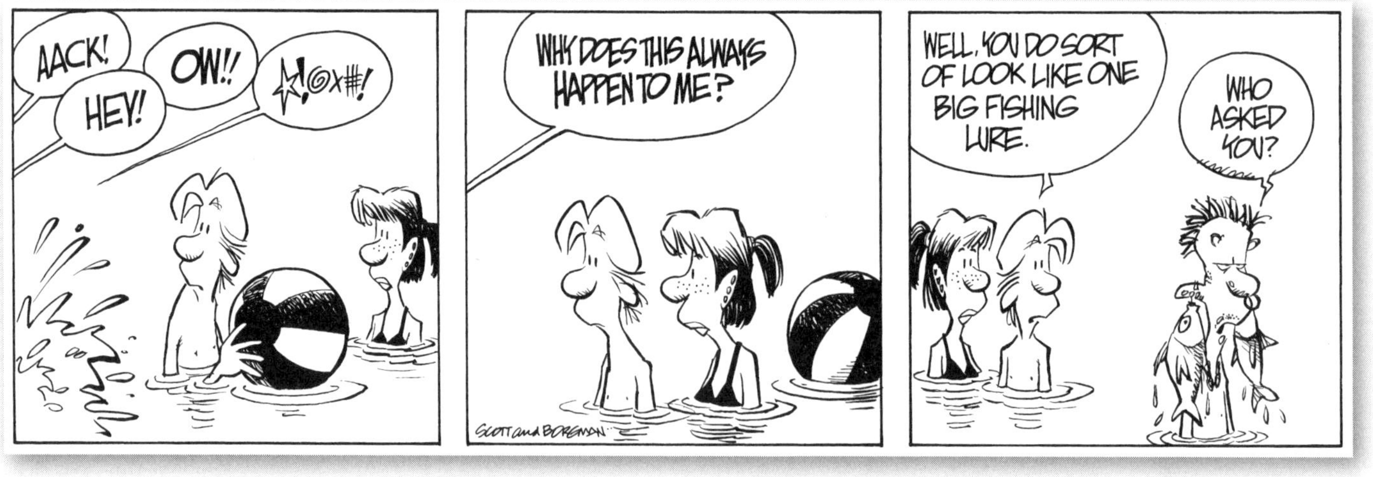
AACK!
HEY!
OW!!
WHY DOES THIS ALWAYS HAPPEN TO ME?
SCOTT and BORGMAN
WELL, YOU DO SORT OF LOOK LIKE ONE BIG FISHING LURE.
WHO ASKED YOU?

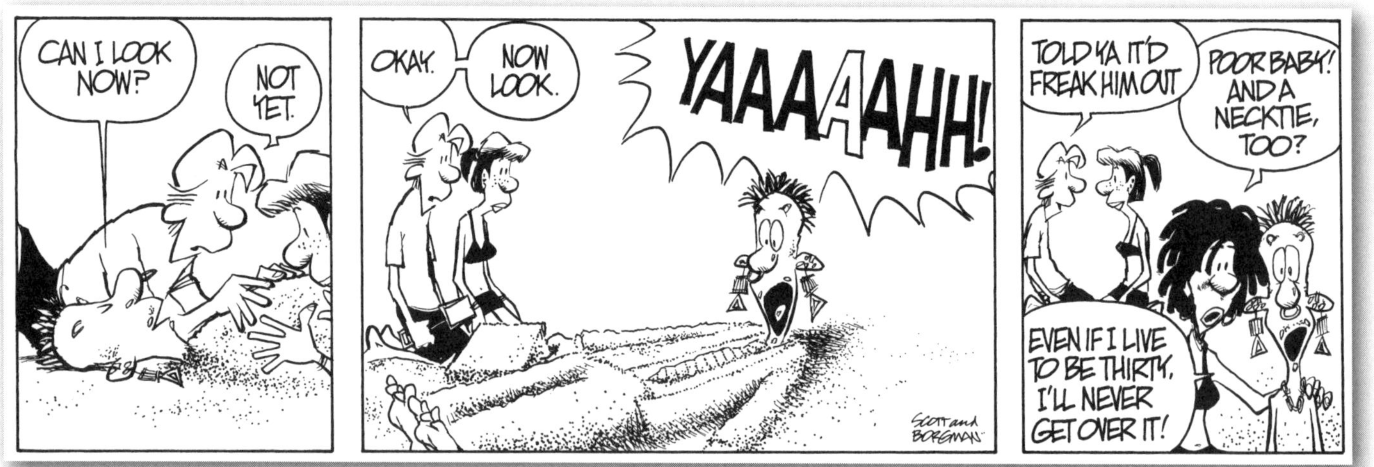
CAN I LOOK NOW?
NOT YET.
OKAY.
NOW LOOK.
YAAAAAHH!
SCOTT and BORGMAN
TOLD YA IT'D FREAK HIM OUT
POOR BABY! AND A NECKTIE, TOO?
EVEN IF I LIVE TO BE THIRTY, I'LL NEVER GET OVER IT!

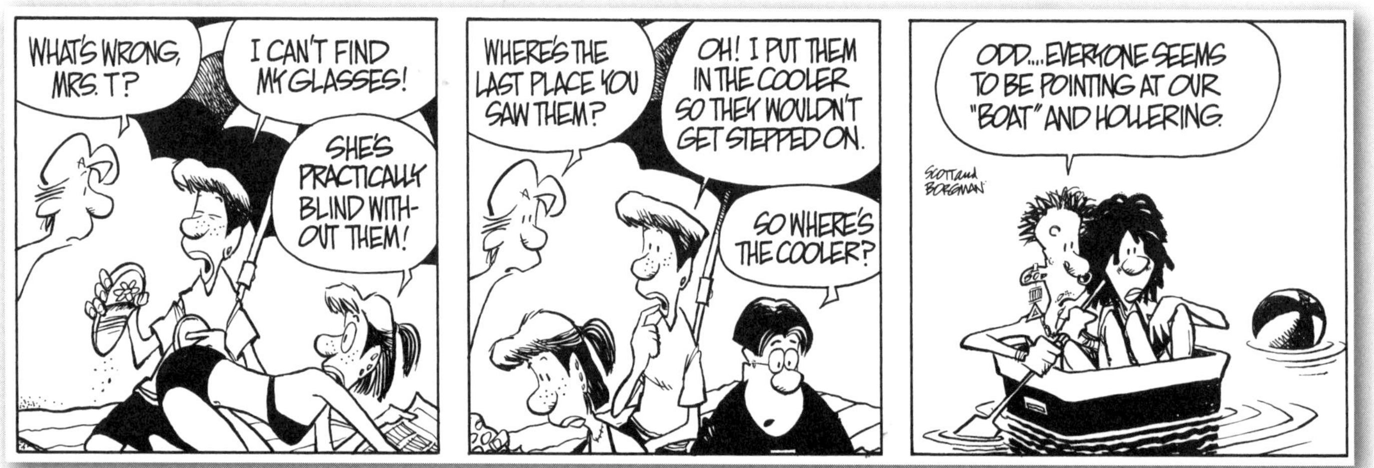
WHAT'S WRONG, MRS. T?
I CAN'T FIND MY GLASSES!
SHE'S PRACTICALLY BLIND WITH-OUT THEM!
WHERE'S THE LAST PLACE YOU SAW THEM?
OH! I PUT THEM IN THE COOLER SO THEY WOULDN'T GET STEPPED ON.
SO WHERE'S THE COOLER?
ODD....EVERYONE SEEMS TO BE POINTING AT OUR "BOAT" AND HOLLERING.
SCOTT and BORGMAN

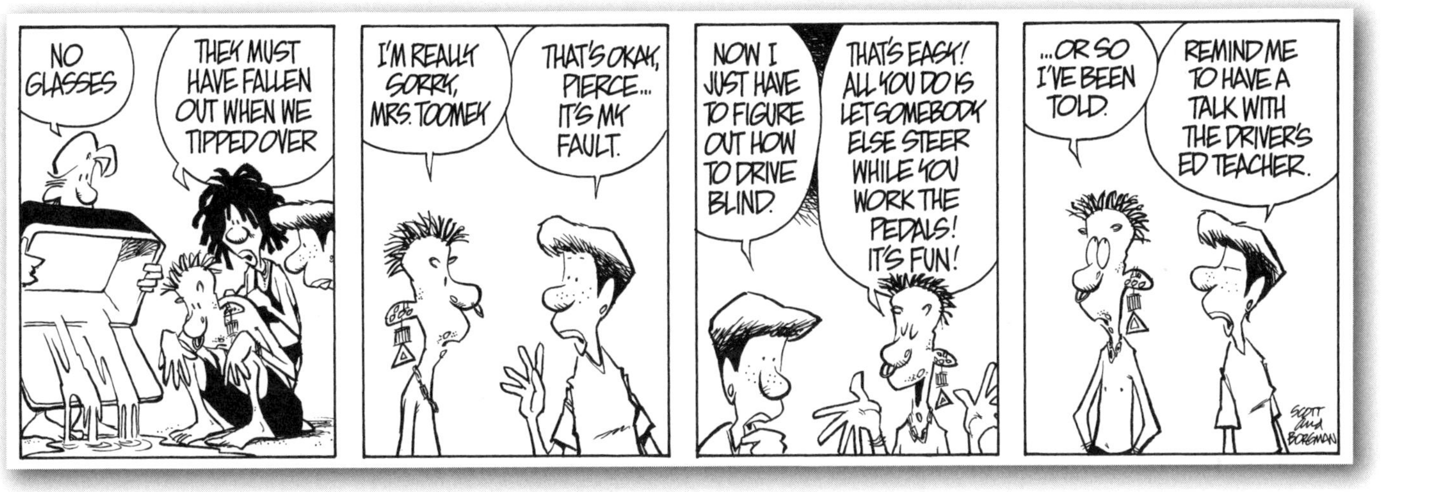
NO GLASSES
THEY MUST HAVE FALLEN OUT WHEN WE TIPPED OVER
I'M REALLY SORRY, MRS. TOOMEY
THAT'S OKAY, PIERCE... IT'S MY FAULT.
NOW I JUST HAVE TO FIGURE OUT HOW TO DRIVE BLIND.
THAT'S EASY! ALL YOU DO IS LET SOMEBODY ELSE STEER WHILE YOU WORK THE PEDALS! IT'S FUN!
...OR SO I'VE BEEN TOLD.
REMIND ME TO HAVE A TALK WITH THE DRIVER'S ED TEACHER.
SCOTT and BORGMAN

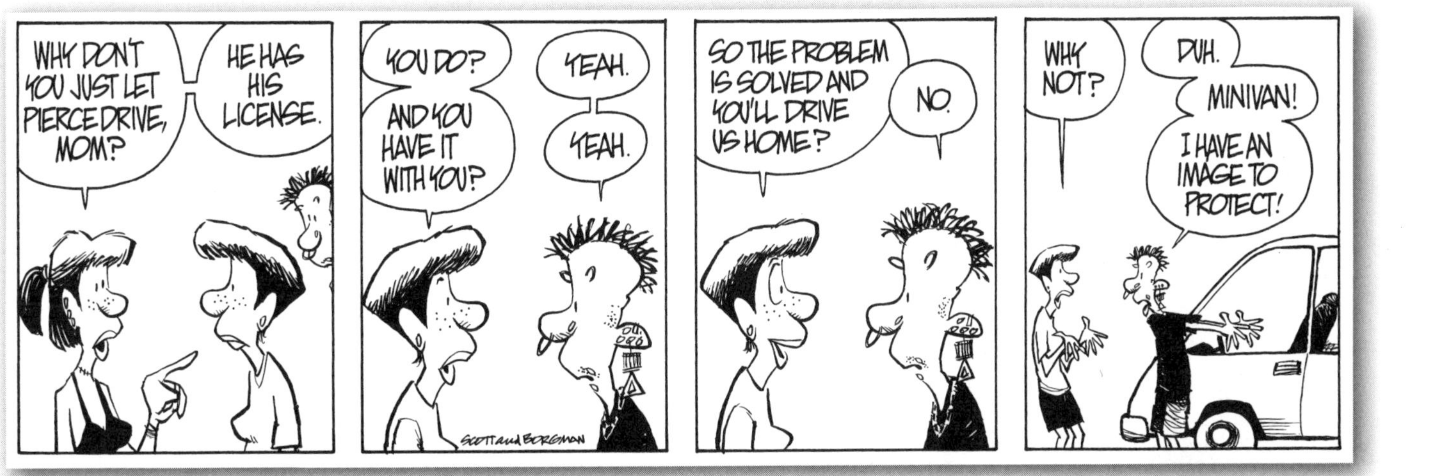
WHY DON'T YOU JUST LET PIERCE DRIVE, MOM?
HE HAS HIS LICENSE.
YOU DO?
AND YOU HAVE IT WITH YOU?
YEAH.
YEAH.
SCOTT and BORGMAN
SO THE PROBLEM IS SOLVED AND YOU'LL DRIVE US HOME?
NO.
WHY NOT?
DUH.
MINIVAN!
I HAVE AN IMAGE TO PROTECT!

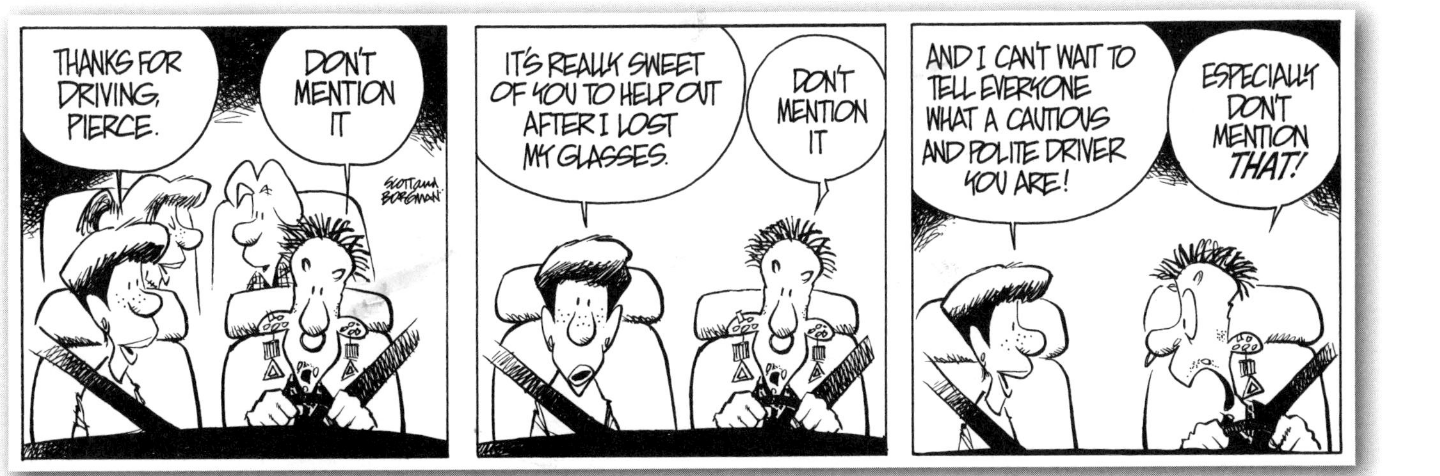
THANKS FOR DRIVING, PIERCE.
DON'T MENTION IT
SCOTT and BORGMAN
IT'S REALLY SWEET OF YOU TO HELP OUT AFTER I LOST MY GLASSES.
DON'T MENTION IT
AND I CAN'T WAIT TO TELL EVERYONE WHAT A CAUTIOUS AND POLITE DRIVER YOU ARE!
ESPECIALLY DON'T MENTION THAT!

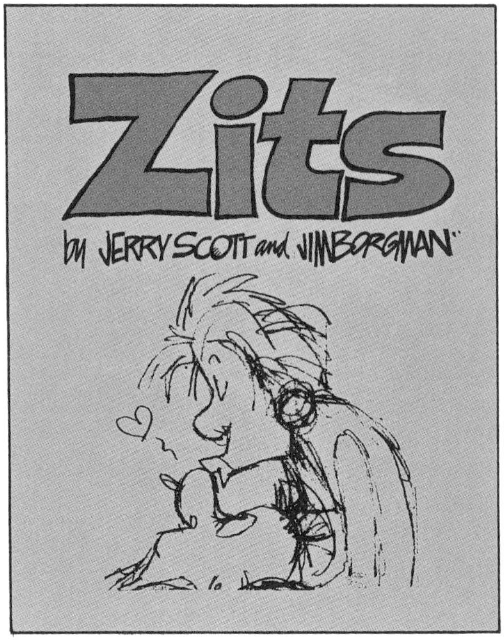
Zits
by JERRY SCOTT and JIM BORGMAN

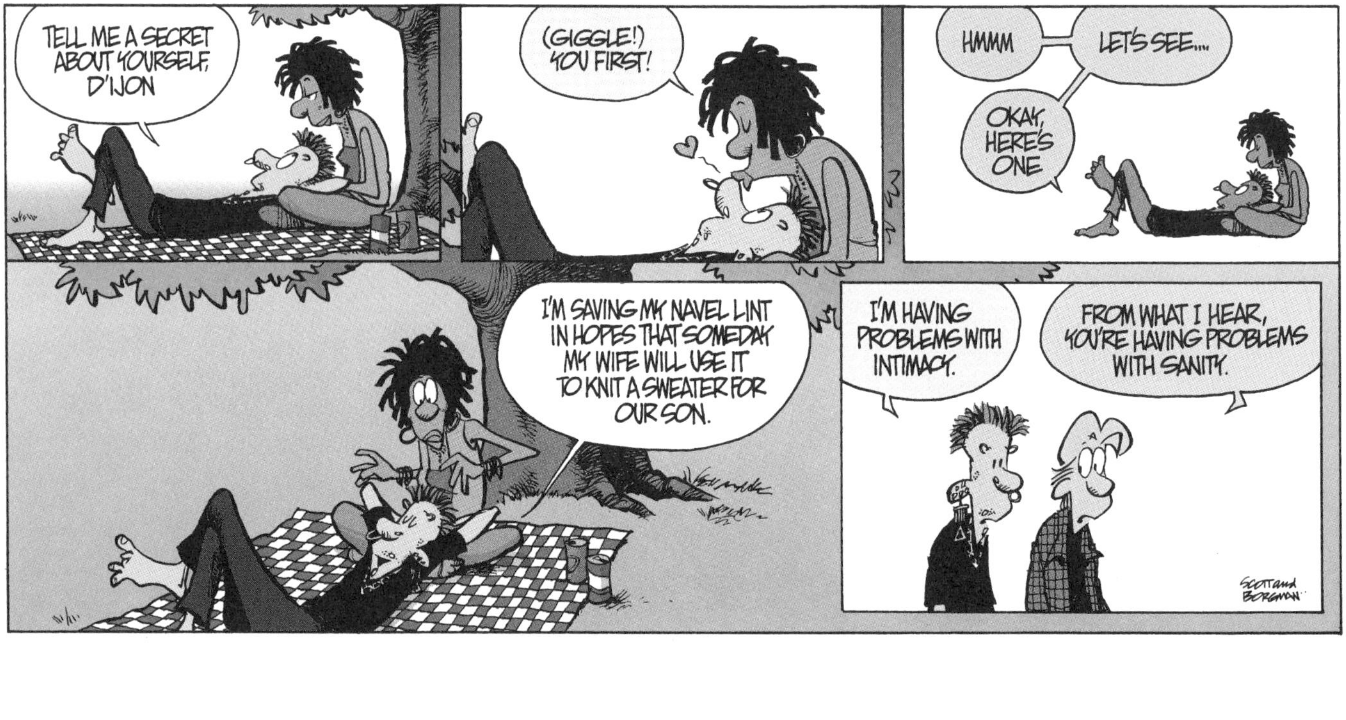
TELL ME A SECRET ABOUT YOURSELF, D'IJON
(GIGGLE!) YOU FIRST!
HMMM
LET'S SEE....
OKAY, HERE'S ONE
I'M SAVING MY NAVEL LINT IN HOPES THAT SOMEDAY MY WIFE WILL USE IT TO KNIT A SWEATER FOR OUR SON.
I'M HAVING PROBLEMS WITH INTIMACY.
FROM WHAT I HEAR, YOU'RE HAVING PROBLEMS WITH SANITY.
SCOTT and BORGMAN

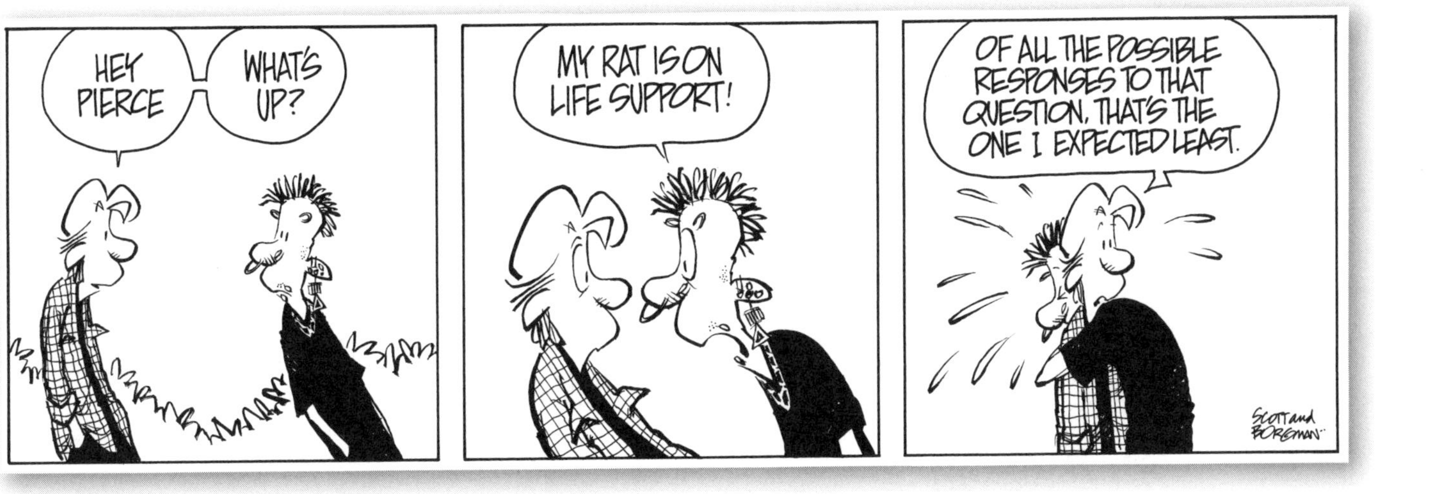
HEY PIERCE
WHAT'S UP?
MY RAT IS ON LIFE SUPPORT!
OF ALL THE POSSIBLE RESPONSES TO THAT QUESTION, THAT'S THE ONE I EXPECTED LEAST.
SCOTT and BORGMAN

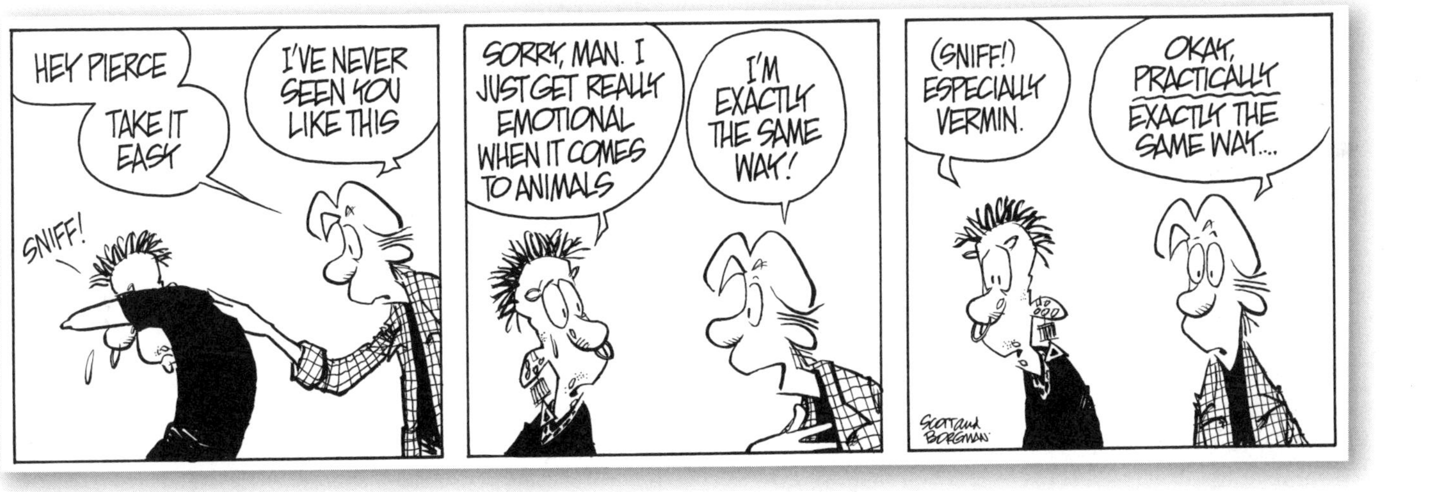
HEY PIERCE
TAKE IT EASY
I'VE NEVER SEEN YOU LIKE THIS
SNIFF!
SORRY, MAN. I JUST GET REALLY EMOTIONAL WHEN IT COMES TO ANIMALS
I'M EXACTLY THE SAME WAY!
(SNIFF!) ESPECIALLY VERMIN.
OKAY, PRACTICALLY EXACTLY THE SAME WAY....
SCOTT and BORGMAN

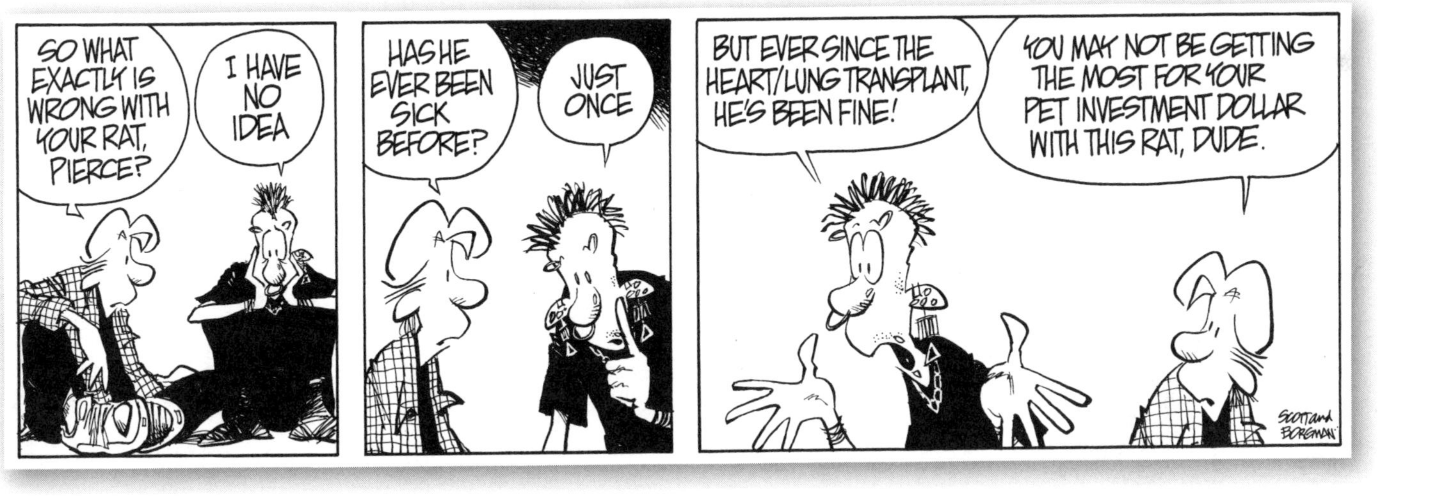
SO WHAT EXACTLY IS WRONG WITH YOUR RAT, PIERCE?
I HAVE NO IDEA
HAS HE EVER BEEN SICK BEFORE?
JUST ONCE
BUT EVER SINCE THE HEART/LUNG TRANSPLANT, HE'S BEEN FINE!
YOU MAY NOT BE GETTING THE MOST FOR YOUR PET INVESTMENT DOLLAR WITH THIS RAT, DUDE.
SCOTT and BORGMAN

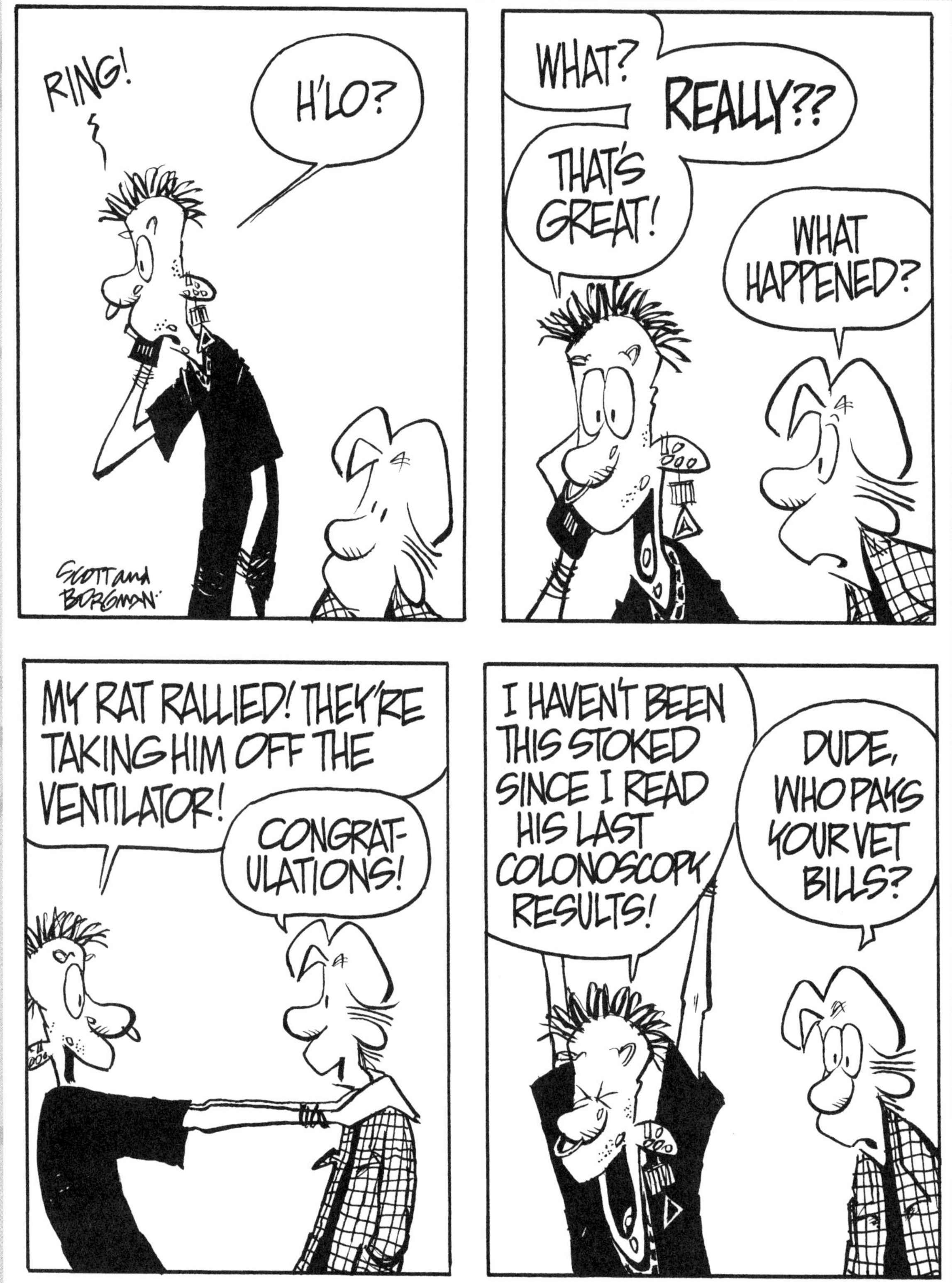
RING!
H'LO?
SCOTT and BORGMAN
WHAT? REALLY??
THAT'S GREAT!
WHAT HAPPENED?
MY RAT RALLIED! THEY'RE TAKING HIM OFF THE VENTILATOR!
CONGRAT-ULATIONS!
I HAVEN'T BEEN THIS STOKED SINCE I READ HIS LAST COLONOSCOPY RESULTS!
DUDE, WHO PAYS YOUR VET BILLS?

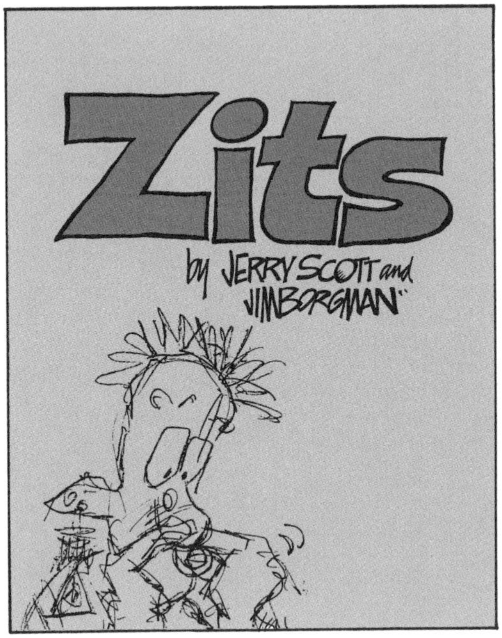
Zits
by JERRY SCOTT and JIM BORGMAN

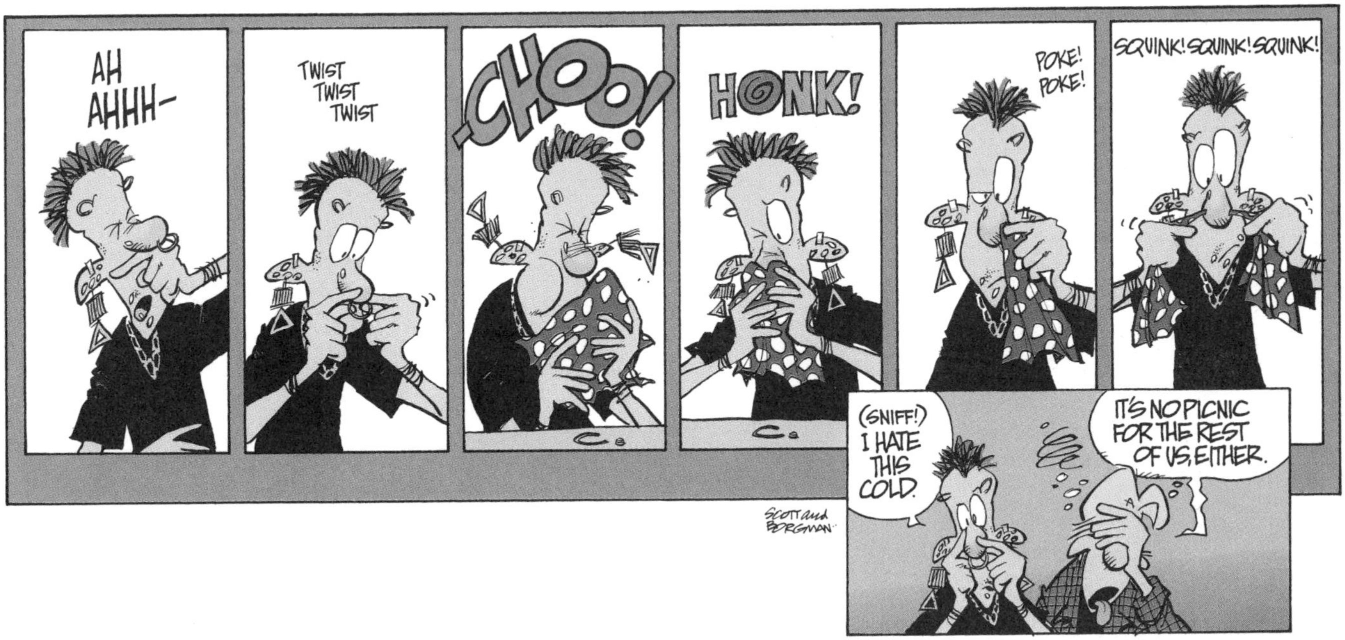
AH AHHH-
TWIST TWIST TWIST
-CHOO!
HONK!
POKE! POKE!
SQUINK! SQUINK! SQUINK!
(SNIFF!) I HATE THIS COLD.
IT'S NO PICNIC FOR THE REST OF US, EITHER.
SCOTT and BORGMAN

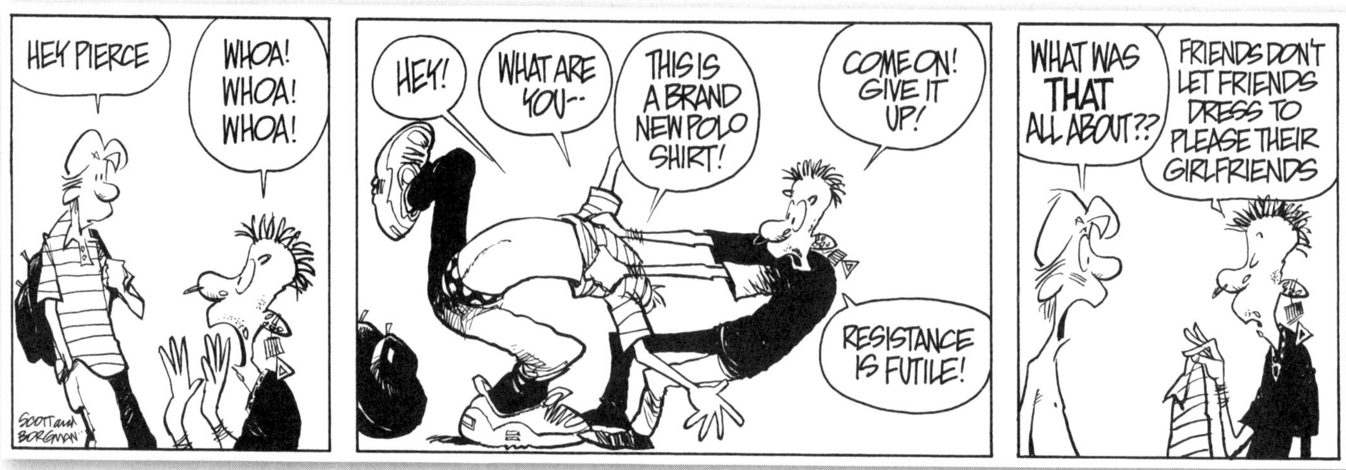
HEY PIERCE
WHOA! WHOA! WHOA!
HEY!
WHAT ARE YOU--
THIS IS A BRAND NEW POLO SHIRT!
COME ON! GIVE IT UP!
RESISTANCE IS FUTILE!
WHAT WAS **THAT** ALL ABOUT??
FRIENDS DON'T LET FRIENDS DRESS TO PLEASE THEIR GIRLFRIENDS

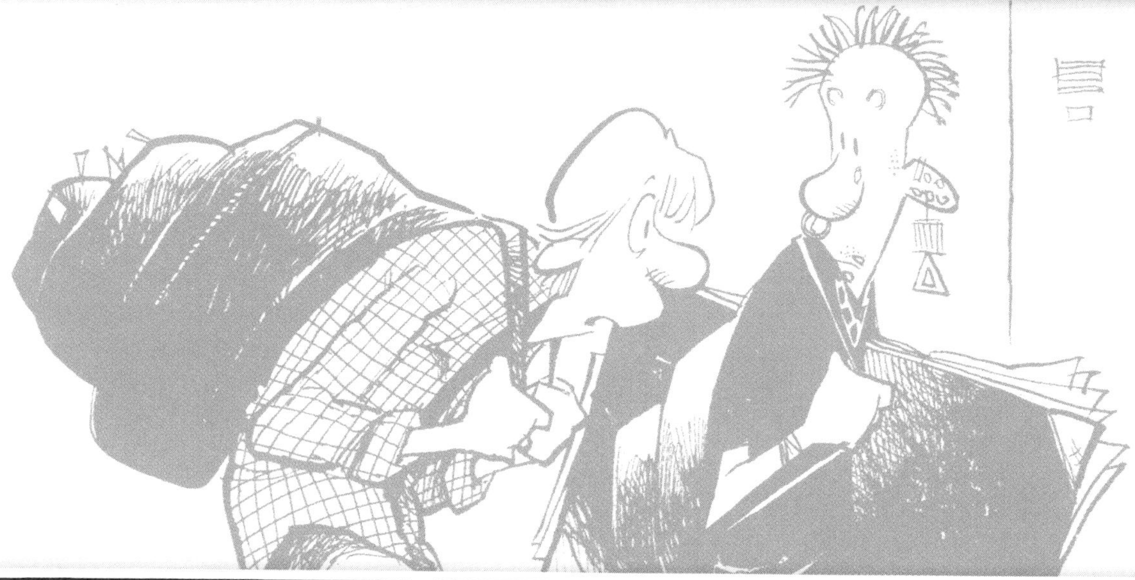

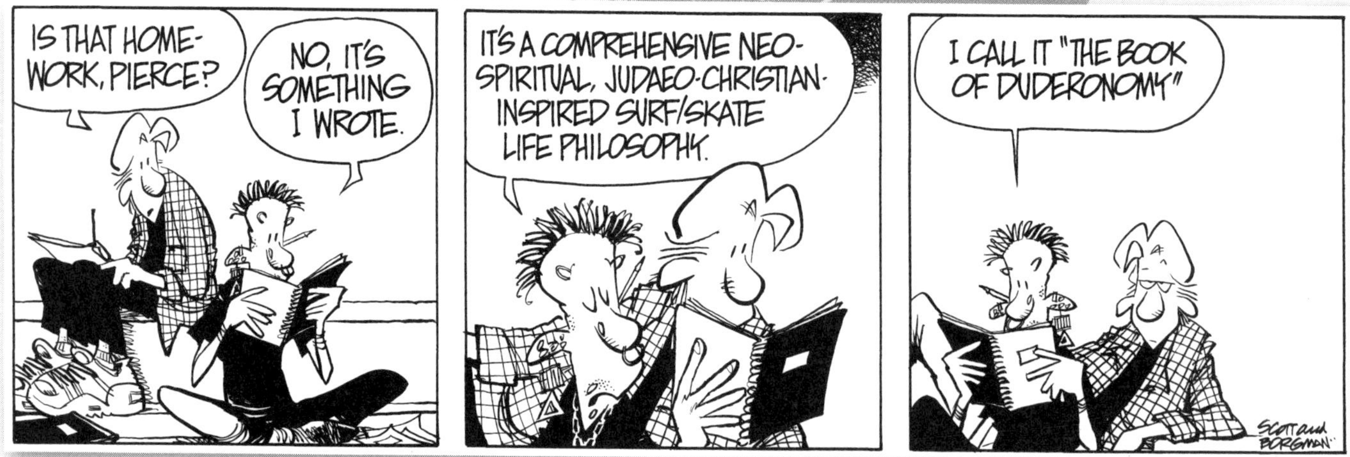
IS THAT HOME-WORK, PIERCE?
NO, IT'S SOMETHING I WROTE.
IT'S A COMPREHENSIVE NEO-SPIRITUAL, JUDAEO-CHRISTIAN-INSPIRED SURF/SKATE LIFE PHILOSOPHY.
I CALL IT "THE BOOK OF DUDERONOMY"

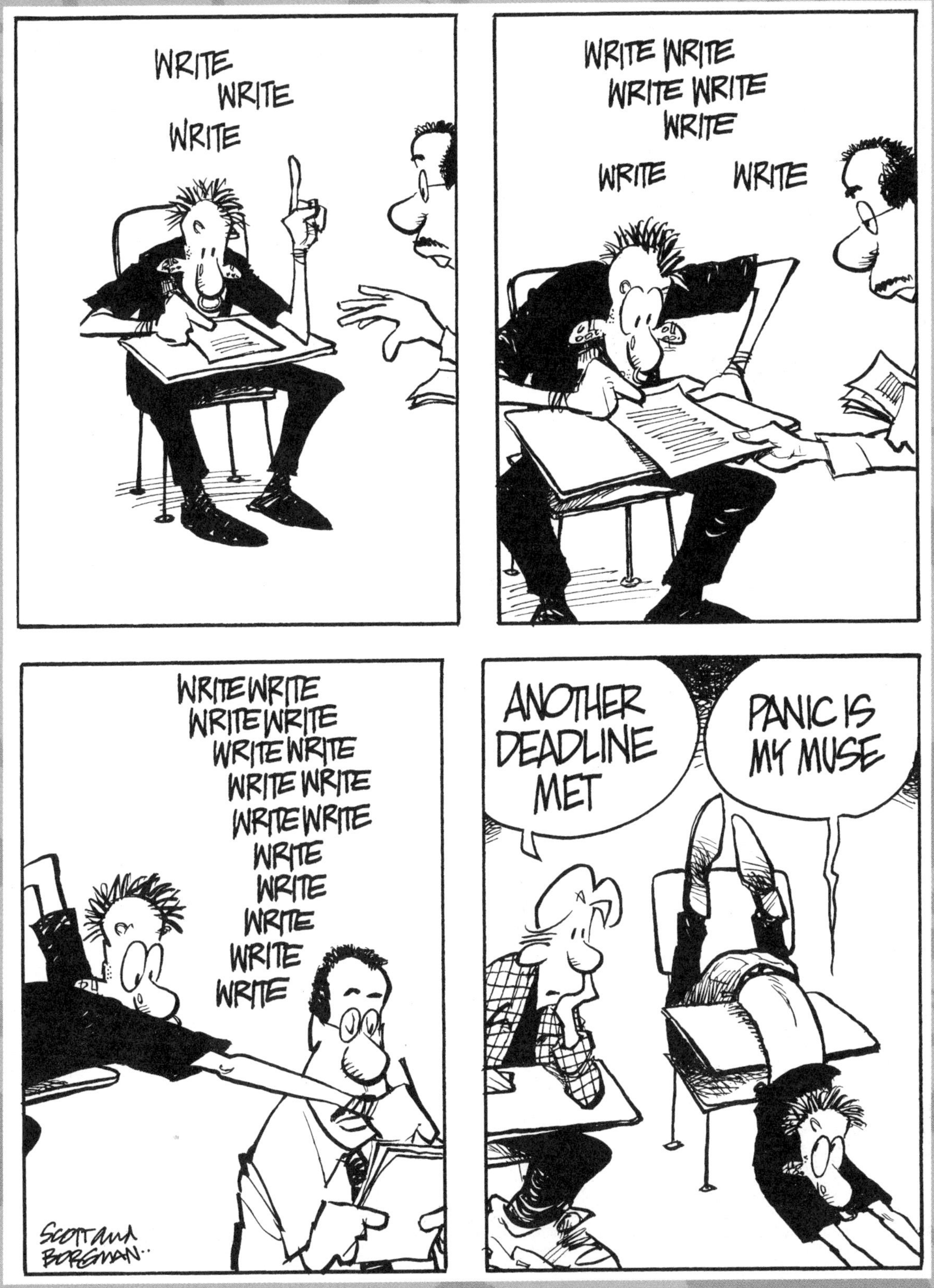
WRITE WRITE WRITE
WRITE WRITE WRITE WRITE WRITE WRITE WRITE
WRITE WRITE WRITE WRITE WRITE WRITE WRITE WRITE WRITE WRITE WRITE WRITE WRITE WRITE
ANOTHER DEADLINE MET
PANIC IS MY MUSE
SCOTT AND BORGMAN

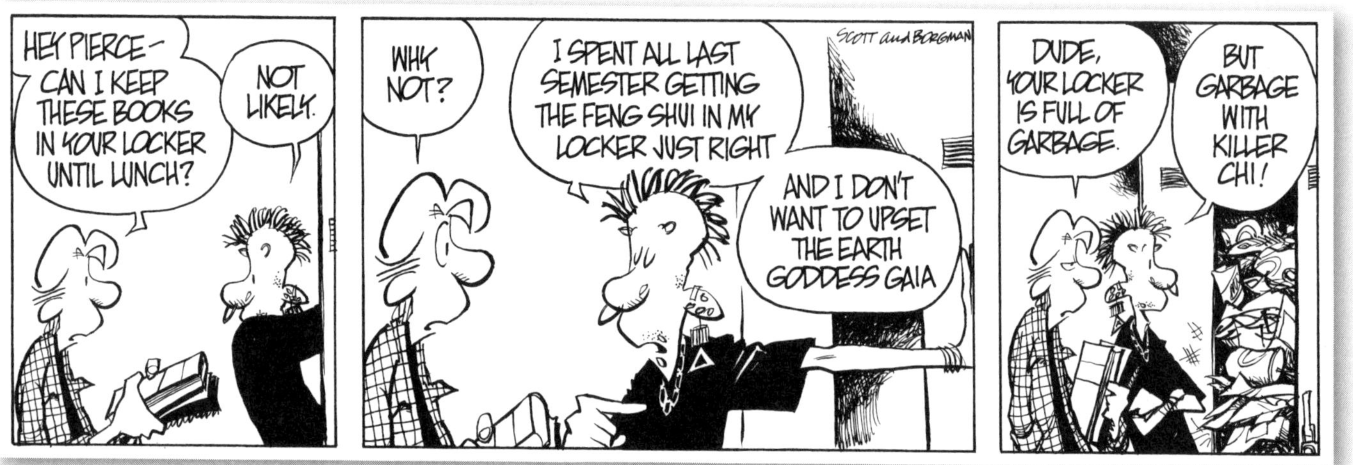
HEY PIERCE- CAN I KEEP THESE BOOKS IN YOUR LOCKER UNTIL LUNCH?
NOT LIKELY.
WHY NOT?
I SPENT ALL LAST SEMESTER GETTING THE FENG SHUI IN MY LOCKER JUST RIGHT
AND I DON'T WANT TO UPSET THE EARTH GODDESS GAIA
SCOTT and BORGMAN
DUDE, YOUR LOCKER IS FULL OF GARBAGE.
BUT GARBAGE WITH KILLER CHI!

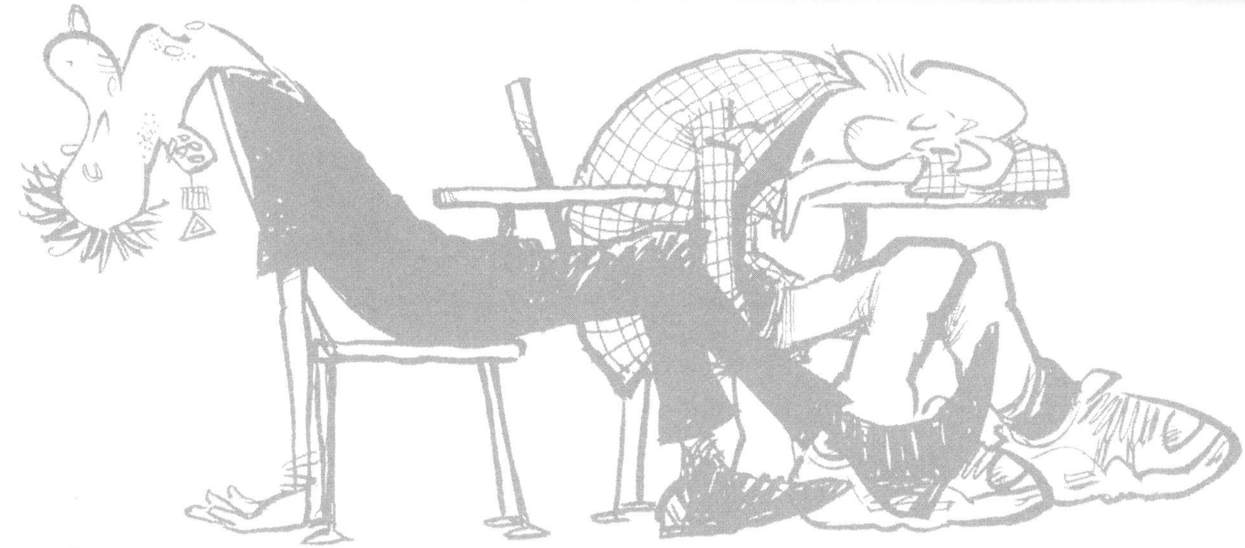

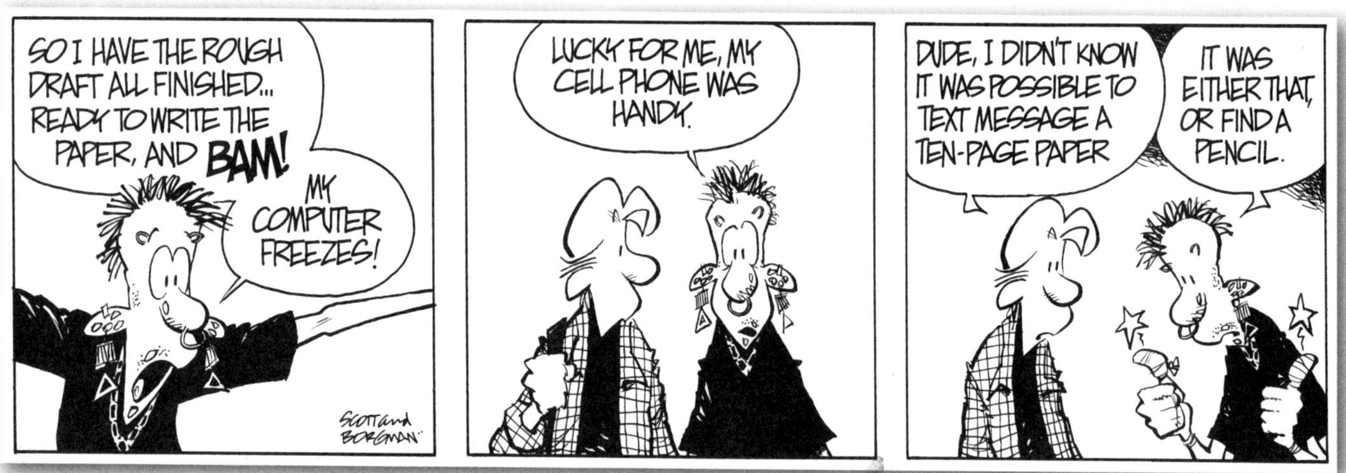
SO I HAVE THE ROUGH DRAFT ALL FINISHED... READY TO WRITE THE PAPER, AND BAM!
MY COMPUTER FREEZES!
SCOTT and BORGMAN
LUCKY FOR ME, MY CELL PHONE WAS HANDY.
DUDE, I DIDN'T KNOW IT WAS POSSIBLE TO TEXT MESSAGE A TEN-PAGE PAPER
IT WAS EITHER THAT, OR FIND A PENCIL.

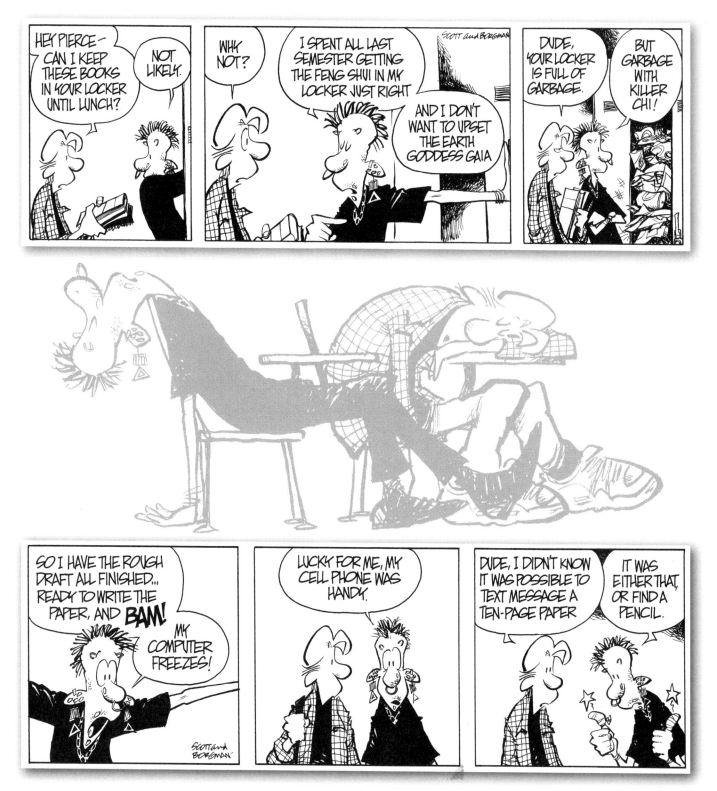

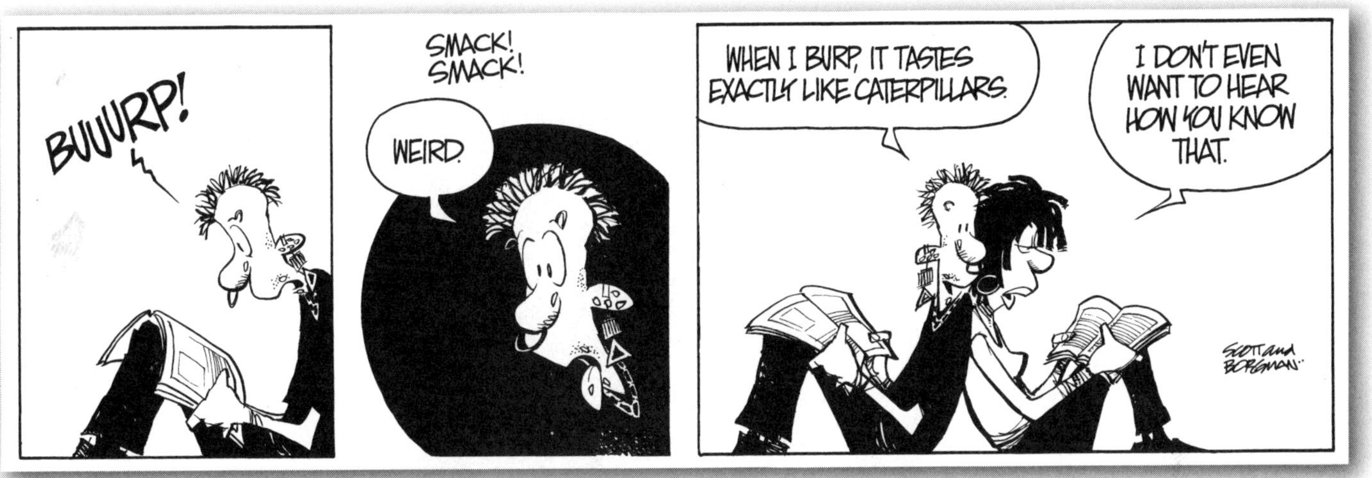
BUUURP!
SMACK! SMACK!
WEIRD.
WHEN I BURP, IT TASTES EXACTLY LIKE CATERPILLARS.
I DON'T EVEN WANT TO HEAR HOW YOU KNOW THAT.
SCOTT AND BORGMAN

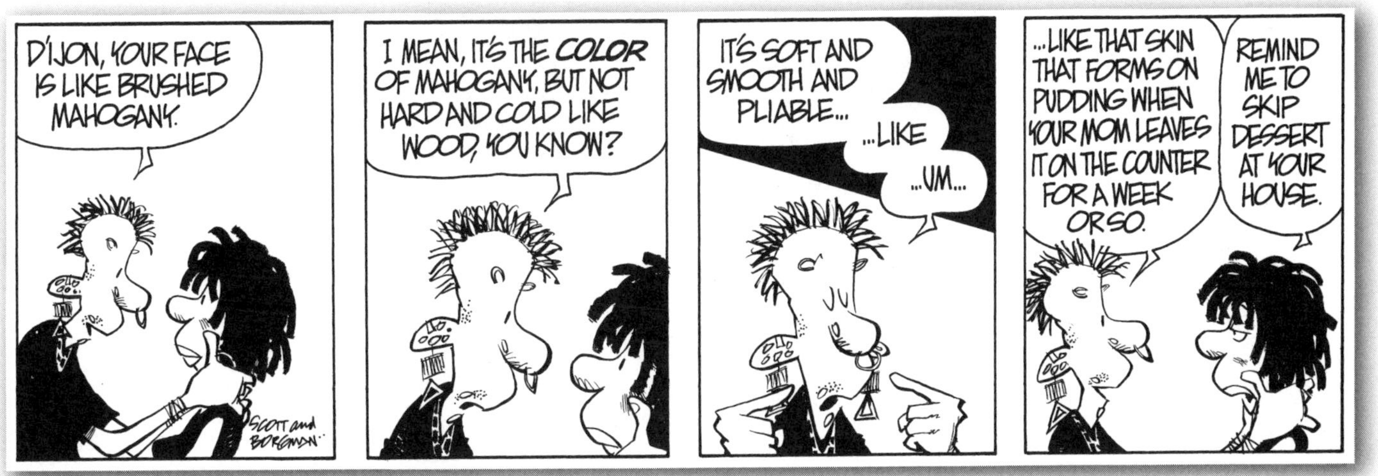
D'JON, YOUR FACE IS LIKE BRUSHED MAHOGANY.
SCOTT AND BORGMAN
I MEAN, IT'S THE ***COLOR*** OF MAHOGANY, BUT NOT HARD AND COLD LIKE WOOD, YOU KNOW?
IT'S SOFT AND SMOOTH AND PLIABLE...
...LIKE
...UM...
...LIKE THAT SKIN THAT FORMS ON PUDDING WHEN YOUR MOM LEAVES IT ON THE COUNTER FOR A WEEK OR SO.
REMIND ME TO SKIP DESSERT AT YOUR HOUSE.

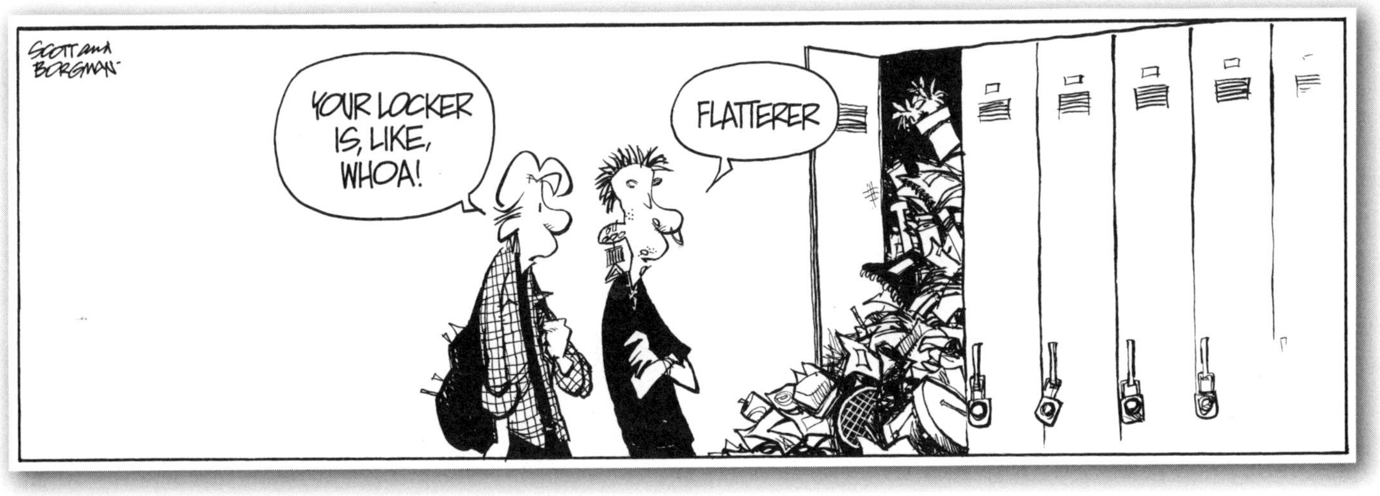
SCOTT AND BORGMAN
YOUR LOCKER IS, LIKE, WHOA!
FLATTERER

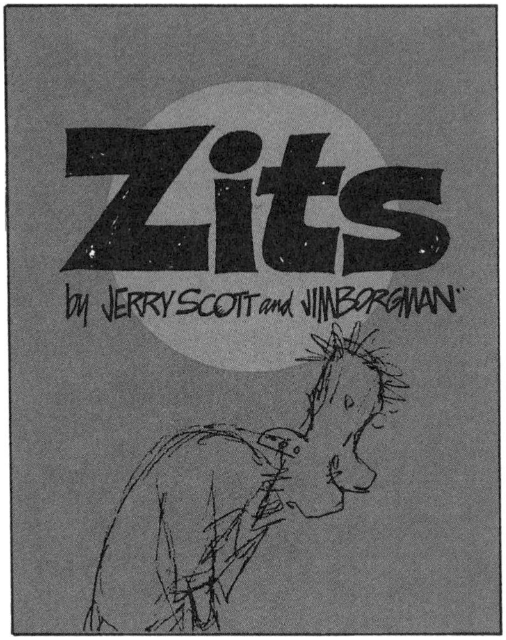
Zits
by JERRY SCOTT and JIM BORGMAN

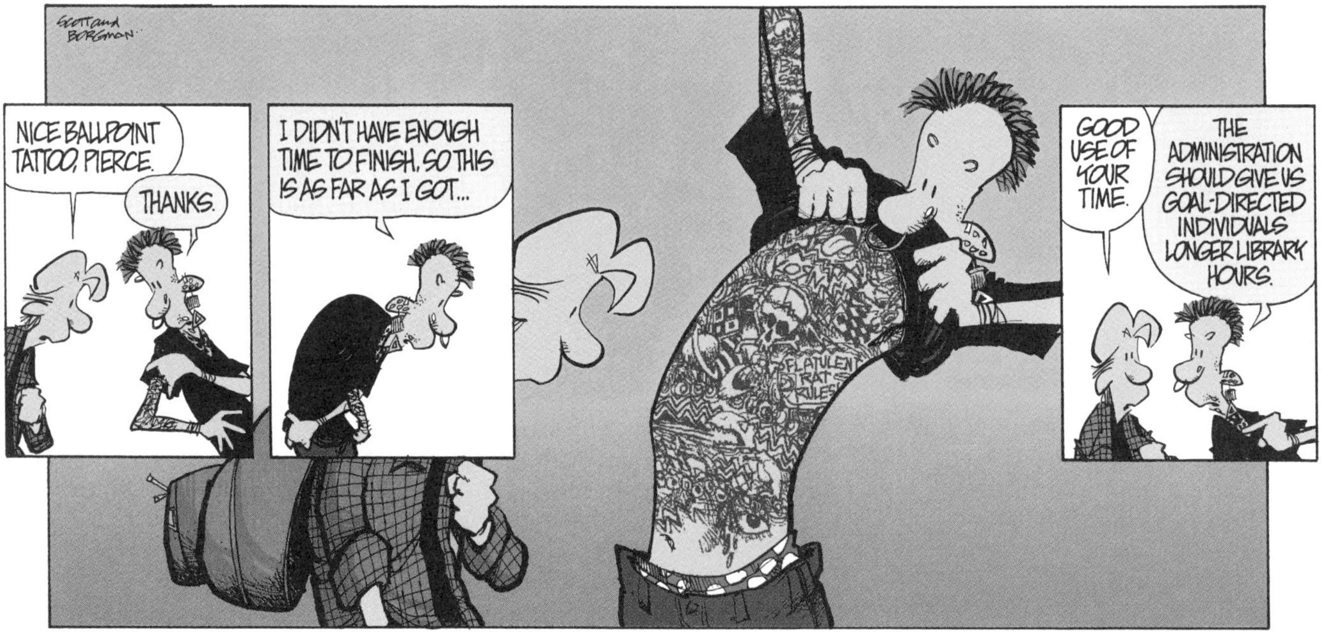
SCOTT and BORGMAN
NICE BALLPOINT TATTOO, PIERCE.
THANKS.
I DIDN'T HAVE ENOUGH TIME TO FINISH, SO THIS IS AS FAR AS I GOT...
FLATULEN RAT RULES
GOOD USE OF YOUR TIME.
THE ADMINISTRATION SHOULD GIVE US GOAL-DIRECTED INDIVIDUALS LONGER LIBRARY HOURS.

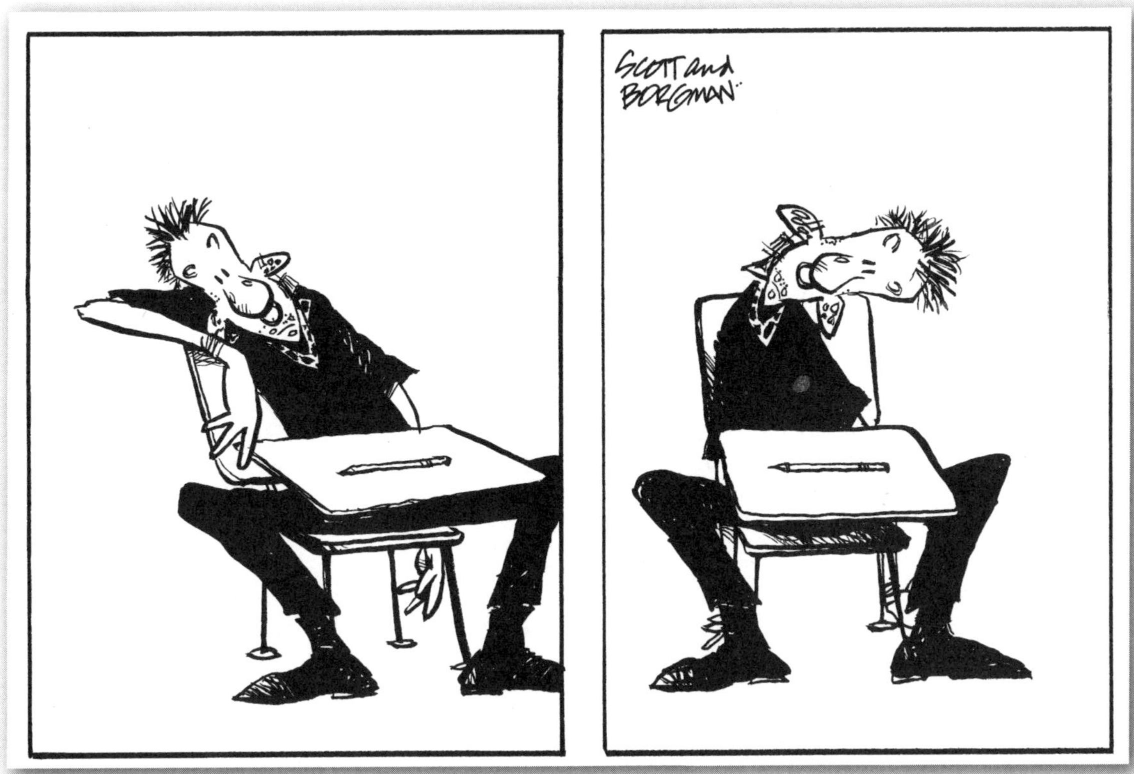
SCOTT and BORGMAN

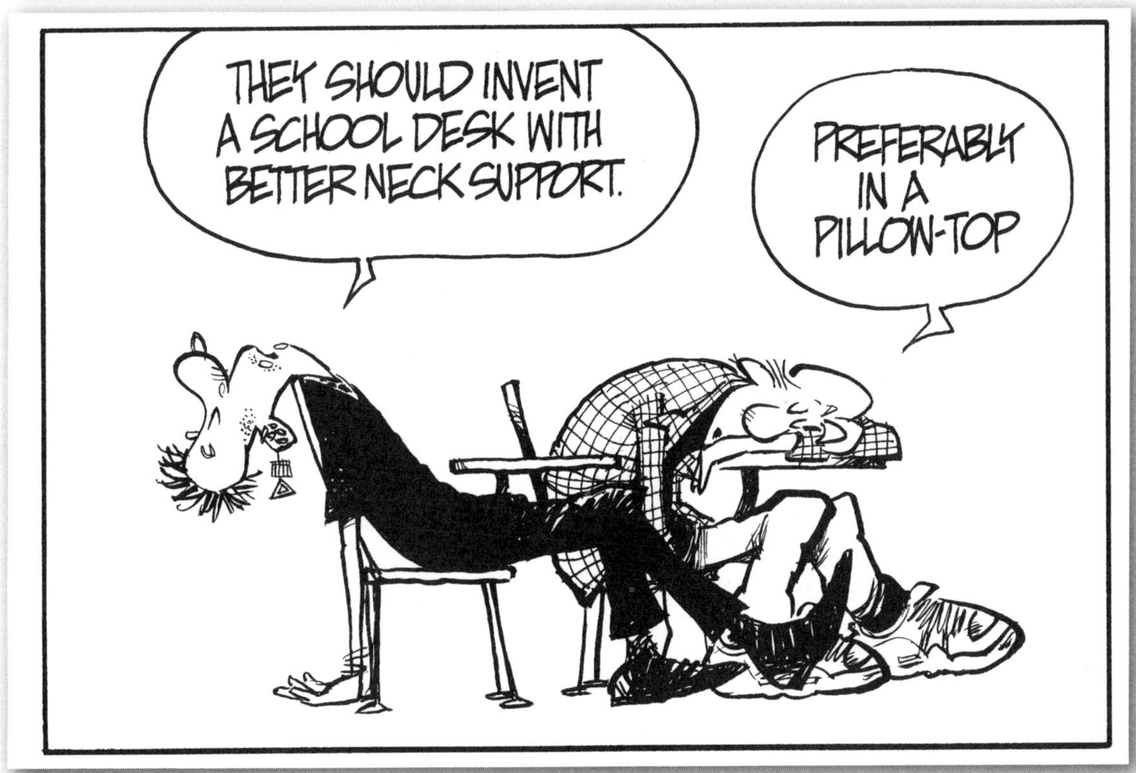
THEY SHOULD INVENT A SCHOOL DESK WITH BETTER NECK SUPPORT.
PREFERABLY IN A PILLOW-TOP

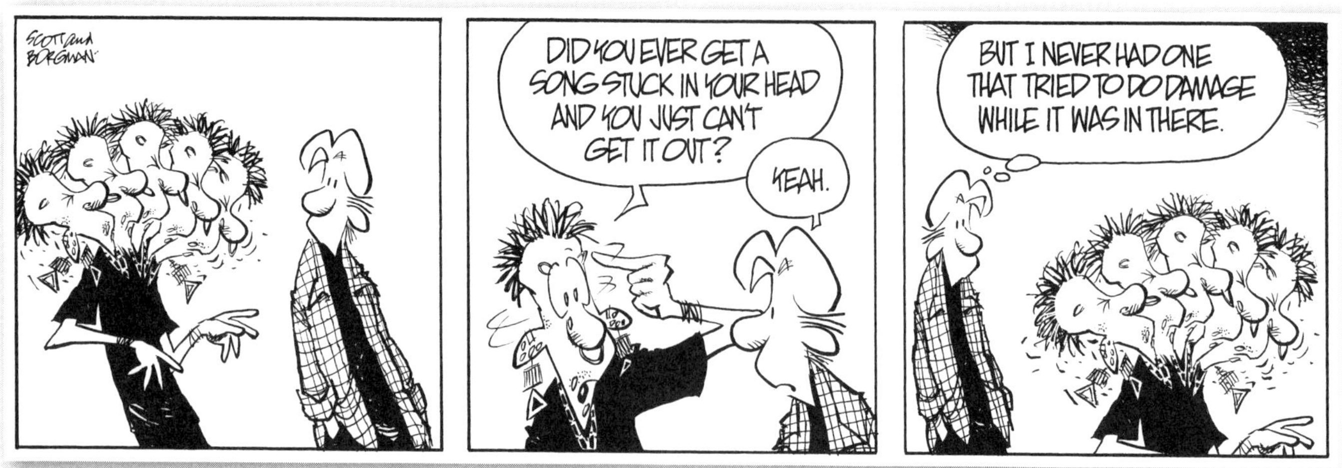
SCOTT and BORGMAN
DID YOU EVER GET A SONG STUCK IN YOUR HEAD AND YOU JUST CAN'T GET IT OUT?
YEAH.
BUT I NEVER HAD ONE THAT TRIED TO DO DAMAGE WHILE IT WAS IN THERE.

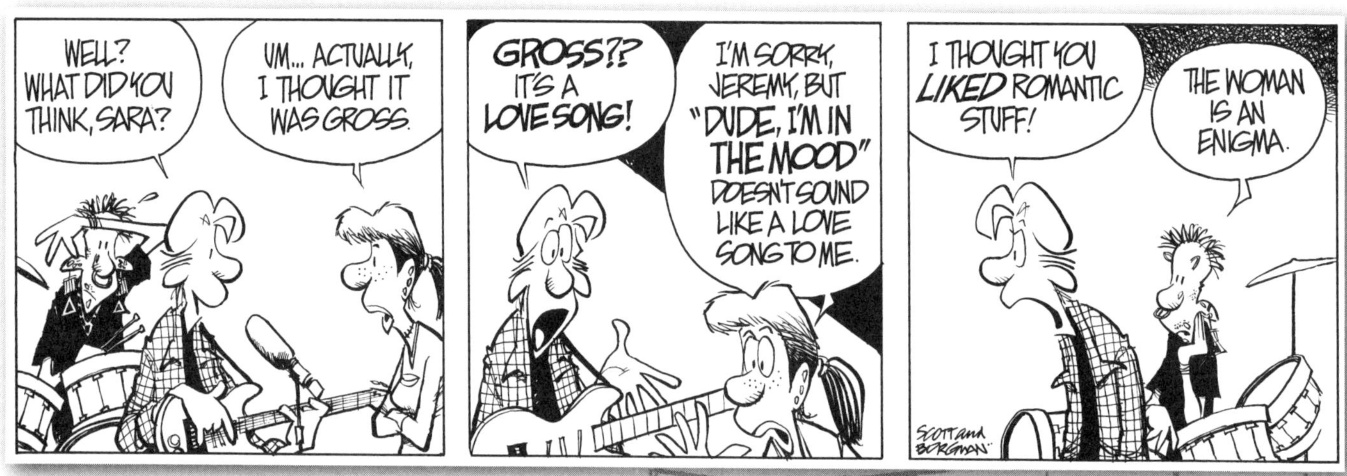
WELL? WHAT DID YOU THINK, SARA?
UM... ACTUALLY, I THOUGHT IT WAS GROSS.
GROSS?!? IT'S A LOVE SONG!
I'M SORRY, JEREMY, BUT "DUDE, I'M IN THE MOOD" DOESN'T SOUND LIKE A LOVE SONG TO ME.
I THOUGHT YOU LIKED ROMANTIC STUFF!
THE WOMAN IS AN ENIGMA.
SCOTT and BORGMAN

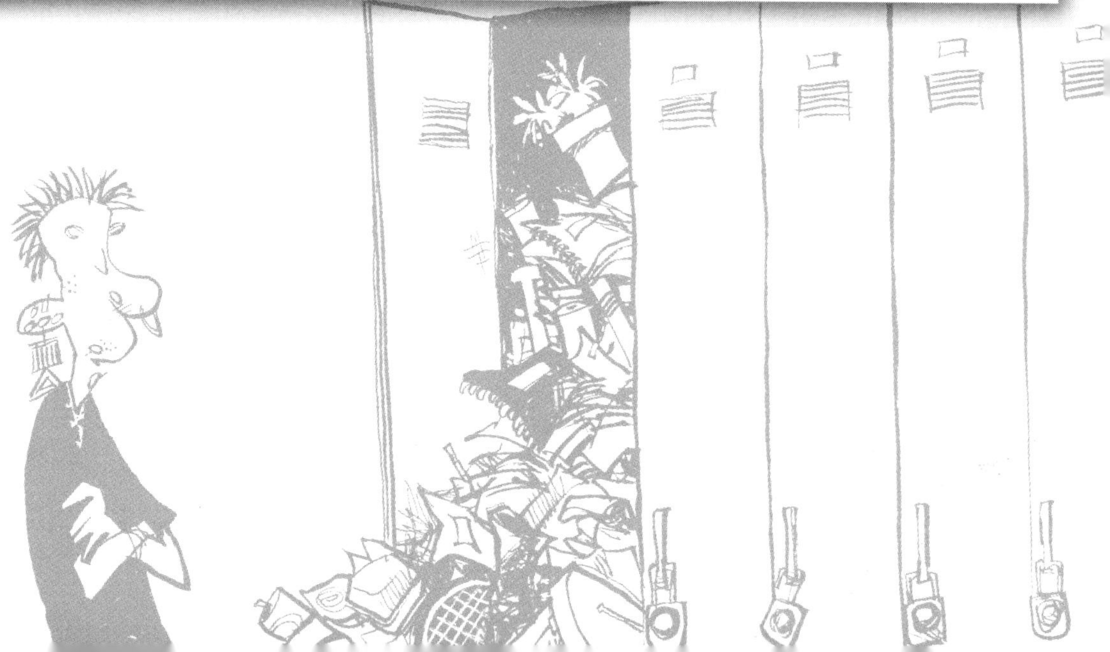

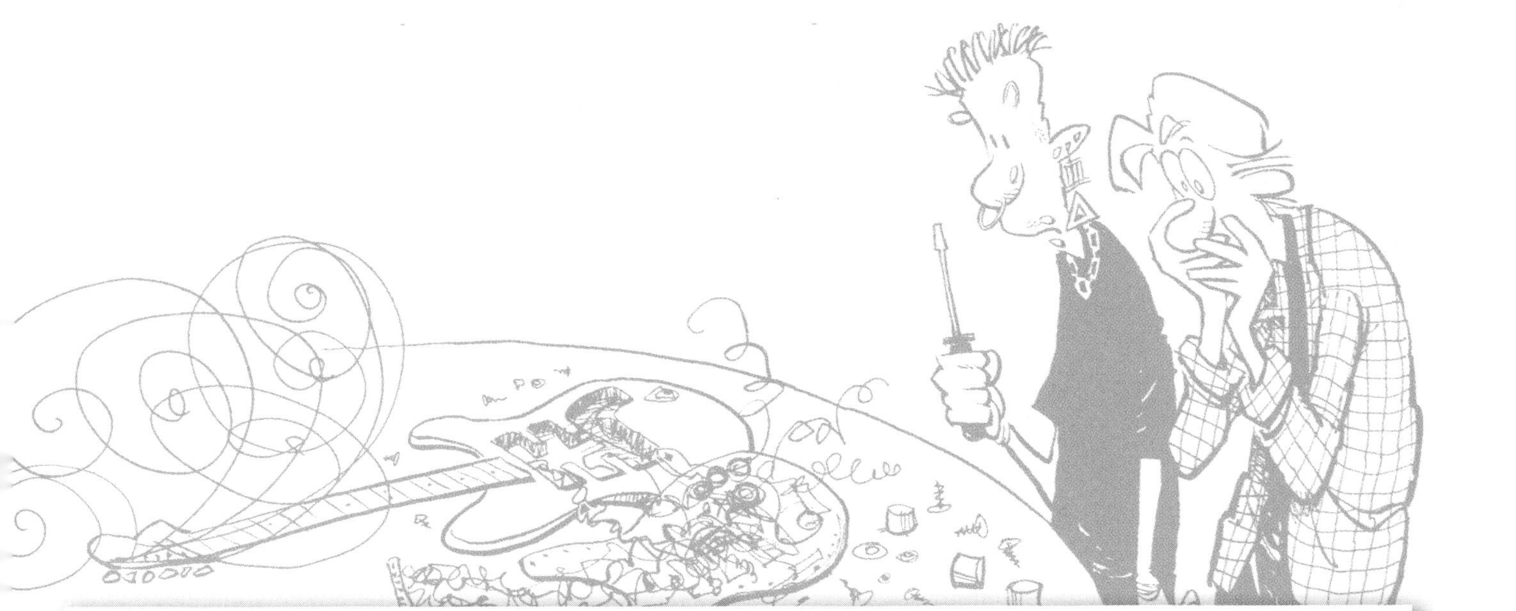

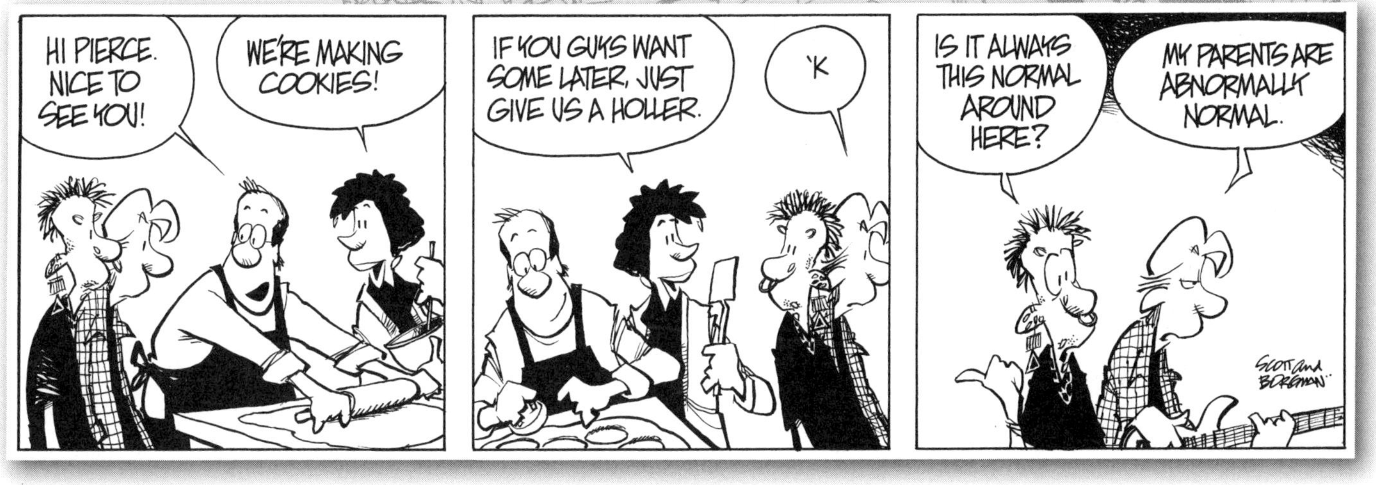
HI PIERCE. NICE TO SEE YOU!
WE'RE MAKING COOKIES!
IF YOU GUYS WANT SOME LATER, JUST GIVE US A HOLLER.
'K
IS IT ALWAYS THIS NORMAL AROUND HERE?
MY PARENTS ARE ABNORMALLY NORMAL.
SCOTT and BORGMAN

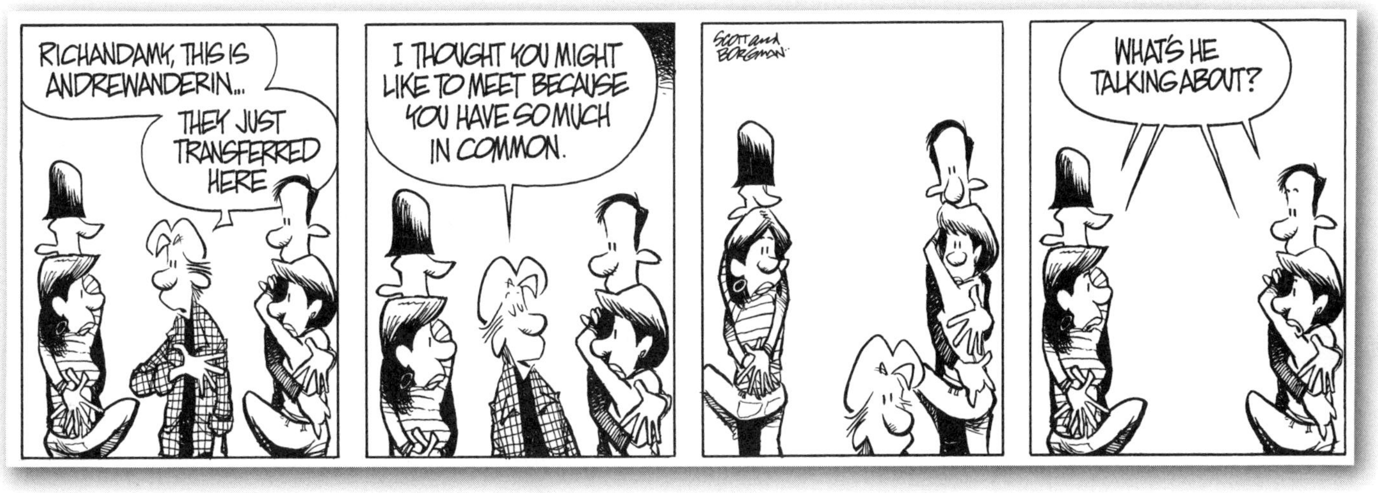
RICHANDAMY, THIS IS ANDREWANDERIN...
THEY JUST TRANSFERRED HERE
I THOUGHT YOU MIGHT LIKE TO MEET BECAUSE YOU HAVE SO MUCH IN COMMON.
SCOTT and BORGMAN
WHAT'S HE TALKING ABOUT?

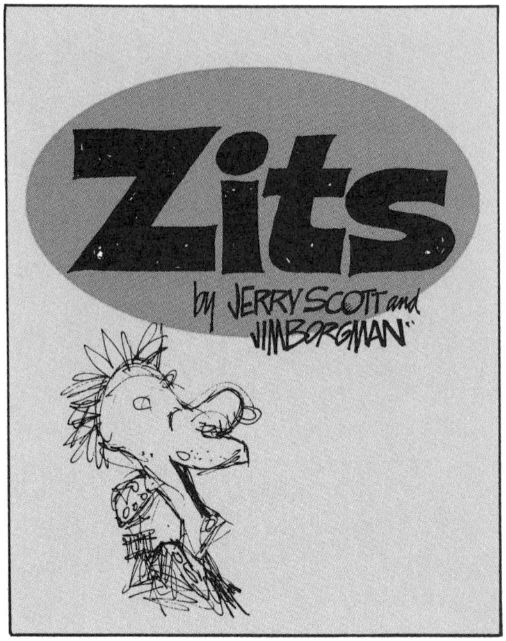
Zits
by JERRY SCOTT and JIM BORGMAN

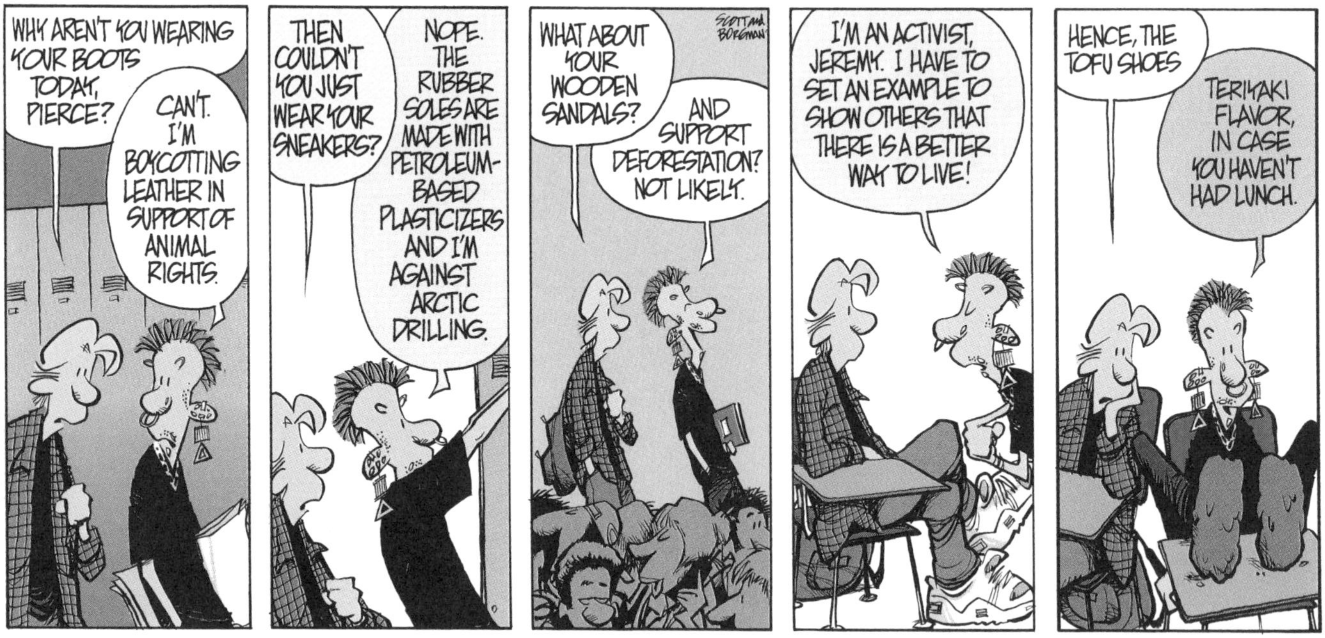
WHY AREN'T YOU WEARING YOUR BOOTS TODAY, PIERCE?
CAN'T. I'M BOYCOTTING LEATHER IN SUPPORT OF ANIMAL RIGHTS.
THEN COULDN'T YOU JUST WEAR YOUR SNEAKERS?
NOPE. THE RUBBER SOLES ARE MADE WITH PETROLEUM-BASED PLASTICIZERS AND I'M AGAINST ARCTIC DRILLING.
SCOTT AND BORGMAN
WHAT ABOUT YOUR WOODEN SANDALS?
AND SUPPORT DEFORESTATION? NOT LIKELY.
I'M AN ACTIVIST, JEREMY. I HAVE TO SET AN EXAMPLE TO SHOW OTHERS THAT THERE IS A BETTER WAY TO LIVE!
HENCE, THE TOFU SHOES
TERIYAKI FLAVOR, IN CASE YOU HAVEN'T HAD LUNCH.

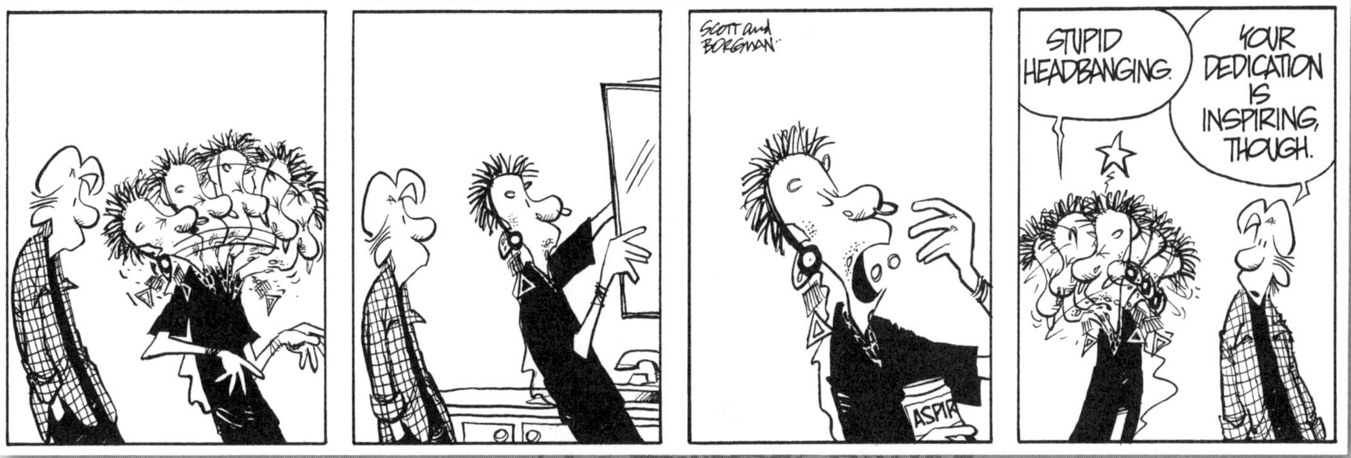
SCOTT and BORGMAN
STUPID HEADBANGING.
YOUR DEDICATION IS INSPIRING, THOUGH.
ASPIR

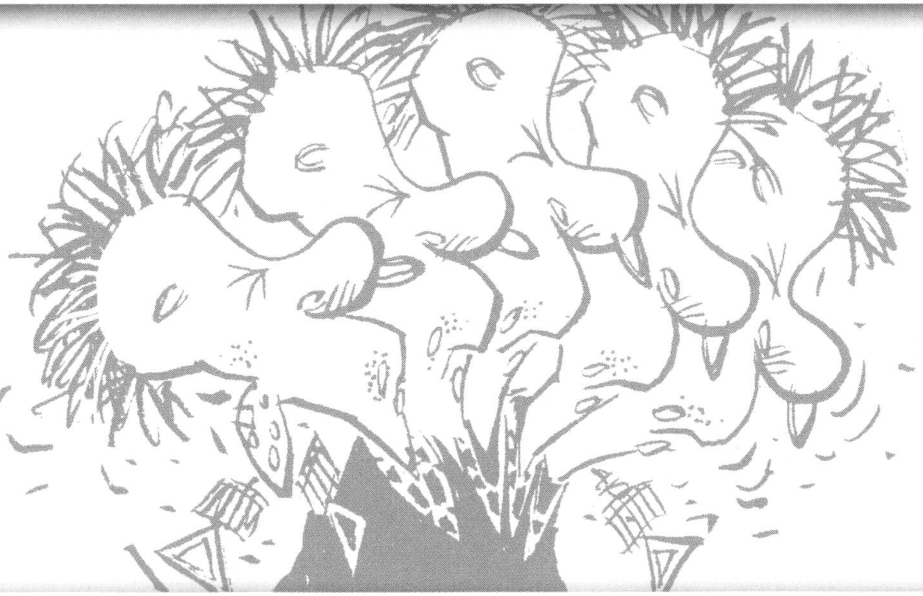

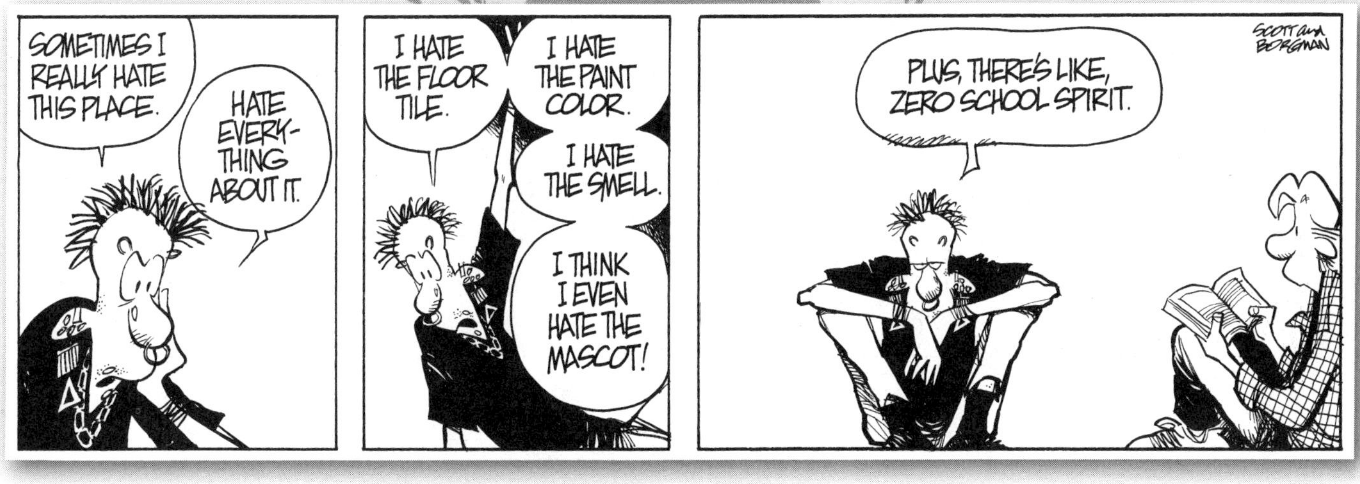
SOMETIMES I REALLY HATE THIS PLACE.
HATE EVERY-THING ABOUT IT.
I HATE THE FLOOR TILE.
I HATE THE PAINT COLOR.
I HATE THE SMELL.
I THINK I EVEN HATE THE MASCOT!
SCOTT and BORGMAN
PLUS, THERE'S LIKE, ZERO SCHOOL SPIRIT.

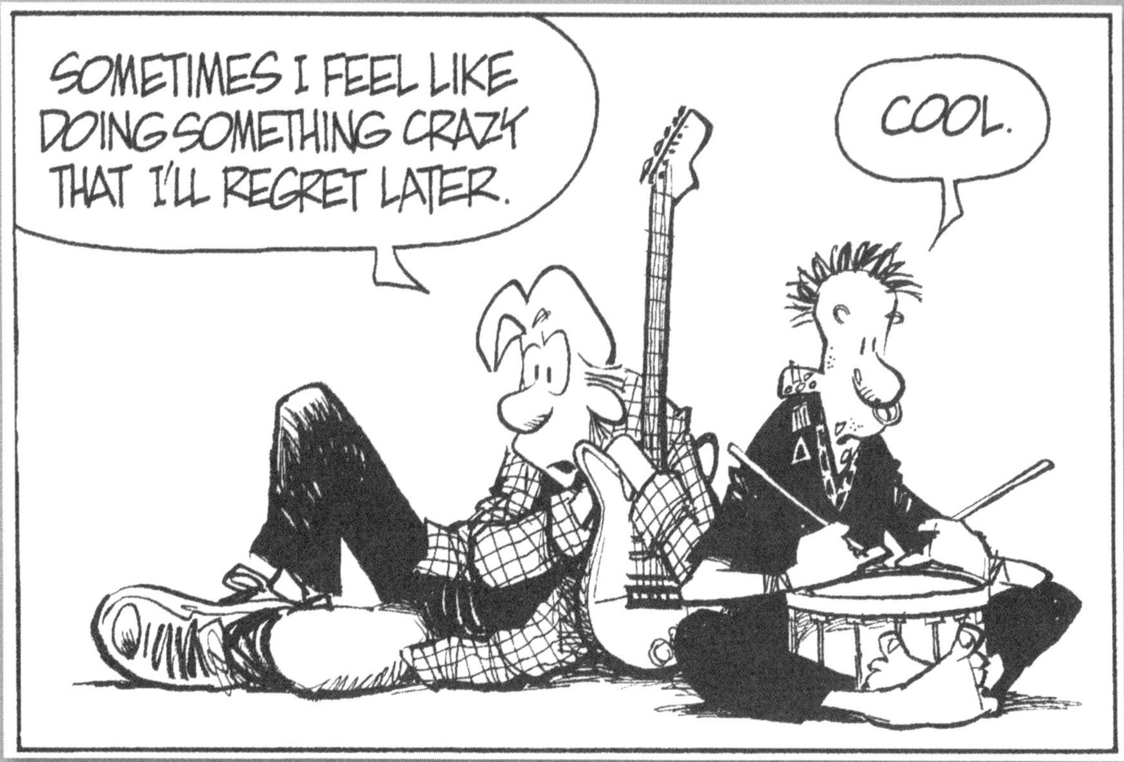
SOMETIMES I FEEL LIKE DOING SOMETHING CRAZY THAT I'LL REGRET LATER.
COOL.

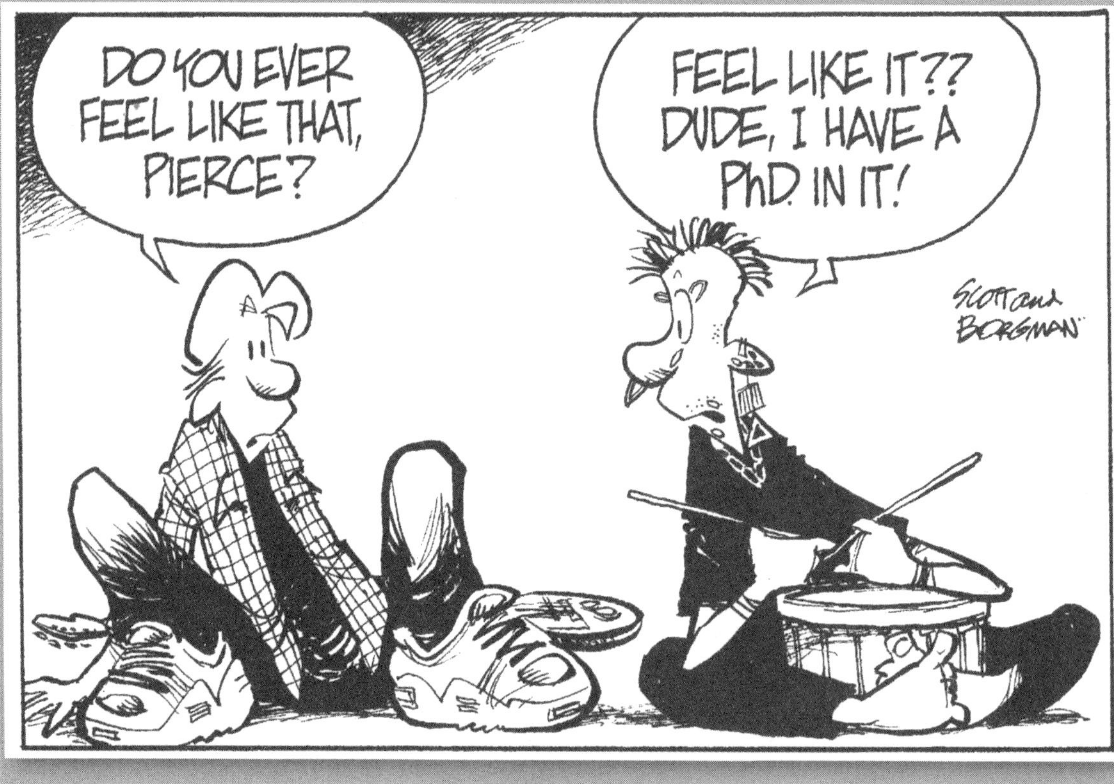
DO YOU EVER FEEL LIKE THAT, PIERCE?
FEEL LIKE IT?? DUDE, I HAVE A PhD. IN IT!
SCOTT and BORGMAN

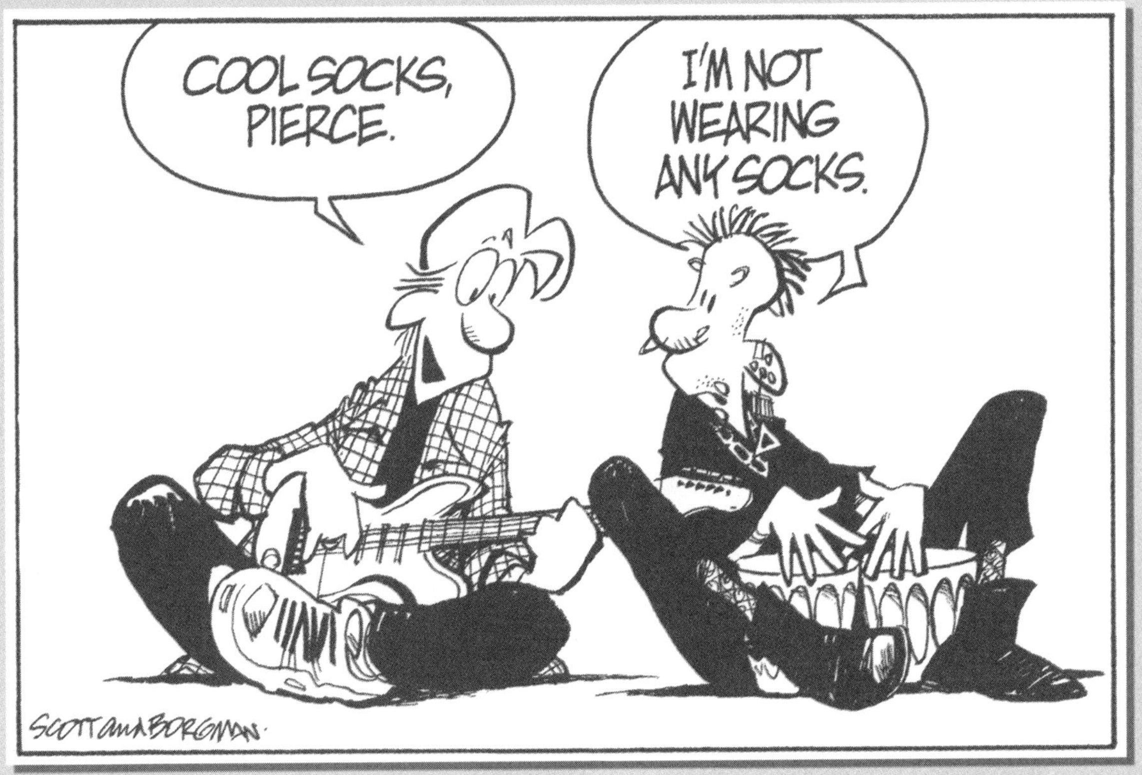
COOL SOCKS, PIERCE.
I'M NOT WEARING ANY SOCKS.
SCOTT and BORGMAN

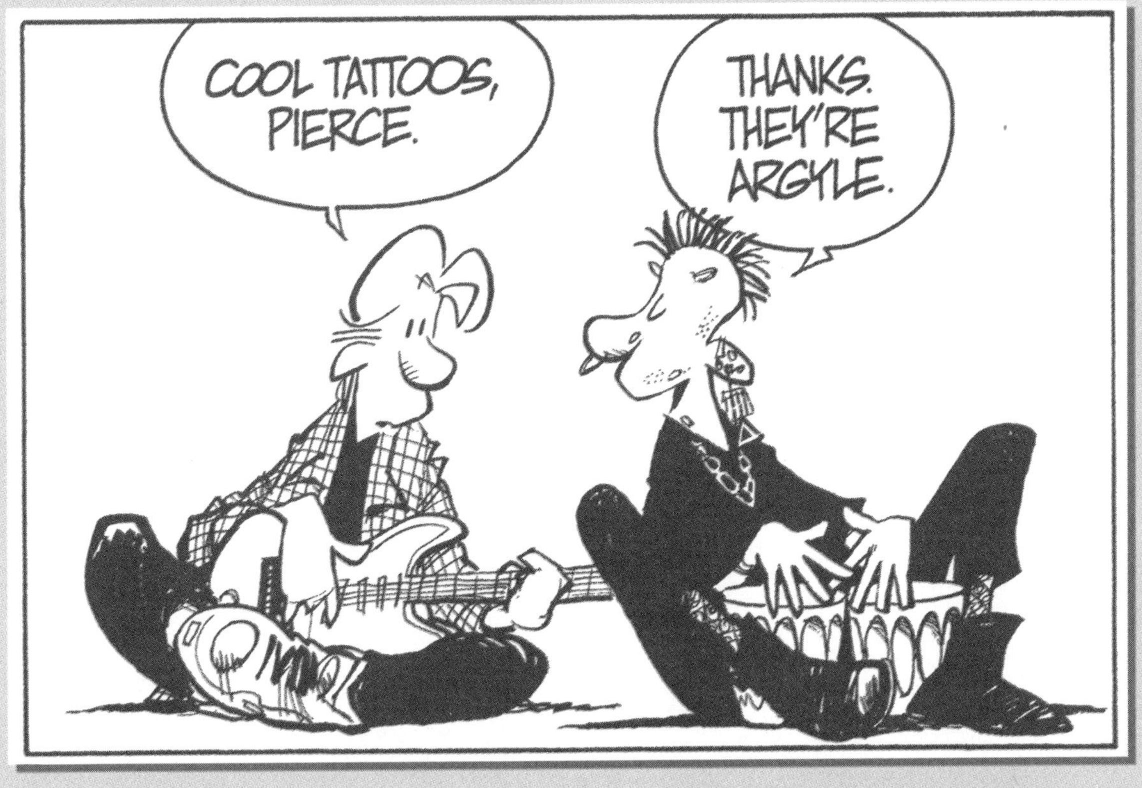
COOL TATTOOS, PIERCE.
THANKS. THEY'RE ARGYLE.

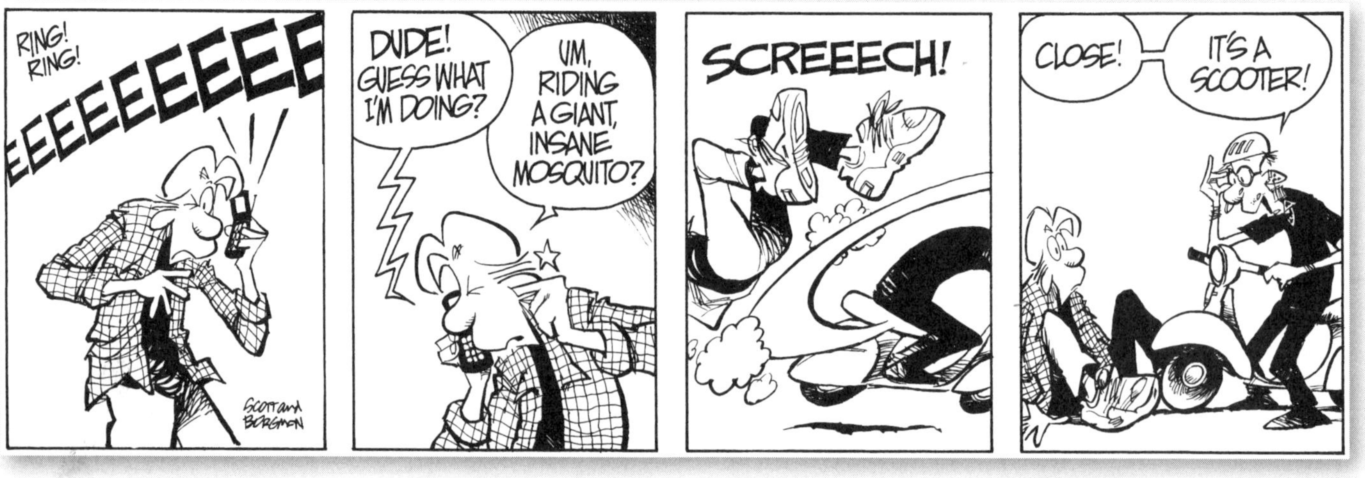
RING! RING!
EEEEEEEEEEEE
DUDE! GUESS WHAT I'M DOING?
UM, RIDING A GIANT, INSANE MOSQUITO?
SCREEECH!
CLOSE!
IT'S A SCOOTER!

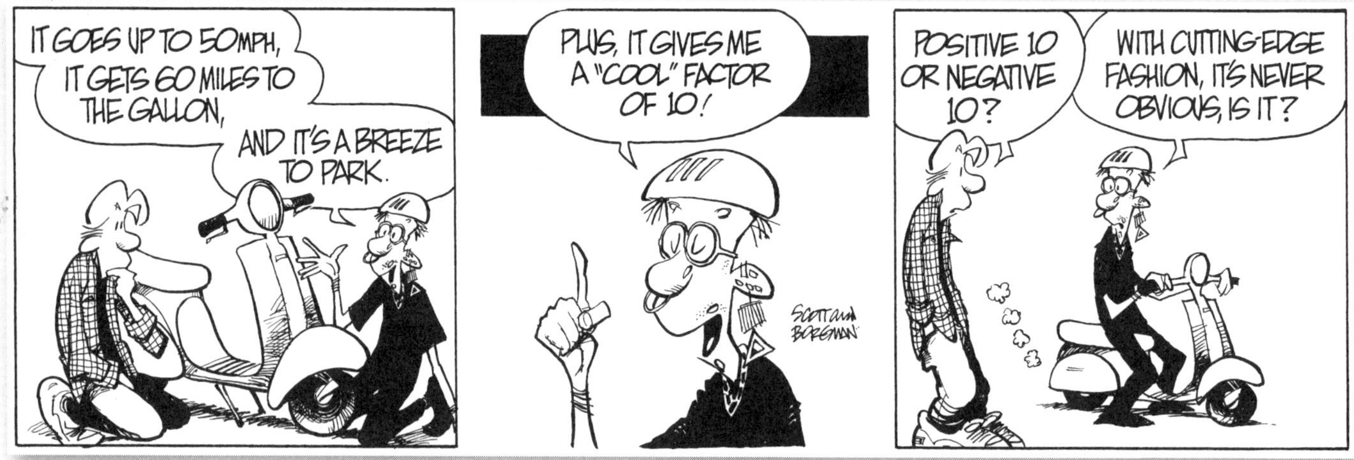
IT GOES UP TO 50MPH, IT GETS 60 MILES TO THE GALLON,
AND IT'S A BREEZE TO PARK.
PLUS, IT GIVES ME A "COOL" FACTOR OF 10!
POSITIVE 10 OR NEGATIVE 10?
WITH CUTTING-EDGE FASHION, IT'S NEVER OBVIOUS, IS IT?

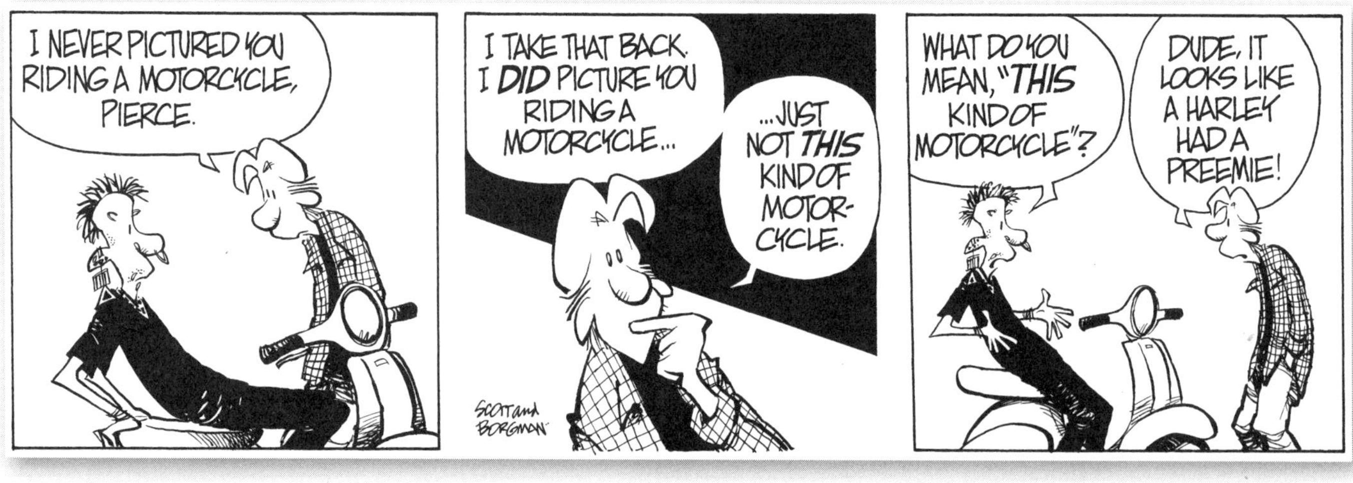
I NEVER PICTURED YOU RIDING A MOTORCYCLE, PIERCE.
I TAKE THAT BACK. I DID PICTURE YOU RIDING A MOTORCYCLE...
...JUST NOT THIS KIND OF MOTOR-CYCLE.
WHAT DO YOU MEAN, "THIS KIND OF MOTORCYCLE"?
DUDE, IT LOOKS LIKE A HARLEY HAD A PREEMIE!

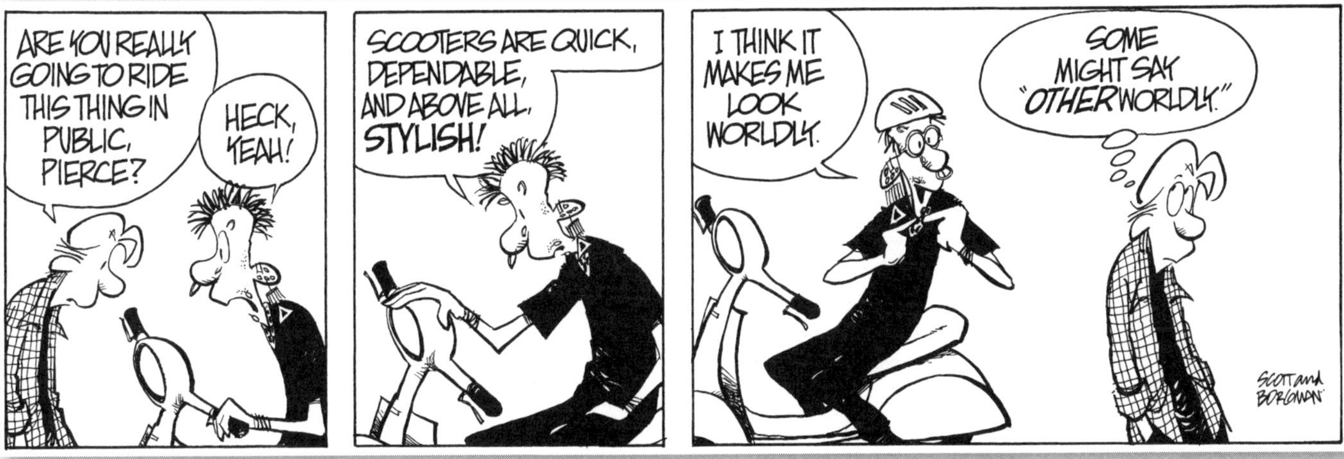
ARE YOU REALLY GOING TO RIDE THIS THING IN PUBLIC, PIERCE?
HECK, YEAH!
SCOOTERS ARE QUICK, DEPENDABLE, AND ABOVE ALL, STYLISH!
I THINK IT MAKES ME LOOK WORLDLY.
SOME MIGHT SAY "OTHERWORLDLY."
SCOTT AND BORGMAN

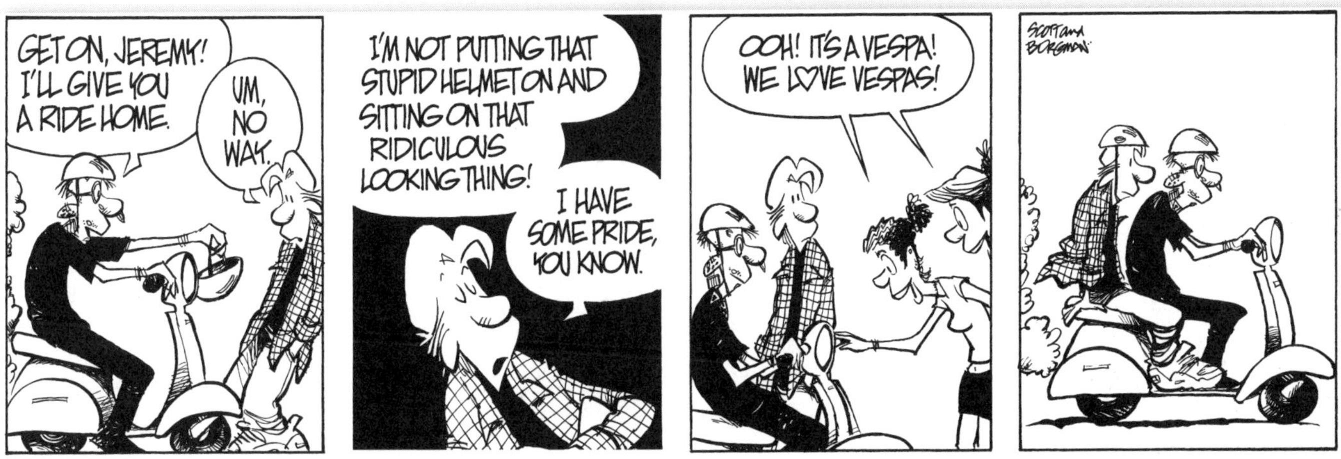
GET ON, JEREMY! I'LL GIVE YOU A RIDE HOME.
UM, NO WAY.
I'M NOT PUTTING THAT STUPID HELMET ON AND SITTING ON THAT RIDICULOUS LOOKING THING!
I HAVE SOME PRIDE, YOU KNOW.
OOH! IT'S A VESPA! WE LOVE VESPAS!
SCOTT AND BORGMAN

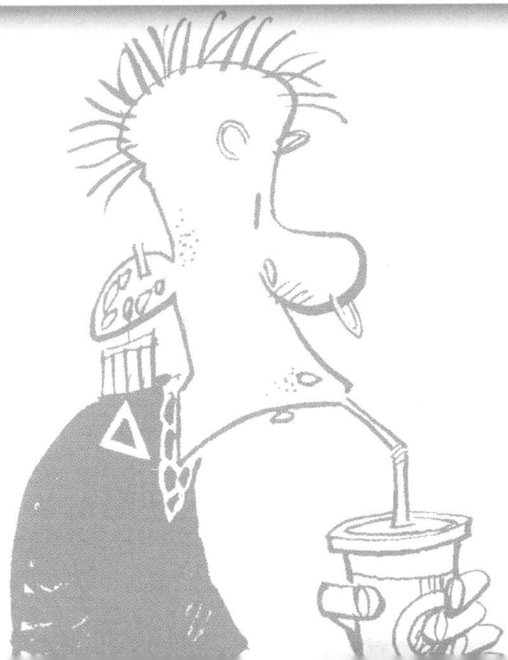

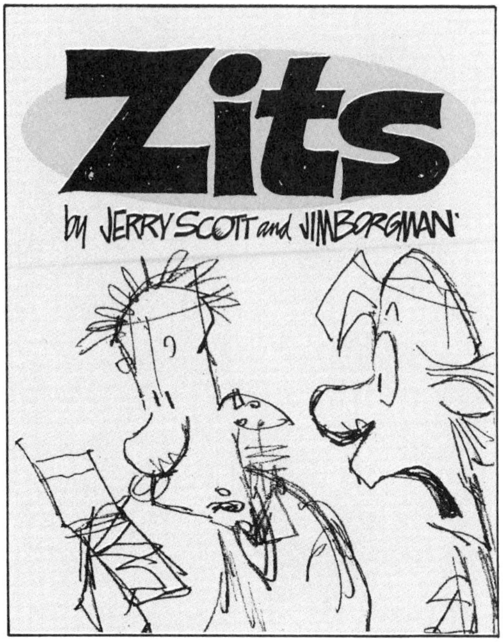
Zits
by JERRY SCOTT and JIM BORGMAN

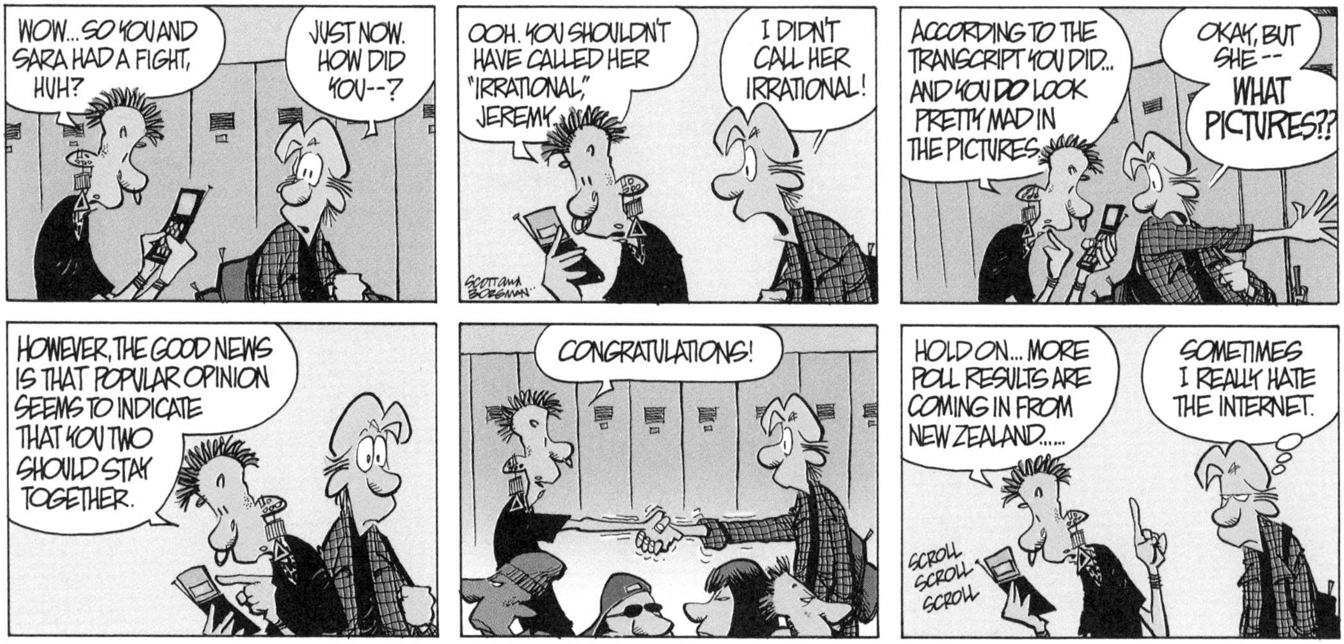
WOW... SO YOU AND SARA HAD A FIGHT, HUH?
JUST NOW. HOW DID YOU--?
OOH. YOU SHOULDN'T HAVE CALLED HER "IRRATIONAL," JEREMY.
I DIDN'T CALL HER IRRATIONAL!
ACCORDING TO THE TRANSCRIPT YOU DID... AND YOU DO LOOK PRETTY MAD IN THE PICTURES.
OKAY, BUT SHE -- WHAT PICTURES??
HOWEVER, THE GOOD NEWS IS THAT POPULAR OPINION SEEMS TO INDICATE THAT YOU TWO SHOULD STAY TOGETHER.
CONGRATULATIONS!
HOLD ON... MORE POLL RESULTS ARE COMING IN FROM NEW ZEALAND.....
SCROLL SCROLL SCROLL
SOMETIMES I REALLY HATE THE INTERNET.

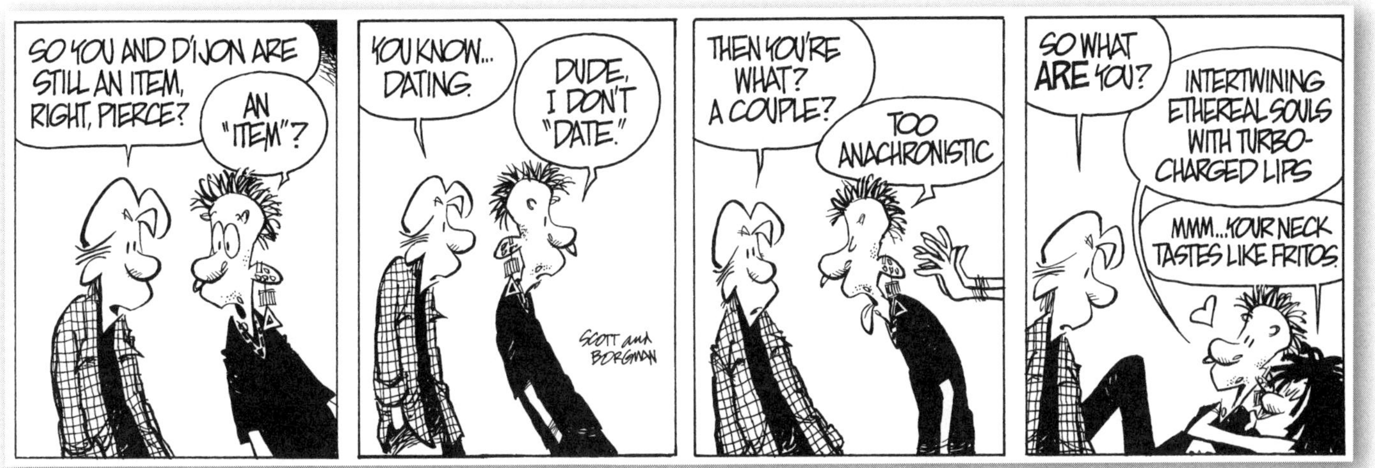
SO YOU AND D'JON ARE STILL AN ITEM, RIGHT, PIERCE?
AN "ITEM"?
YOU KNOW... DATING.
DUDE, I DON'T "DATE."
SCOTT and BORGMAN
THEN YOU'RE WHAT? A COUPLE?
TOO ANACHRONISTIC
SO WHAT ARE YOU?
INTERTWINING ETHEREAL SOULS WITH TURBO-CHARGED LIPS
MMM... YOUR NECK TASTES LIKE FRITOS.

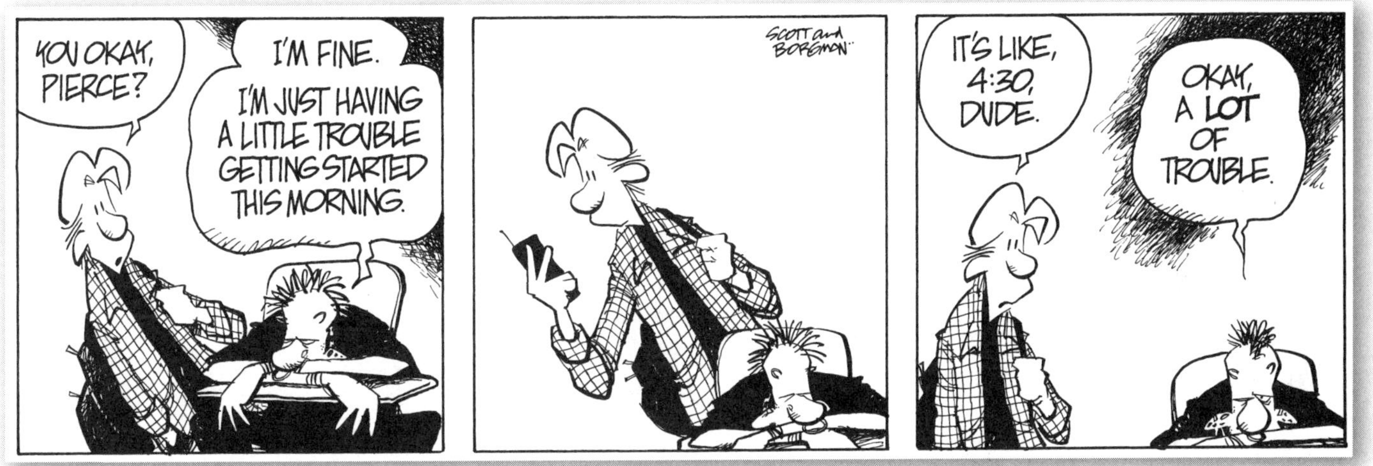
YOU OKAY, PIERCE?
I'M FINE.
I'M JUST HAVING A LITTLE TROUBLE GETTING STARTED THIS MORNING.
SCOTT and BORGMAN
IT'S LIKE, 4:30, DUDE.
OKAY, A LOT OF TROUBLE.

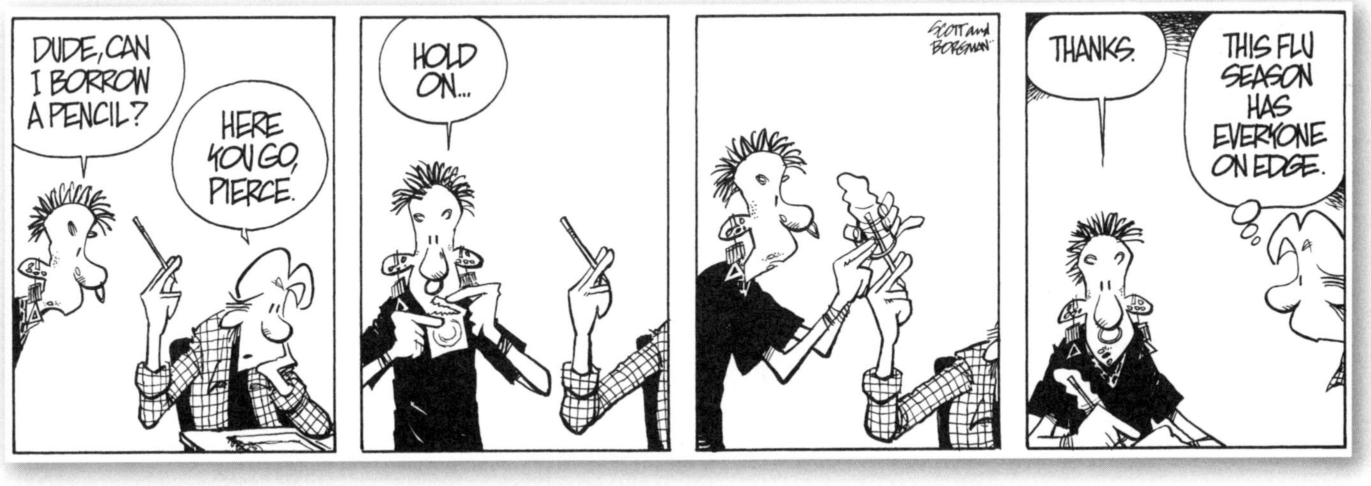
DUDE, CAN I BORROW A PENCIL?
HERE YOU GO, PIERCE.
HOLD ON...
SCOTT and BORGMAN
THANKS.
THIS FLU SEASON HAS EVERYONE ON EDGE.

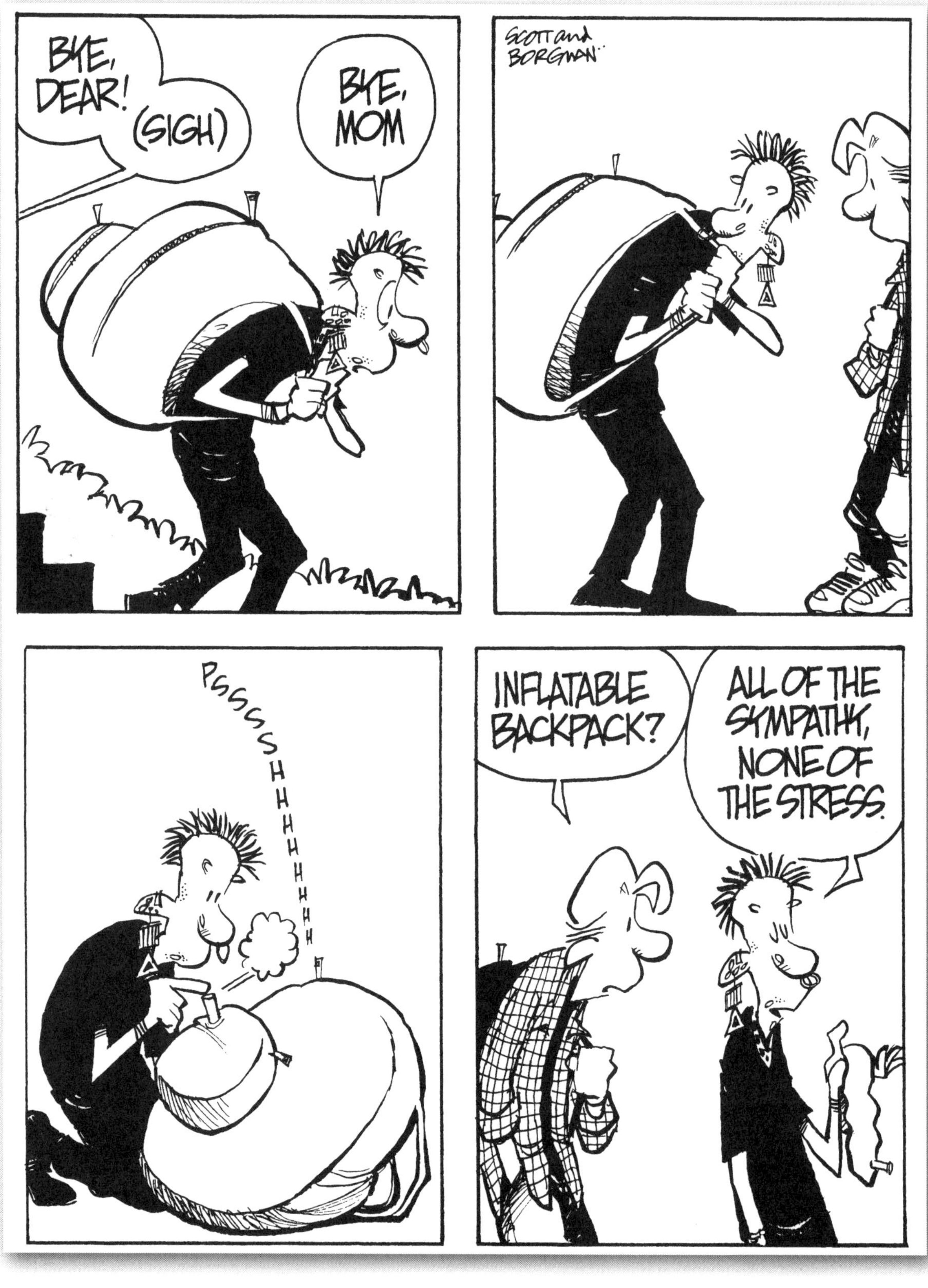
BYE, DEAR!
(SIGH)
BYE, MOM
SCOTT and BORGMAN
PSSSSHHHHHHHHHH
INFLATABLE BACKPACK?
ALL OF THE SYMPATHY, NONE OF THE STRESS.

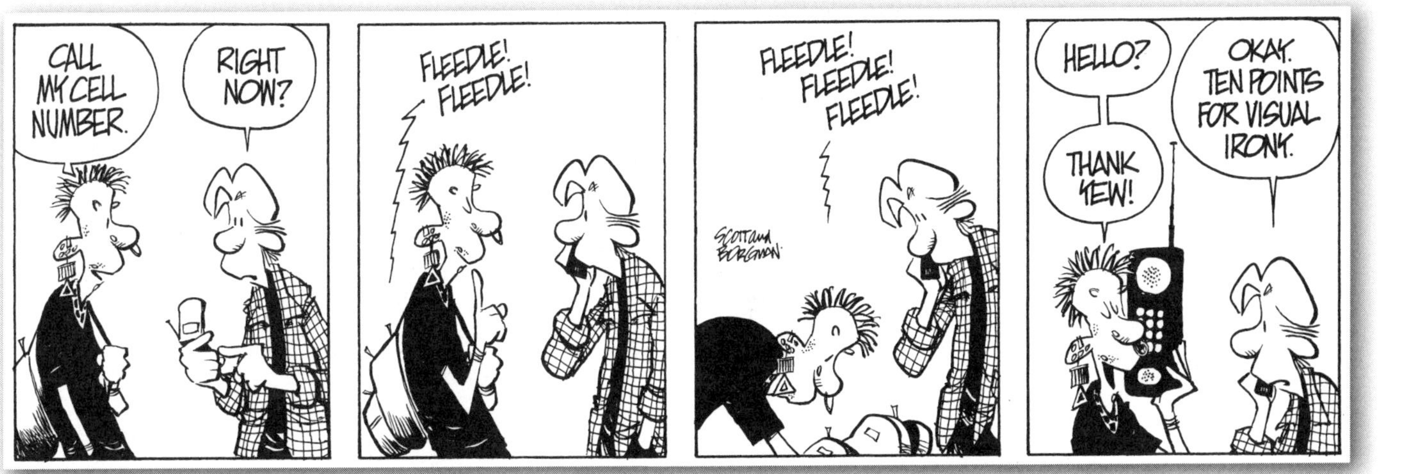
CALL MY CELL NUMBER.
RIGHT NOW?
FLEEDLE! FLEEDLE!
FLEEDLE! FLEEDLE! FLEEDLE!
HELLO?
THANK YEW!
OKAY. TEN POINTS FOR VISUAL IRONY.

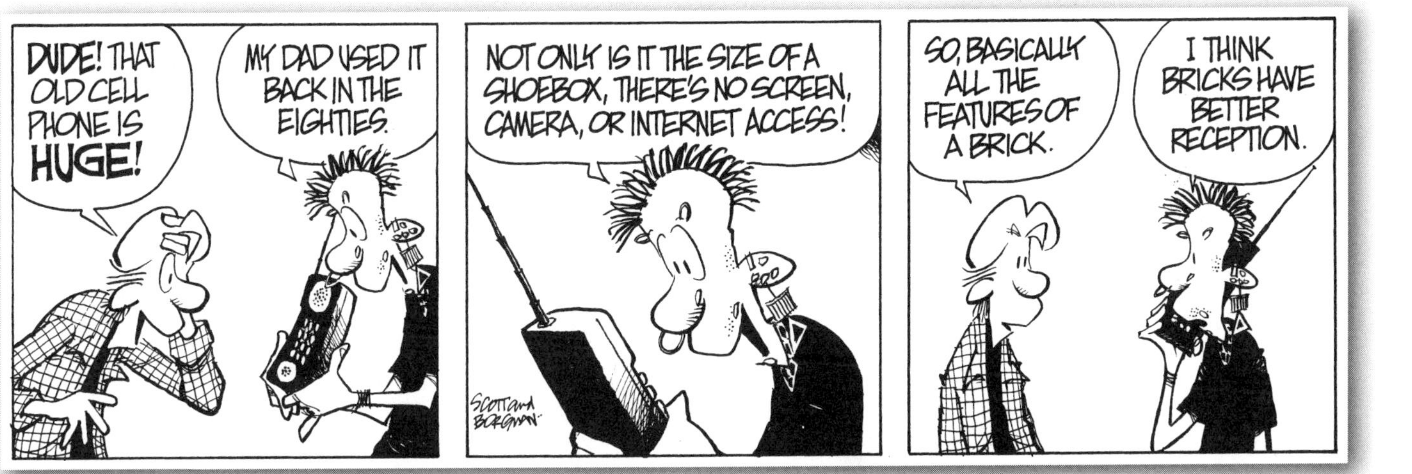
DUDE! THAT OLD CELL PHONE IS HUGE!
MY DAD USED IT BACK IN THE EIGHTIES.
NOT ONLY IS IT THE SIZE OF A SHOEBOX, THERE'S NO SCREEN, CAMERA, OR INTERNET ACCESS!
SO, BASICALLY ALL THE FEATURES OF A BRICK.
I THINK BRICKS HAVE BETTER RECEPTION.

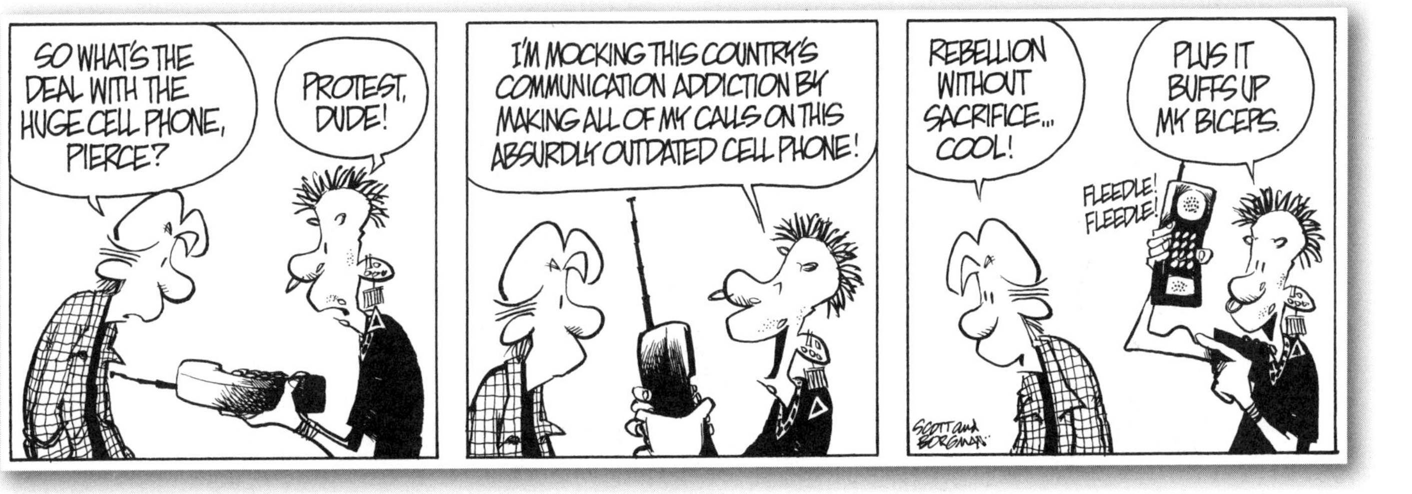
SO WHAT'S THE DEAL WITH THE HUGE CELL PHONE, PIERCE?
PROTEST, DUDE!
I'M MOCKING THIS COUNTRY'S COMMUNICATION ADDICTION BY MAKING ALL OF MY CALLS ON THIS ABSURDLY OUTDATED CELL PHONE!
REBELLION WITHOUT SACRIFICE... COOL!
FLEEDLE! FLEEDLE!
PLUS IT BUFFS UP MY BICEPS.

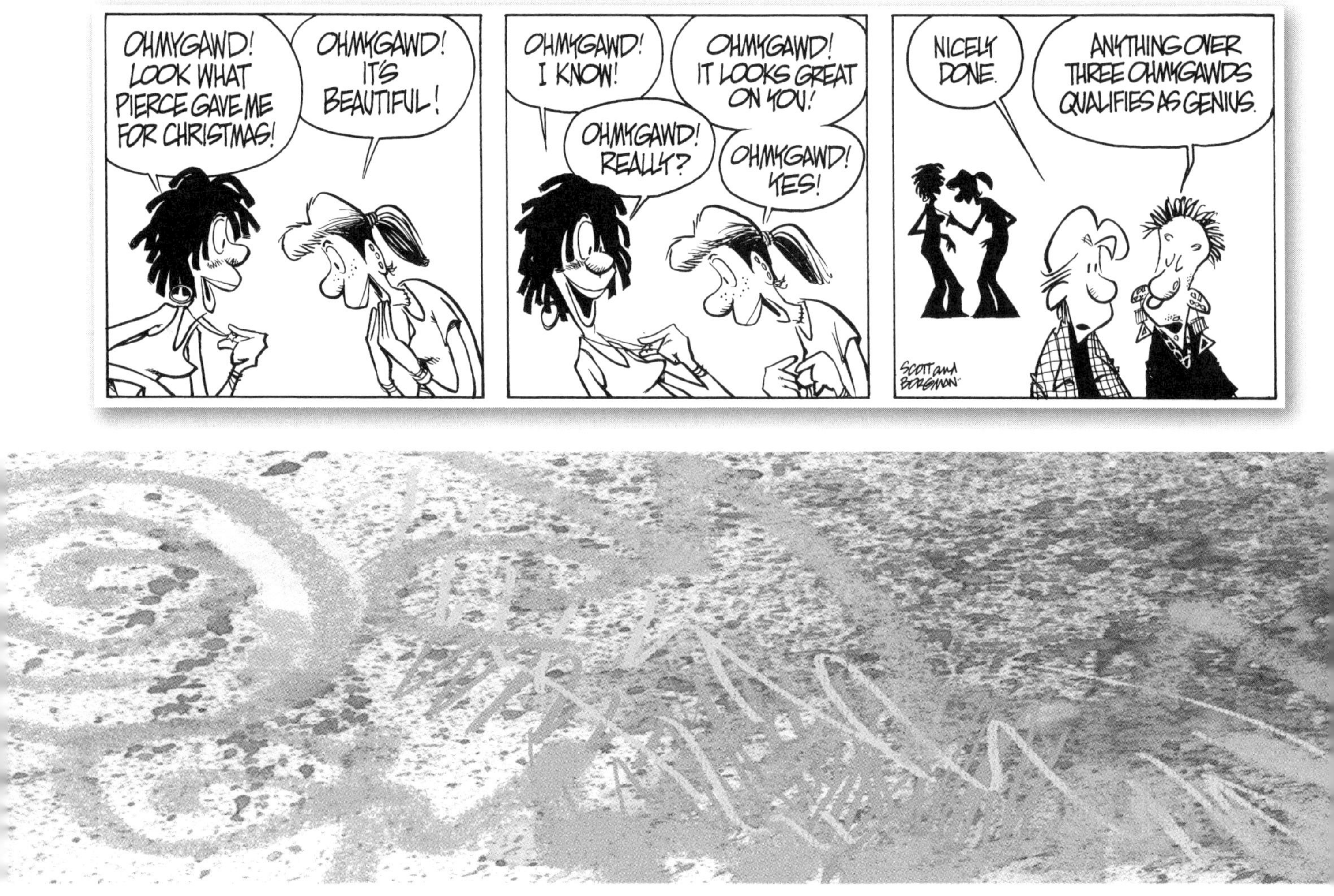
OHMYGAWD! LOOK WHAT PIERCE GAVE ME FOR CHRISTMAS!
OHMYGAWD! IT'S BEAUTIFUL!
OHMYGAWD! I KNOW!
OHMYGAWD! IT LOOKS GREAT ON YOU!
OHMYGAWD! REALLY?
OHMYGAWD! YES!
NICELY DONE.
ANYTHING OVER THREE OHMYGAWDS QUALIFIES AS GENIUS.
SCOTT and BORGMAN

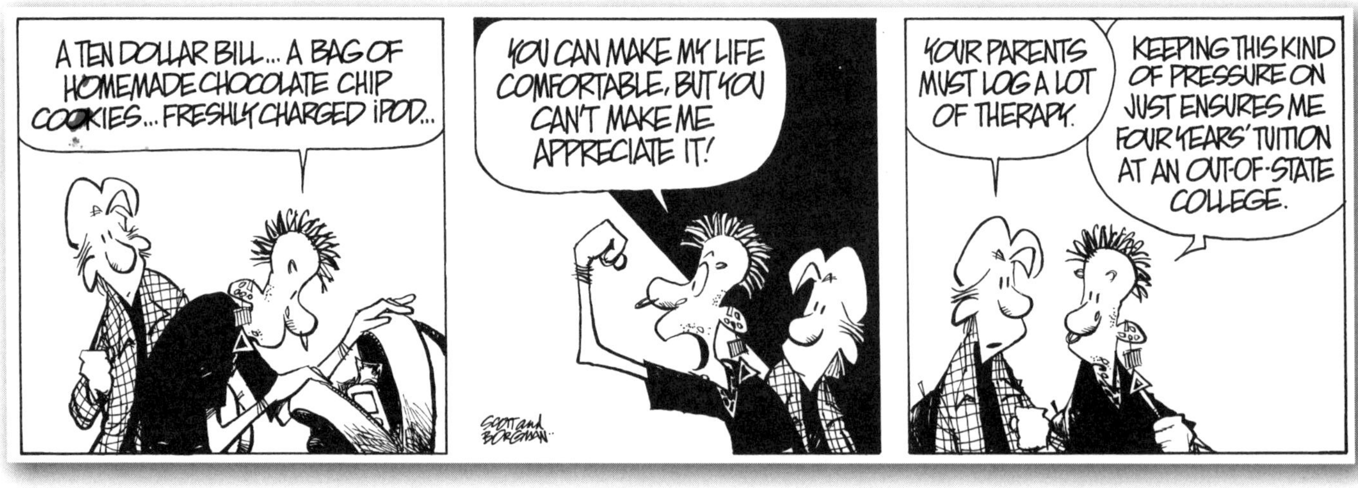
A TEN DOLLAR BILL... A BAG OF HOMEMADE CHOCOLATE CHIP COOKIES... FRESHLY CHARGED iPOD...
YOU CAN MAKE MY LIFE COMFORTABLE, BUT YOU CAN'T MAKE ME APPRECIATE IT!
SCOTT and BORGMAN
YOUR PARENTS MUST LOG A LOT OF THERAPY.
KEEPING THIS KIND OF PRESSURE ON JUST ENSURES ME FOUR YEARS' TUITION AT AN OUT-OF-STATE COLLEGE.

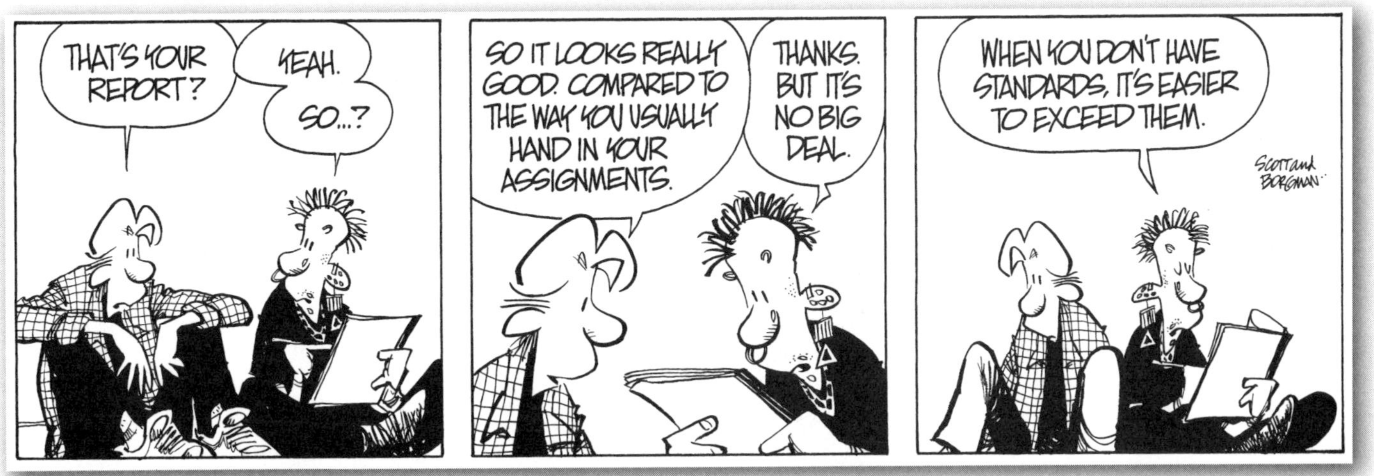
THAT'S YOUR REPORT?
YEAH.
SO...?
SO IT LOOKS REALLY GOOD. COMPARED TO THE WAY YOU USUALLY HAND IN YOUR ASSIGNMENTS.
THANKS. BUT IT'S NO BIG DEAL.
WHEN YOU DON'T HAVE STANDARDS, IT'S EASIER TO EXCEED THEM.
SCOTT AND BORGMAN

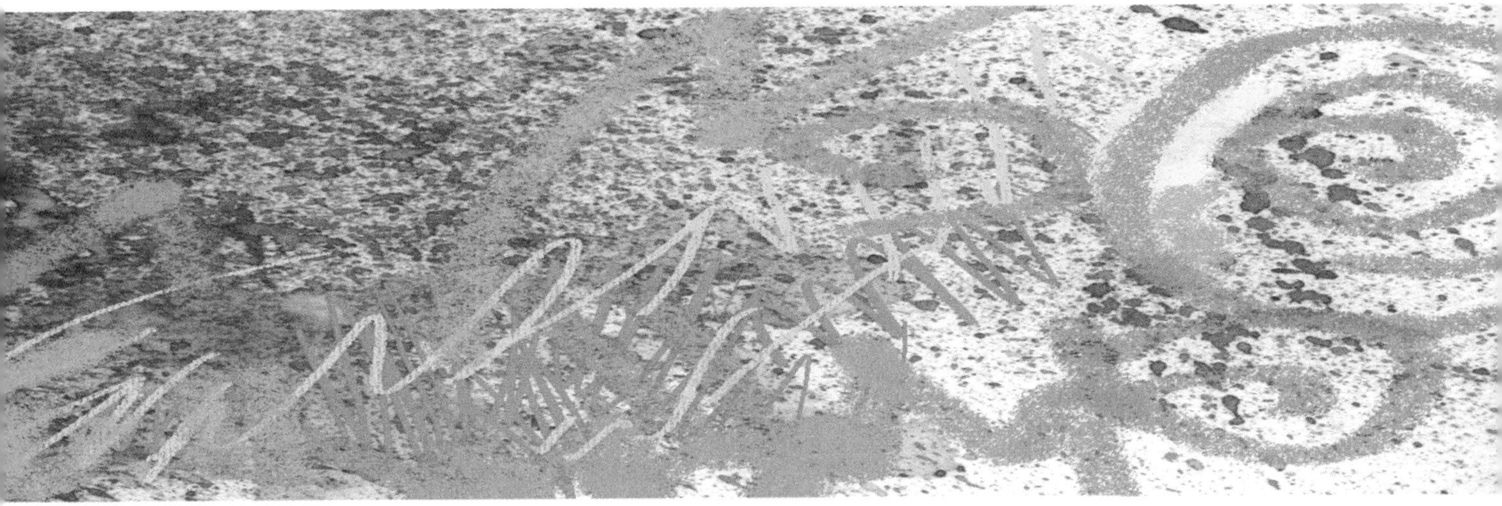

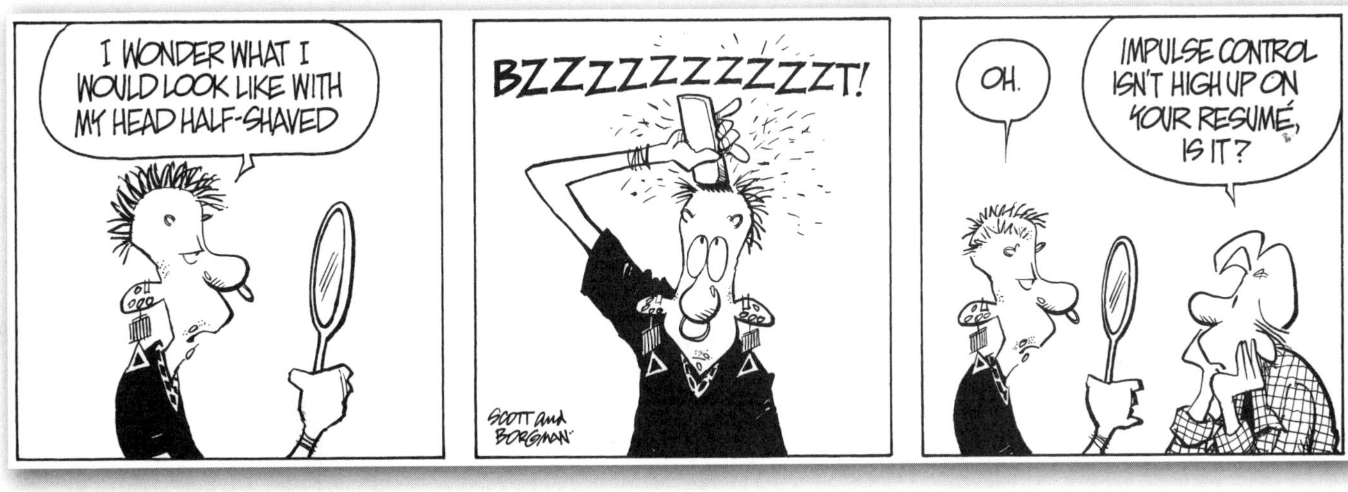
I WONDER WHAT I WOULD LOOK LIKE WITH MY HEAD HALF-SHAVED
BZZZZZZZZZZT!
SCOTT AND BORGMAN
OH.
IMPULSE CONTROL ISN'T HIGH UP ON YOUR RESUMÉ, IS IT?

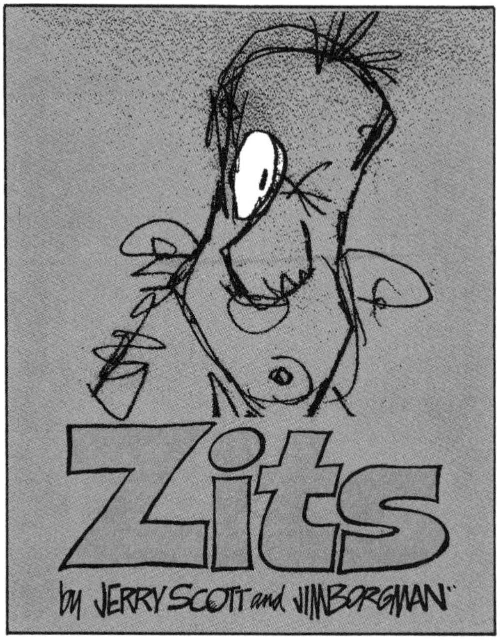
Zits
by JERRY SCOTT and JIM BORGMAN

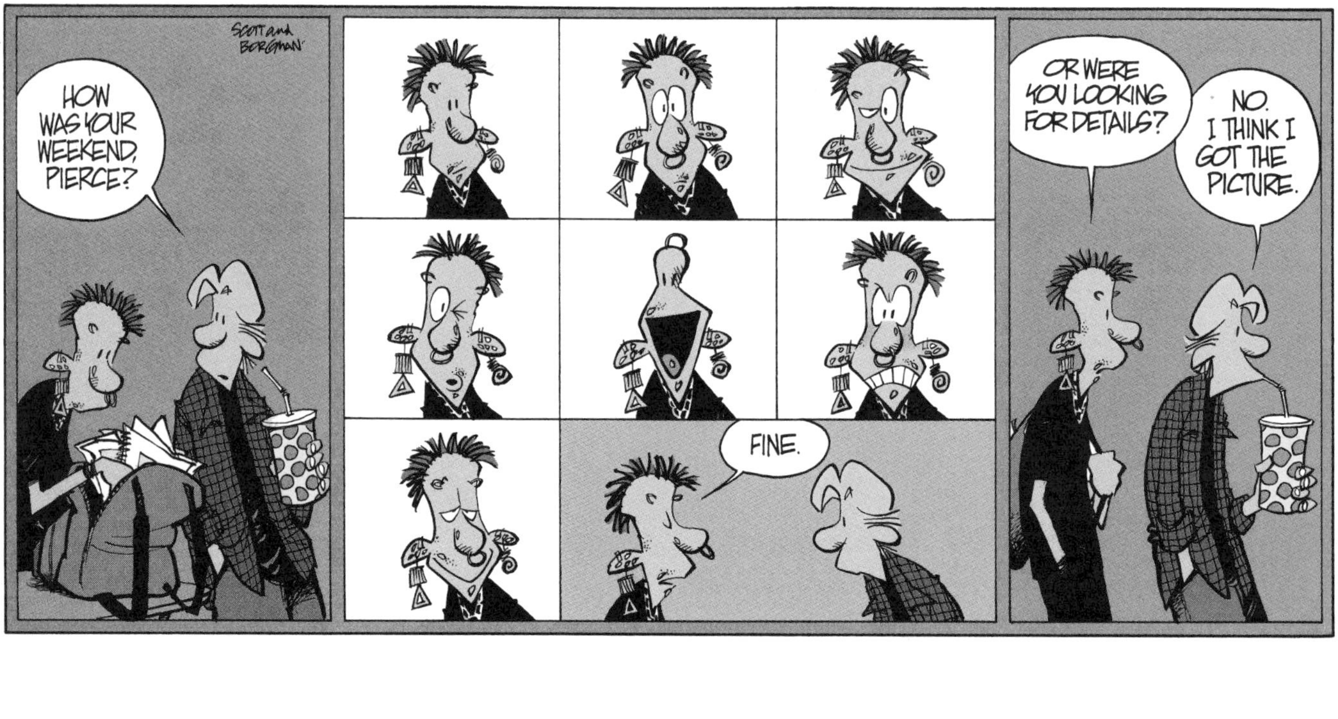
SCOTT and BORGMAN
HOW WAS YOUR WEEKEND, PIERCE?
FINE.
OR WERE YOU LOOKING FOR DETAILS?
NO. I THINK I GOT THE PICTURE.

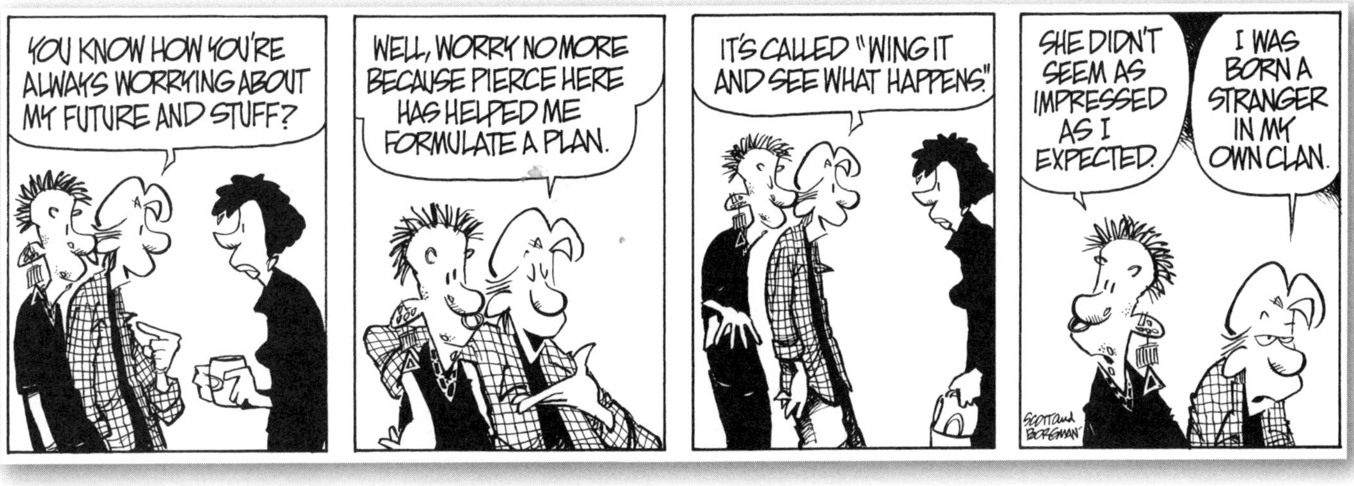
YOU KNOW HOW YOU'RE ALWAYS WORRYING ABOUT MY FUTURE AND STUFF?
WELL, WORRY NO MORE BECAUSE PIERCE HERE HAS HELPED ME FORMULATE A PLAN.
IT'S CALLED "WING IT AND SEE WHAT HAPPENS."
SHE DIDN'T SEEM AS IMPRESSED AS I EXPECTED.
I WAS BORN A STRANGER IN MY OWN CLAN.
SCOTT AND BORGMAN

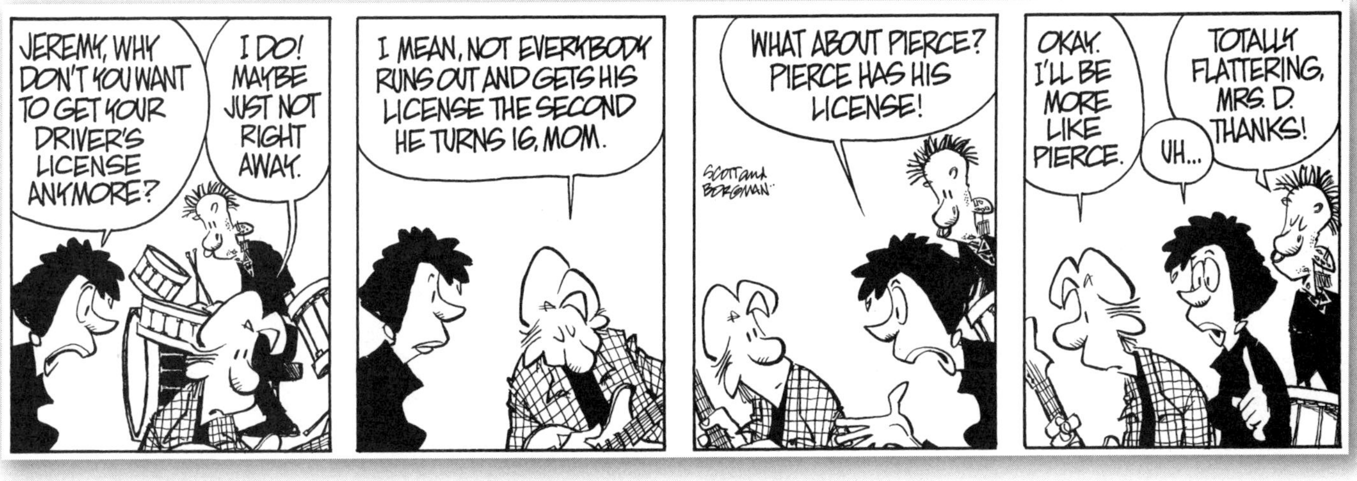
JEREMY, WHY DON'T YOU WANT TO GET YOUR DRIVER'S LICENSE ANYMORE?
I DO! MAYBE JUST NOT RIGHT AWAY.
I MEAN, NOT EVERYBODY RUNS OUT AND GETS HIS LICENSE THE SECOND HE TURNS 16, MOM.
WHAT ABOUT PIERCE? PIERCE HAS HIS LICENSE!
SCOTT AND BORGMAN
OKAY. I'LL BE MORE LIKE PIERCE.
UH...
TOTALLY FLATTERING, MRS. D. THANKS!

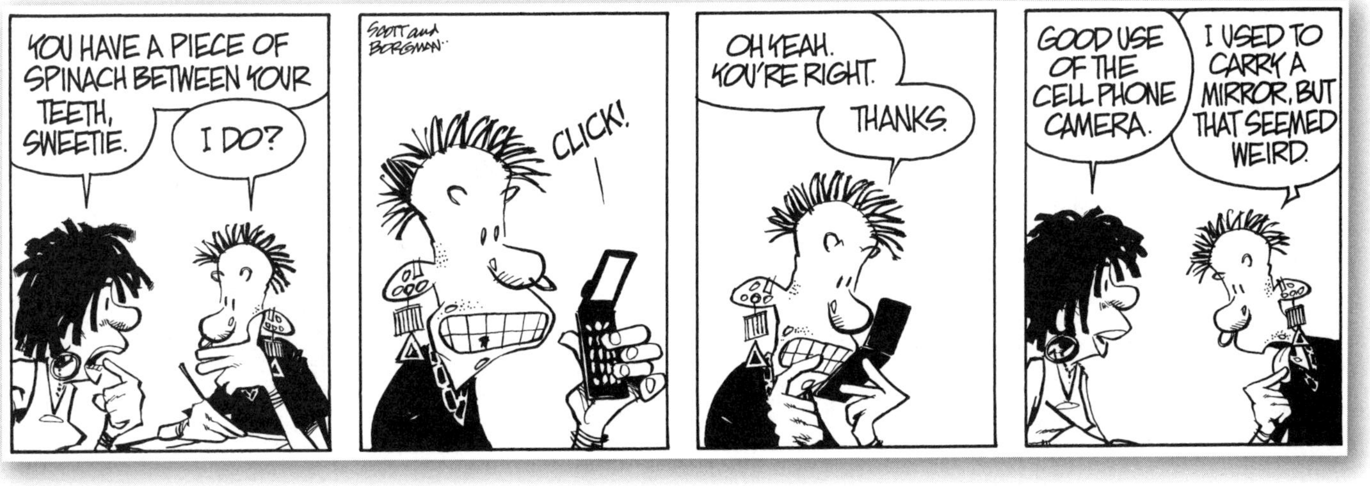
YOU HAVE A PIECE OF SPINACH BETWEEN YOUR TEETH, SWEETIE.
I DO?
SCOTT AND BORGMAN
CLICK!
OH YEAH. YOU'RE RIGHT.
THANKS.
GOOD USE OF THE CELL PHONE CAMERA.
I USED TO CARRY A MIRROR, BUT THAT SEEMED WEIRD.

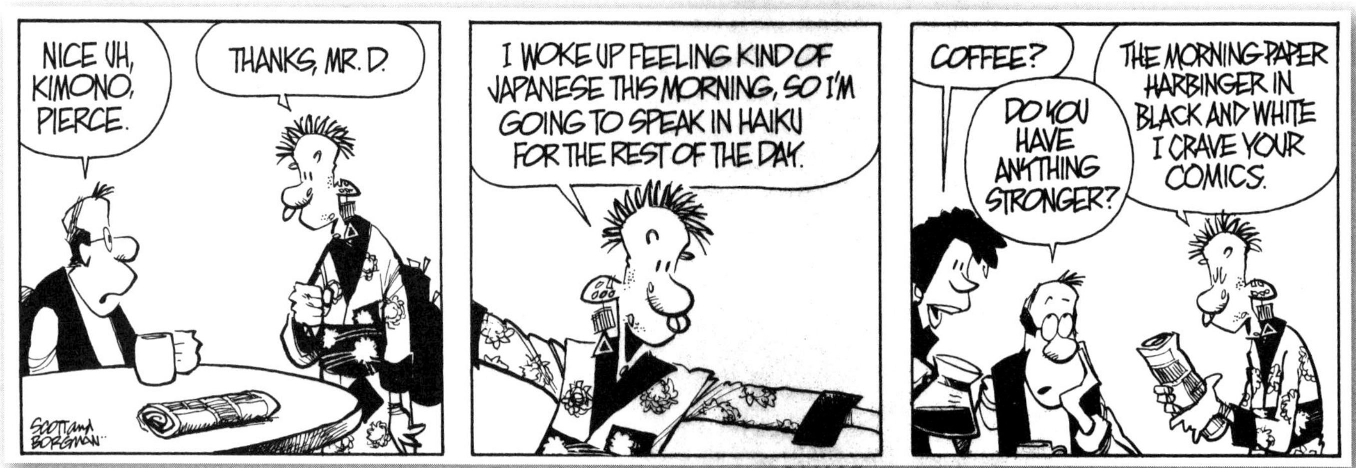
NICE UH, KIMONO, PIERCE.
THANKS, MR. D.
I WOKE UP FEELING KIND OF JAPANESE THIS MORNING, SO I'M GOING TO SPEAK IN HAIKU FOR THE REST OF THE DAY.
COFFEE?
DO YOU HAVE ANYTHING STRONGER?
THE MORNING PAPER HARBINGER IN BLACK AND WHITE I CRAVE YOUR COMICS.

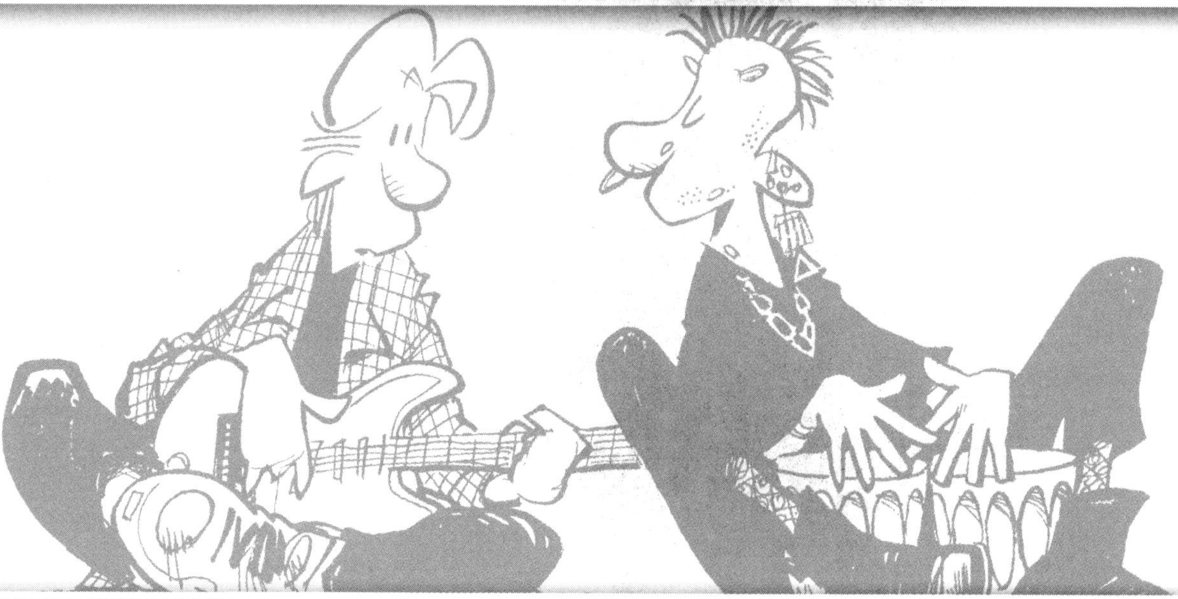

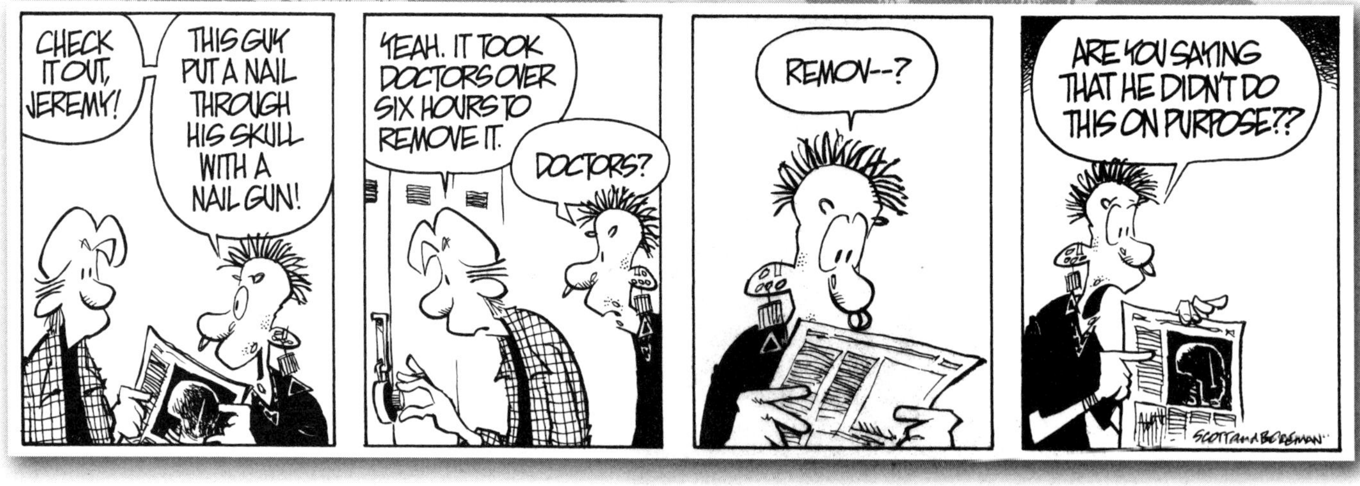
CHECK IT OUT, JEREMY!
THIS GUY PUT A NAIL THROUGH HIS SKULL WITH A NAIL GUN!
YEAH. IT TOOK DOCTORS OVER SIX HOURS TO REMOVE IT.
DOCTORS?
REMOV--?
ARE YOU SAYING THAT HE DIDN'T DO THIS ON PURPOSE??

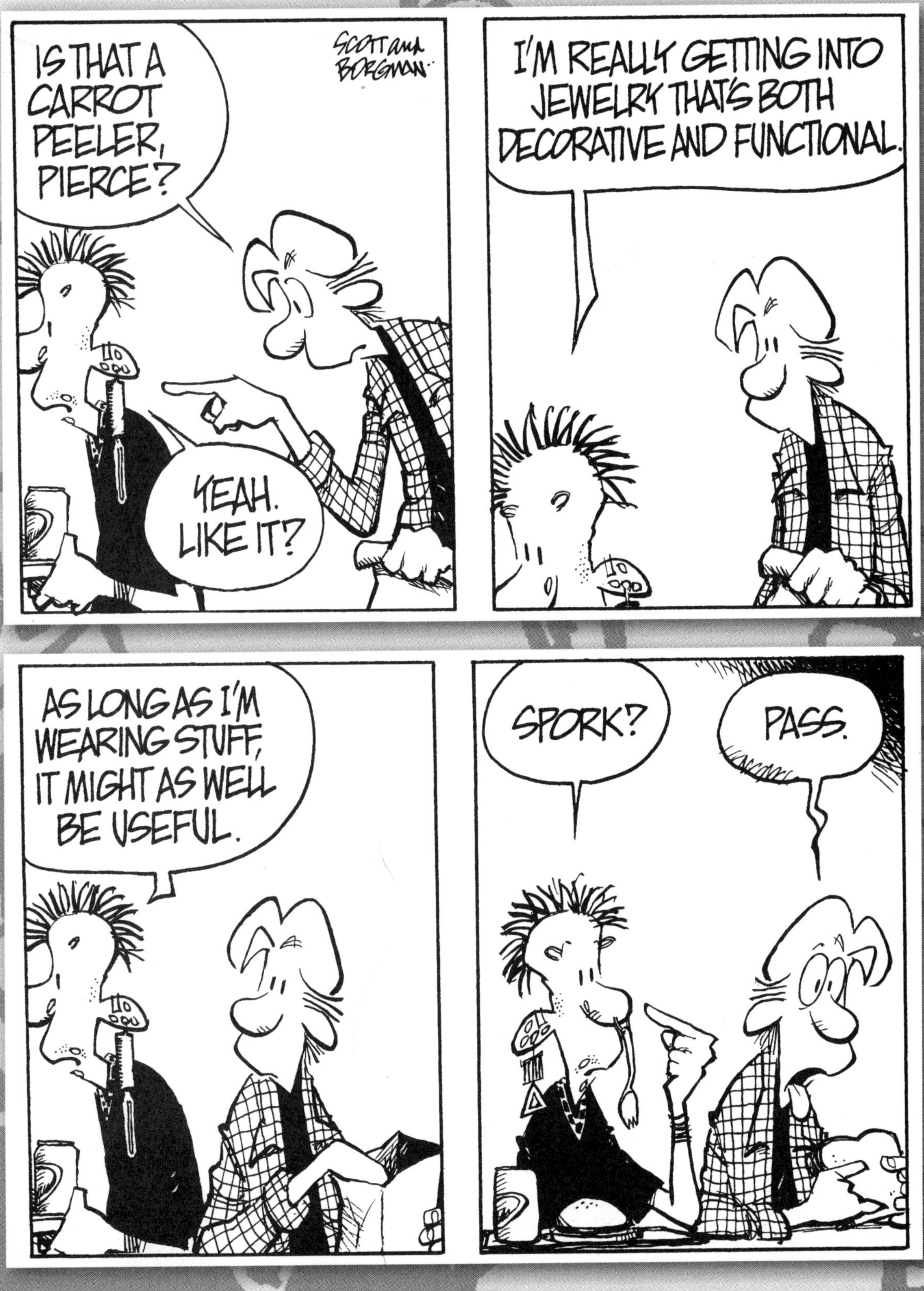
SCOTT AND BORGMAN
IS THAT A CARROT PEELER, PIERCE?
YEAH. LIKE IT?
I'M REALLY GETTING INTO JEWELRY THAT'S BOTH DECORATIVE AND FUNCTIONAL.
AS LONG AS I'M WEARING STUFF, IT MIGHT AS WELL BE USEFUL.
SPORK?
PASS.

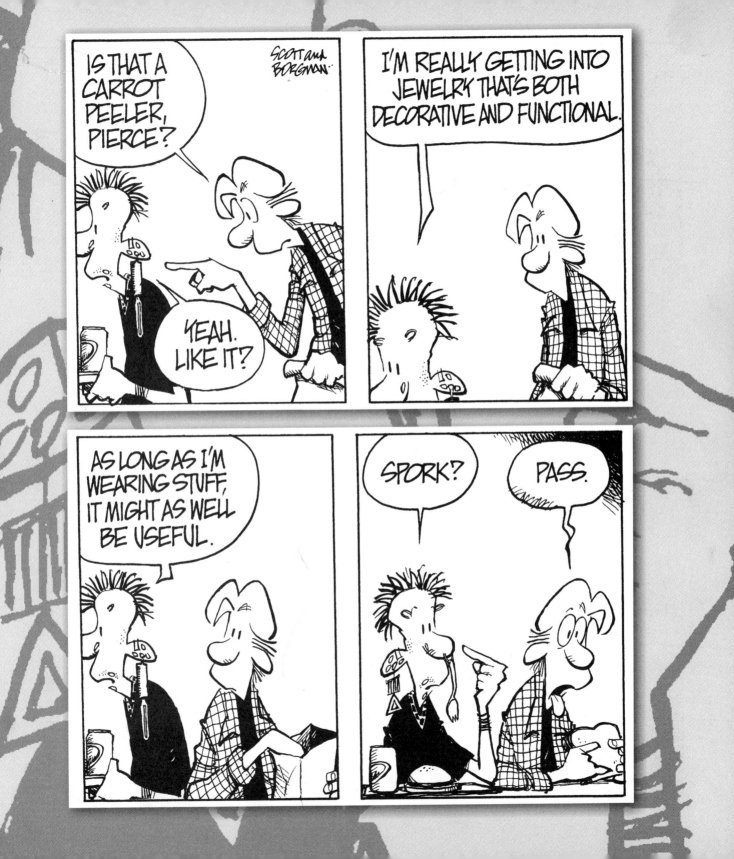

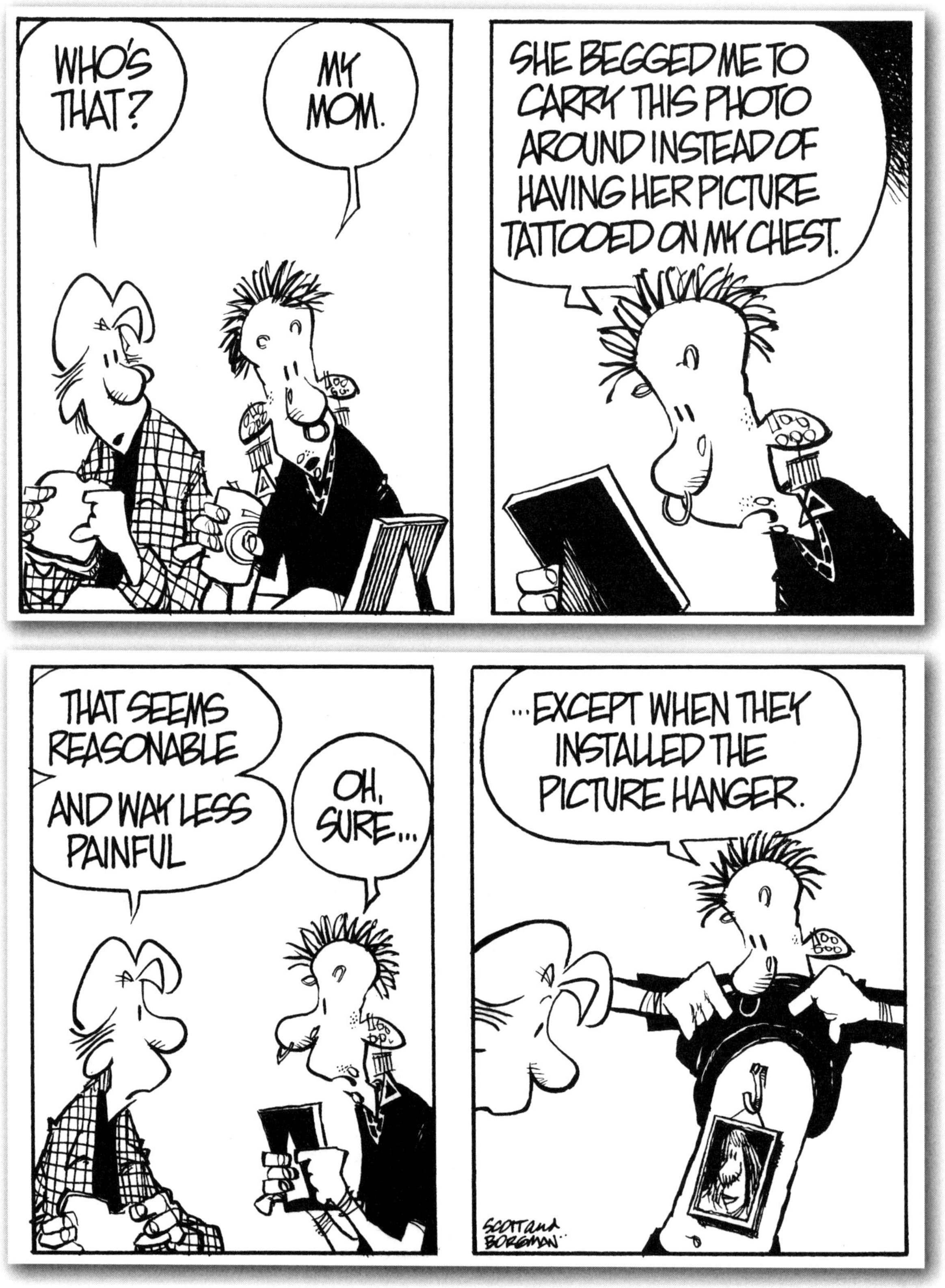
WHO'S THAT?
MY MOM.
SHE BEGGED ME TO CARRY THIS PHOTO AROUND INSTEAD OF HAVING HER PICTURE TATTOOED ON MY CHEST.
THAT SEEMS REASONABLE
AND WAY LESS PAINFUL
OH, SURE...
...EXCEPT WHEN THEY INSTALLED THE PICTURE HANGER.
SCOTT AND BORGMAN

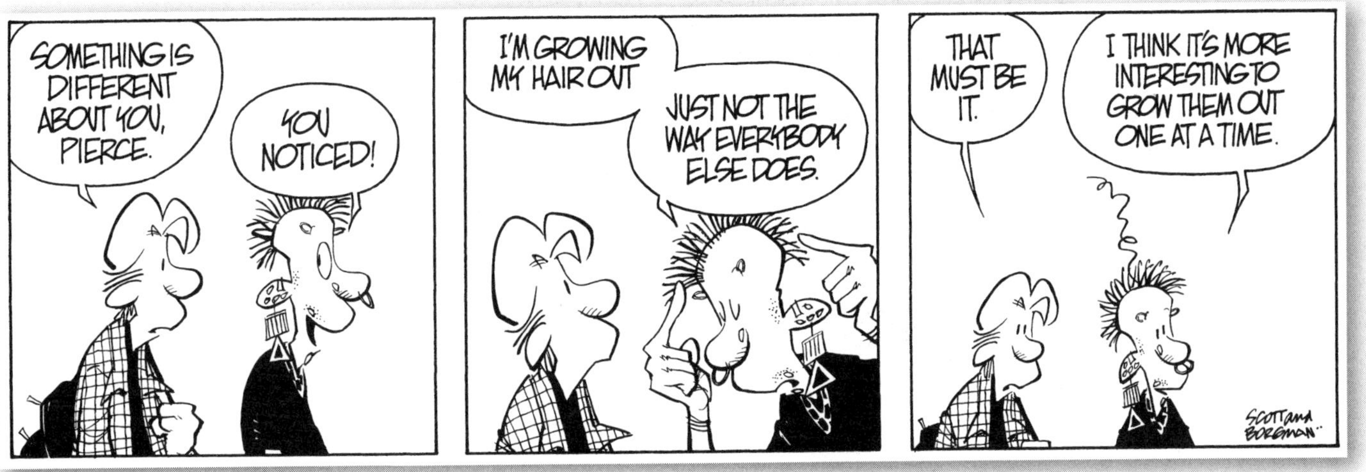
SOMETHING IS DIFFERENT ABOUT YOU, PIERCE.
YOU NOTICED!
I'M GROWING MY HAIR OUT
JUST NOT THE WAY EVERYBODY ELSE DOES.
THAT MUST BE IT.
I THINK IT'S MORE INTERESTING TO GROW THEM OUT ONE AT A TIME.
SCOTT and BORGMAN

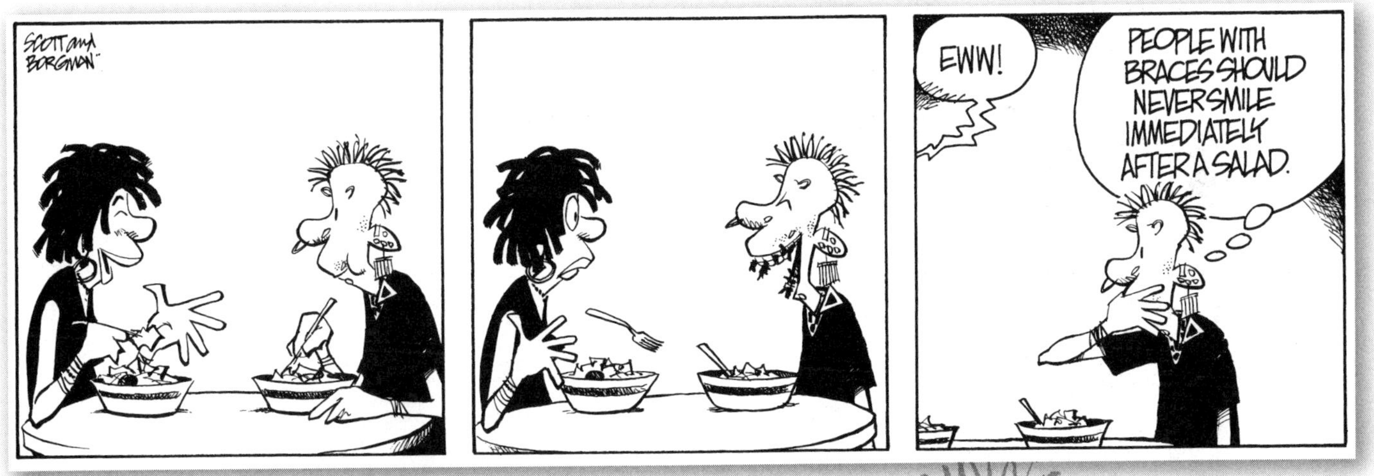
SCOTT and BORGMAN
EWW!
PEOPLE WITH BRACES SHOULD NEVER SMILE IMMEDIATELY AFTER A SALAD.

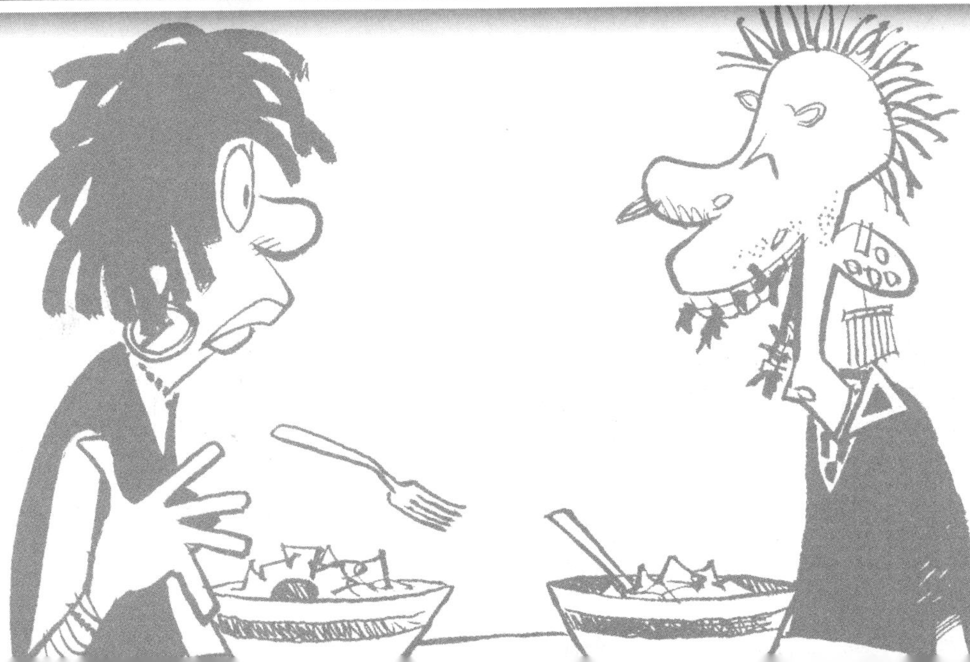

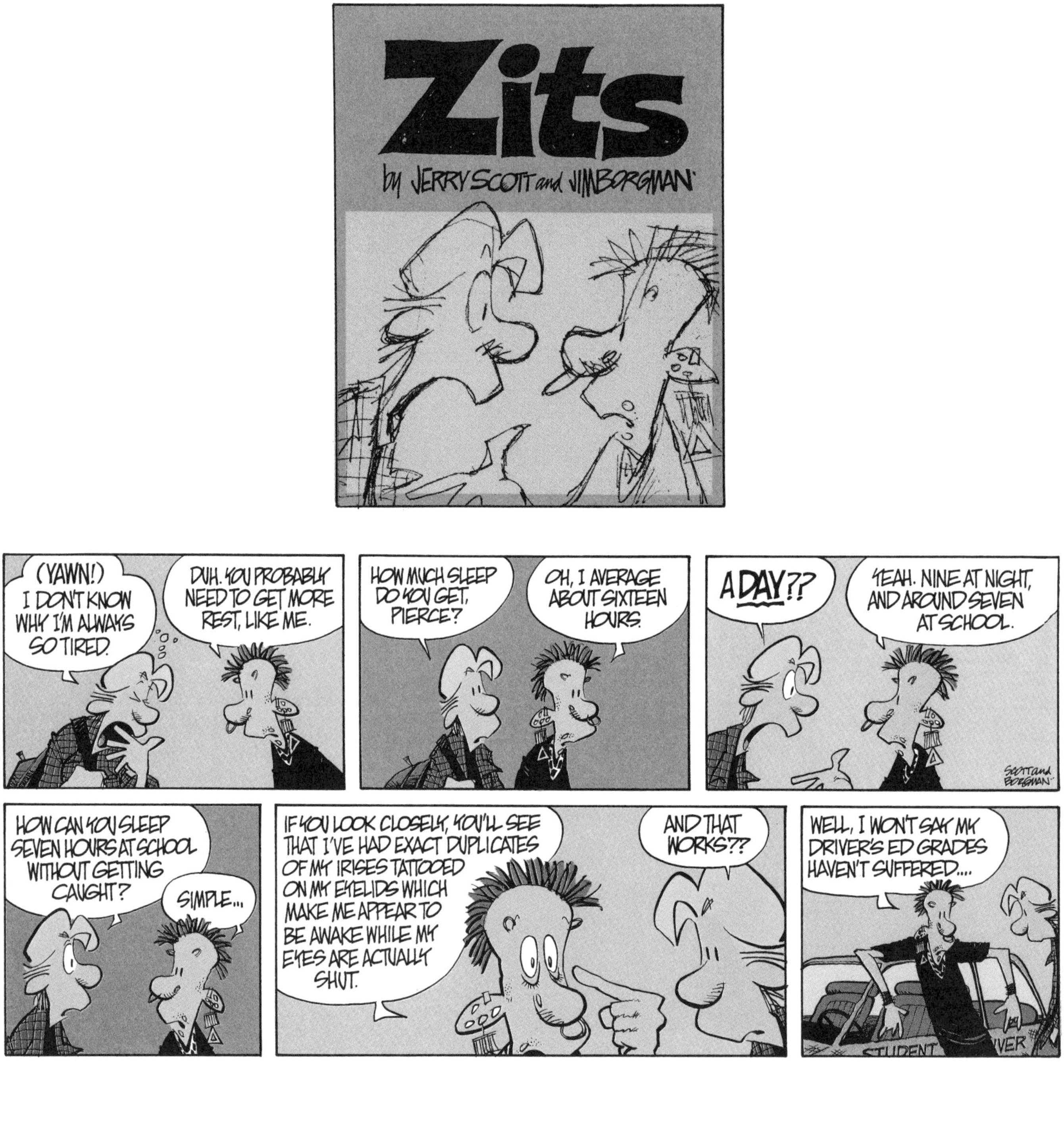
Zits
by JERRY SCOTT and JIM BORGMAN
(YAWN!) I DON'T KNOW WHY I'M ALWAYS SO TIRED.
DUH. YOU PROBABLY NEED TO GET MORE REST, LIKE ME.
HOW MUCH SLEEP DO YOU GET, PIERCE?
OH, I AVERAGE ABOUT SIXTEEN HOURS.
A DAY??
YEAH. NINE AT NIGHT, AND AROUND SEVEN AT SCHOOL.
SCOTT and BORGMAN
HOW CAN YOU SLEEP SEVEN HOURS AT SCHOOL WITHOUT GETTING CAUGHT?
SIMPLE...
IF YOU LOOK CLOSELY, YOU'LL SEE THAT I'VE HAD EXACT DUPLICATES OF MY IRISES TATTOOED ON MY EYELIDS WHICH MAKE ME APPEAR TO BE AWAKE WHILE MY EYES ARE ACTUALLY SHUT.
AND THAT WORKS??
WELL, I WON'T SAY MY DRIVER'S ED GRADES HAVEN'T SUFFERED....

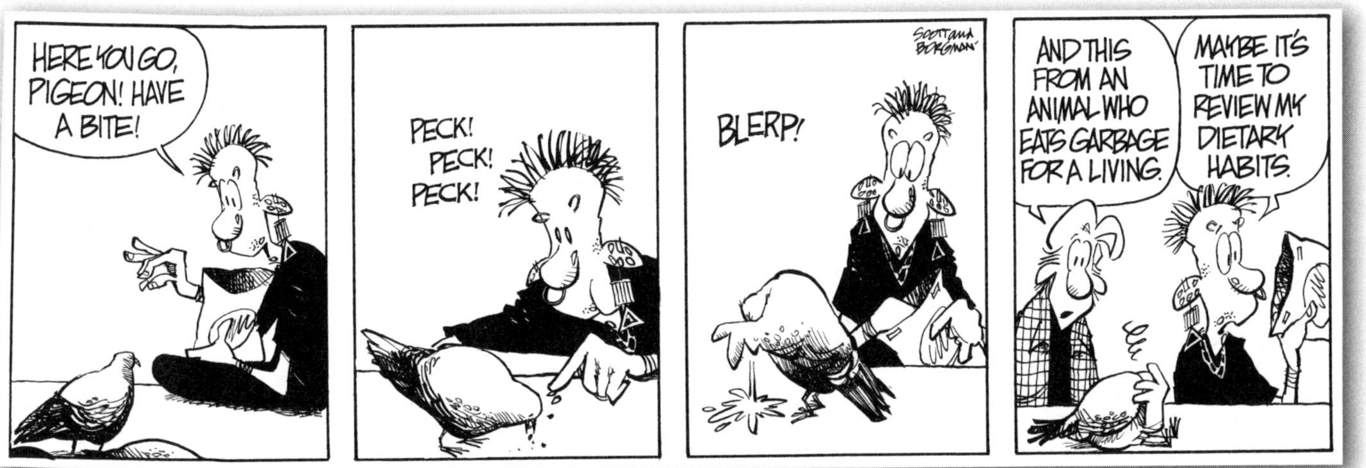

HERE YOU GO, PIGEON! HAVE A BITE!
PECK! PECK! PECK!
SCOTT AND BORGMAN
BLERP!
AND THIS FROM AN ANIMAL WHO EATS GARBAGE FOR A LIVING.
MAYBE IT'S TIME TO REVIEW MY DIETARY HABITS.

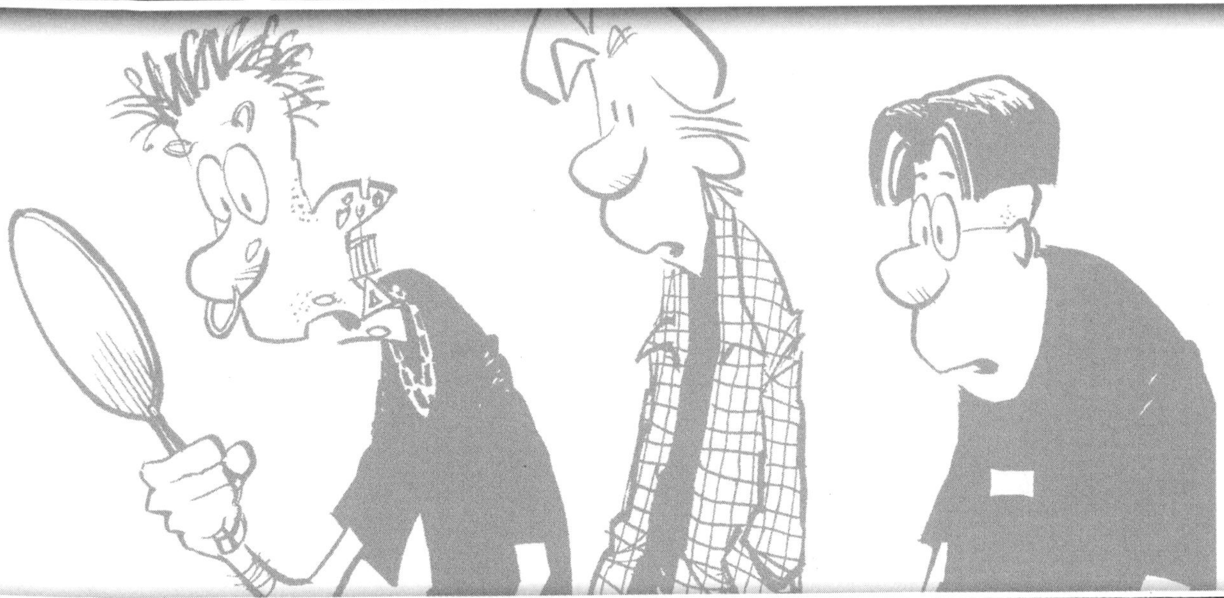

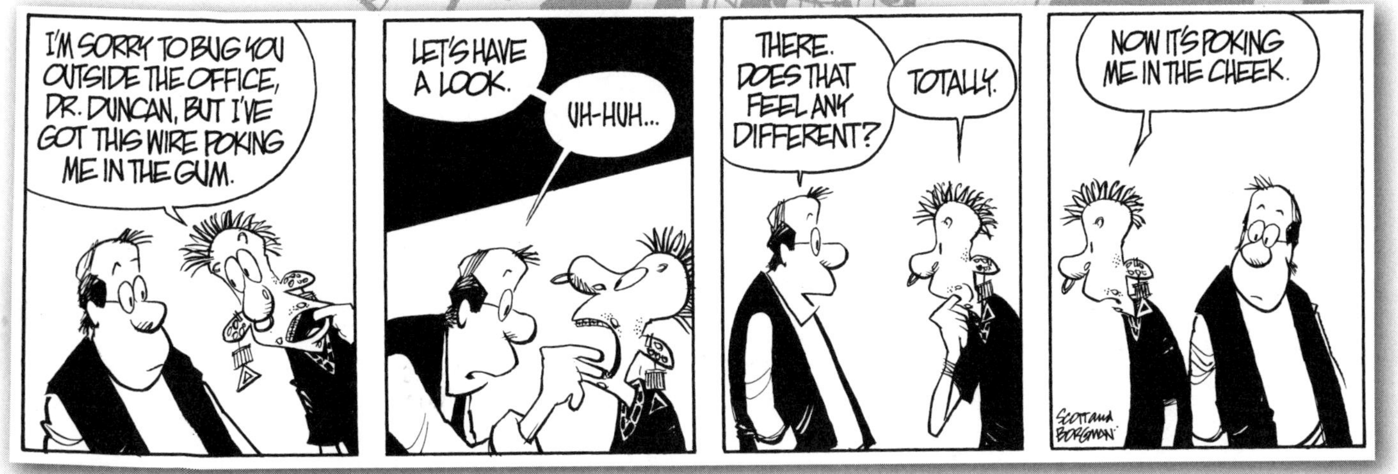

I'M SORRY TO BUG YOU OUTSIDE THE OFFICE, DR. DUNCAN, BUT I'VE GOT THIS WIRE POKING ME IN THE GUM.
LET'S HAVE A LOOK.
UH-HUH...
THERE. DOES THAT FEEL ANY DIFFERENT?
TOTALLY.
NOW IT'S POKING ME IN THE CHEEK.
SCOTT AND BORGMAN

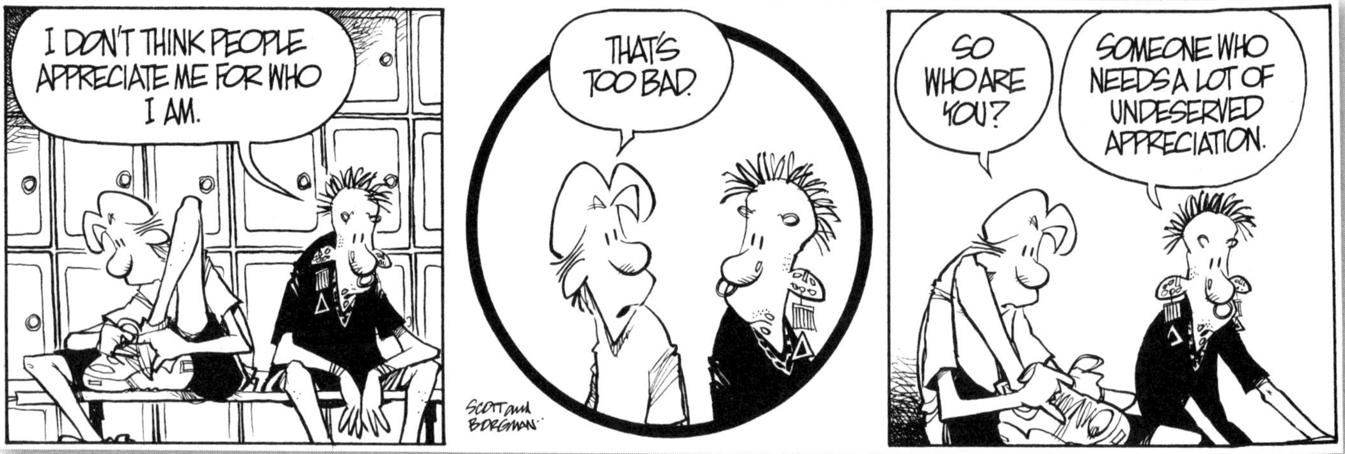
I DON'T THINK PEOPLE APPRECIATE ME FOR WHO I AM.
THAT'S TOO BAD.
SCOTT and BORGMAN
SO WHO ARE YOU?
SOMEONE WHO NEEDS A LOT OF UNDESERVED APPRECIATION.

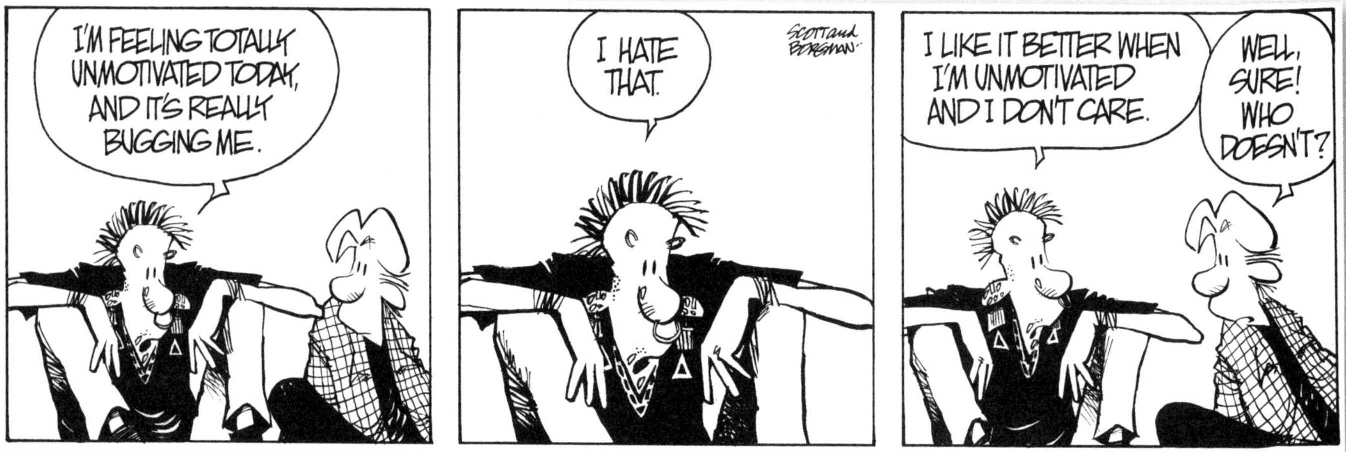
I'M FEELING TOTALLY UNMOTIVATED TODAY, AND IT'S REALLY BUGGING ME.
I HATE THAT.
SCOTT and BORGMAN
I LIKE IT BETTER WHEN I'M UNMOTIVATED AND I DON'T CARE.
WELL, SURE! WHO DOESN'T?

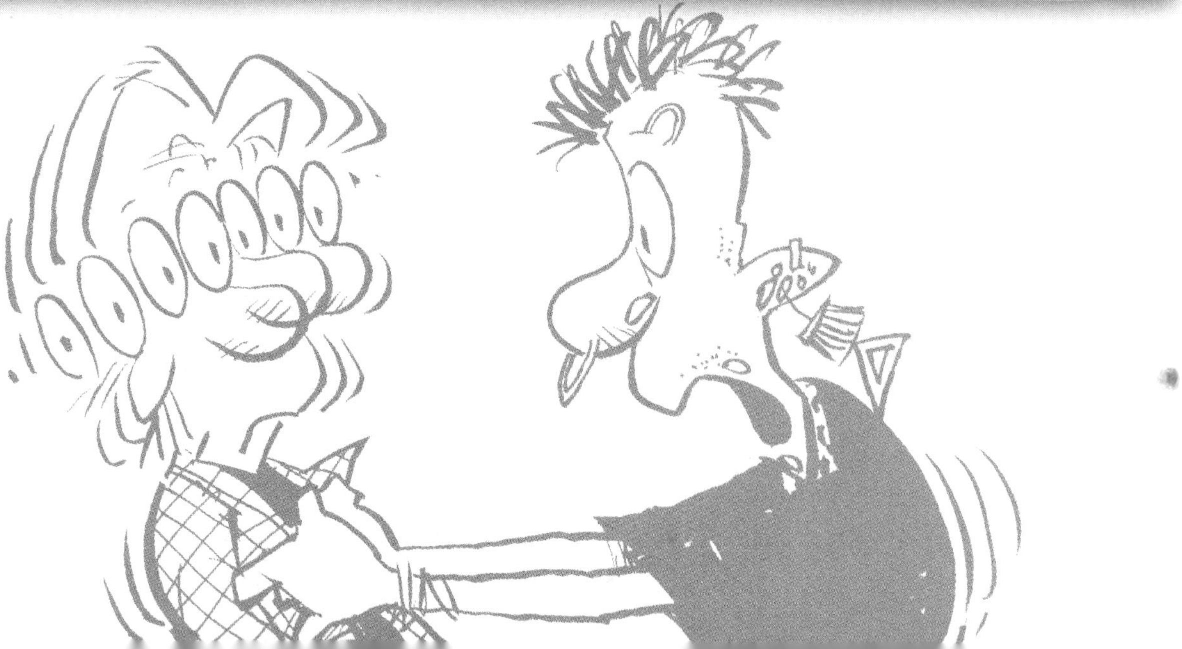

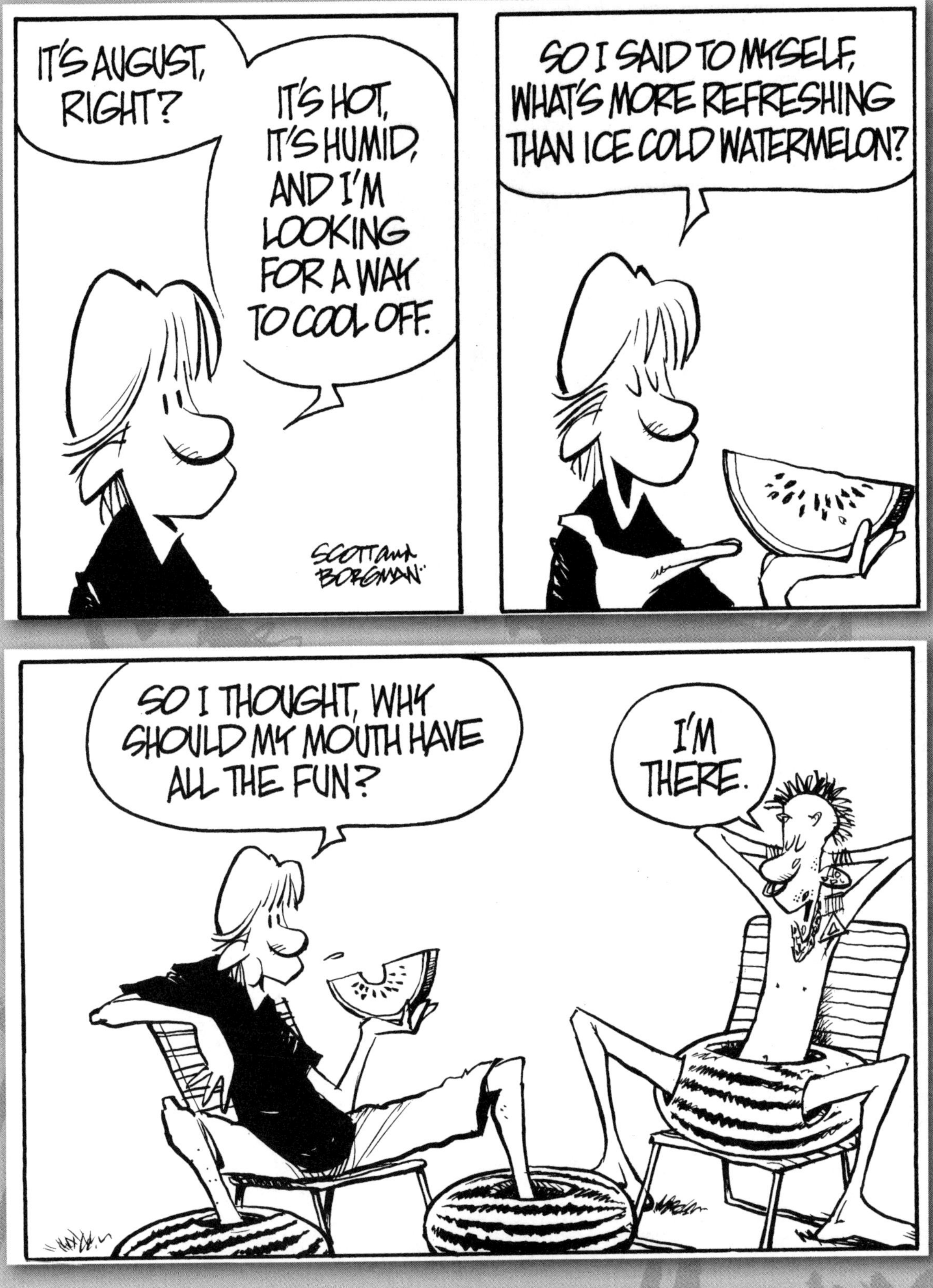
IT'S AUGUST, RIGHT?
IT'S HOT, IT'S HUMID, AND I'M LOOKING FOR A WAY TO COOL OFF.
SCOTT AND BORGMAN
SO I SAID TO MYSELF, WHAT'S MORE REFRESHING THAN ICE COLD WATERMELON?
SO I THOUGHT, WHY SHOULD MY MOUTH HAVE ALL THE FUN?
I'M THERE.

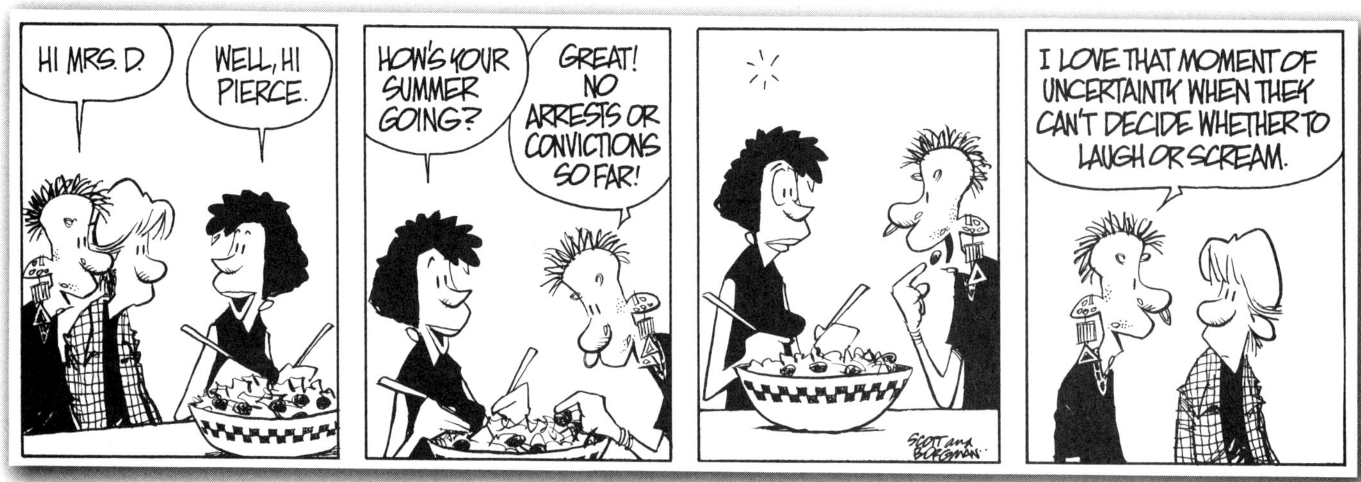
HI MRS. D.
WELL, HI PIERCE.
HOW'S YOUR SUMMER GOING?
GREAT! NO ARRESTS OR CONVICTIONS SO FAR!
SCOTT and BORGMAN
I LOVE THAT MOMENT OF UNCERTAINTY WHEN THEY CAN'T DECIDE WHETHER TO LAUGH OR SCREAM.

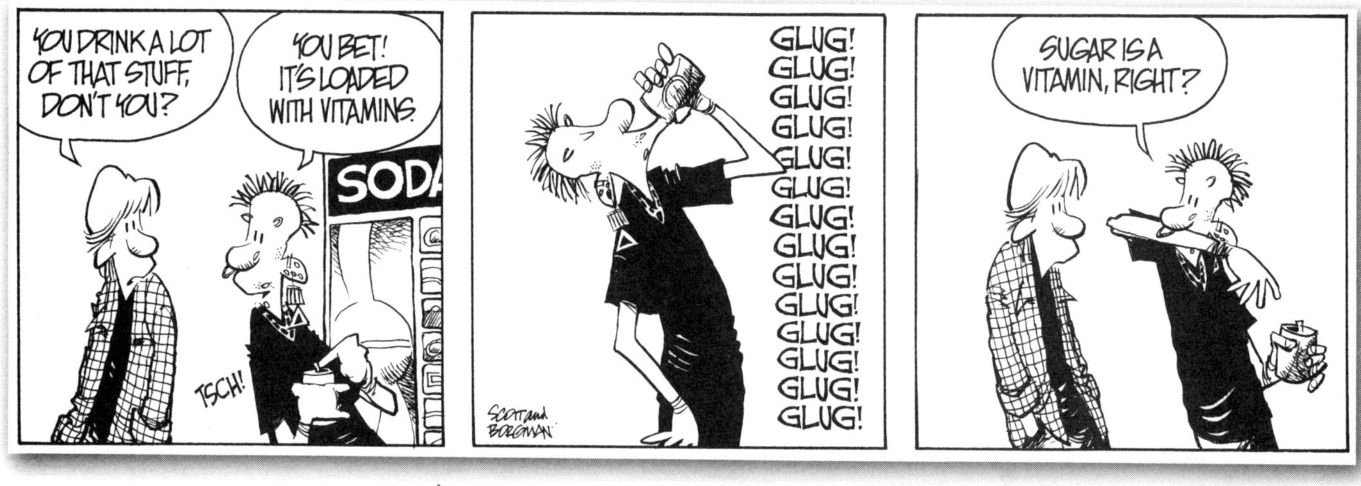
YOU DRINK A LOT OF THAT STUFF, DON'T YOU?
YOU BET! IT'S LOADED WITH VITAMINS.
SODA
TSCH!
GLUG! GLUG! GLUG! GLUG! GLUG! GLUG! GLUG! GLUG! GLUG! GLUG! GLUG! GLUG! GLUG! GLUG!
SCOTT and BORGMAN
SUGAR IS A VITAMIN, RIGHT?

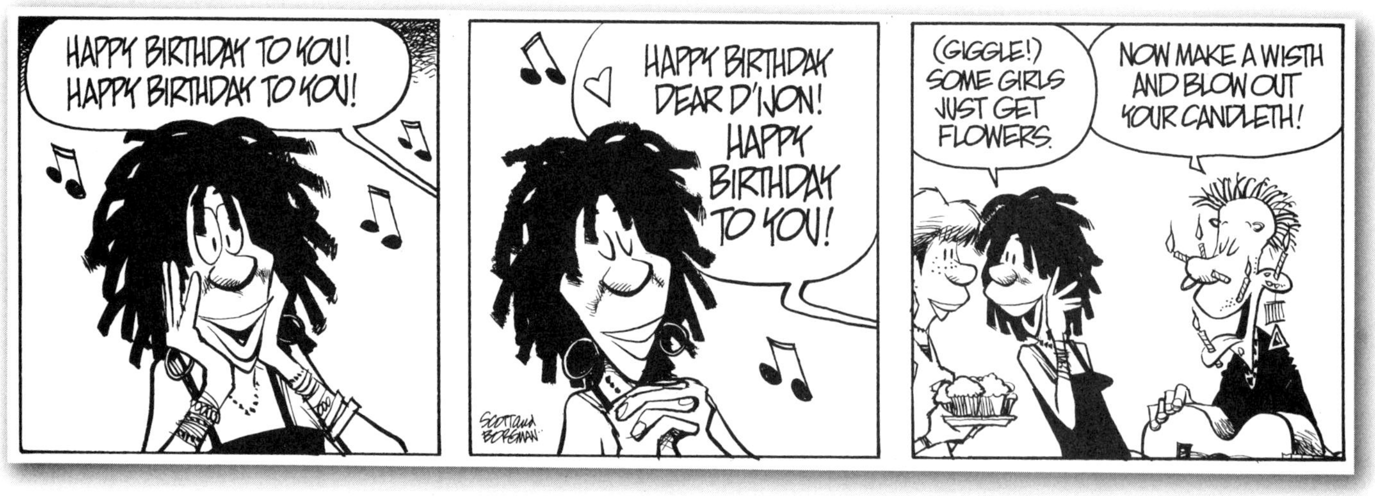
HAPPY BIRTHDAY TO YOU! HAPPY BIRTHDAY TO YOU!
HAPPY BIRTHDAY DEAR D'JON! HAPPY BIRTHDAY TO YOU!
SCOTT and BORGMAN
(GIGGLE!) SOME GIRLS JUST GET FLOWERS.
NOW MAKE A WISTH AND BLOW OUT YOUR CANDLETH!

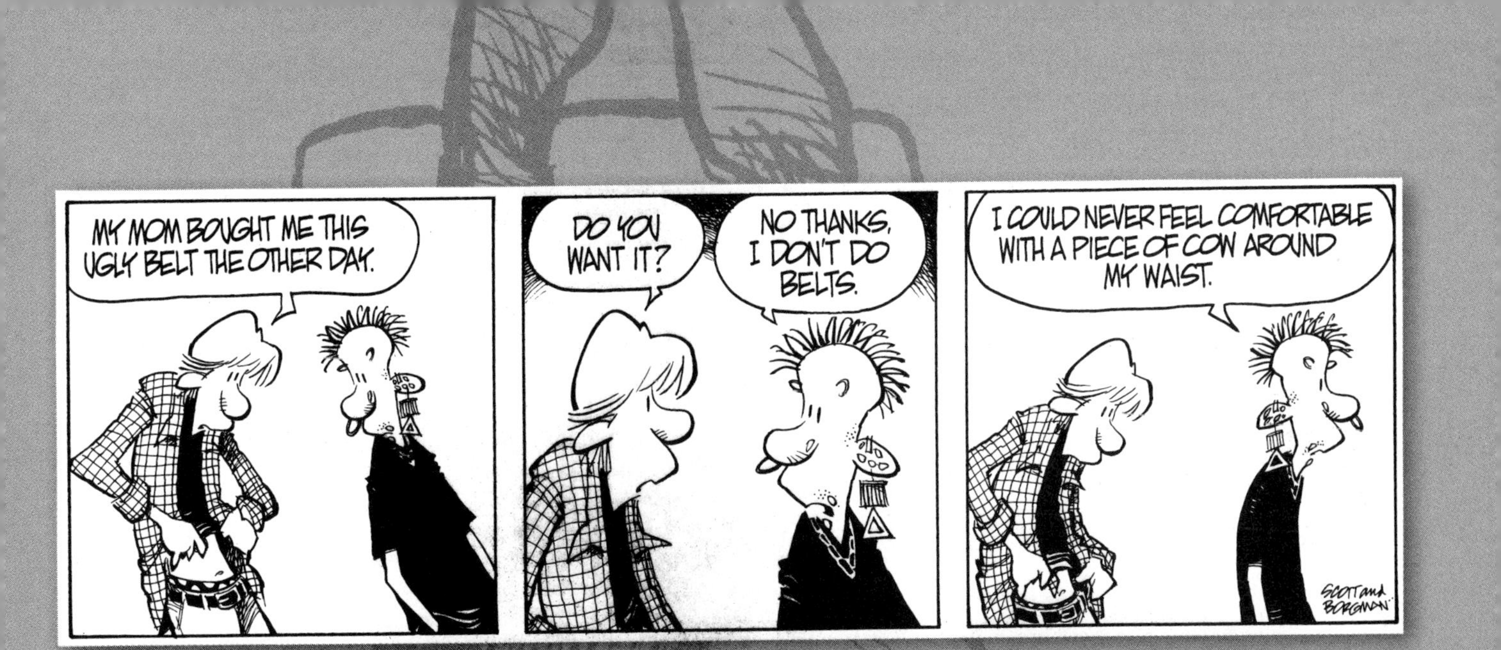
MY MOM BOUGHT ME THIS UGLY BELT THE OTHER DAY.
DO YOU WANT IT?
NO THANKS, I DON'T DO BELTS.
I COULD NEVER FEEL COMFORTABLE WITH A PIECE OF COW AROUND MY WAIST.
SCOTT AND BORGMAN

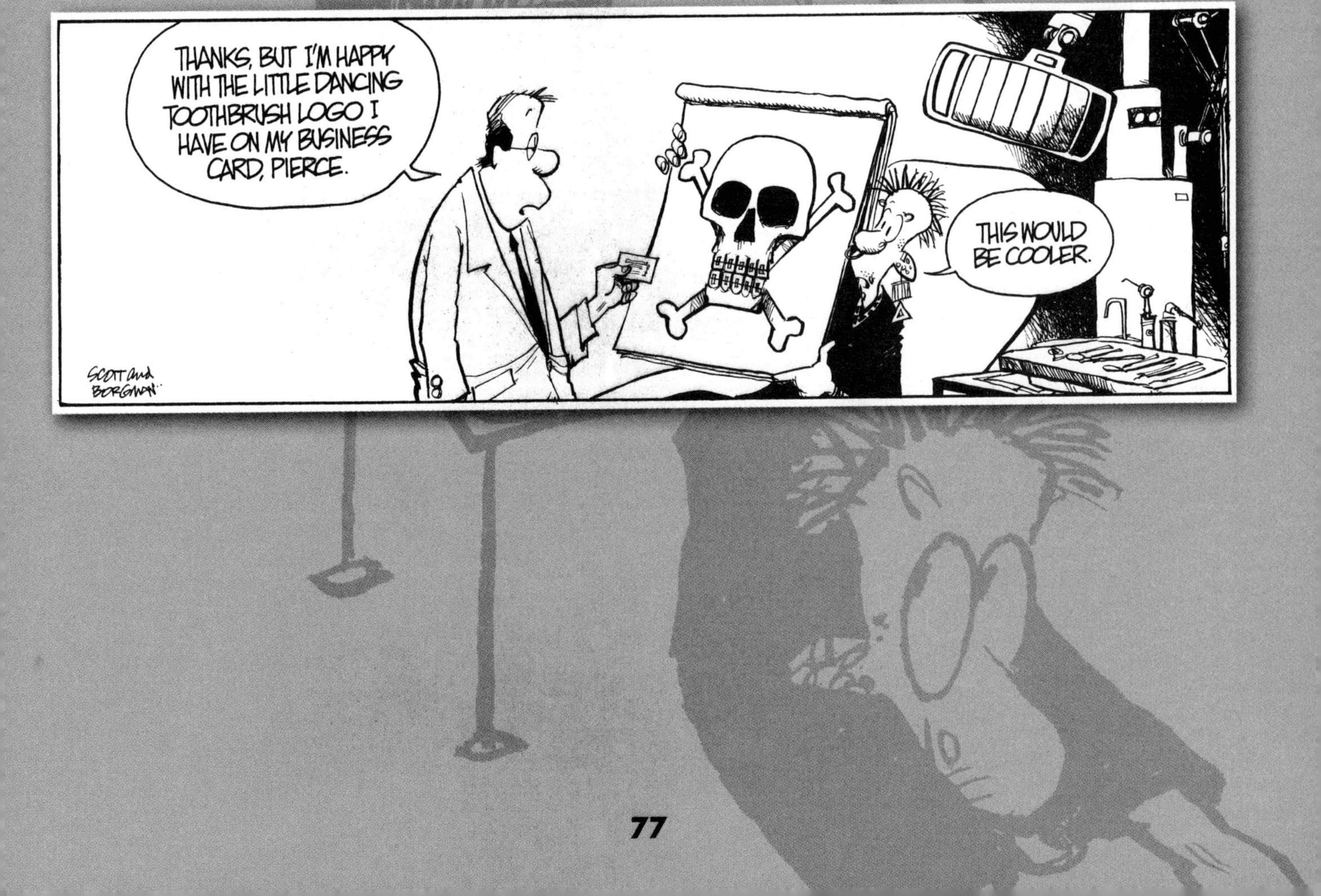
THANKS, BUT I'M HAPPY WITH THE LITTLE DANCING TOOTHBRUSH LOGO I HAVE ON MY BUSINESS CARD, PIERCE.
THIS WOULD BE COOLER.
SCOTT AND BORGMAN

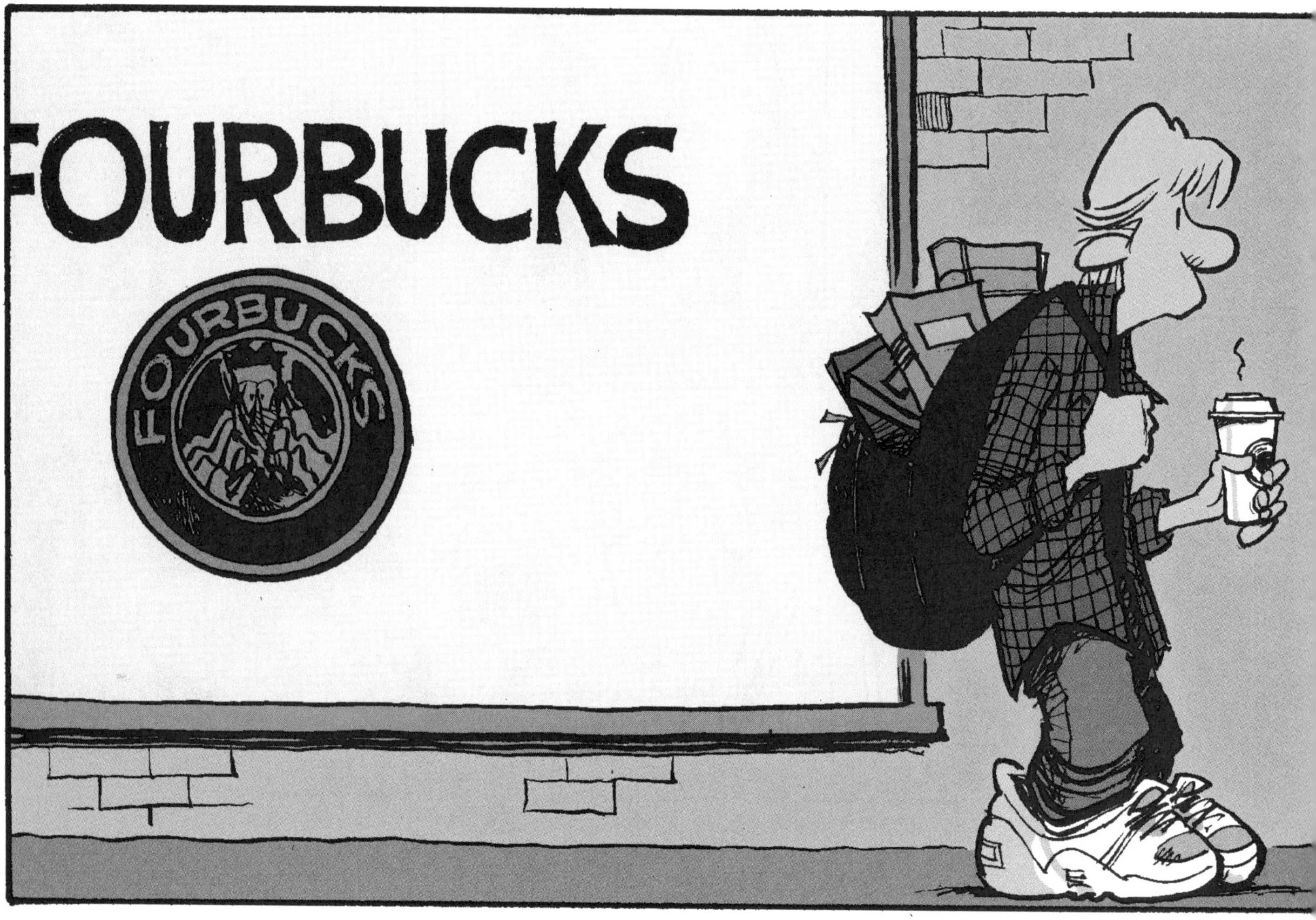
FOURBUCKS
FOURBUCKS

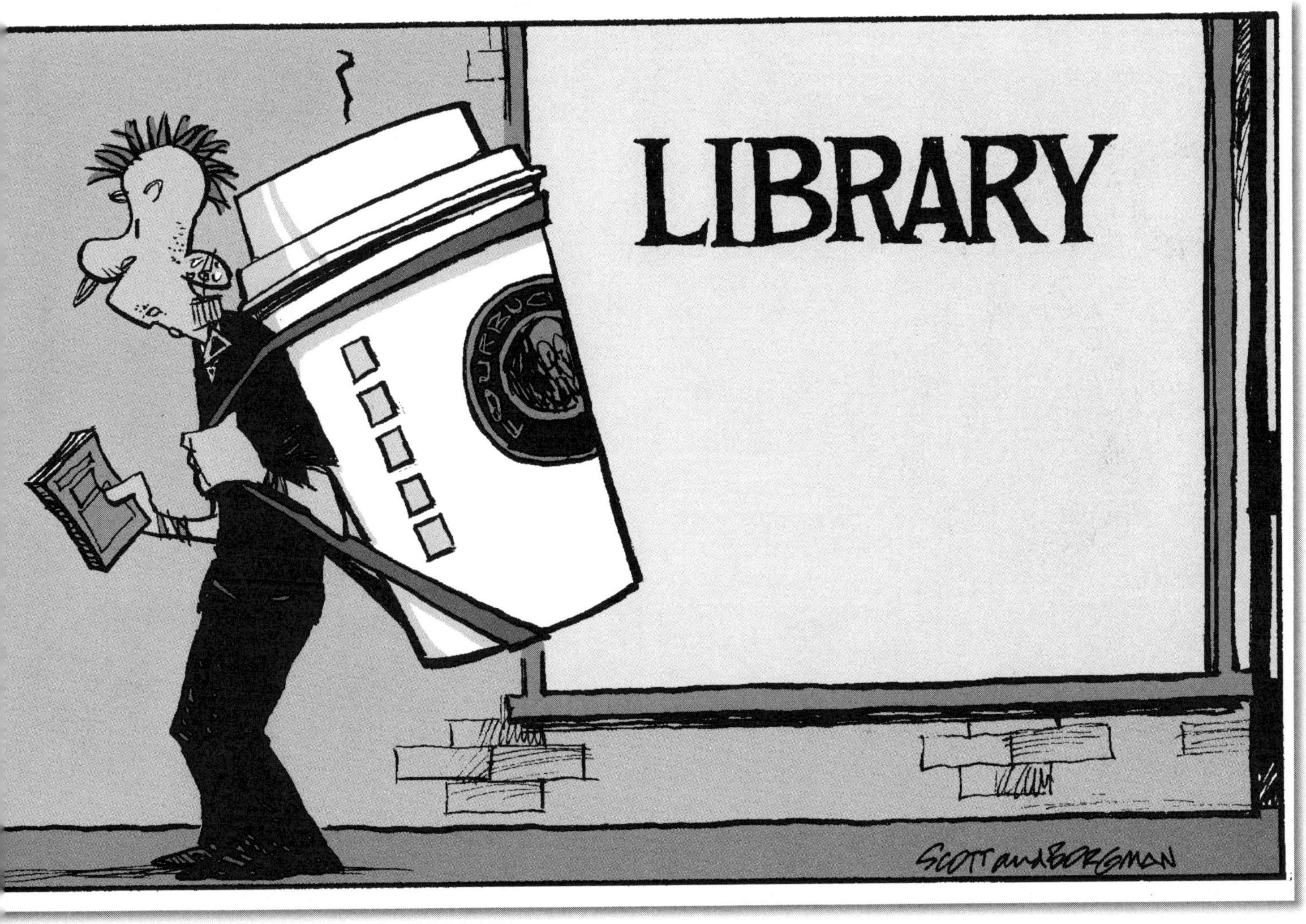
LIBRARY
SCOTT and BORGMAN

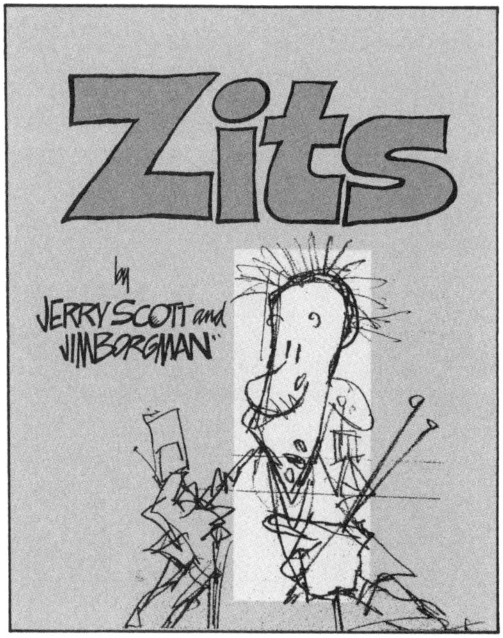
Zits
by
JERRY SCOTT and
JIM BORGMAN

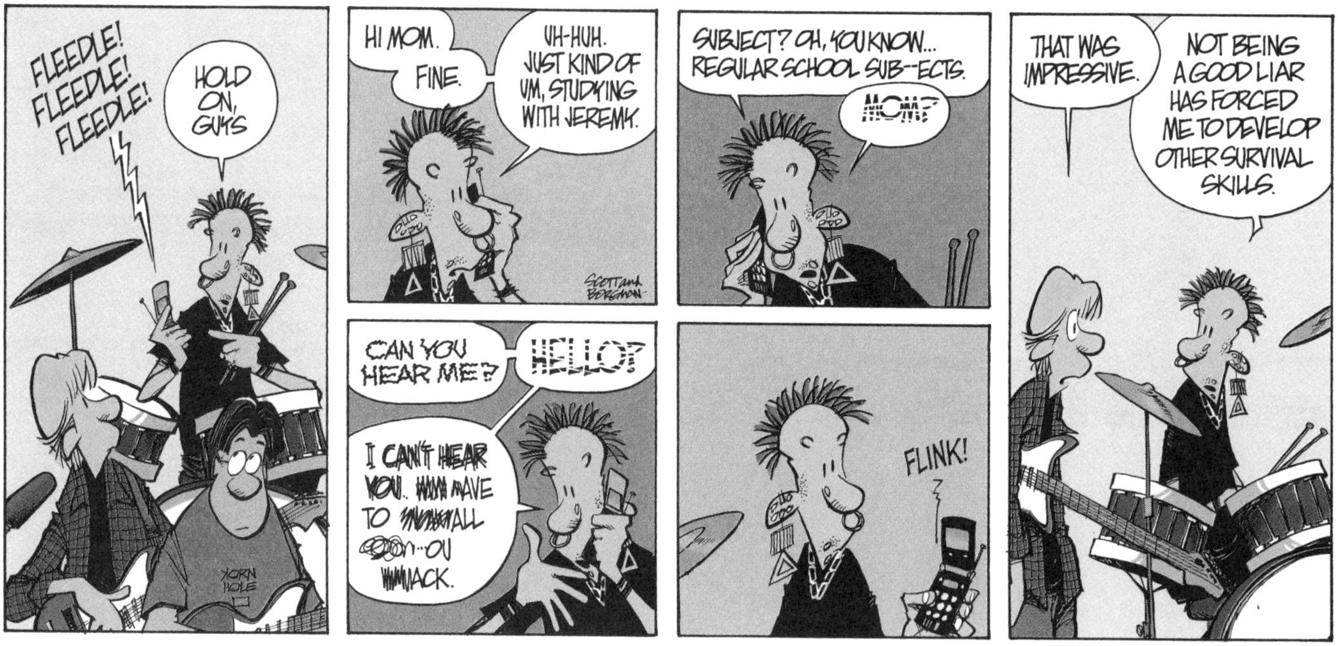
FLEEDLE! FLEEDLE! FLEEDLE!
HOLD ON, GUYS
HI MOM.
FINE.
UH-HUH. JUST KIND OF UM, STUDYING WITH JEREMY.
SUBJECT? OH, YOU KNOW... REGULAR SCHOOL SUB--ECTS.
MOM?
THAT WAS IMPRESSIVE.
NOT BEING A GOOD LIAR HAS FORCED ME TO DEVELOP OTHER SURVIVAL SKILLS.
CAN YOU HEAR ME?
HELLO?
FLINK!
SCOTT and BORGMAN

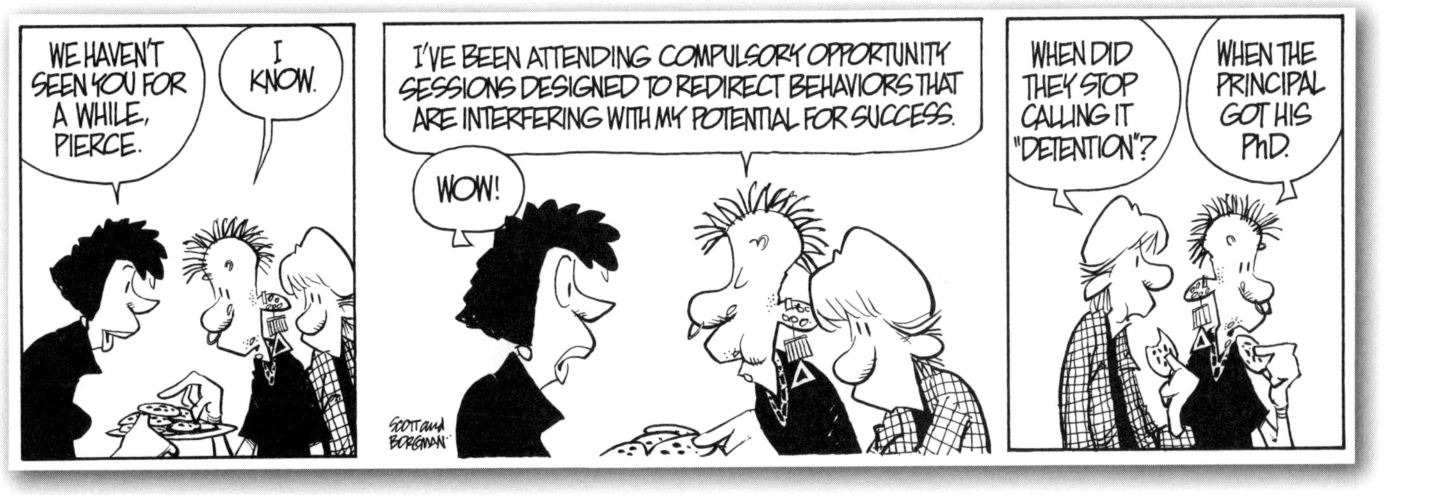
WE HAVEN'T SEEN YOU FOR A WHILE, PIERCE.
I KNOW.
I'VE BEEN ATTENDING COMPULSORY OPPORTUNITY SESSIONS DESIGNED TO REDIRECT BEHAVIORS THAT ARE INTERFERING WITH MY POTENTIAL FOR SUCCESS.
WOW!
WHEN DID THEY STOP CALLING IT "DETENTION"?
WHEN THE PRINCIPAL GOT HIS PhD.

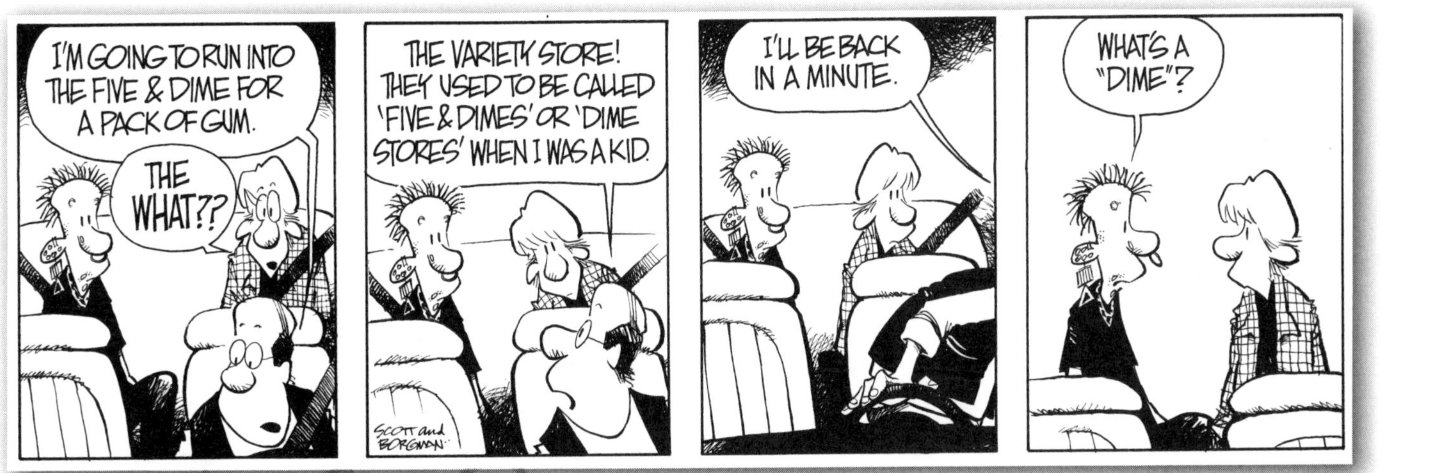
I'M GOING TO RUN INTO THE FIVE & DIME FOR A PACK OF GUM.
THE WHAT??
THE VARIETY STORE! THEY USED TO BE CALLED 'FIVE & DIMES' OR 'DIME STORES' WHEN I WAS A KID.
I'LL BE BACK IN A MINUTE.
WHAT'S A "DIME"?

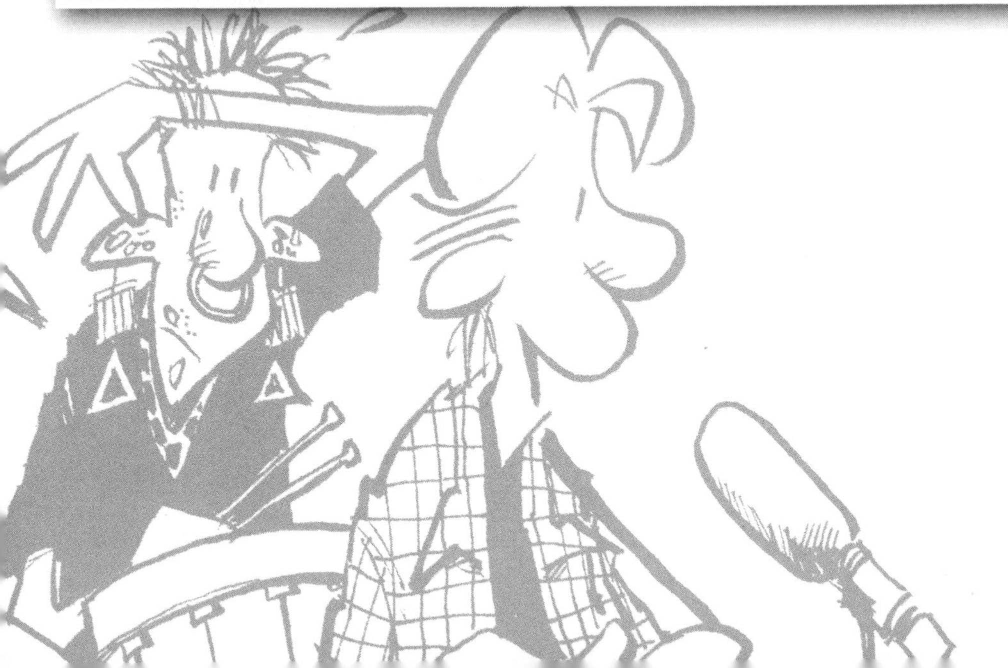

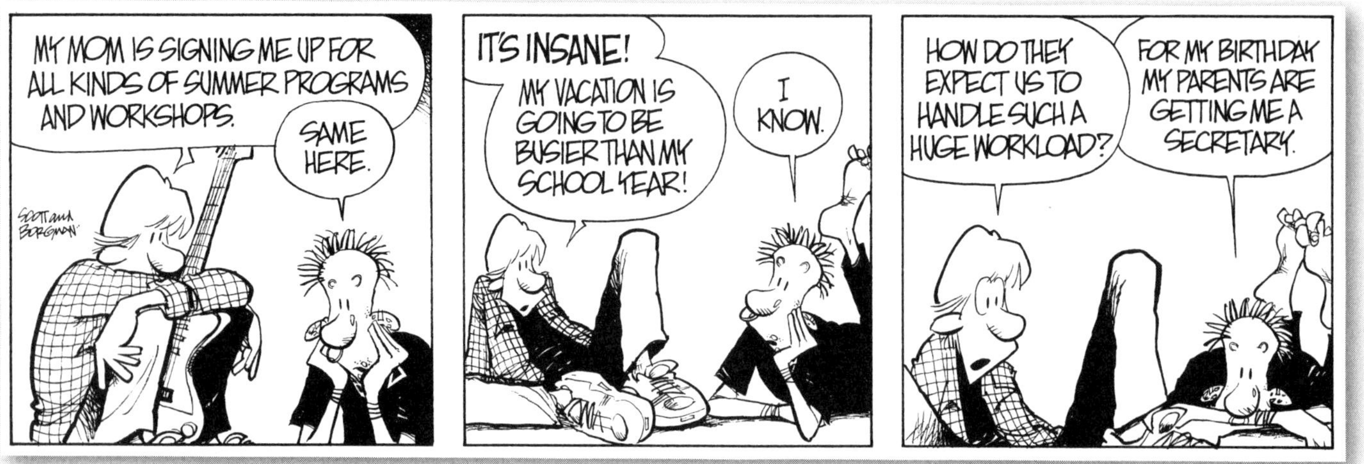
MY MOM IS SIGNING ME UP FOR ALL KINDS OF SUMMER PROGRAMS AND WORKSHOPS.
SAME HERE.
IT'S INSANE!
MY VACATION IS GOING TO BE BUSIER THAN MY SCHOOL YEAR!
I KNOW.
HOW DO THEY EXPECT US TO HANDLE SUCH A HUGE WORKLOAD?
FOR MY BIRTHDAY MY PARENTS ARE GETTING ME A SECRETARY.

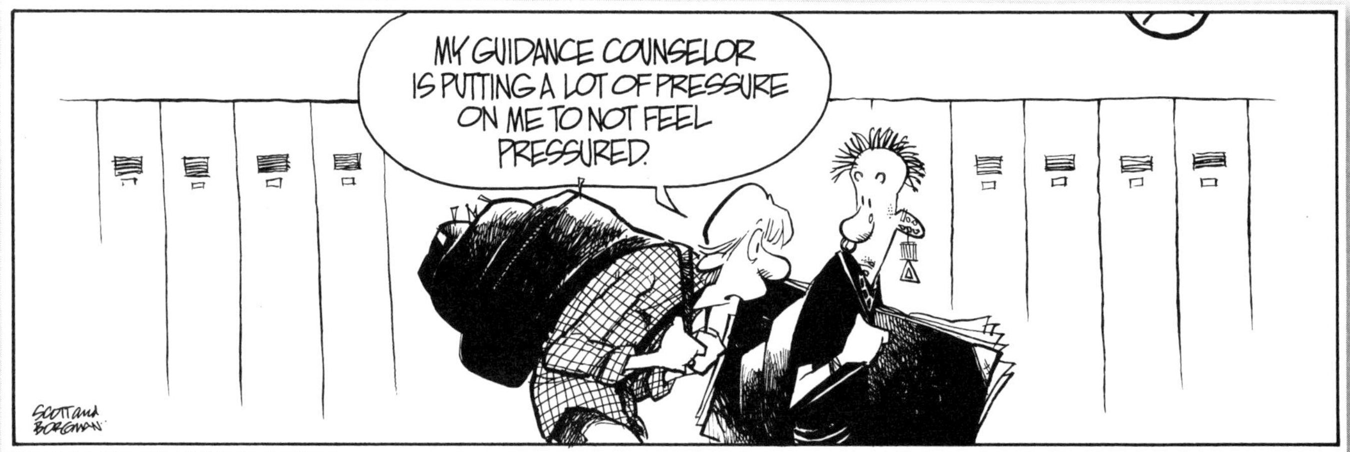
MY GUIDANCE COUNSELOR IS PUTTING A LOT OF PRESSURE ON ME TO NOT FEEL PRESSURED.

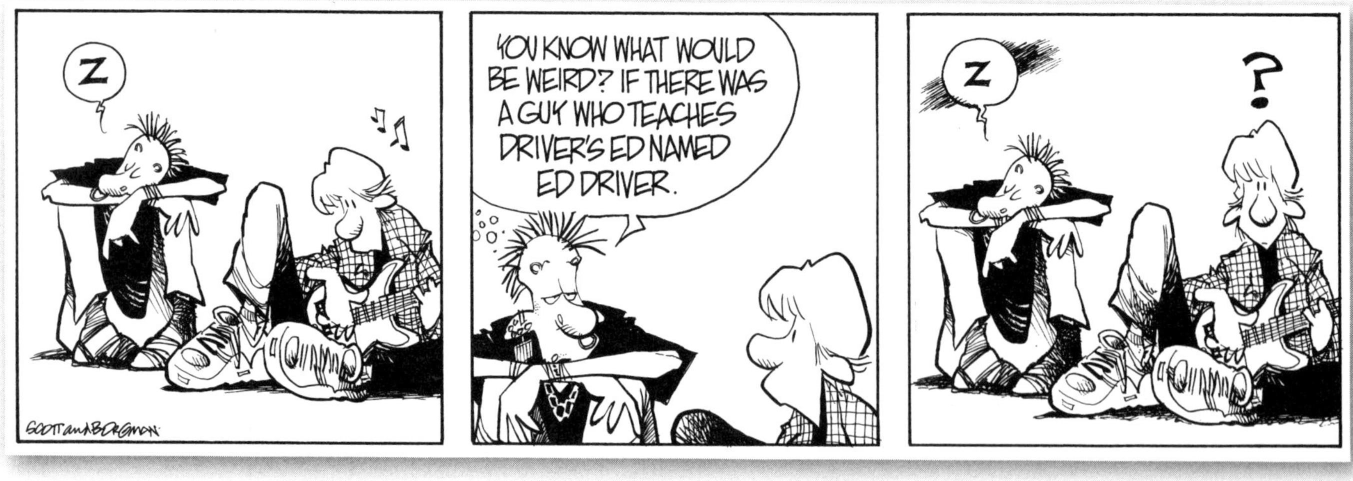
Z
YOU KNOW WHAT WOULD BE WEIRD? IF THERE WAS A GUY WHO TEACHES DRIVER'S ED NAMED ED DRIVER.
Z
?

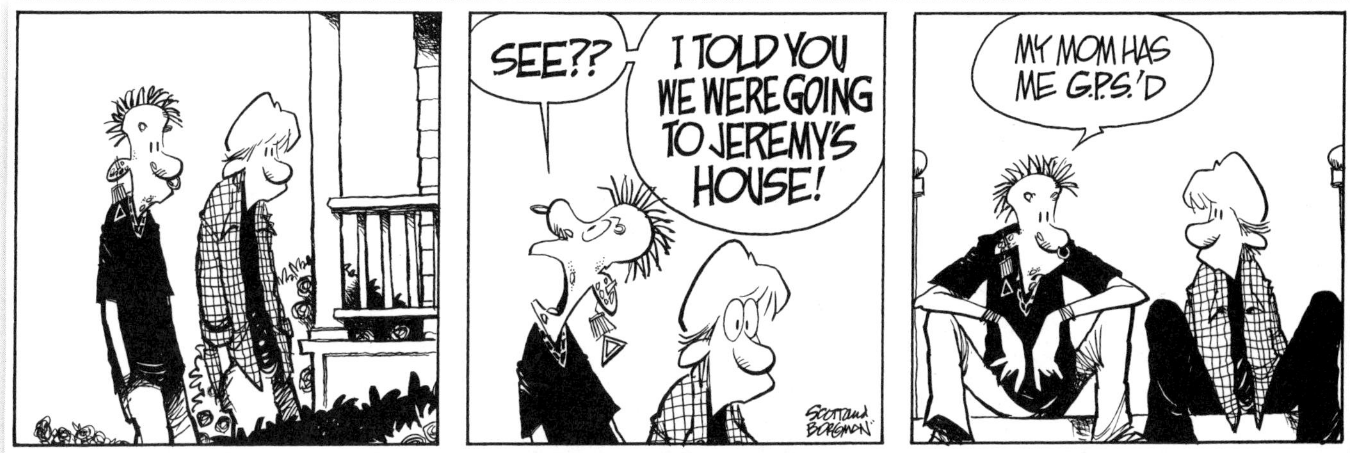
SEE??
I TOLD YOU WE WERE GOING TO JEREMY'S HOUSE!
MY MOM HAS ME G.P.S.'D

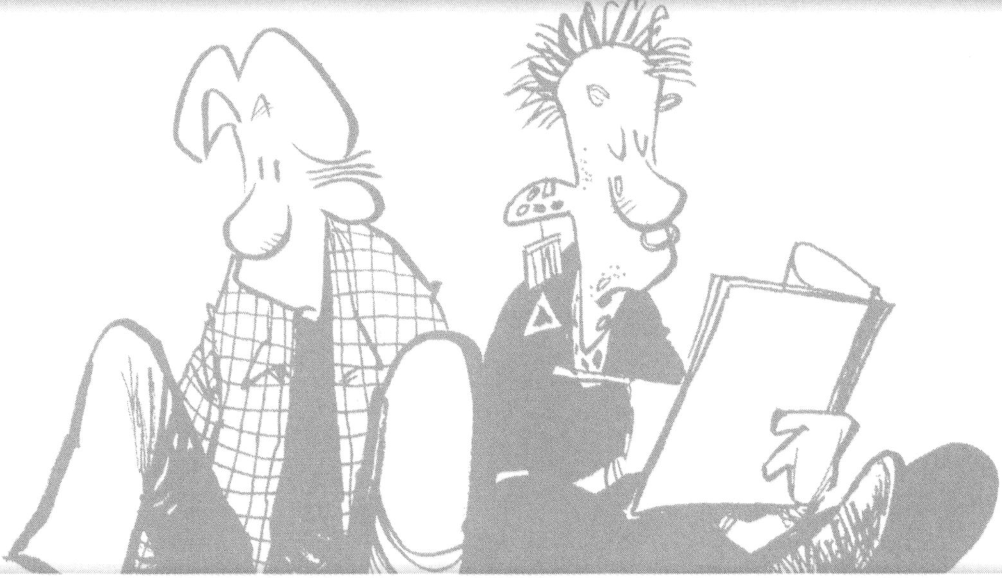

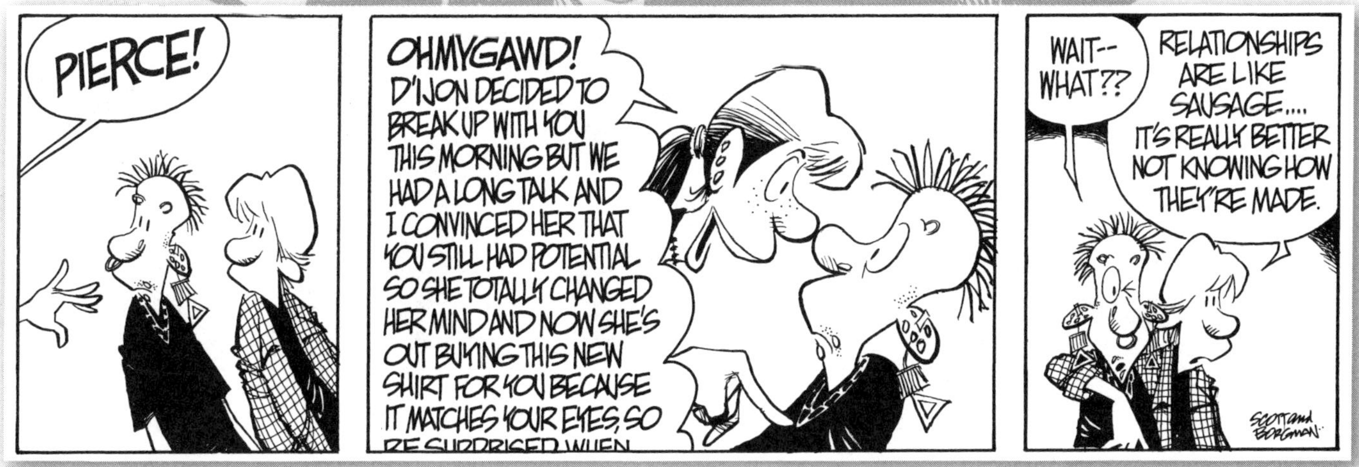
PIERCE!
OHMYGAWD! D'JON DECIDED TO BREAK UP WITH YOU THIS MORNING BUT WE HAD A LONG TALK AND I CONVINCED HER THAT YOU STILL HAD POTENTIAL SO SHE TOTALLY CHANGED HER MIND AND NOW SHE'S OUT BUYING THIS NEW SHIRT FOR YOU BECAUSE IT MATCHES YOUR EYES, SO
WAIT-- WHAT??
RELATIONSHIPS ARE LIKE SAUSAGE.... IT'S REALLY BETTER NOT KNOWING HOW THEY'RE MADE.

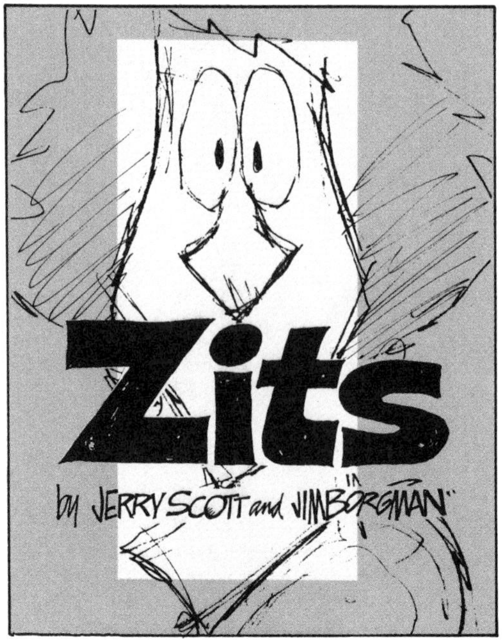
Zits
by JERRY SCOTT and JIM BORGMAN

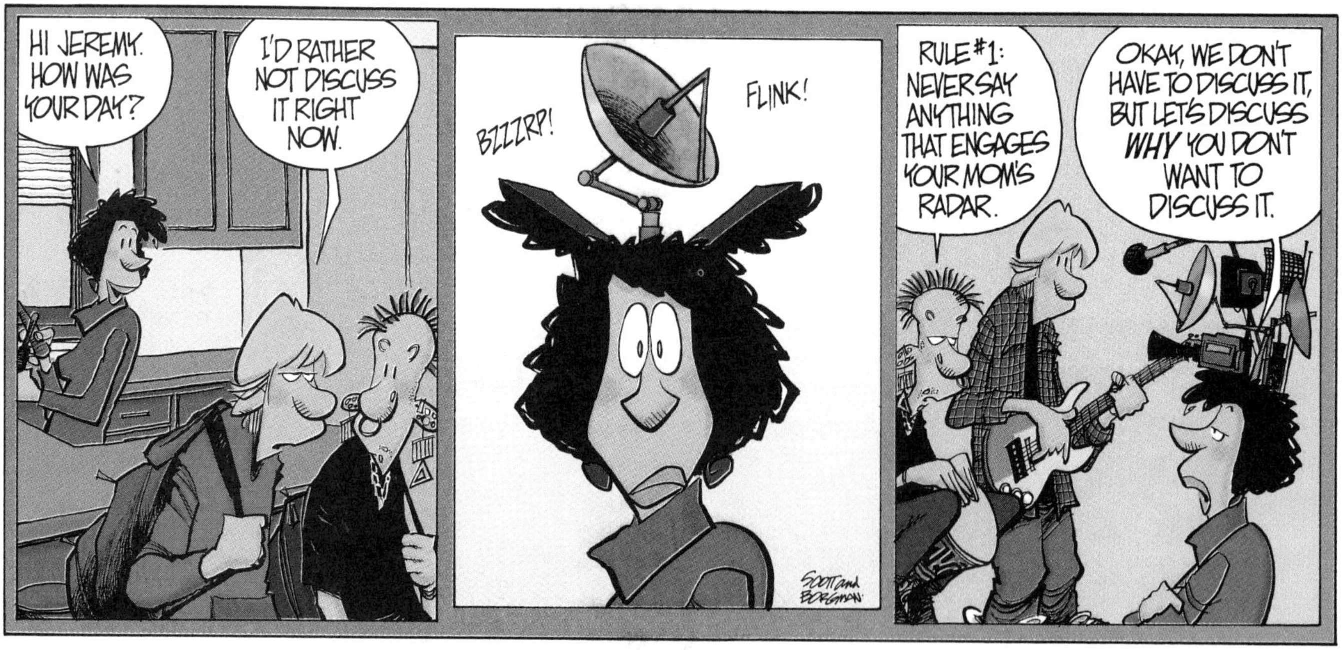
HI JEREMY. HOW WAS YOUR DAY?
I'D RATHER NOT DISCUSS IT RIGHT NOW.
BZZZRP!
FLINK!
RULE #1: NEVER SAY ANYTHING THAT ENGAGES YOUR MOM'S RADAR.
OKAY, WE DON'T HAVE TO DISCUSS IT, BUT LET'S DISCUSS *WHY* YOU DON'T WANT TO DISCUSS IT.
SCOTT and BORGMAN

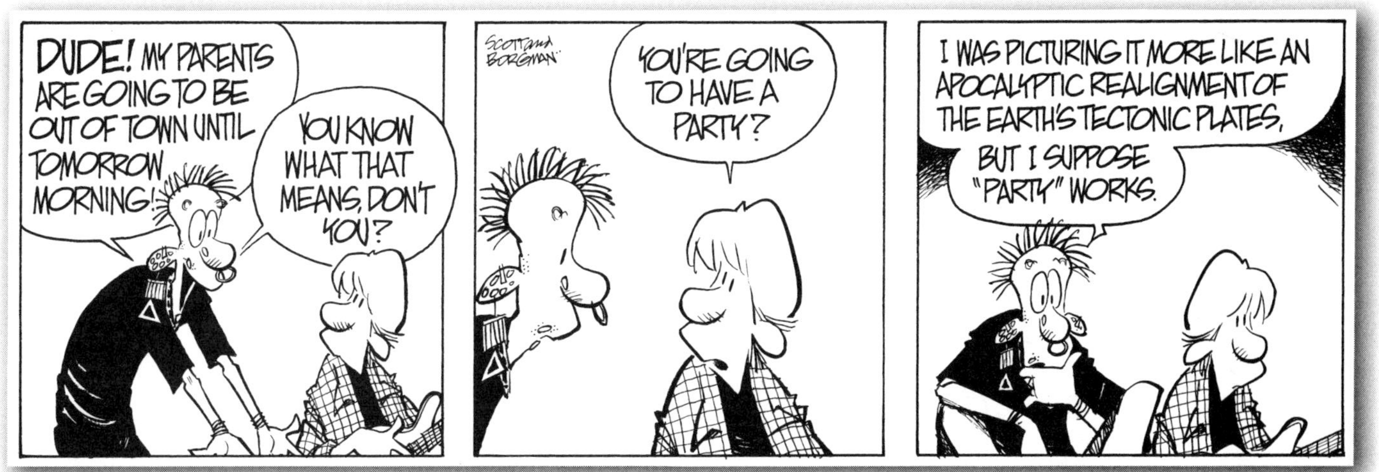
DUDE! MY PARENTS ARE GOING TO BE OUT OF TOWN UNTIL TOMORROW MORNING!
YOU KNOW WHAT THAT MEANS, DON'T YOU?
YOU'RE GOING TO HAVE A PARTY?
I WAS PICTURING IT MORE LIKE AN APOCALYPTIC REALIGNMENT OF THE EARTH'S TECTONIC PLATES,
BUT I SUPPOSE "PARTY" WORKS.

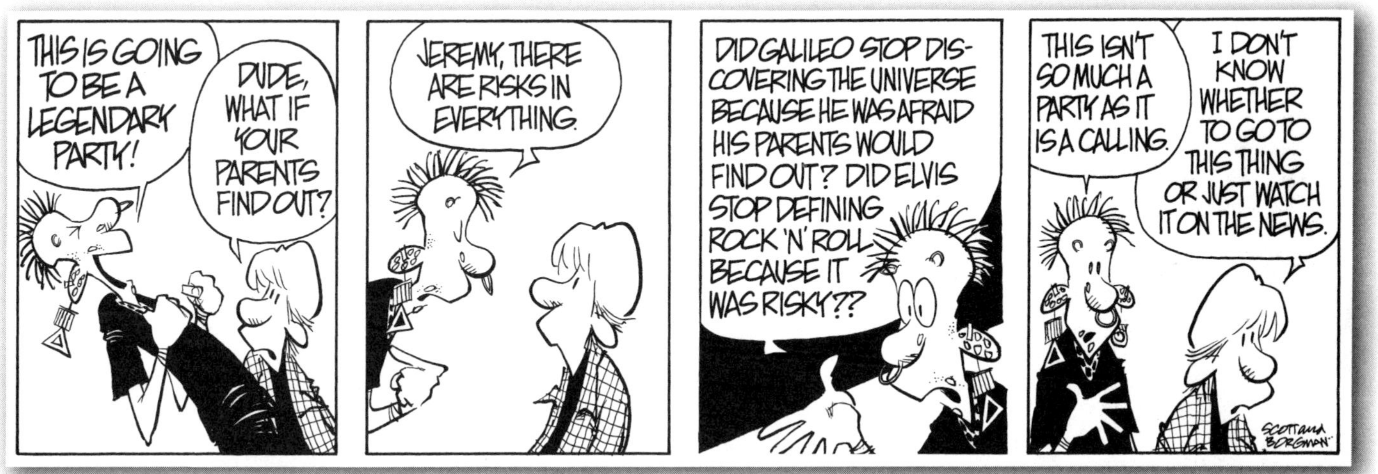
THIS IS GOING TO BE A LEGENDARY PARTY!
DUDE, WHAT IF YOUR PARENTS FIND OUT?
JEREMY, THERE ARE RISKS IN EVERYTHING.
DID GALILEO STOP DISCOVERING THE UNIVERSE BECAUSE HE WAS AFRAID HIS PARENTS WOULD FIND OUT? DID ELVIS STOP DEFINING ROCK 'N' ROLL BECAUSE IT WAS RISKY??
THIS ISN'T SO MUCH A PARTY AS IT IS A CALLING.
I DON'T KNOW WHETHER TO GO TO THIS THING OR JUST WATCH IT ON THE NEWS.

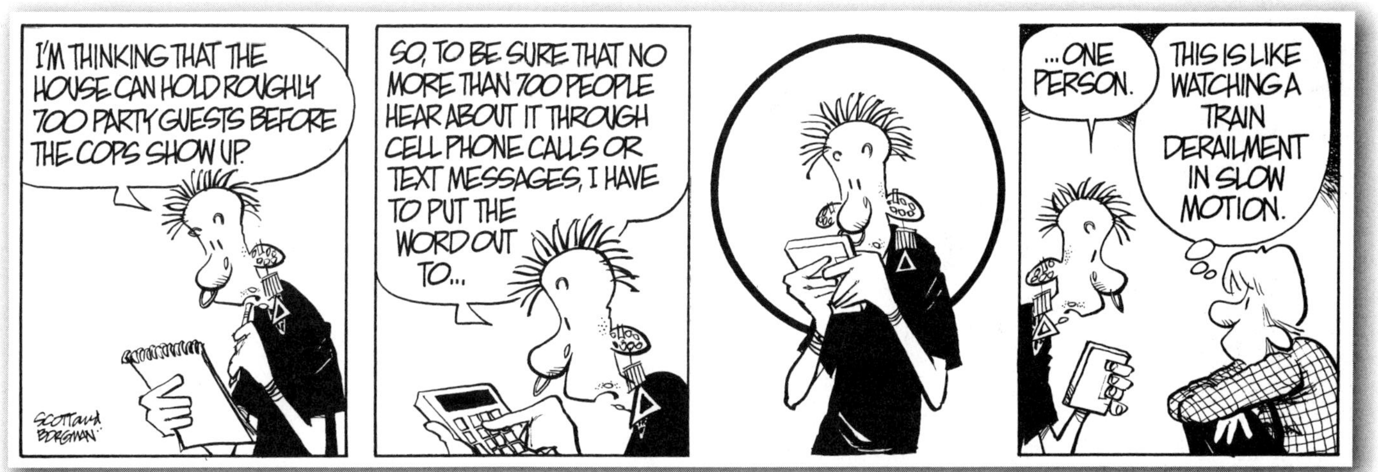
I'M THINKING THAT THE HOUSE CAN HOLD ROUGHLY 700 PARTY GUESTS BEFORE THE COPS SHOW UP.
SO, TO BE SURE THAT NO MORE THAN 700 PEOPLE HEAR ABOUT IT THROUGH CELL PHONE CALLS OR TEXT MESSAGES, I HAVE TO PUT THE WORD OUT TO...
...ONE PERSON.
THIS IS LIKE WATCHING A TRAIN DERAILMENT IN SLOW MOTION.

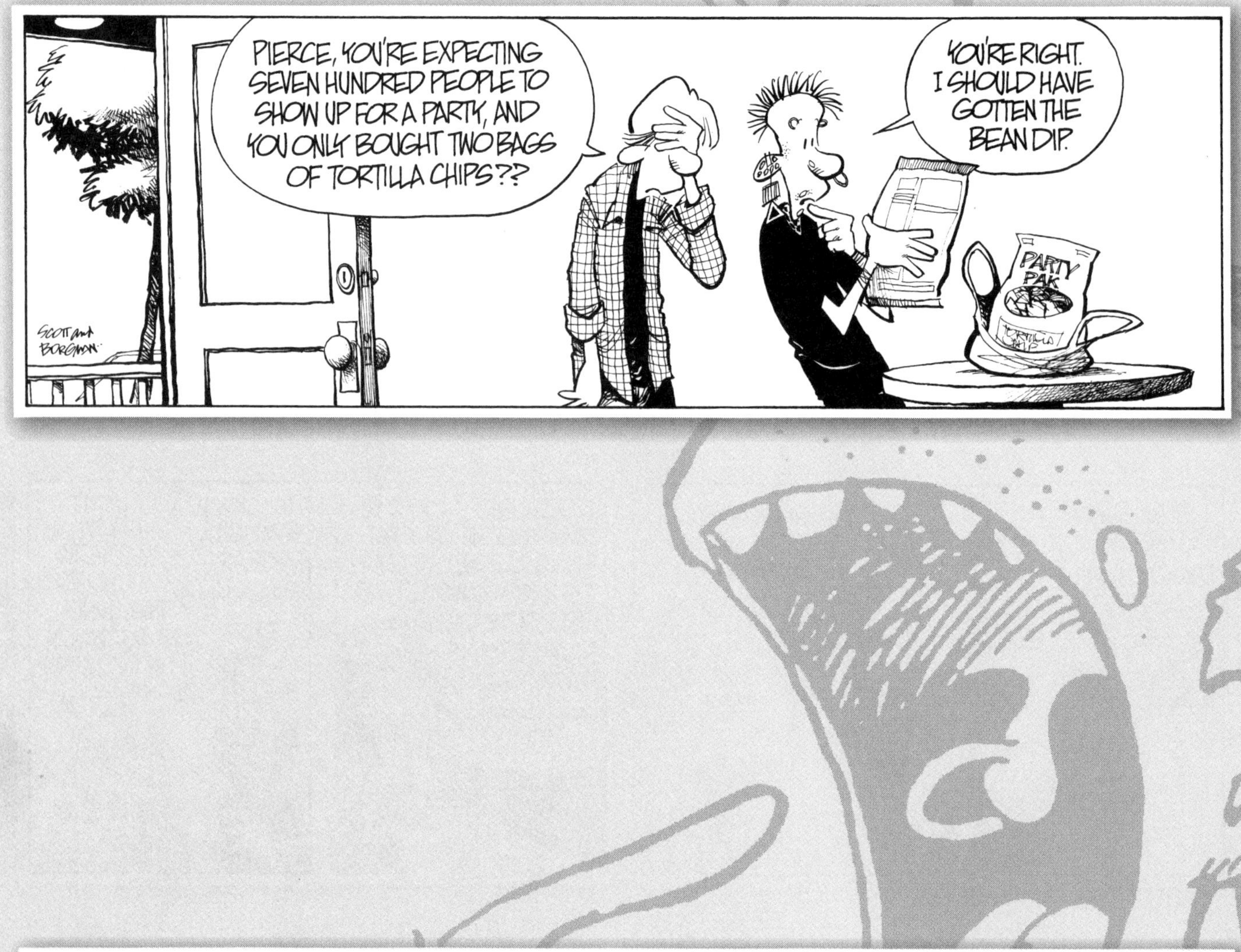
PIERCE, YOU'RE EXPECTING SEVEN HUNDRED PEOPLE TO SHOW UP FOR A PARTY, AND YOU ONLY BOUGHT TWO BAGS OF TORTILLA CHIPS??
YOU'RE RIGHT. I SHOULD HAVE GOTTEN THE BEAN DIP.
PARTY PAK
SCOTT and BORGMAN

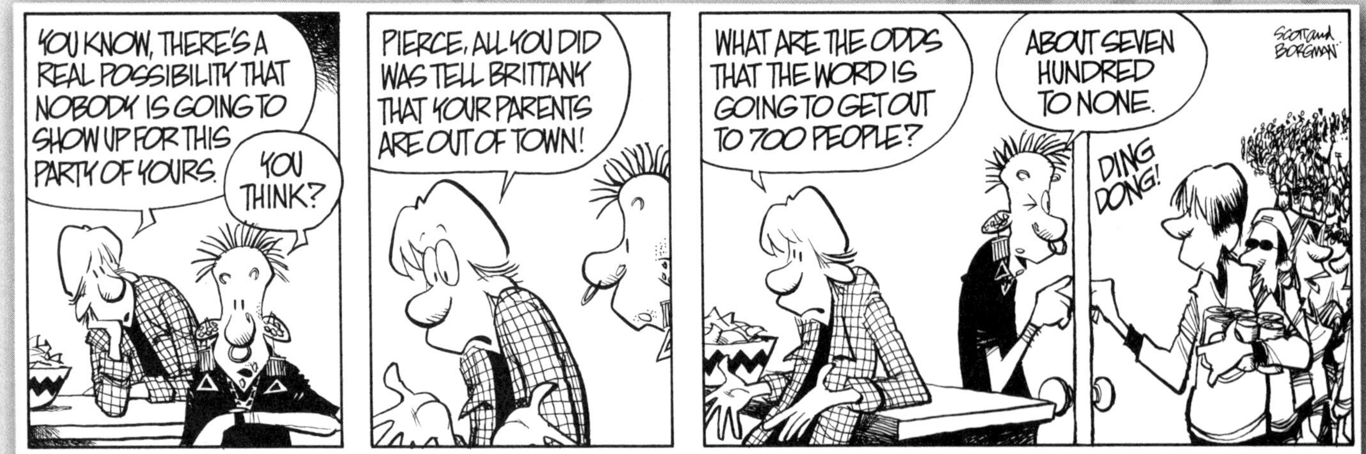
YOU KNOW, THERE'S A REAL POSSIBILITY THAT NOBODY IS GOING TO SHOW UP FOR THIS PARTY OF YOURS.
YOU THINK?
PIERCE, ALL YOU DID WAS TELL BRITTANY THAT YOUR PARENTS ARE OUT OF TOWN!
WHAT ARE THE ODDS THAT THE WORD IS GOING TO GET OUT TO 700 PEOPLE?
ABOUT SEVEN HUNDRED TO NONE.
DING DONG!
SCOTT and BORGMAN

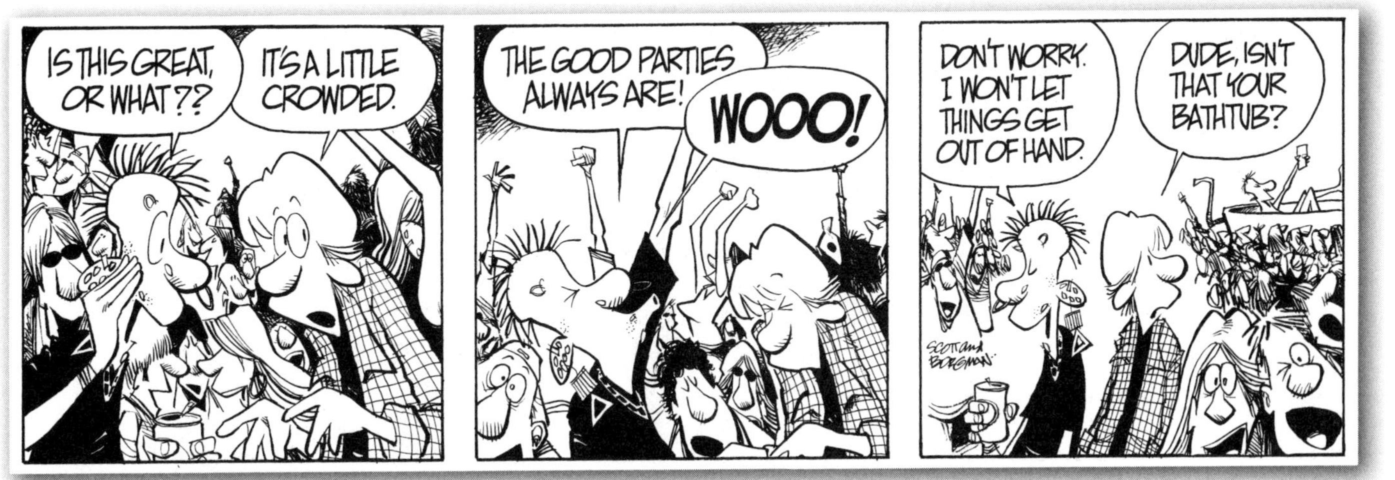
IS THIS GREAT, OR WHAT??
IT'S A LITTLE CROWDED.
THE GOOD PARTIES ALWAYS ARE!
WOOO!
DON'T WORRY. I WON'T LET THINGS GET OUT OF HAND.
DUDE, ISN'T THAT YOUR BATHTUB?
SCOTT and BORGMAN

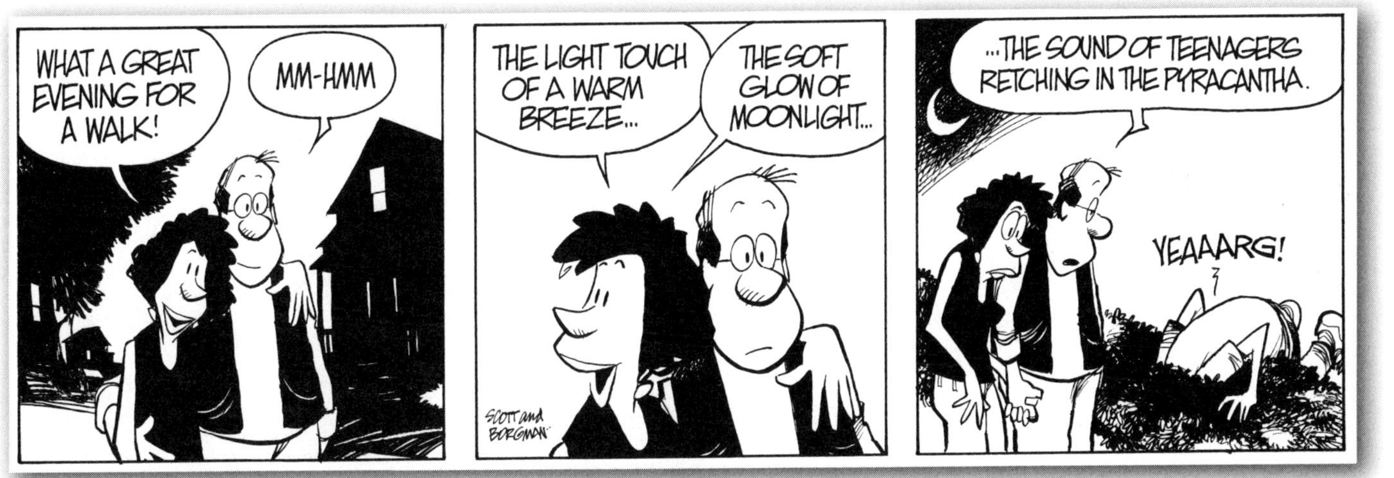
WHAT A GREAT EVENING FOR A WALK!
MM-HMM
THE LIGHT TOUCH OF A WARM BREEZE...
THE SOFT GLOW OF MOONLIGHT...
SCOTT and BORGMAN
...THE SOUND OF TEENAGERS RETCHING IN THE PYRACANTHA.
YEAAARG!

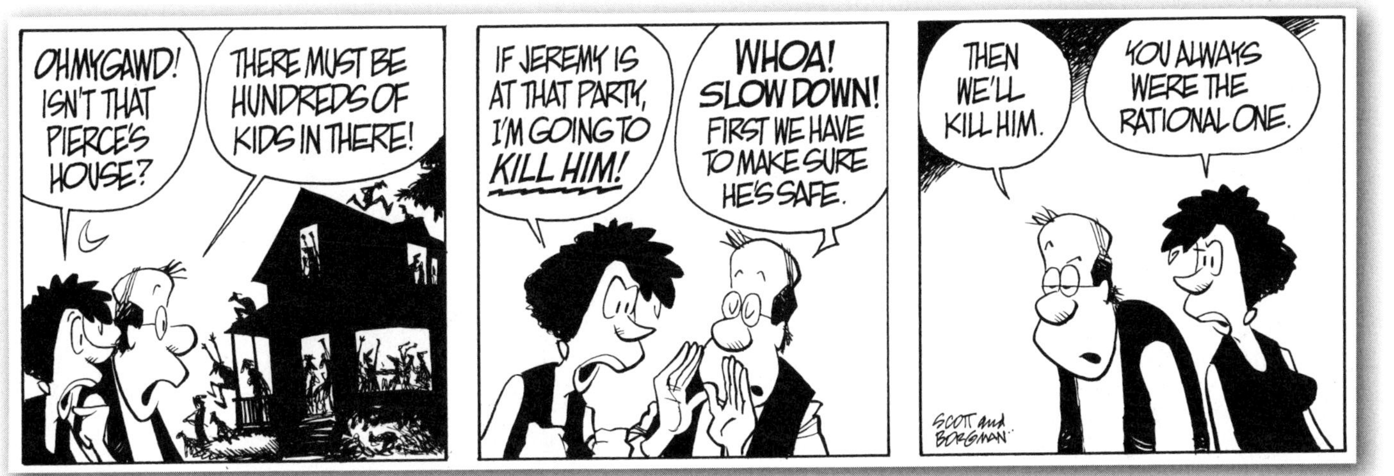
OHMYGAWD! ISN'T THAT PIERCE'S HOUSE?
THERE MUST BE HUNDREDS OF KIDS IN THERE!
IF JEREMY IS AT THAT PARTY, I'M GOING TO KILL HIM!
WHOA! SLOW DOWN! FIRST WE HAVE TO MAKE SURE HE'S SAFE.
THEN WE'LL KILL HIM.
YOU ALWAYS WERE THE RATIONAL ONE.
SCOTT and BORGMAN

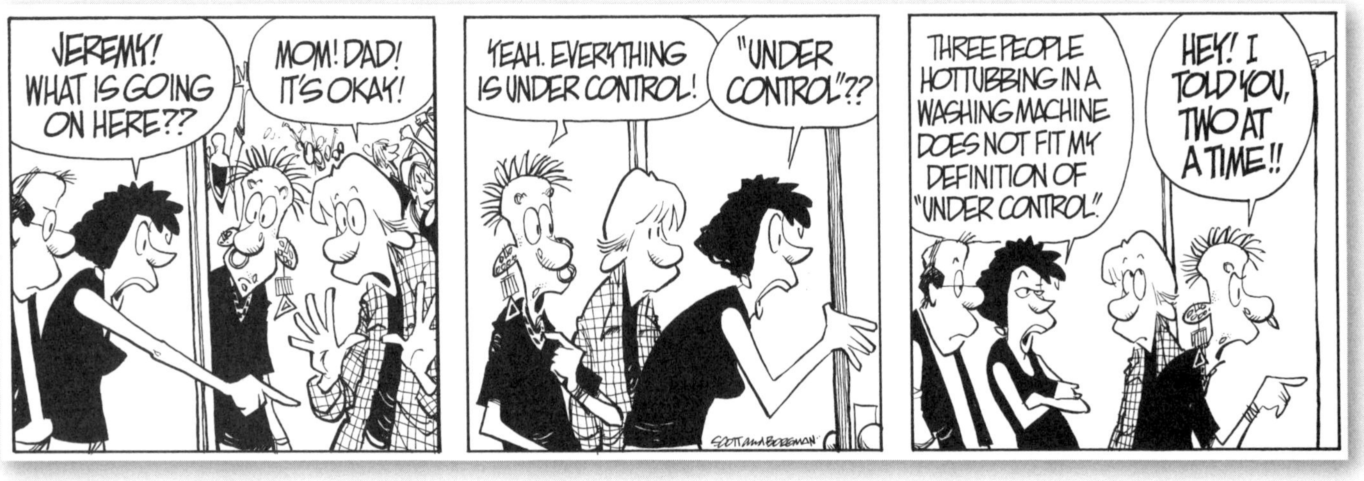
JEREMY! WHAT IS GOING ON HERE??
MOM! DAD! IT'S OKAY!
YEAH. EVERYTHING IS UNDER CONTROL!
"UNDER CONTROL"??
THREE PEOPLE HOTTUBBING IN A WASHING MACHINE DOES NOT FIT MY DEFINITION OF "UNDER CONTROL."
HEY! I TOLD YOU, TWO AT A TIME!!

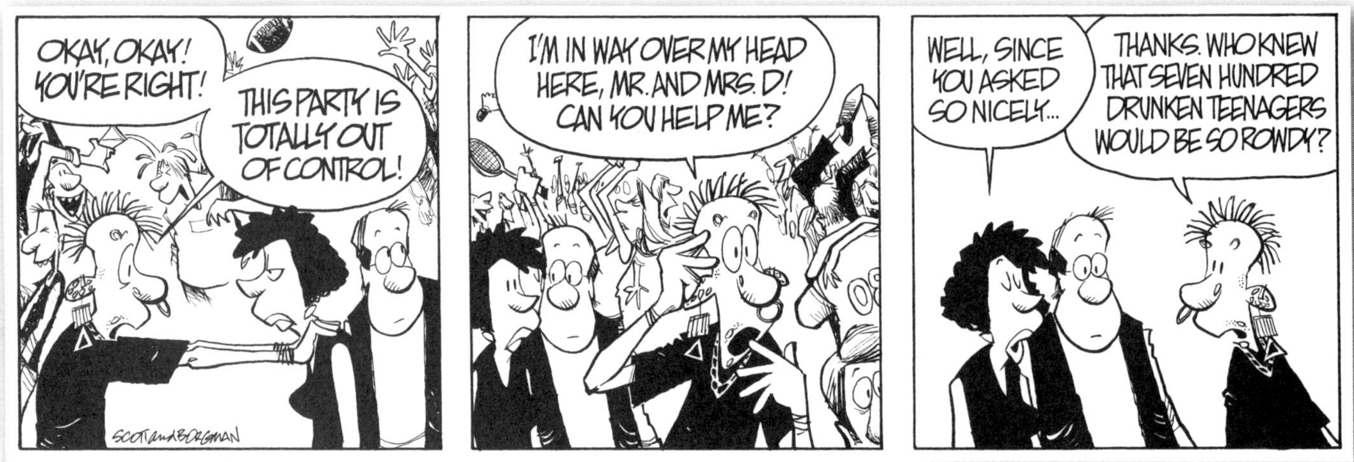
OKAY, OKAY! YOU'RE RIGHT!
THIS PARTY IS TOTALLY OUT OF CONTROL!
I'M IN WAY OVER MY HEAD HERE, MR. AND MRS. D! CAN YOU HELP ME?
WELL, SINCE YOU ASKED SO NICELY...
THANKS. WHO KNEW THAT SEVEN HUNDRED DRUNKEN TEENAGERS WOULD BE SO ROWDY?

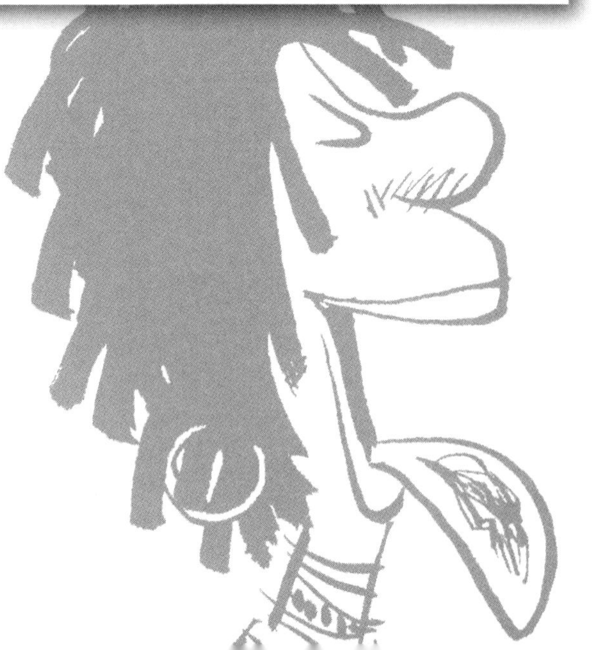

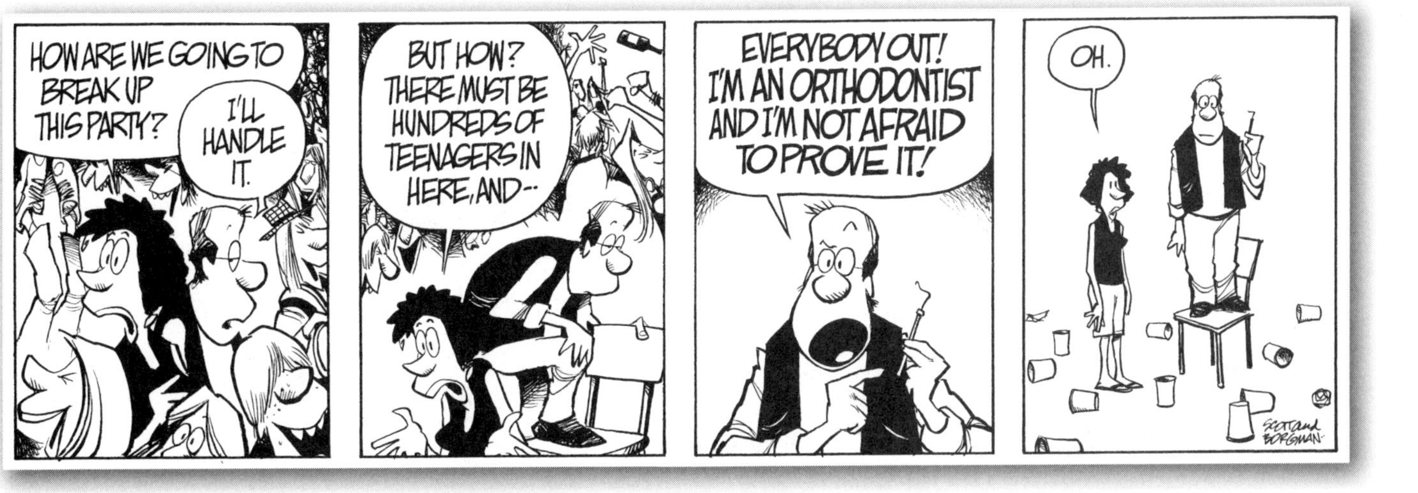

HOW ARE WE GOING TO BREAK UP THIS PARTY?
I'LL HANDLE IT.
BUT HOW? THERE MUST BE HUNDREDS OF TEENAGERS IN HERE, AND--
EVERYBODY OUT! I'M AN ORTHODONTIST AND I'M NOT AFRAID TO PROVE IT!
OH.
SCOTT and BORGMAN

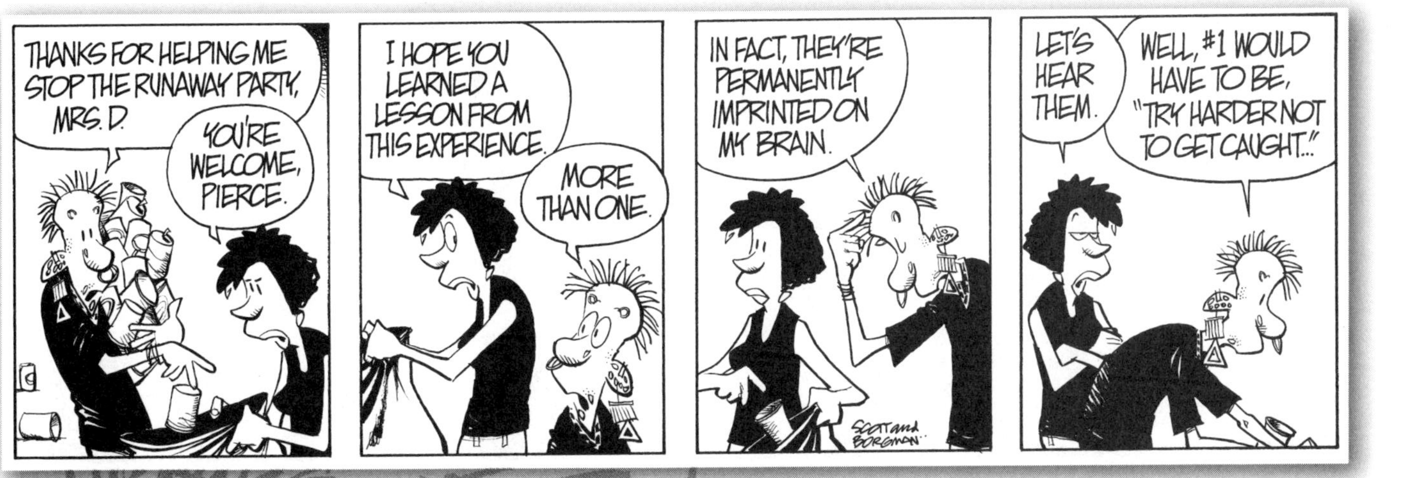

THANKS FOR HELPING ME STOP THE RUNAWAY PARTY, MRS. D.
YOU'RE WELCOME, PIERCE.
I HOPE YOU LEARNED A LESSON FROM THIS EXPERIENCE.
MORE THAN ONE.
IN FACT, THEY'RE PERMANENTLY IMPRINTED ON MY BRAIN.
SCOTT and BORGMAN
LET'S HEAR THEM.
WELL, #1 WOULD HAVE TO BE, "TRY HARDER NOT TO GET CAUGHT..."

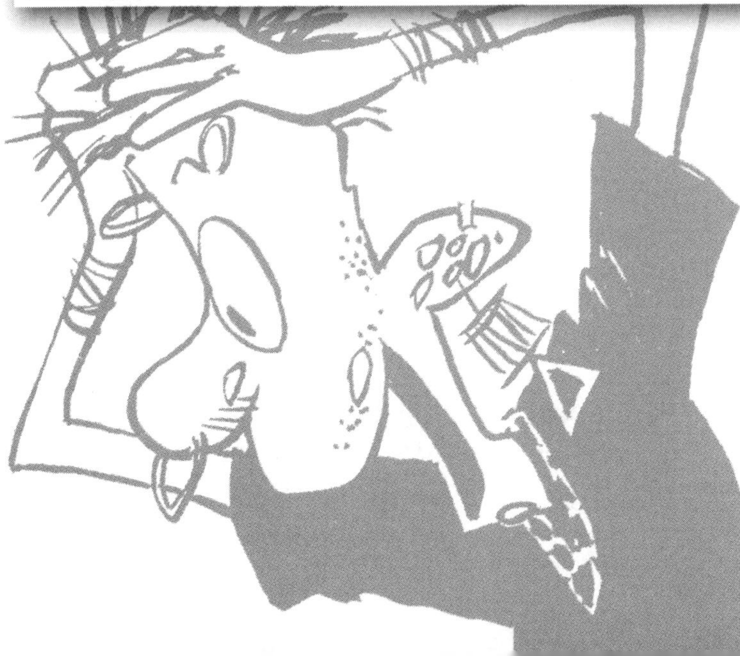

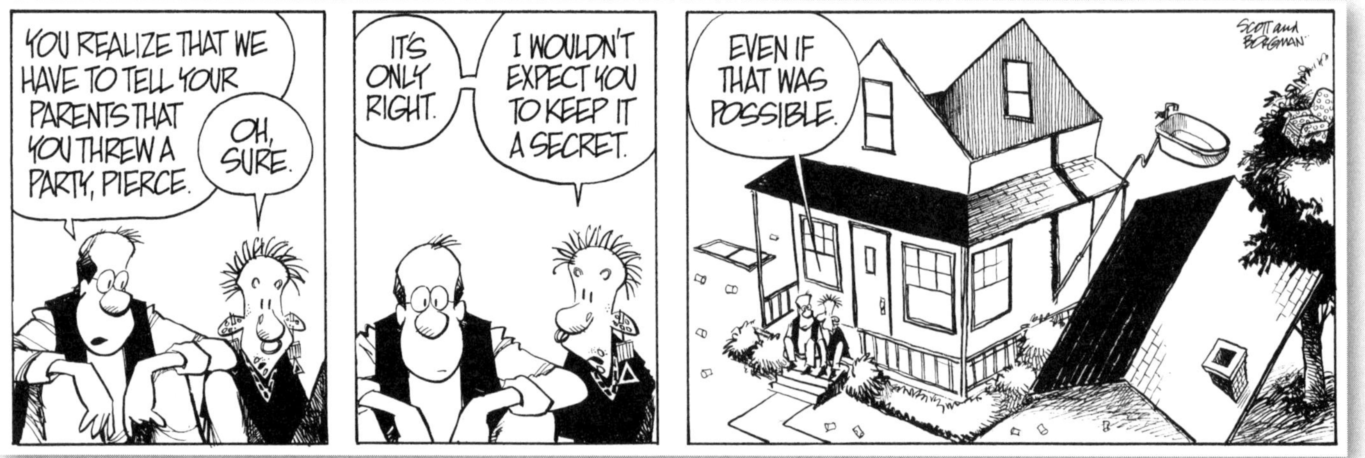
YOU REALIZE THAT WE HAVE TO TELL YOUR PARENTS THAT YOU THREW A PARTY, PIERCE.
OH, SURE.
IT'S ONLY RIGHT.
I WOULDN'T EXPECT YOU TO KEEP IT A SECRET.
EVEN IF THAT WAS POSSIBLE.

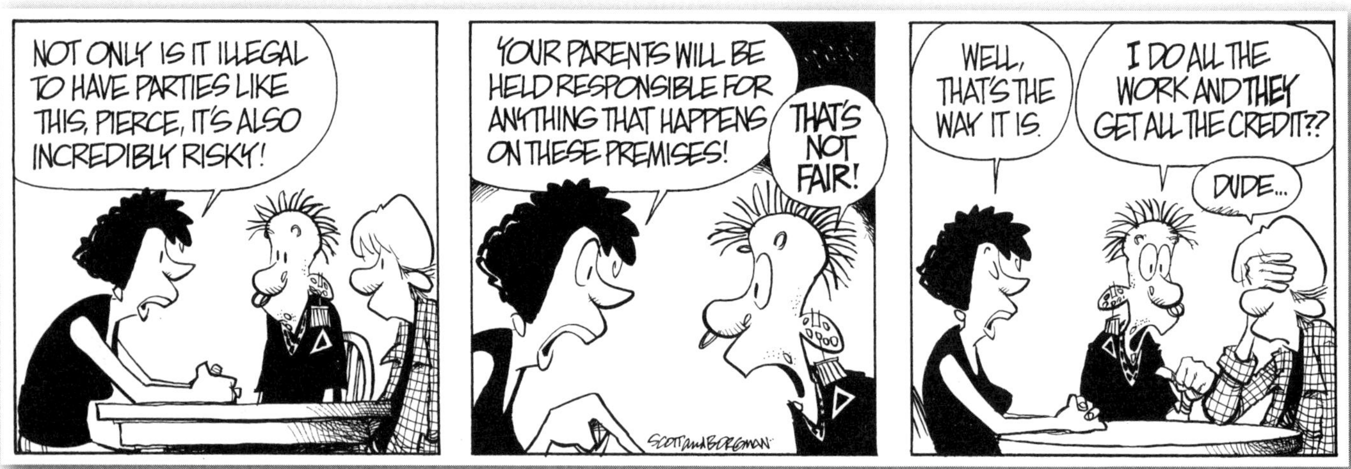
NOT ONLY IS IT ILLEGAL TO HAVE PARTIES LIKE THIS, PIERCE, IT'S ALSO INCREDIBLY RISKY!
YOUR PARENTS WILL BE HELD RESPONSIBLE FOR ANYTHING THAT HAPPENS ON THESE PREMISES!
THAT'S NOT FAIR!
WELL, THAT'S THE WAY IT IS.
I DO ALL THE WORK AND THEY GET ALL THE CREDIT??
DUDE...

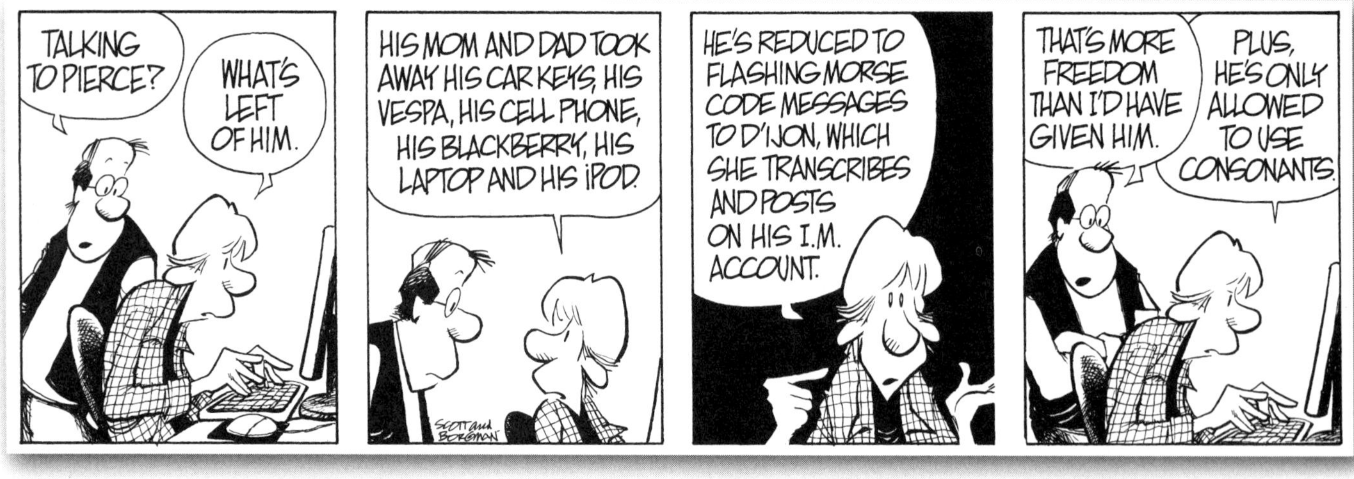
TALKING TO PIERCE?
WHAT'S LEFT OF HIM.
HIS MOM AND DAD TOOK AWAY HIS CAR KEYS, HIS VESPA, HIS CELL PHONE, HIS BLACKBERRY, HIS LAPTOP AND HIS iPOD.
HE'S REDUCED TO FLASHING MORSE CODE MESSAGES TO D'JON, WHICH SHE TRANSCRIBES AND POSTS ON HIS I.M. ACCOUNT.
THAT'S MORE FREEDOM THAN I'D HAVE GIVEN HIM.
PLUS, HE'S ONLY ALLOWED TO USE CONSONANTS.

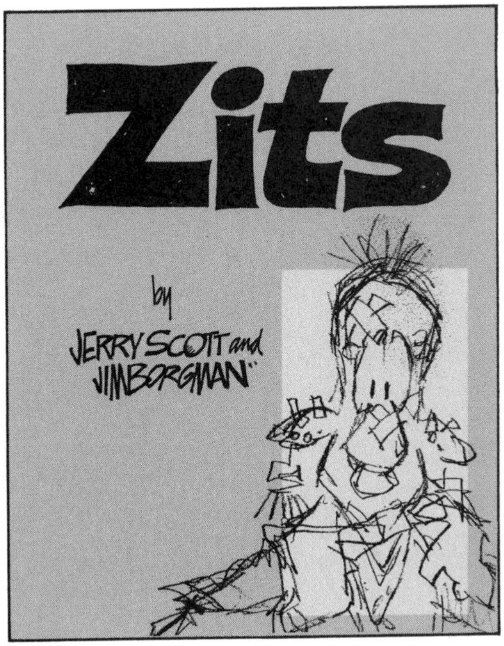
Zits
by
JERRY SCOTT and
JIM BORGMAN

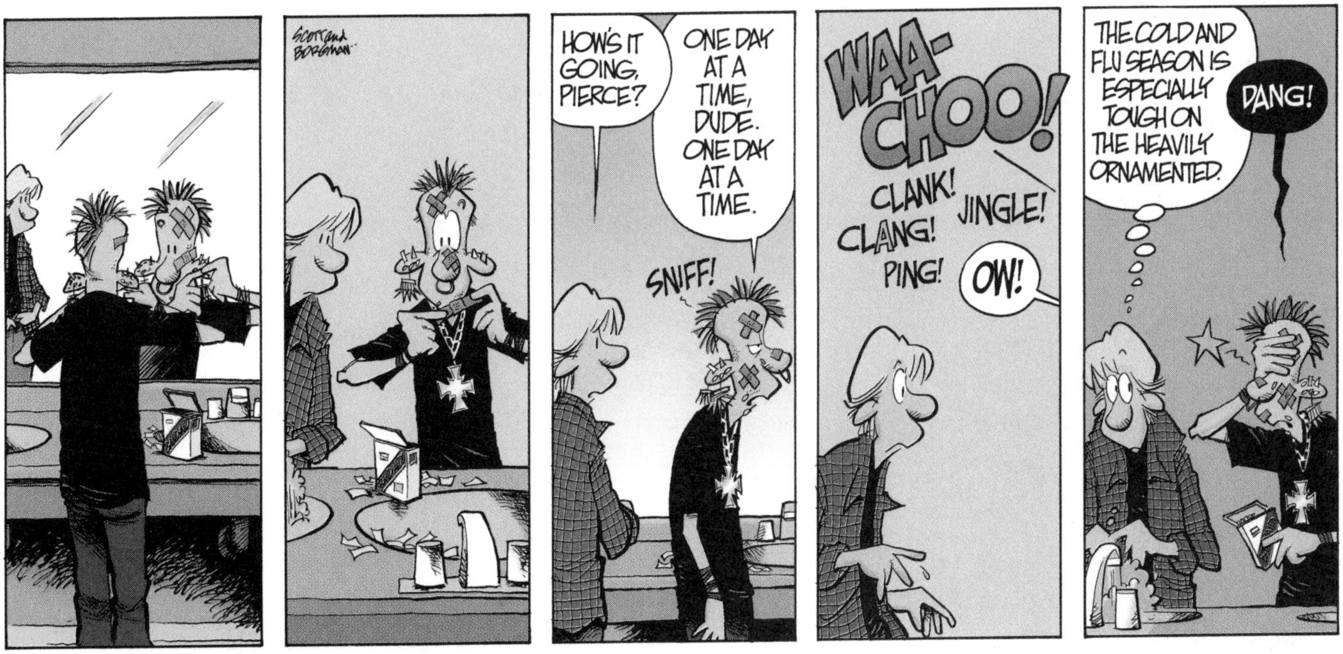
SCOTT and BORGMAN
HOW'S IT GOING, PIERCE?
ONE DAY AT A TIME, DUDE. ONE DAY AT A TIME.
SNIFF!
WAA-CHOO!
CLANK!
JINGLE!
CLANG!
PING!
OW!
THE COLD AND FLU SEASON IS ESPECIALLY TOUGH ON THE HEAVILY ORNAMENTED.
DANG!

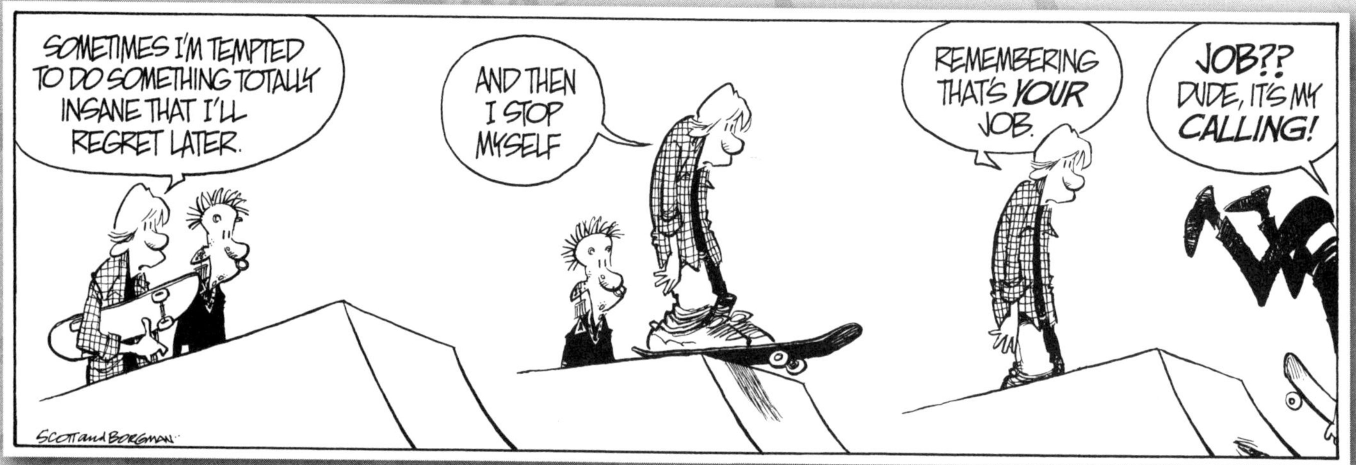
SOMETIMES I'M TEMPTED TO DO SOMETHING TOTALLY INSANE THAT I'LL REGRET LATER.
AND THEN I STOP MYSELF
REMEMBERING THAT'S *YOUR* JOB.
JOB?? DUDE, IT'S MY *CALLING!*
SCOTT and BORGMAN

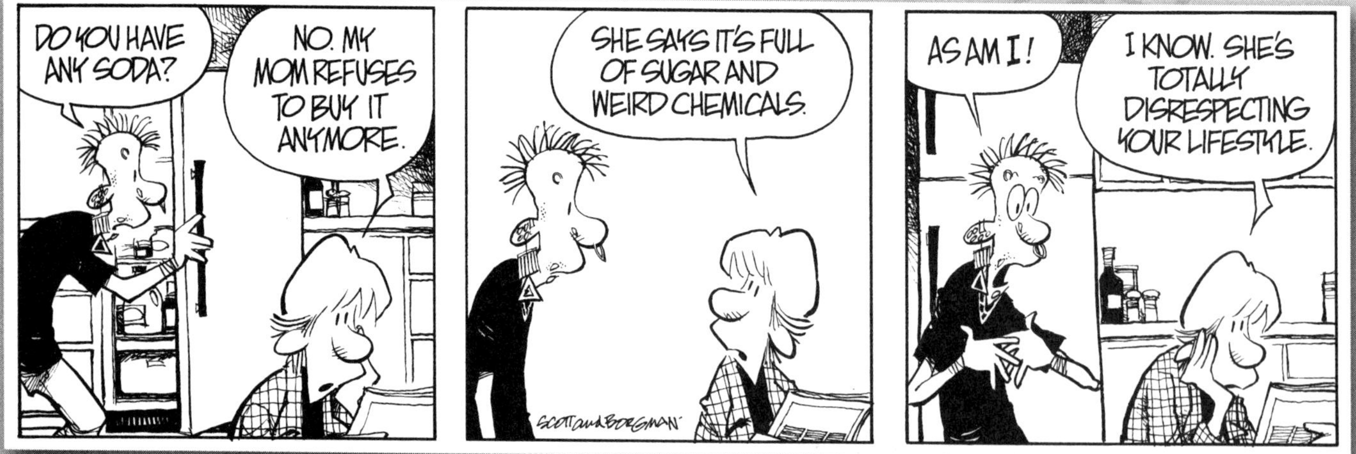
DO YOU HAVE ANY SODA?
NO. MY MOM REFUSES TO BUY IT ANYMORE.
SHE SAYS IT'S FULL OF SUGAR AND WEIRD CHEMICALS.
SCOTT and BORGMAN
AS AM **I**!
I KNOW. SHE'S TOTALLY DISRESPECTING YOUR LIFESTYLE.

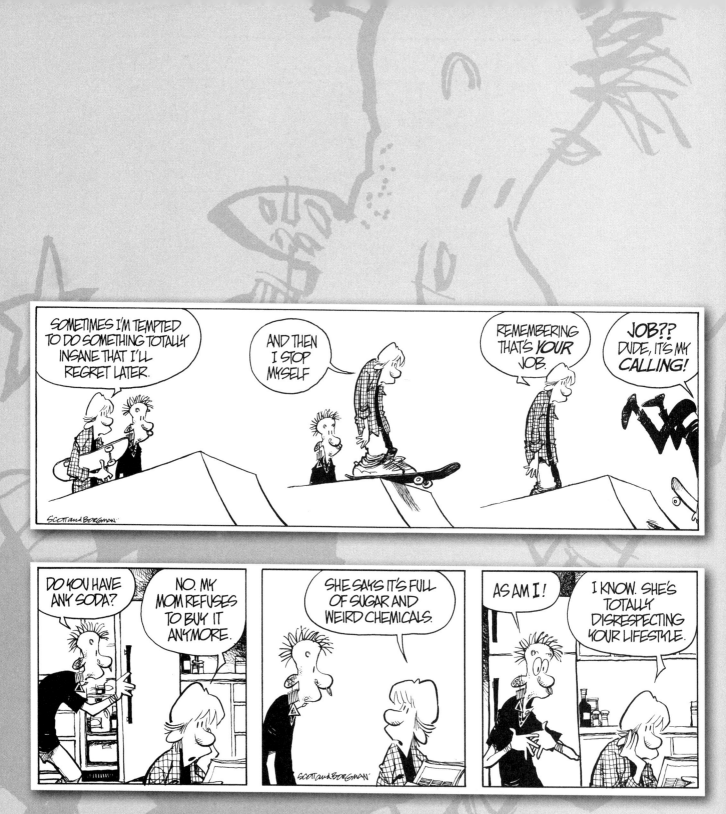

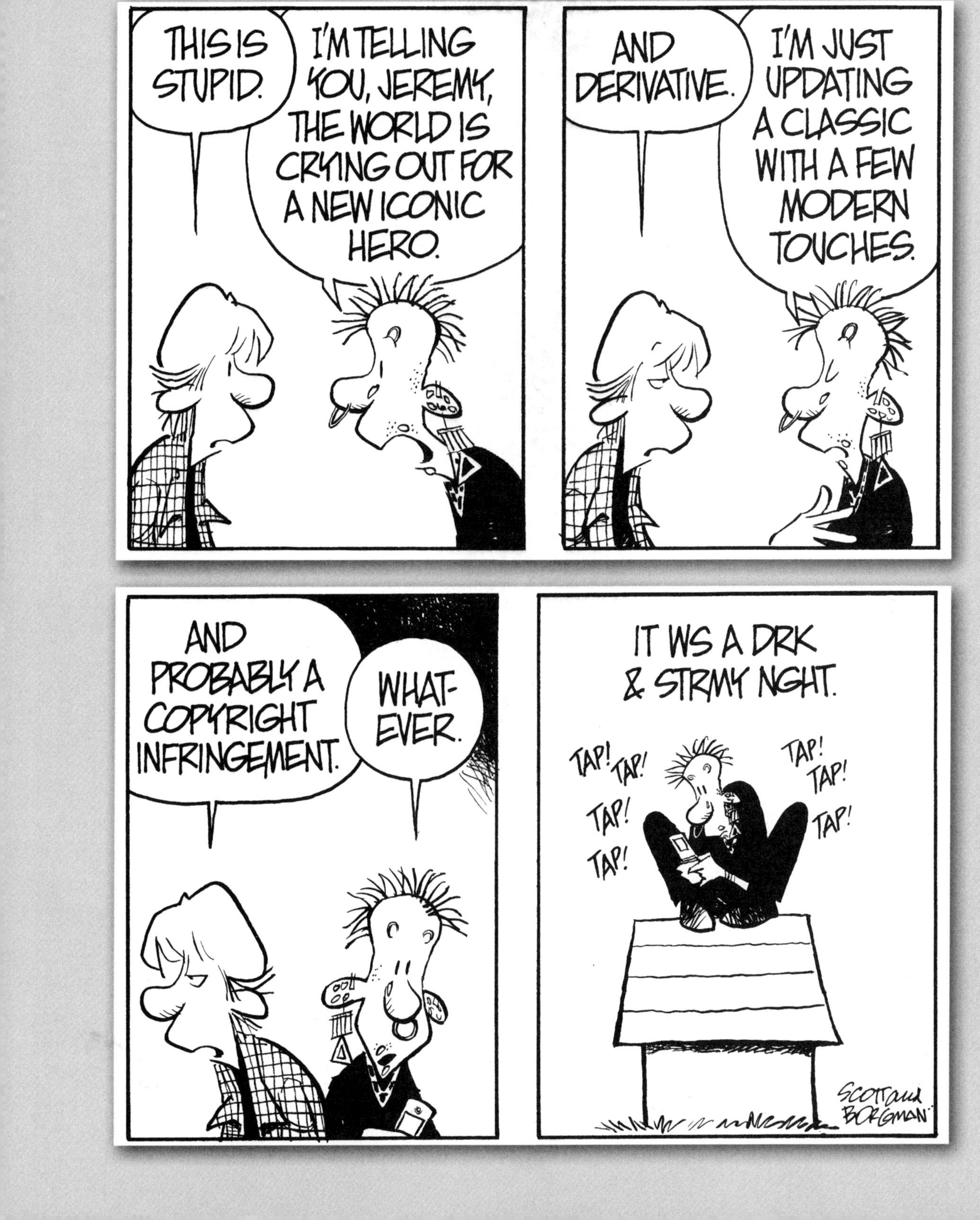
THIS IS STUPID.
I'M TELLING YOU, JEREMY, THE WORLD IS CRYING OUT FOR A NEW ICONIC HERO.
AND DERIVATIVE.
I'M JUST UPDATING A CLASSIC WITH A FEW MODERN TOUCHES.
AND PROBABLY A COPYRIGHT INFRINGEMENT.
WHAT-EVER.
IT WS A DRK & STRMY NGHT.
TAP! TAP! TAP! TAP!
TAP! TAP! TAP!
SCOTT and BORGMAN

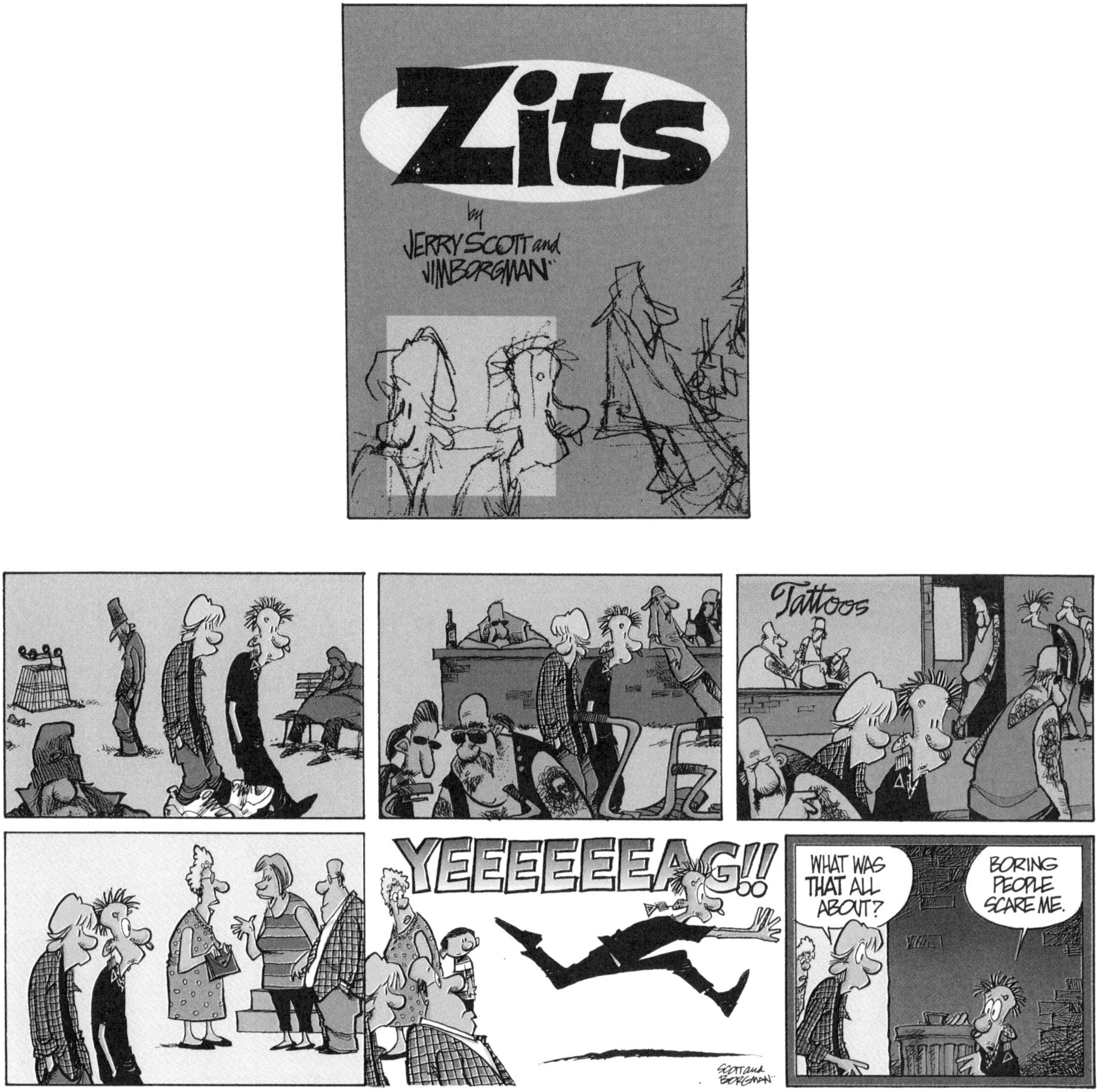
Zits
by
JERRY SCOTT and
JIM BORGMAN
Tattoos
YEEEEEEEAG!!
WHAT WAS THAT ALL ABOUT?
BORING PEOPLE SCARE ME.
SCOTT and BORGMAN

Zits
by
JERRY SCOTT and
JIM BORGMAN

DUDE-
HELP ME
OUT HERE.
CAN YOU READ
QUESTION 8?
WHAT IS
THIS?
THE HISTORY TEST WE'RE
TAKING IN TEN MINUTES.
SCOTT and
BORGMAN
MOE TOOK A PICTURE OF IT LAST PERIOD
WITH HER CELL PHONE CAMERA AND POSTED
IT ON HER MYSPACE PAGE,
WHICH I'VE BEEN TRYING TO
MAKE OUT ON MY TEENIE
BLACKBERRY SCREEN FOR
THE PAST FORTY-FIVE
MINUTES.
GOOD USE
OF YOUR
STUDY HOUR.
WHY DO
PEOPLE KEEP
SAYING THAT
TO ME?

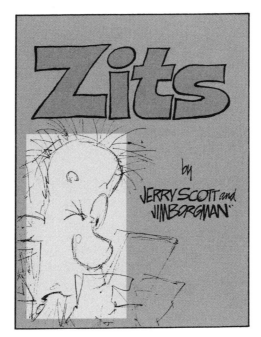

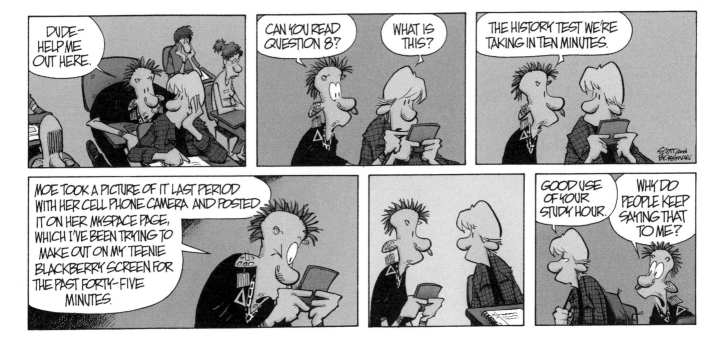

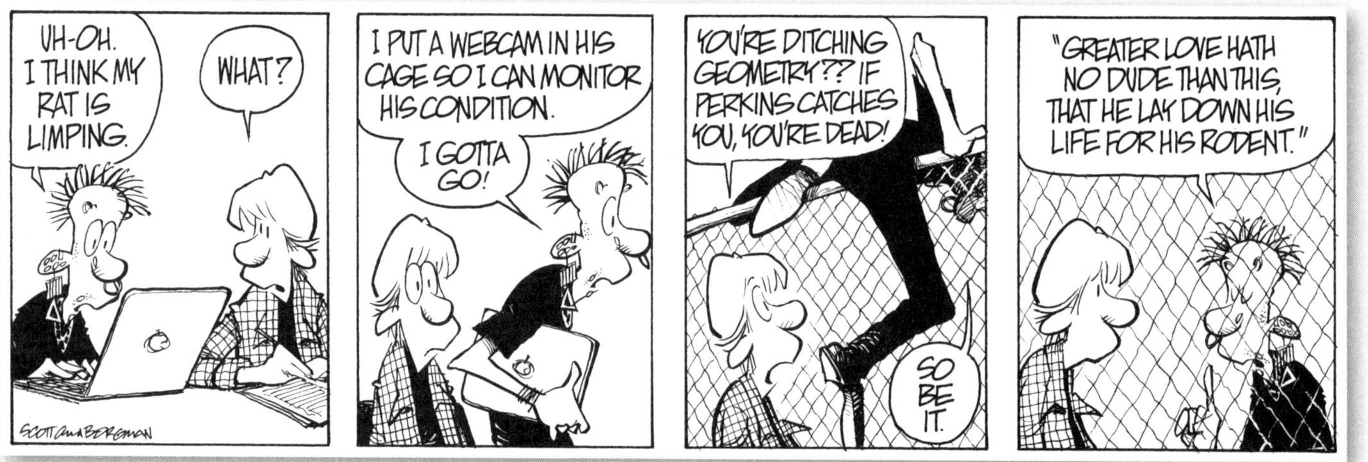
UH-OH. I THINK MY RAT IS LIMPING.
WHAT?
I PUT A WEBCAM IN HIS CAGE SO I CAN MONITOR HIS CONDITION.
I GOTTA GO!
YOU'RE DITCHING GEOMETRY?? IF PERKINS CATCHES YOU, YOU'RE DEAD!
SO BE IT.
"GREATER LOVE HATH NO DUDE THAN THIS, THAT HE LAY DOWN HIS LIFE FOR HIS RODENT."

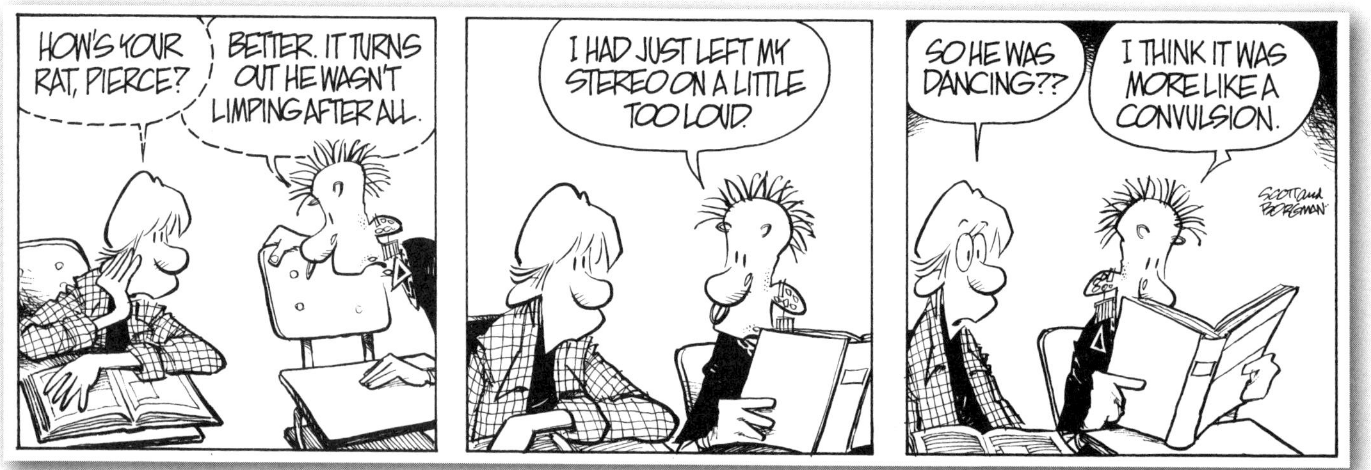
HOW'S YOUR RAT, PIERCE?
BETTER. IT TURNS OUT HE WASN'T LIMPING AFTER ALL.
I HAD JUST LEFT MY STEREO ON A LITTLE TOO LOUD.
SO HE WAS DANCING??
I THINK IT WAS MORE LIKE A CONVULSION.

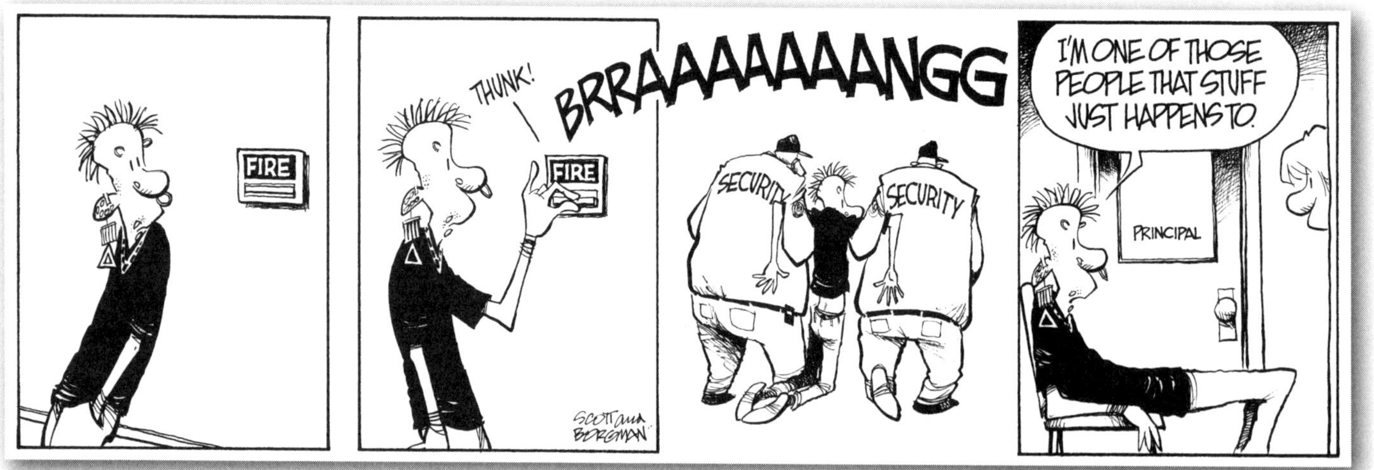
FIRE
THUNK!
FIRE
BRRAAAAAAAANGG
SECURITY
SECURITY
I'M ONE OF THOSE PEOPLE THAT STUFF JUST HAPPENS TO.
PRINCIPAL

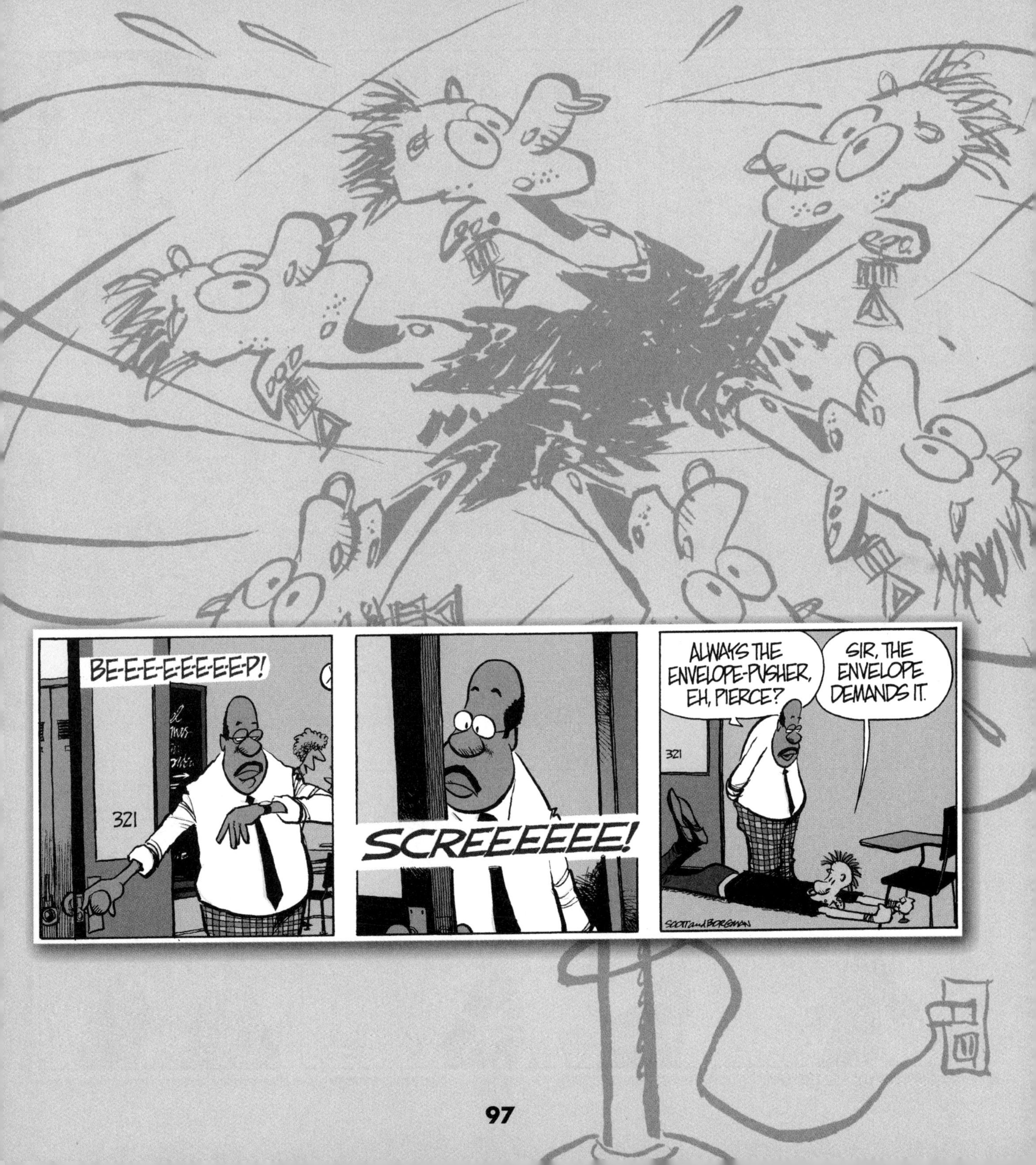
BE-E-E-E-E-E-E-E-P!
321
SCREEEEEEE!
321
ALWAYS THE ENVELOPE-PUSHER, EH, PIERCE?
SIR, THE ENVELOPE DEMANDS IT.
SCOTT and BORGMAN

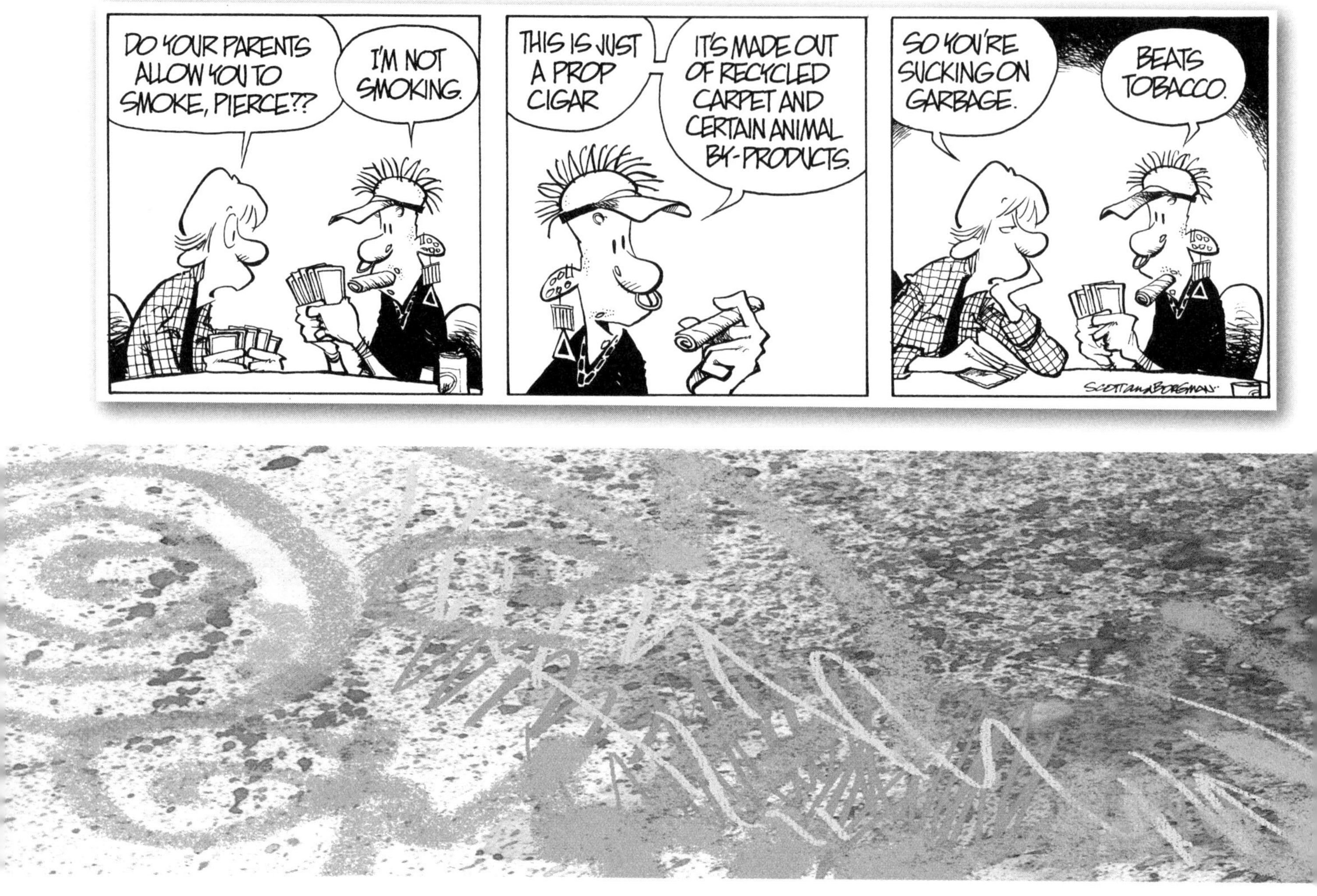
DO YOUR PARENTS ALLOW YOU TO SMOKE, PIERCE??
I'M NOT SMOKING.
THIS IS JUST A PROP CIGAR
IT'S MADE OUT OF RECYCLED CARPET AND CERTAIN ANIMAL BY-PRODUCTS.
SO YOU'RE SUCKING ON GARBAGE.
BEATS TOBACCO.
SCOTT and BORGMAN

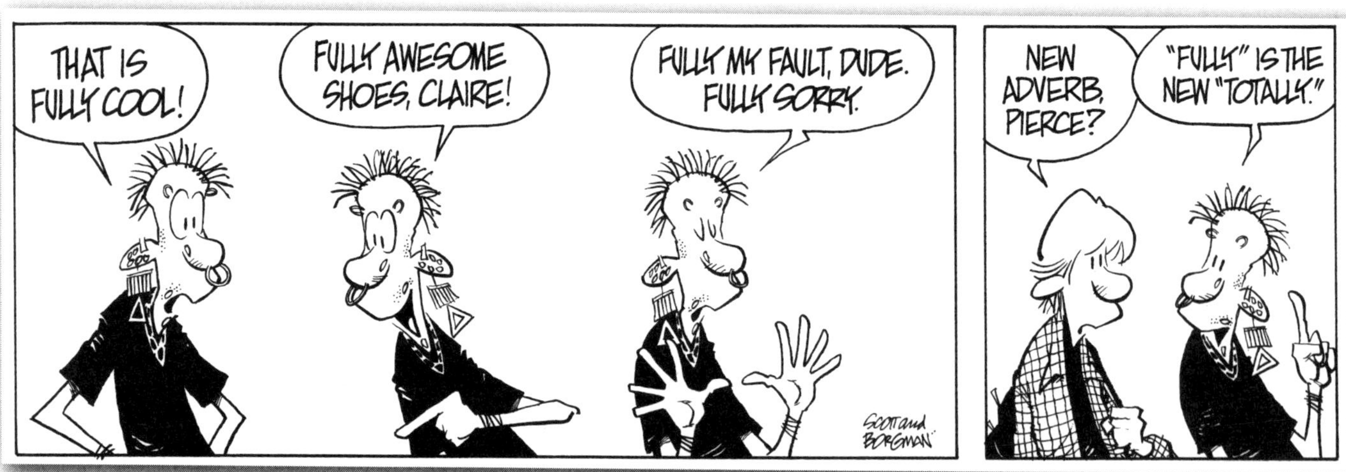
THAT IS FULLY COOL!
FULLY AWESOME SHOES, CLAIRE!
FULLY MY FAULT, DUDE. FULLY SORRY.
SCOTT and BORGMAN
NEW ADVERB, PIERCE?
"FULLY" IS THE NEW "TOTALLY."

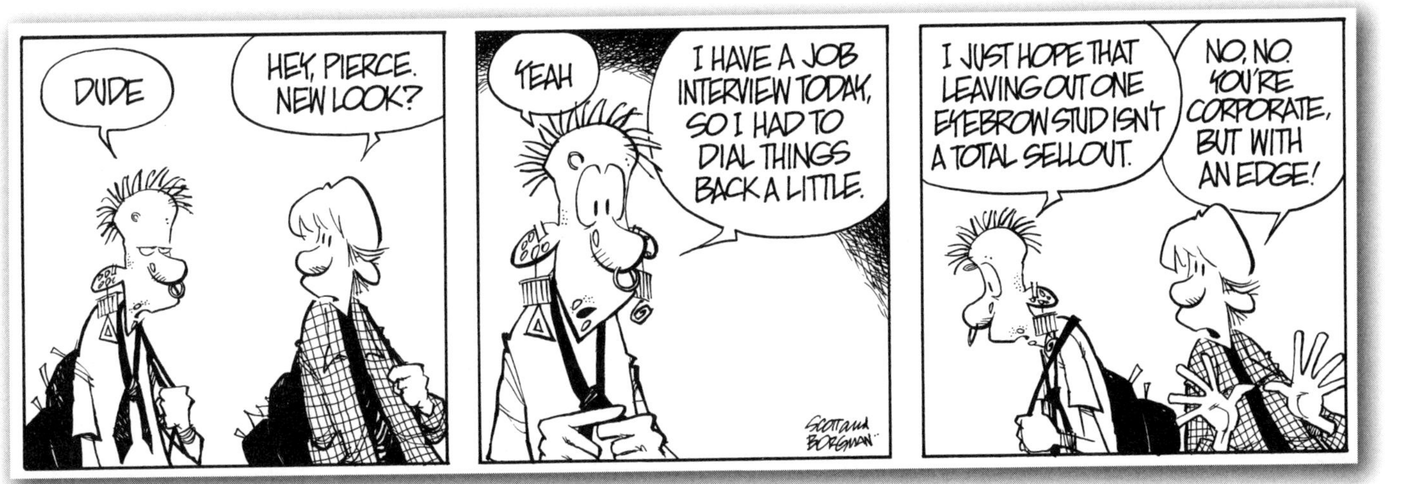
DUDE
HEY, PIERCE. NEW LOOK?
YEAH
I HAVE A JOB INTERVIEW TODAY, SO I HAD TO DIAL THINGS BACK A LITTLE.
I JUST HOPE THAT LEAVING OUT ONE EYEBROW STUD ISN'T A TOTAL SELLOUT.
NO, NO. YOU'RE CORPORATE, BUT WITH AN EDGE!
SCOTT AND BORGMAN

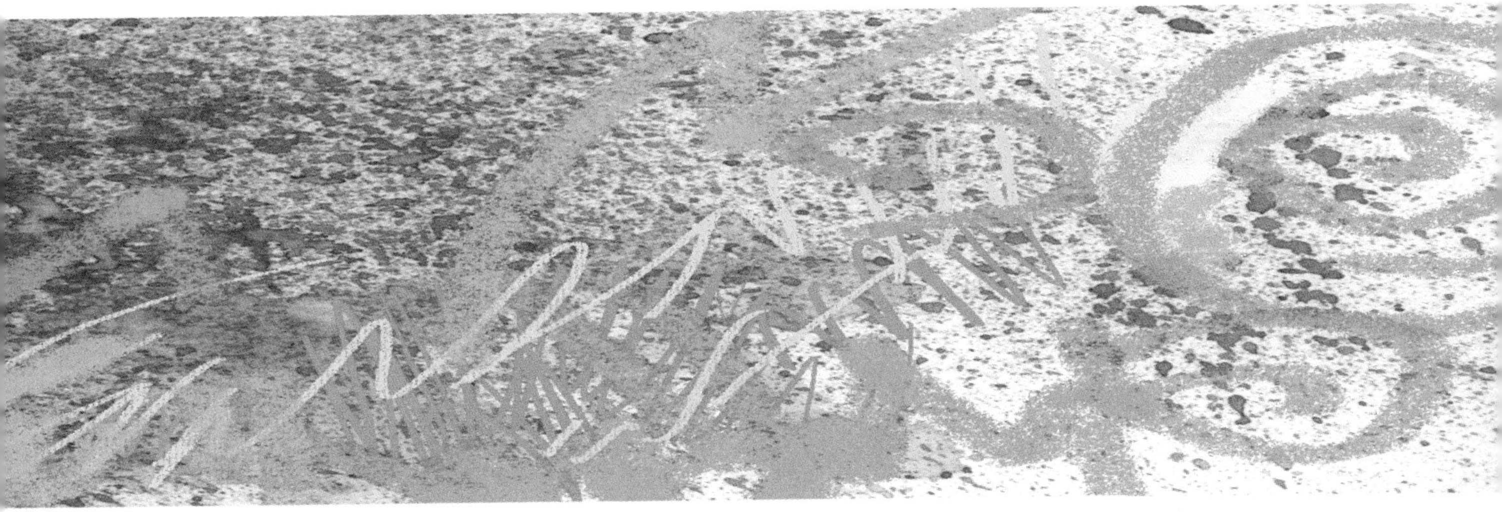

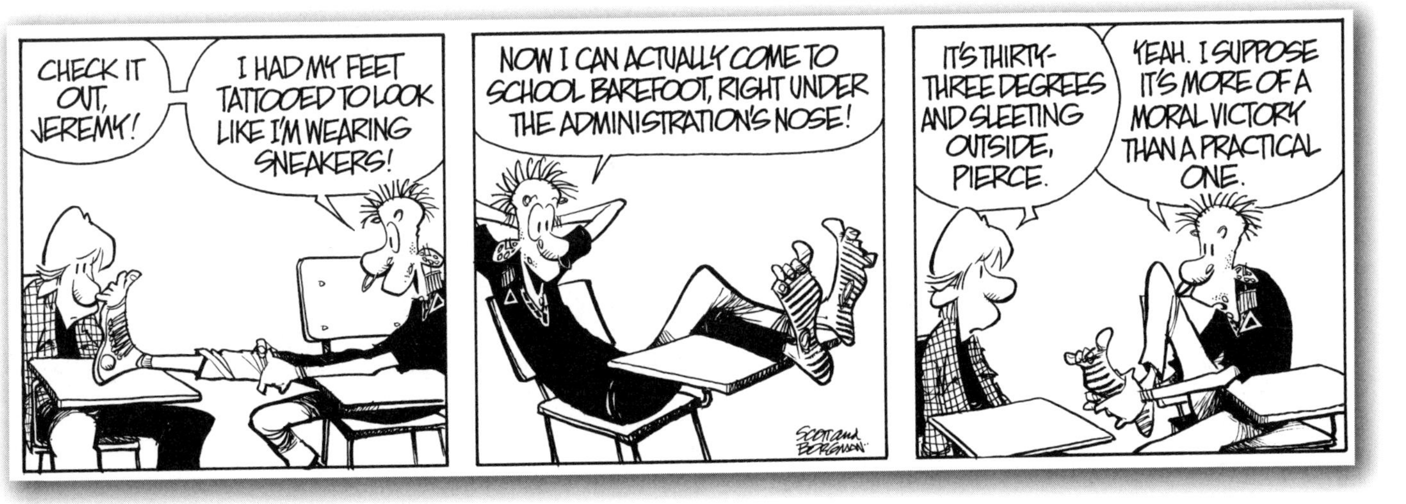
CHECK IT OUT, JEREMY!
I HAD MY FEET TATTOOED TO LOOK LIKE I'M WEARING SNEAKERS!
NOW I CAN ACTUALLY COME TO SCHOOL BAREFOOT, RIGHT UNDER THE ADMINISTRATION'S NOSE!
IT'S THIRTY-THREE DEGREES AND SLEETING OUTSIDE, PIERCE.
YEAH. I SUPPOSE IT'S MORE OF A MORAL VICTORY THAN A PRACTICAL ONE.
SCOTT AND BORGMAN

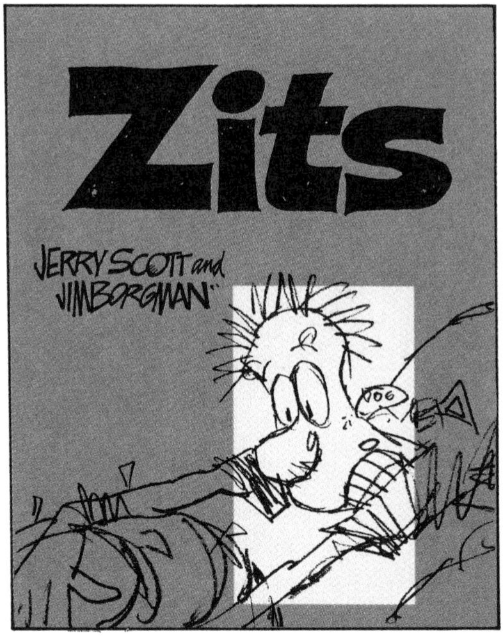
Zits
JERRY SCOTT and
JIM BORGMAN

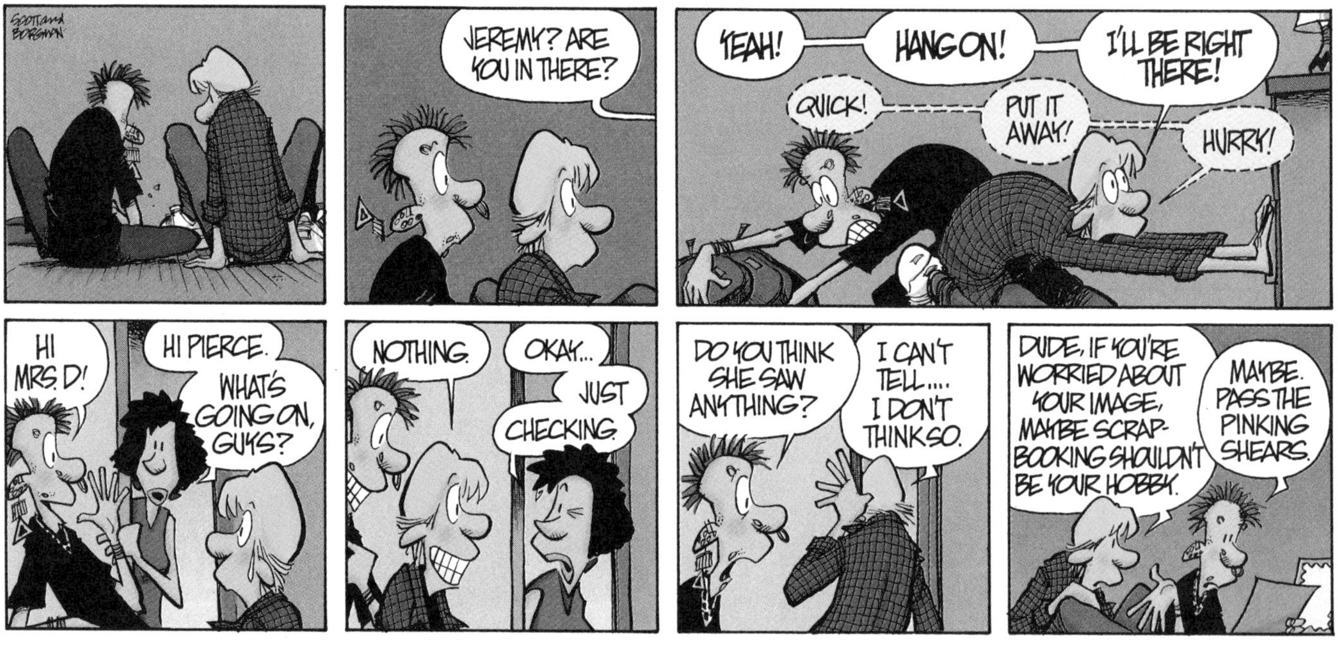
SCOTT and BORGMAN
JEREMY? ARE YOU IN THERE?
YEAH!
HANG ON!
I'LL BE RIGHT THERE!
QUICK!
PUT IT AWAY!
HURRY!
HI MRS. D!
HI PIERCE.
WHAT'S GOING ON, GUYS?
NOTHING.
OKAY... JUST CHECKING.
DO YOU THINK SHE SAW ANYTHING?
I CAN'T TELL.... I DON'T THINK SO.
DUDE, IF YOU'RE WORRIED ABOUT YOUR IMAGE, MAYBE SCRAP-BOOKING SHOULDN'T BE YOUR HOBBY.
MAYBE. PASS THE PINKING SHEARS.

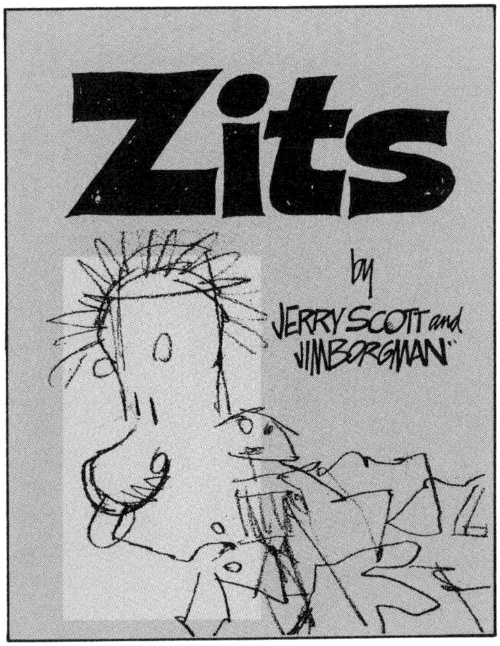
Zits
by
JERRY SCOTT and
JIM BORGMAN

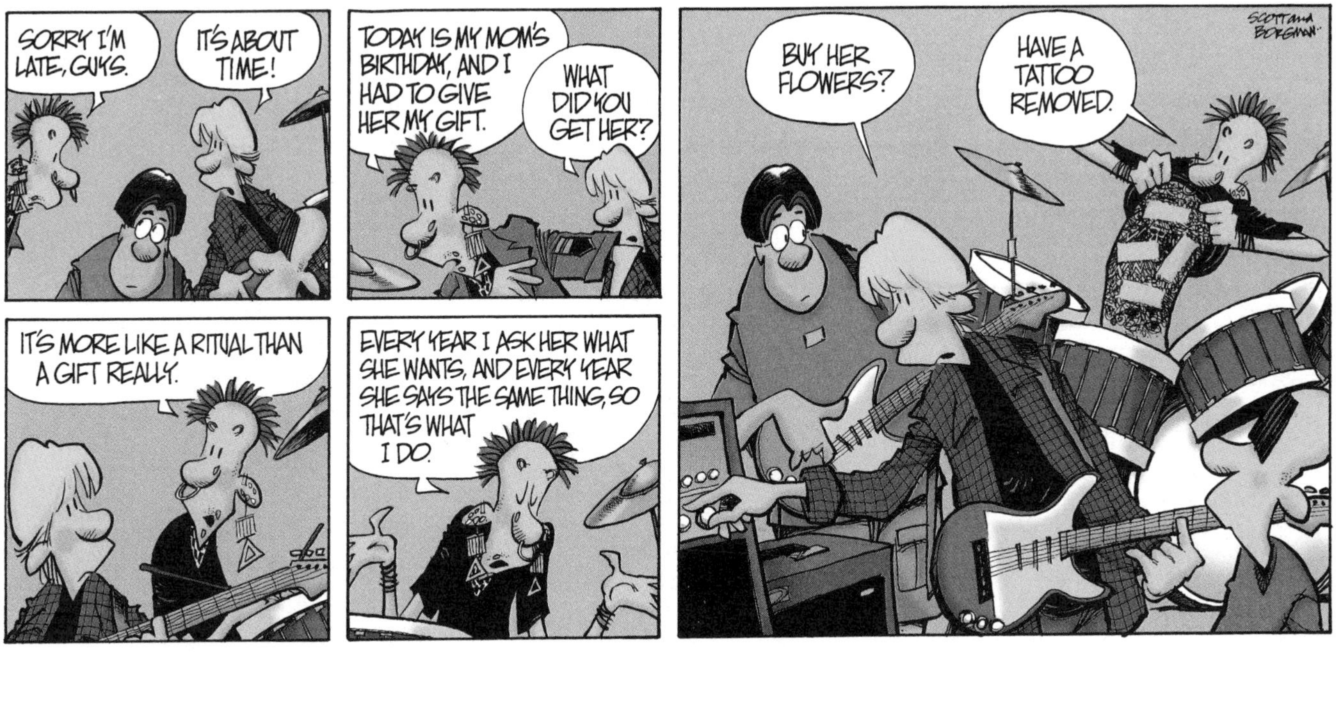
SORRY I'M LATE, GUYS.
IT'S ABOUT TIME!
TODAY IS MY MOM'S BIRTHDAY, AND I HAD TO GIVE HER MY GIFT.
WHAT DID YOU GET HER?
IT'S MORE LIKE A RITUAL THAN A GIFT REALLY.
EVERY YEAR I ASK HER WHAT SHE WANTS, AND EVERY YEAR SHE SAYS THE SAME THING, SO THAT'S WHAT I DO.
BUY HER FLOWERS?
HAVE A TATTOO REMOVED.

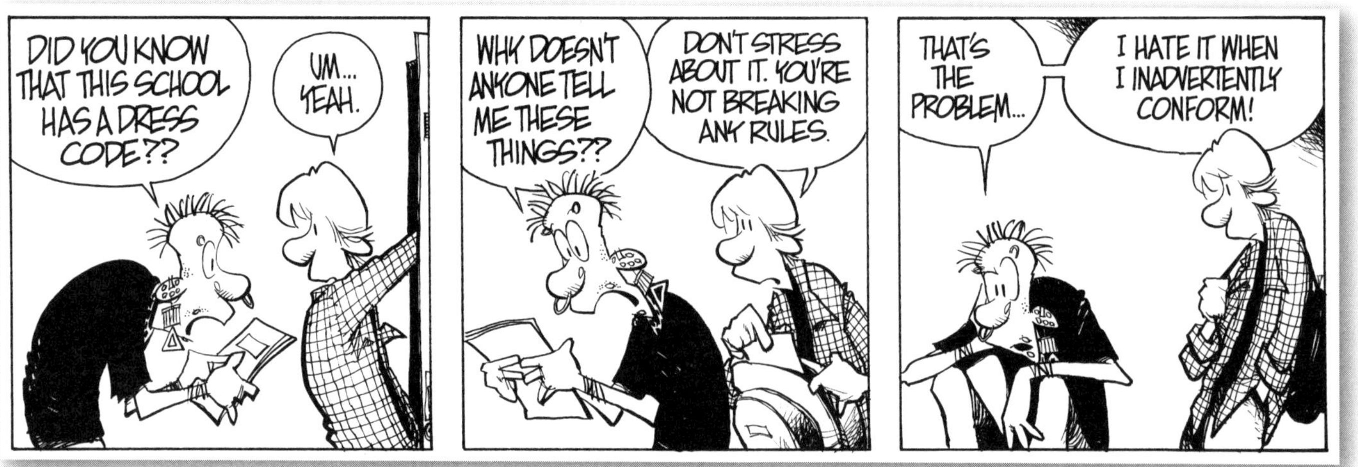
DID YOU KNOW THAT THIS SCHOOL HAS A DRESS CODE??
UM... YEAH.
WHY DOESN'T ANYONE TELL ME THESE THINGS??
DON'T STRESS ABOUT IT. YOU'RE NOT BREAKING ANY RULES.
THAT'S THE PROBLEM...
I HATE IT WHEN I INADVERTENTLY CONFORM!

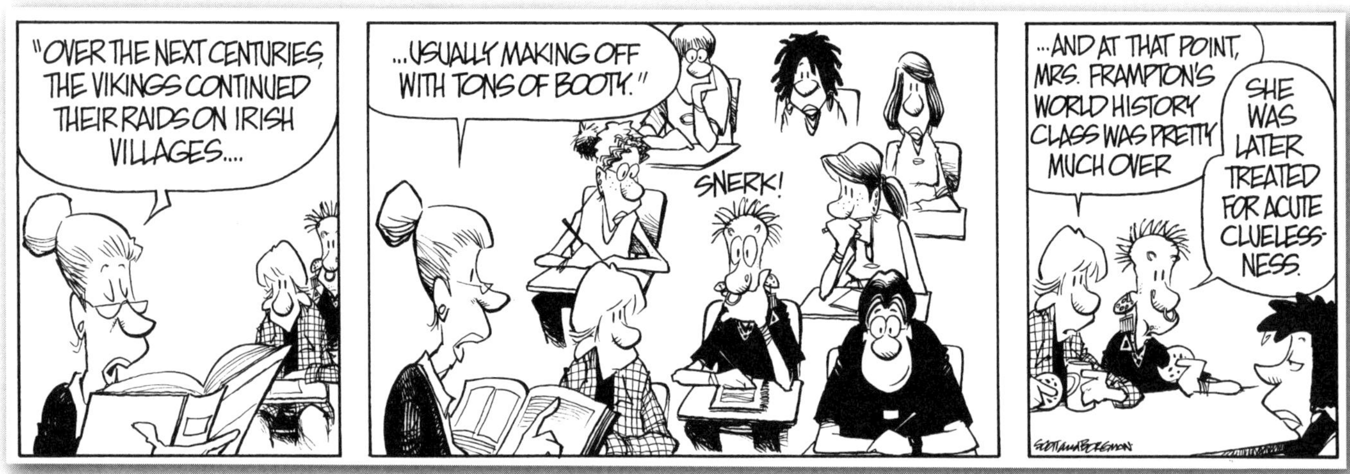
"OVER THE NEXT CENTURIES, THE VIKINGS CONTINUED THEIR RAIDS ON IRISH VILLAGES....
...USUALLY MAKING OFF WITH TONS OF BOOTY."
SNERK!
...AND AT THAT POINT, MRS. FRAMPTON'S WORLD HISTORY CLASS WAS PRETTY MUCH OVER
SHE WAS LATER TREATED FOR ACUTE CLUELESS-NESS.

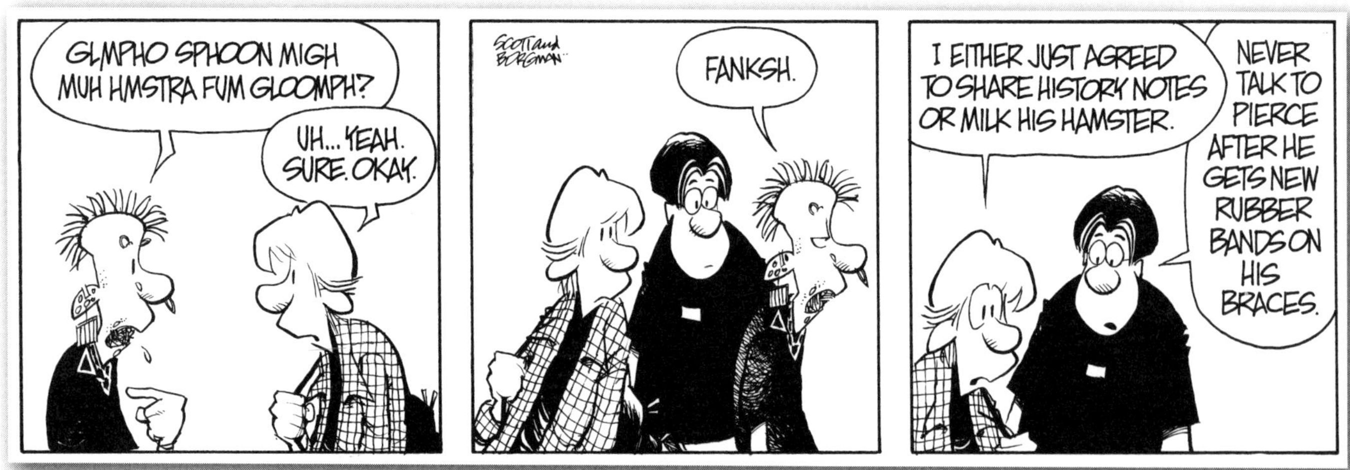
GLMPHO SPHOON MIGH MUH HMSTRA FUM GLOOMPH?
UH... YEAH. SURE. OKAY.
SCOTT and BORGMAN
FANKSH.
I EITHER JUST AGREED TO SHARE HISTORY NOTES OR MILK HIS HAMSTER.
NEVER TALK TO PIERCE AFTER HE GETS NEW RUBBER BANDS ON HIS BRACES.

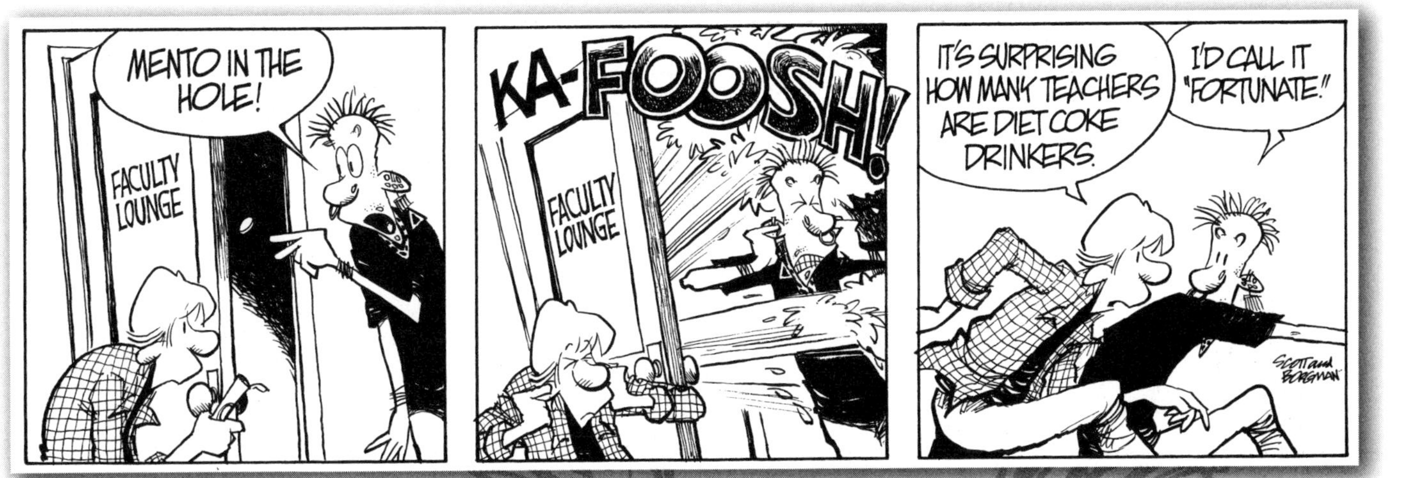
MENTO IN THE HOLE!
FACULTY LOUNGE
KA-FOOSH!
FACULTY LOUNGE
IT'S SURPRISING HOW MANY TEACHERS ARE DIET COKE DRINKERS.
I'D CALL IT "FORTUNATE."
SCOTT and BORGMAN

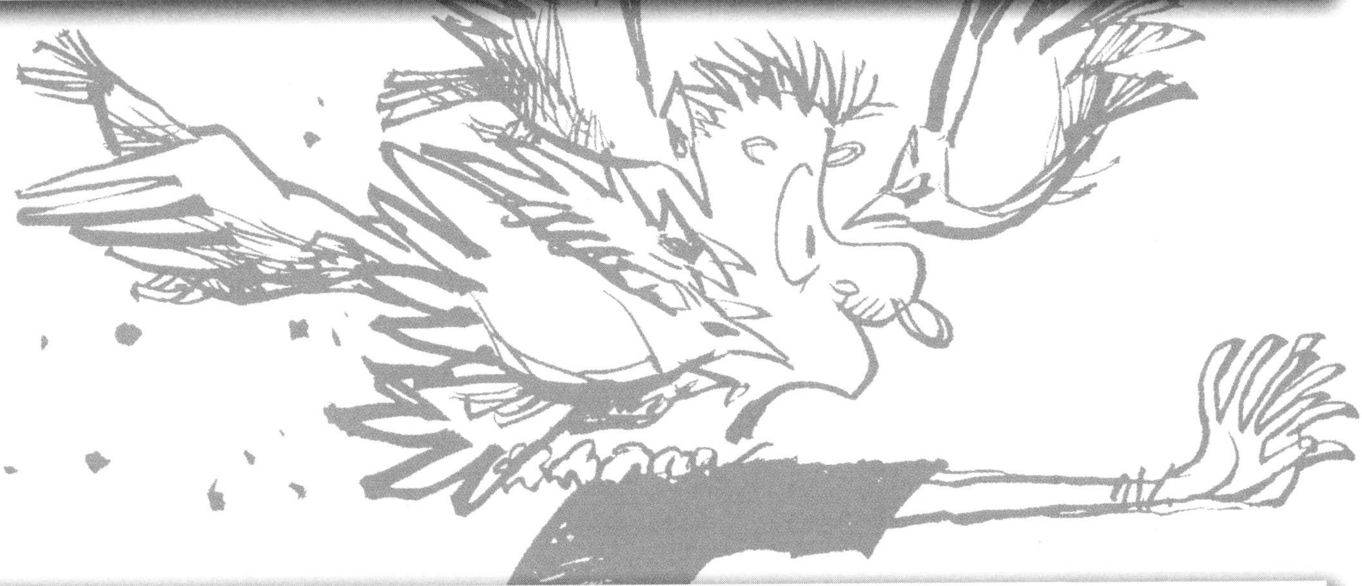

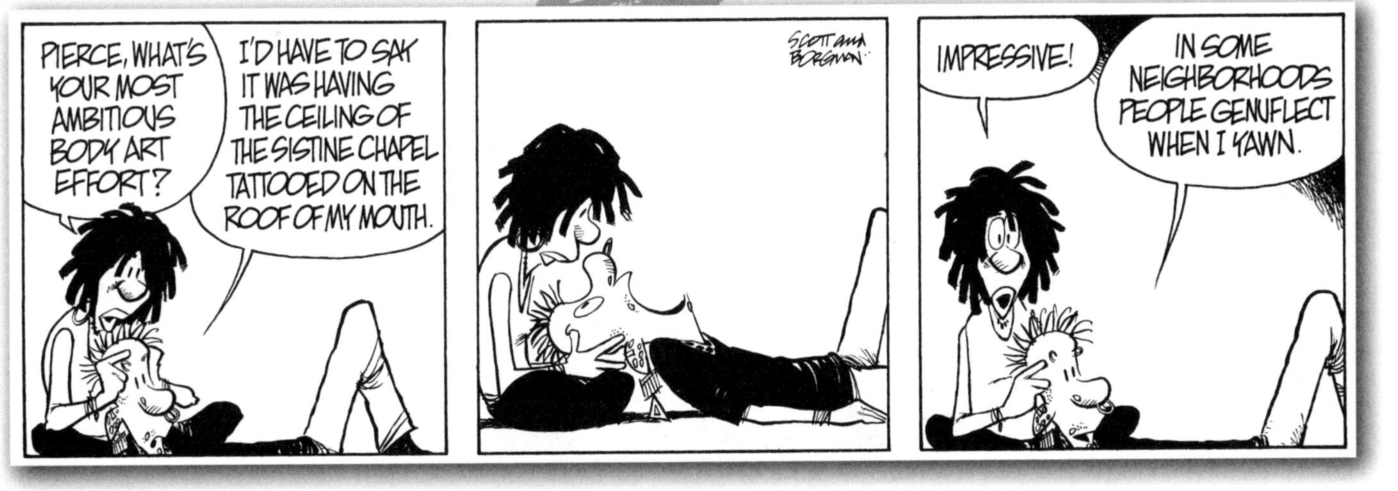
PIERCE, WHAT'S YOUR MOST AMBITIOUS BODY ART EFFORT?
I'D HAVE TO SAY IT WAS HAVING THE CEILING OF THE SISTINE CHAPEL TATTOOED ON THE ROOF OF MY MOUTH.
SCOTT and BORGMAN
IMPRESSIVE!
IN SOME NEIGHBORHOODS PEOPLE GENUFLECT WHEN I YAWN.

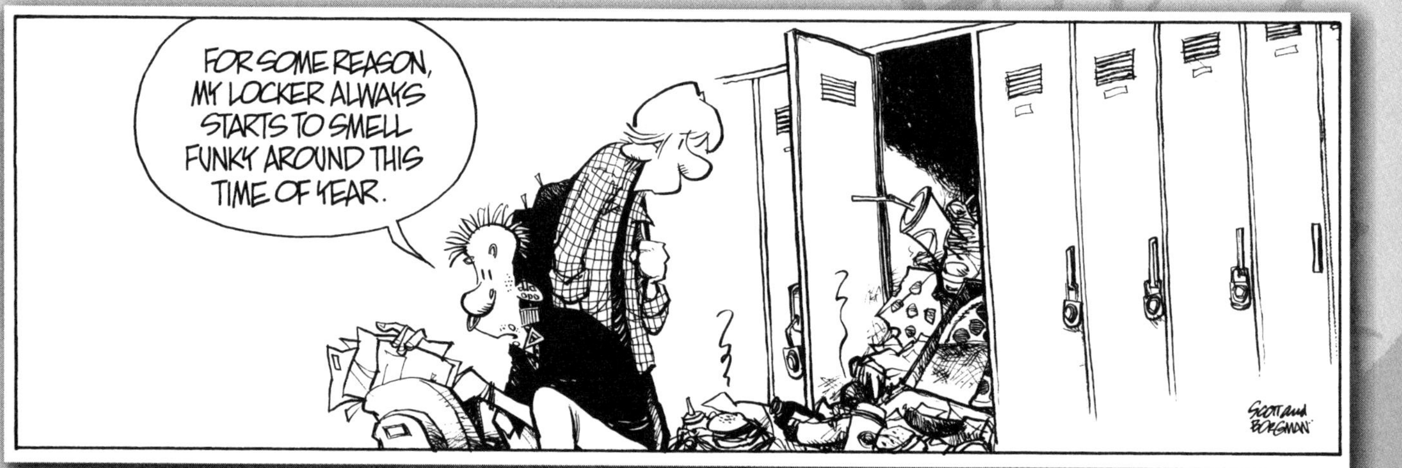
FOR SOME REASON, MY LOCKER ALWAYS STARTS TO SMELL FUNKY AROUND THIS TIME OF YEAR.
SCOTT and BORGMAN

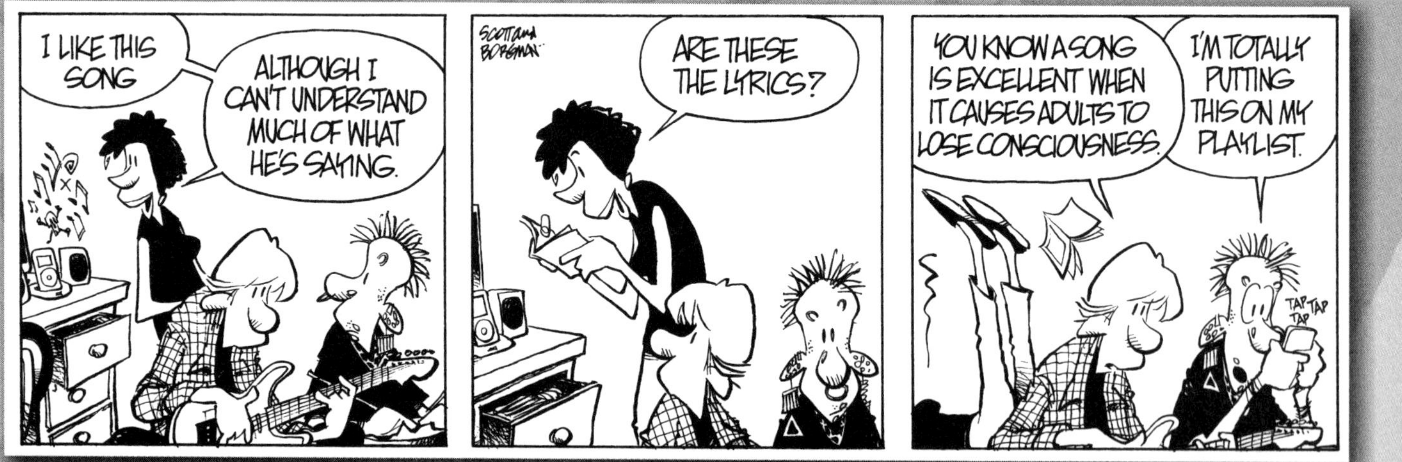
I LIKE THIS SONG
ALTHOUGH I CAN'T UNDERSTAND MUCH OF WHAT HE'S SAYING.
SCOTT and BORGMAN
ARE THESE THE LYRICS?
YOU KNOW A SONG IS EXCELLENT WHEN IT CAUSES ADULTS TO LOSE CONSCIOUSNESS.
I'M TOTALLY PUTTING THIS ON MY PLAYLIST.
TAP TAP TAP

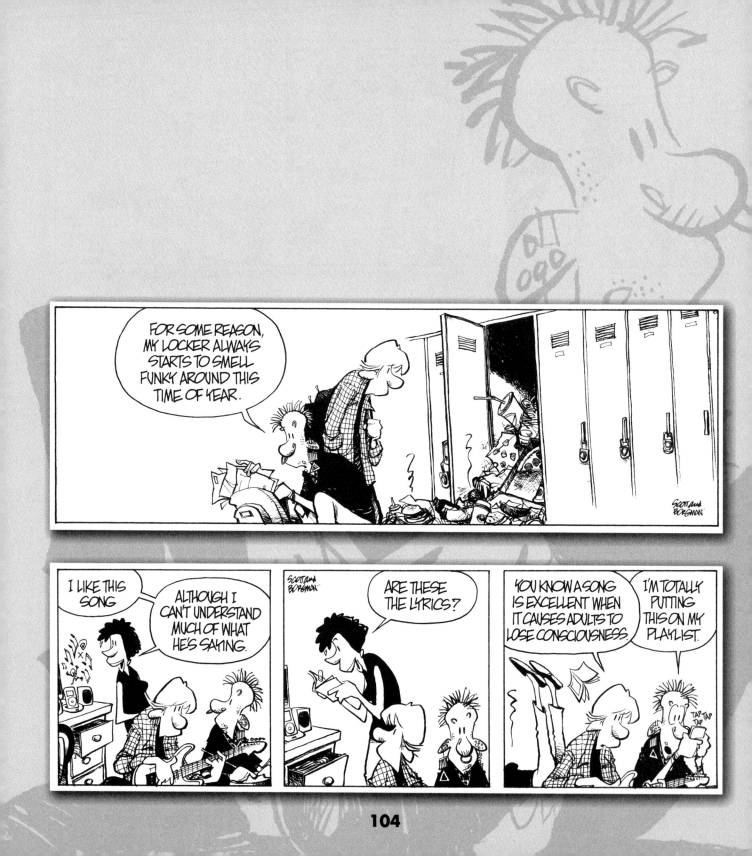

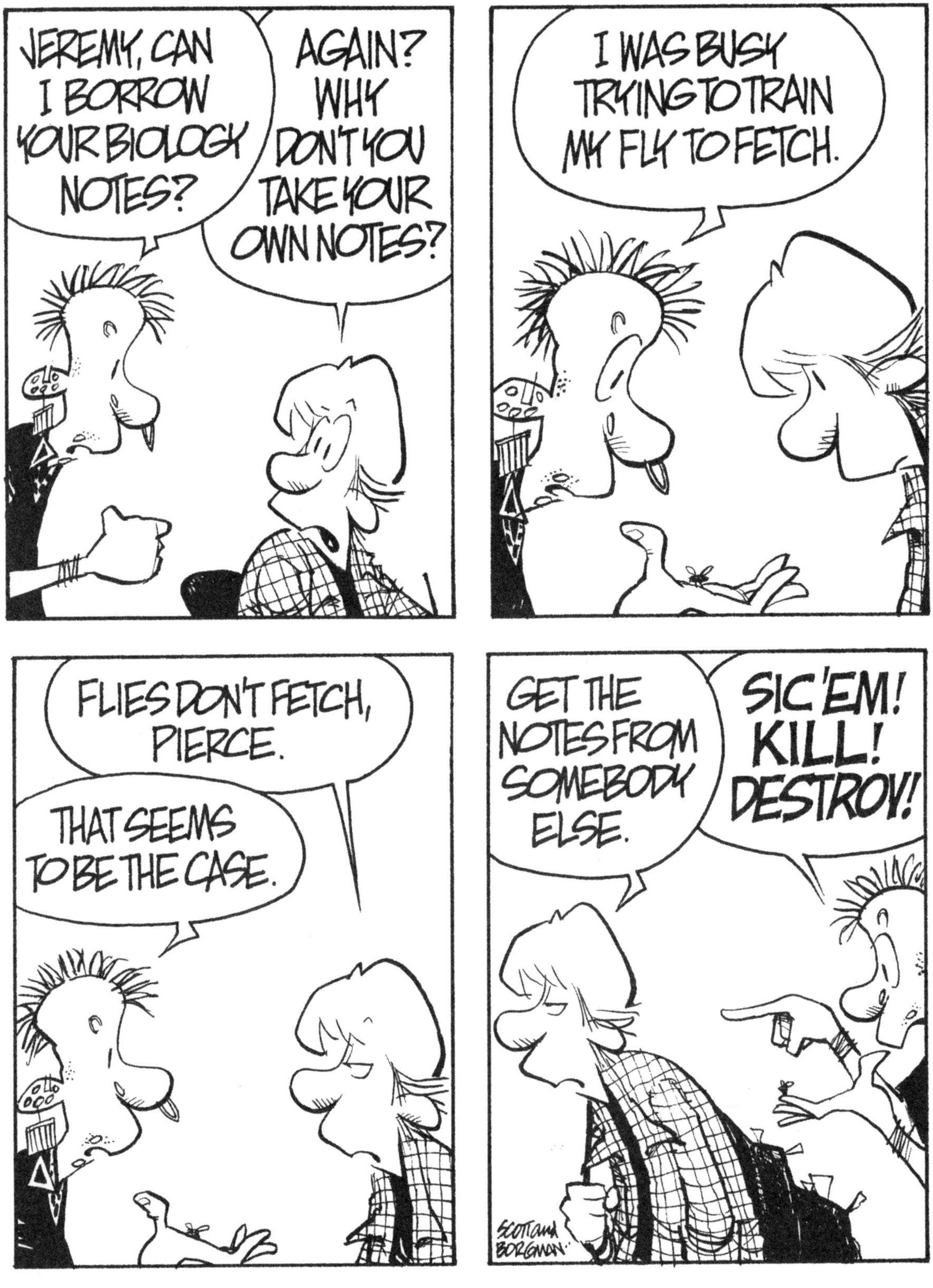
JEREMY, CAN I BORROW YOUR BIOLOGY NOTES?
AGAIN? WHY DON'T YOU TAKE YOUR OWN NOTES?
I WAS BUSY TRYING TO TRAIN MY FLY TO FETCH.
FLIES DON'T FETCH, PIERCE.
THAT SEEMS TO BE THE CASE.
GET THE NOTES FROM SOMEBODY ELSE.
SIC 'EM! KILL! DESTROY!
SCOTT and BORGMAN

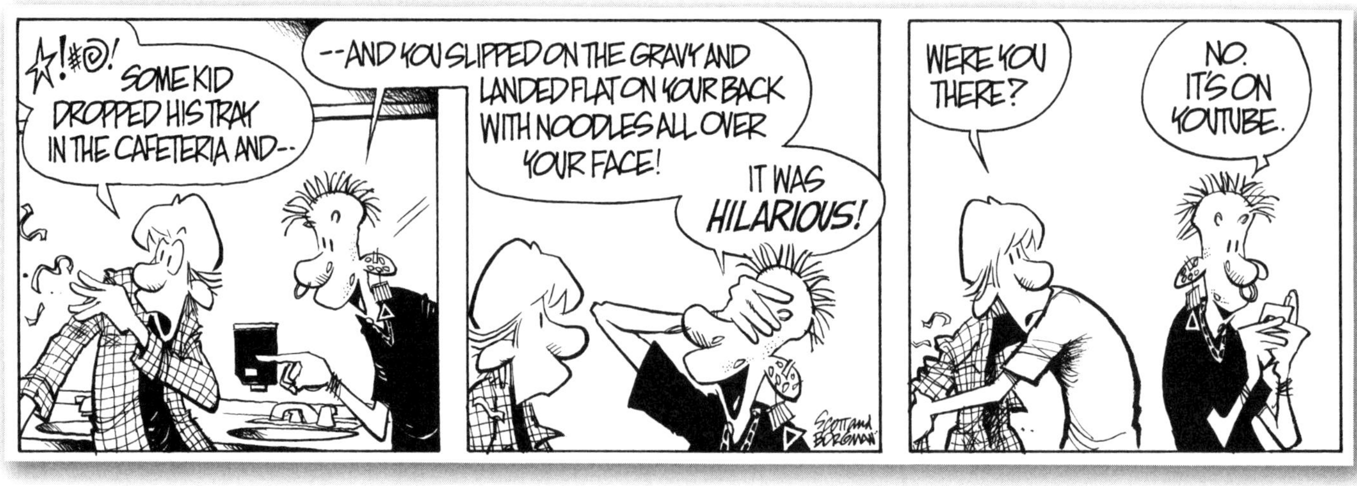
☆!#@! SOME KID DROPPED HIS TRAY IN THE CAFETERIA AND--
--AND YOU SLIPPED ON THE GRAVY AND LANDED FLAT ON YOUR BACK WITH NOODLES ALL OVER YOUR FACE!
IT WAS HILARIOUS!
WERE YOU THERE?
NO. IT'S ON YOUTUBE.
SCOTT AND BORGMAN

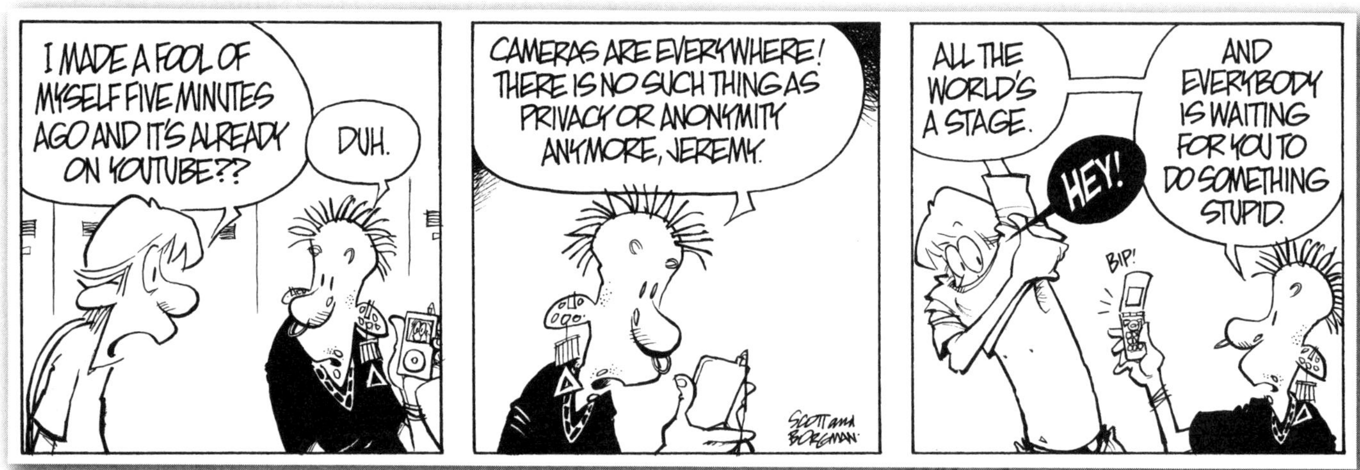
I MADE A FOOL OF MYSELF FIVE MINUTES AGO AND IT'S ALREADY ON YOUTUBE??
DUH.
CAMERAS ARE EVERYWHERE! THERE IS NO SUCH THING AS PRIVACY OR ANONYMITY ANYMORE, JEREMY.
SCOTT AND BORGMAN
ALL THE WORLD'S A STAGE.
AND EVERYBODY IS WAITING FOR YOU TO DO SOMETHING STUPID.
HEY!
BIP!

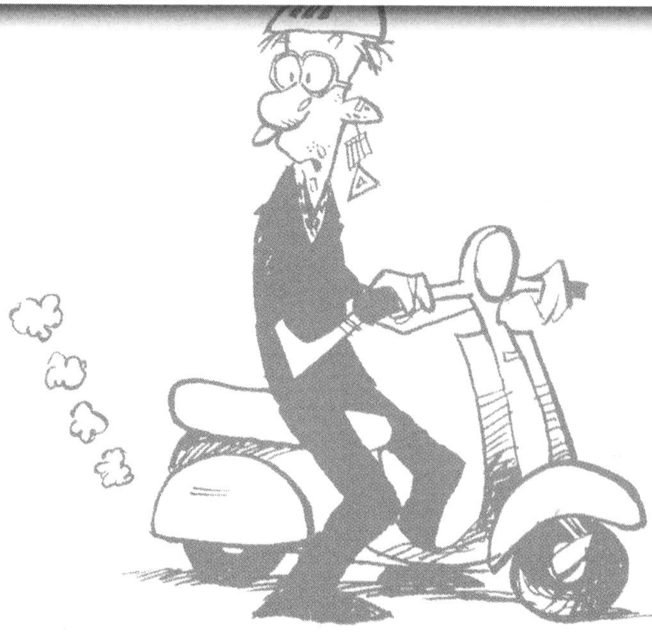

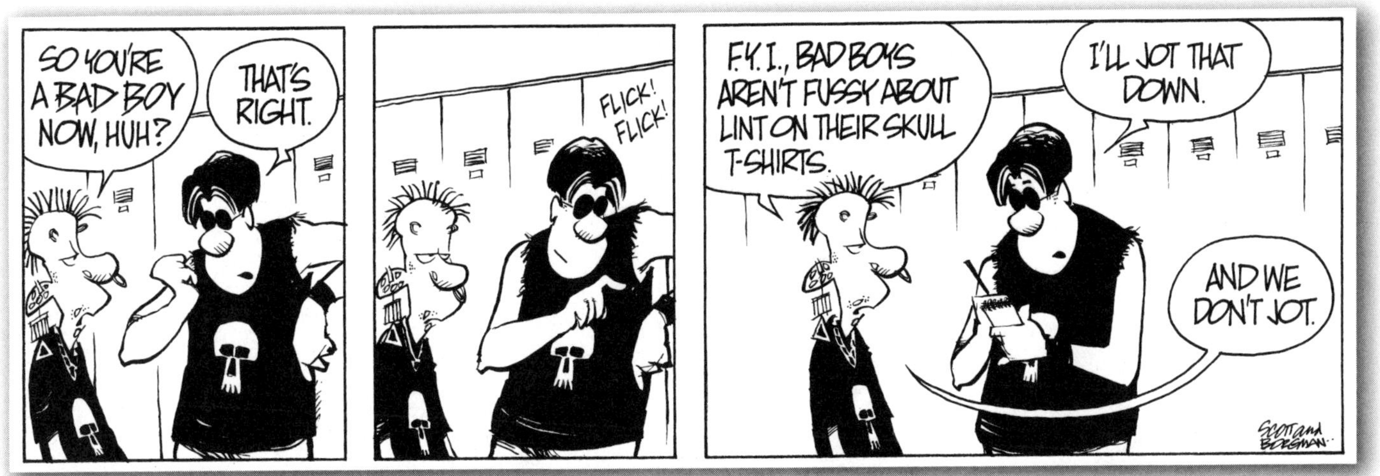
SO YOU'RE A BAD BOY NOW, HUH?
THAT'S RIGHT.
FLICK! FLICK!
F.Y.I., BAD BOYS AREN'T FUSSY ABOUT LINT ON THEIR SKULL T-SHIRTS.
I'LL JOT THAT DOWN.
AND WE DON'T JOT.
SCOTT and BORGMAN

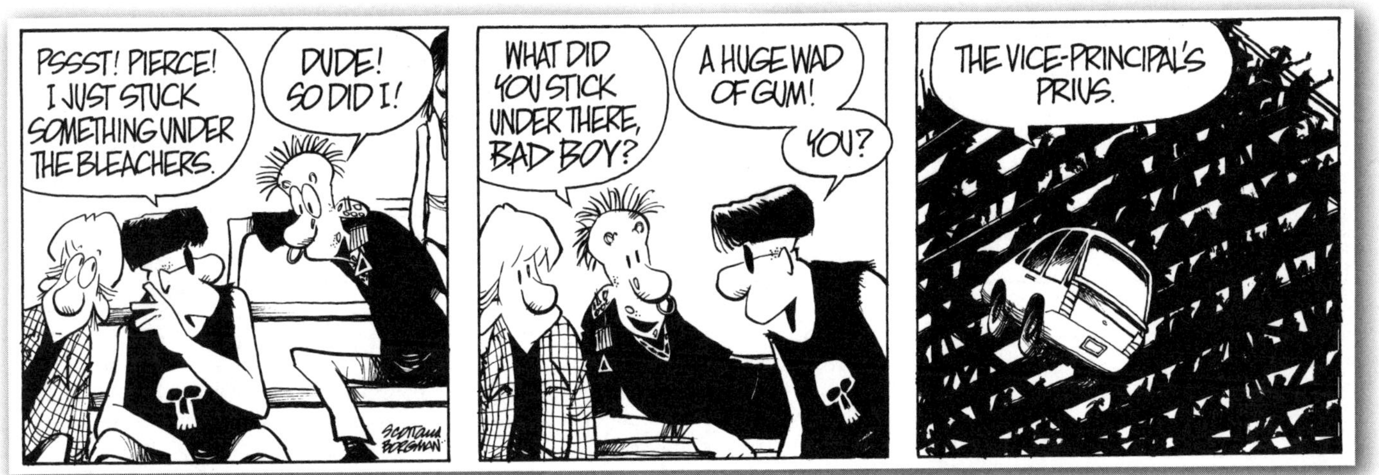
PSSST! PIERCE! I JUST STUCK SOMETHING UNDER THE BLEACHERS.
DUDE! SO DID I!
SCOTT and BORGMAN
WHAT DID YOU STICK UNDER THERE, BAD BOY?
A HUGE WAD OF GUM!
YOU?
THE VICE-PRINCIPAL'S PRIUS.

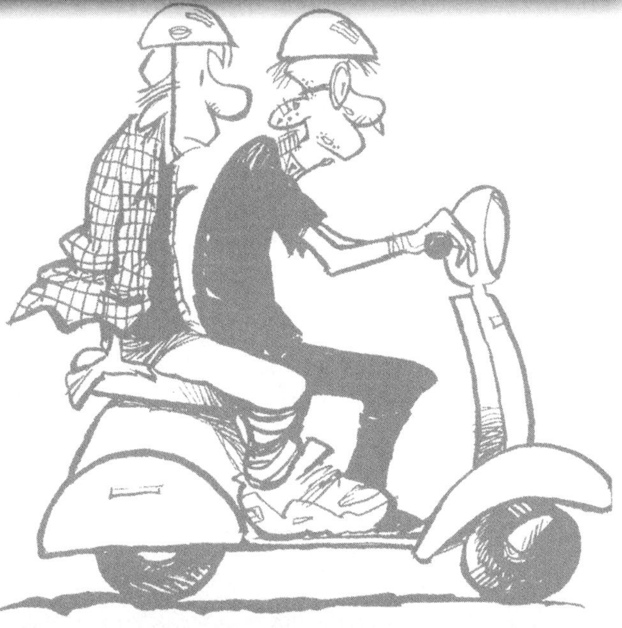

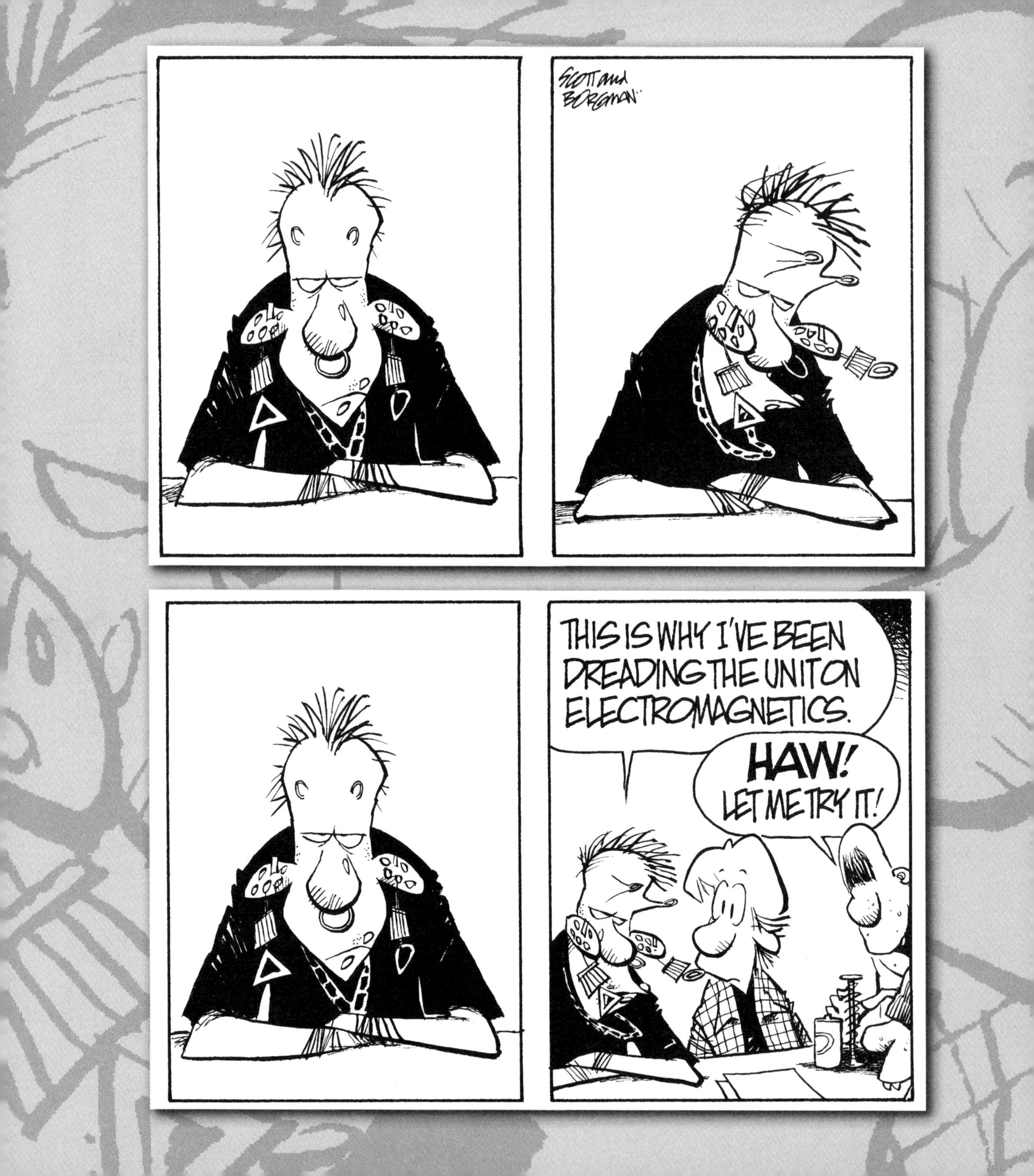
SCOTT AND BORGMAN
THIS IS WHY I'VE BEEN DREADING THE UNIT ON ELECTROMAGNETICS.
HAW! LET ME TRY IT!

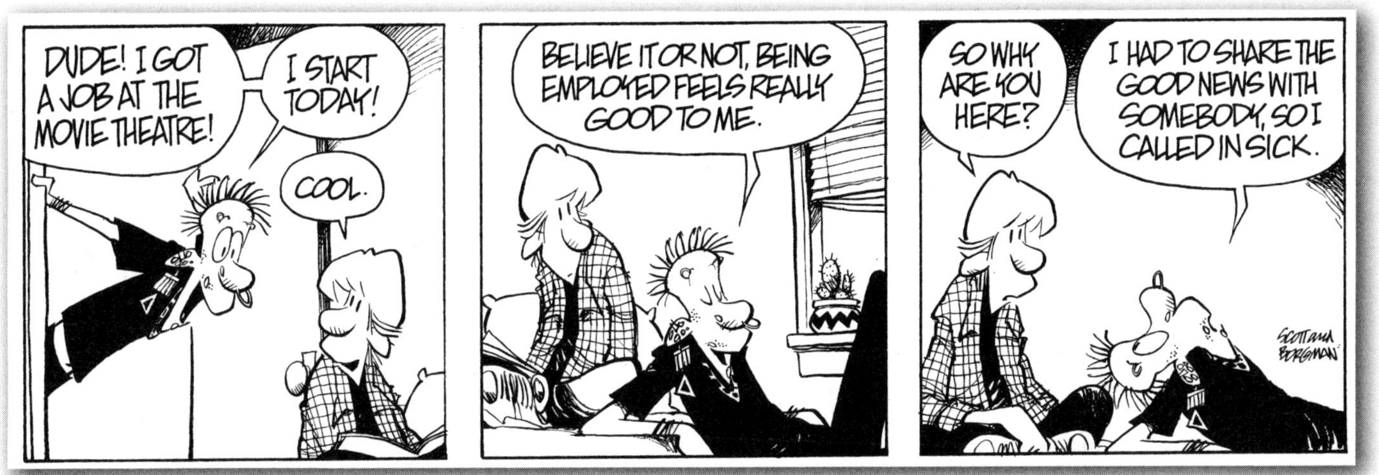
DUDE! I GOT A JOB AT THE MOVIE THEATRE!
I START TODAY!
COOL.
BELIEVE IT OR NOT, BEING EMPLOYED FEELS REALLY GOOD TO ME.
SO WHY ARE YOU HERE?
I HAD TO SHARE THE GOOD NEWS WITH SOMEBODY, SO I CALLED IN SICK.
SCOTT and BORGMAN

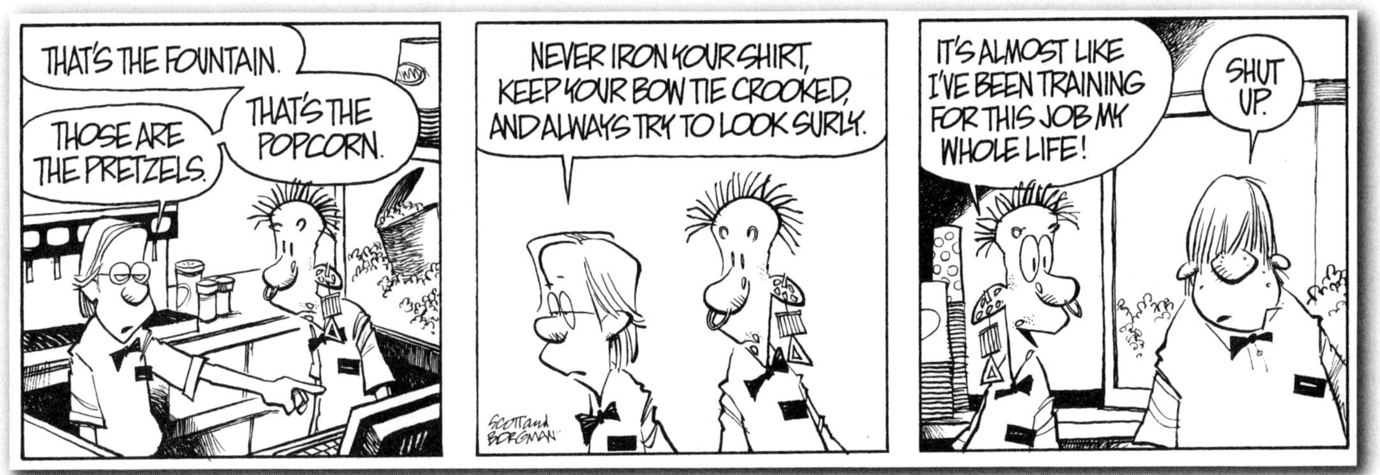
THAT'S THE FOUNTAIN.
THOSE ARE THE PRETZELS.
THAT'S THE POPCORN.
NEVER IRON YOUR SHIRT, KEEP YOUR BOW TIE CROOKED, AND ALWAYS TRY TO LOOK SURLY.
SCOTT and BORGMAN
IT'S ALMOST LIKE I'VE BEEN TRAINING FOR THIS JOB MY WHOLE LIFE!
SHUT UP.

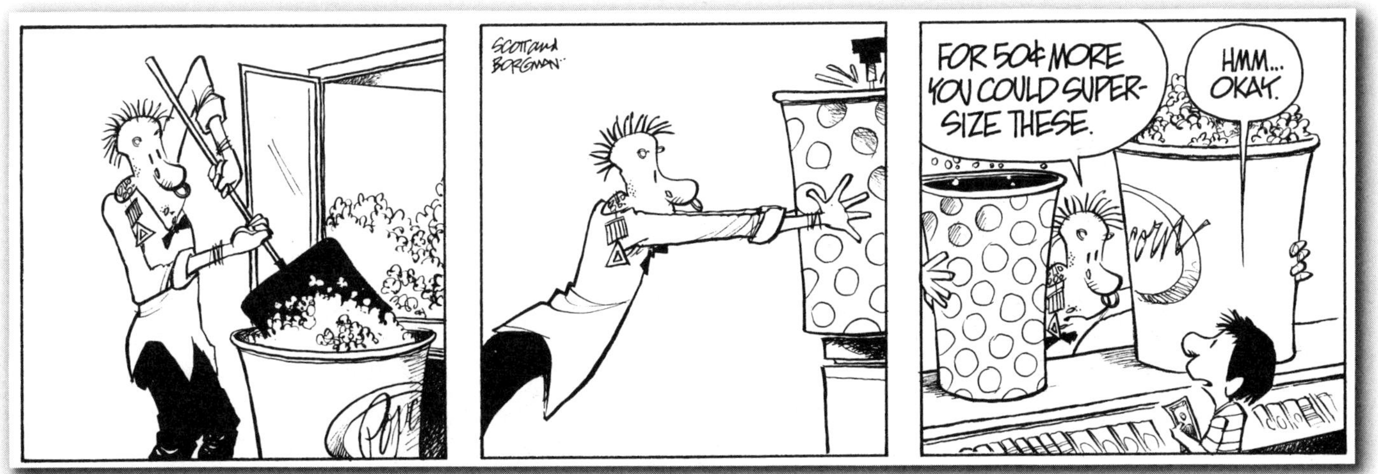
SCOTT and BORGMAN
FOR 50¢ MORE YOU COULD SUPER-SIZE THESE.
HMM... OKAY.

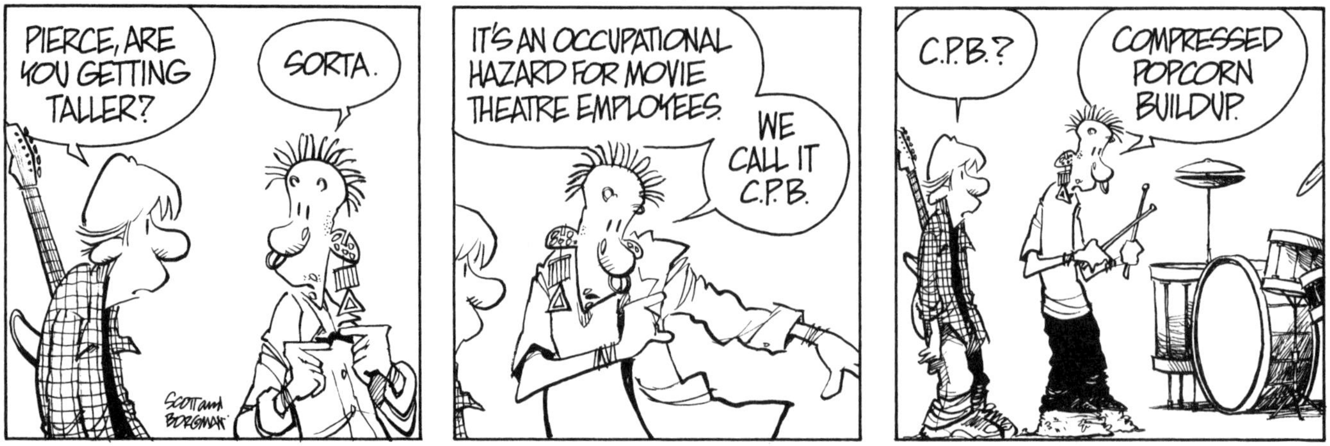
PIERCE, ARE YOU GETTING TALLER?
SORTA.
IT'S AN OCCUPATIONAL HAZARD FOR MOVIE THEATRE EMPLOYEES.
WE CALL IT C.P.B.
C.P.B.?
COMPRESSED POPCORN BUILDUP.

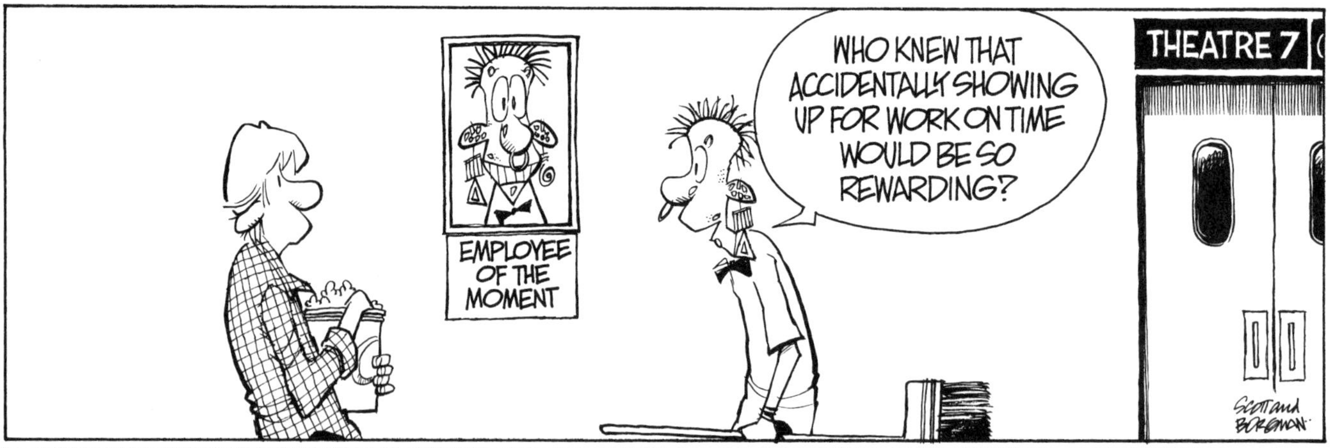
EMPLOYEE OF THE MOMENT
WHO KNEW THAT ACCIDENTALLY SHOWING UP FOR WORK ON TIME WOULD BE SO REWARDING?
THEATRE 7

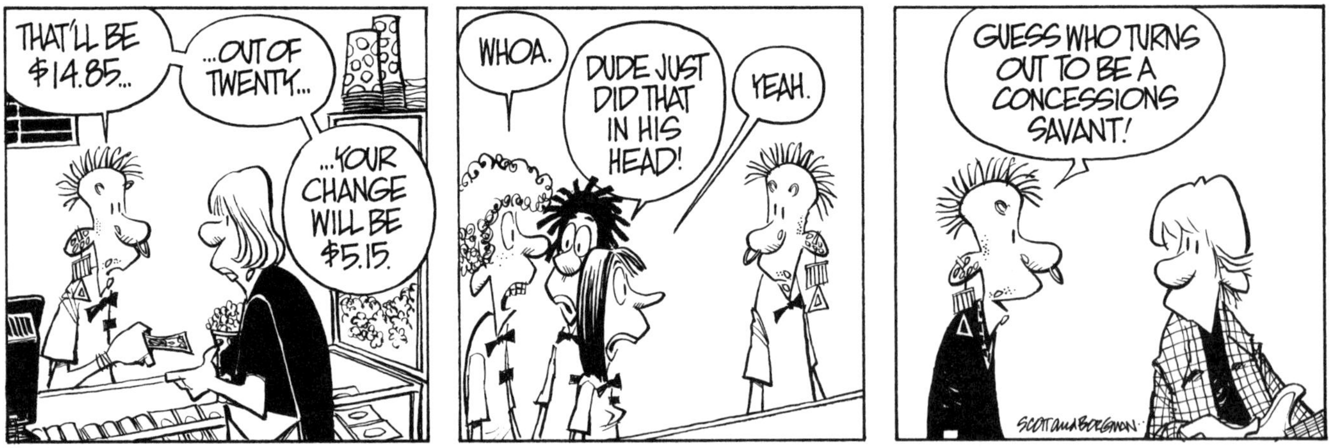
THAT'LL BE $14.85...
...OUT OF TWENTY...
...YOUR CHANGE WILL BE $5.15.
WHOA.
DUDE JUST DID THAT IN HIS HEAD!
YEAH.
GUESS WHO TURNS OUT TO BE A CONCESSIONS SAVANT!

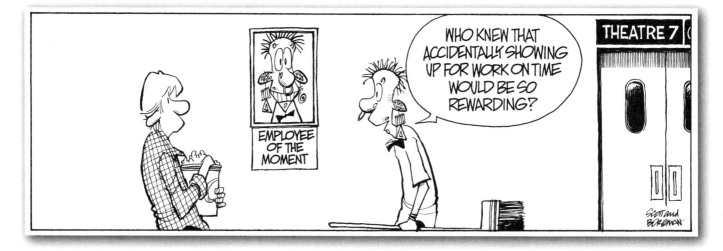

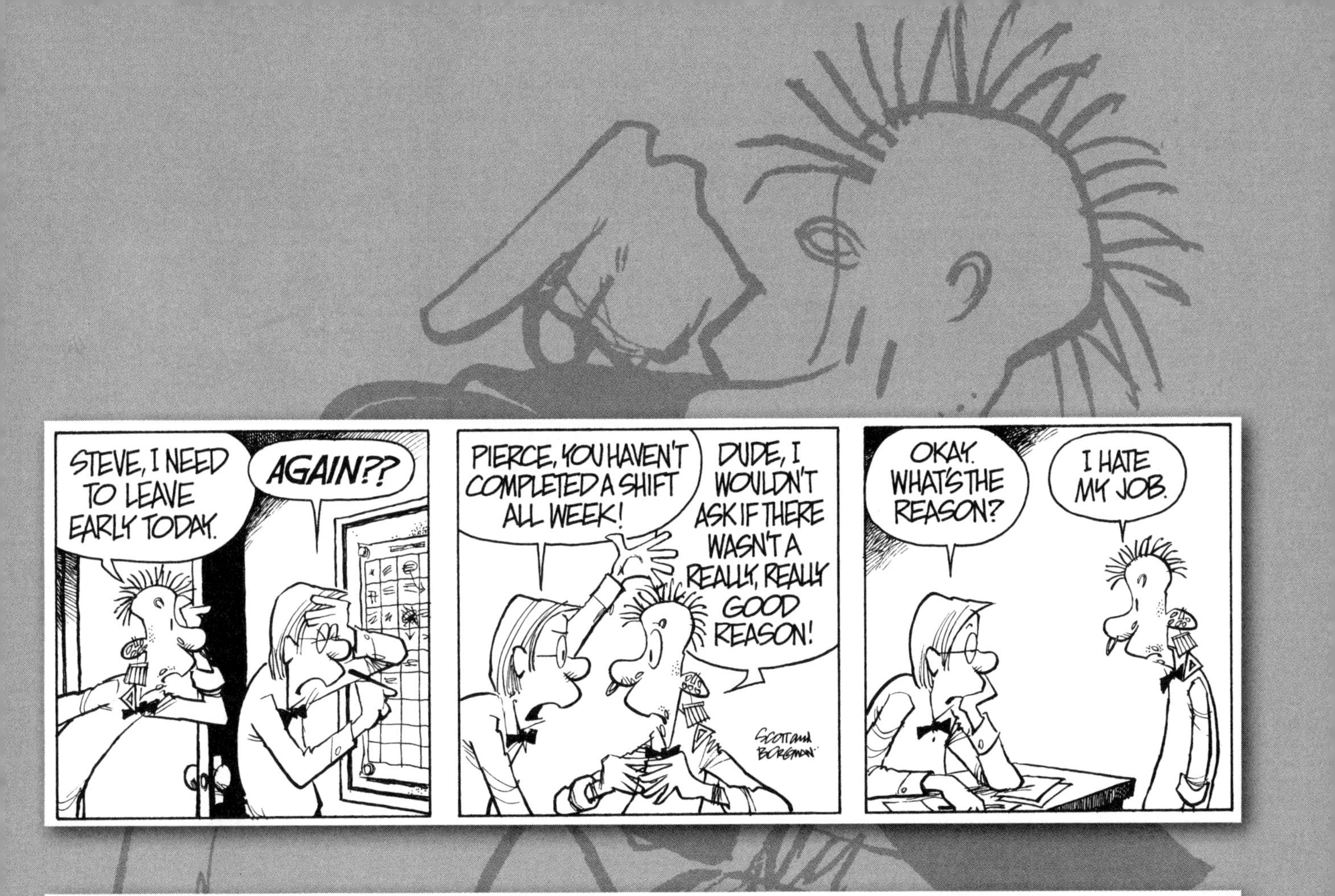
STEVE, I NEED TO LEAVE EARLY TODAY.
AGAIN??
PIERCE, YOU HAVEN'T COMPLETED A SHIFT ALL WEEK!
DUDE, I WOULDN'T ASK IF THERE WASN'T A REALLY, REALLY GOOD REASON!
OKAY. WHAT'S THE REASON?
I HATE MY JOB.

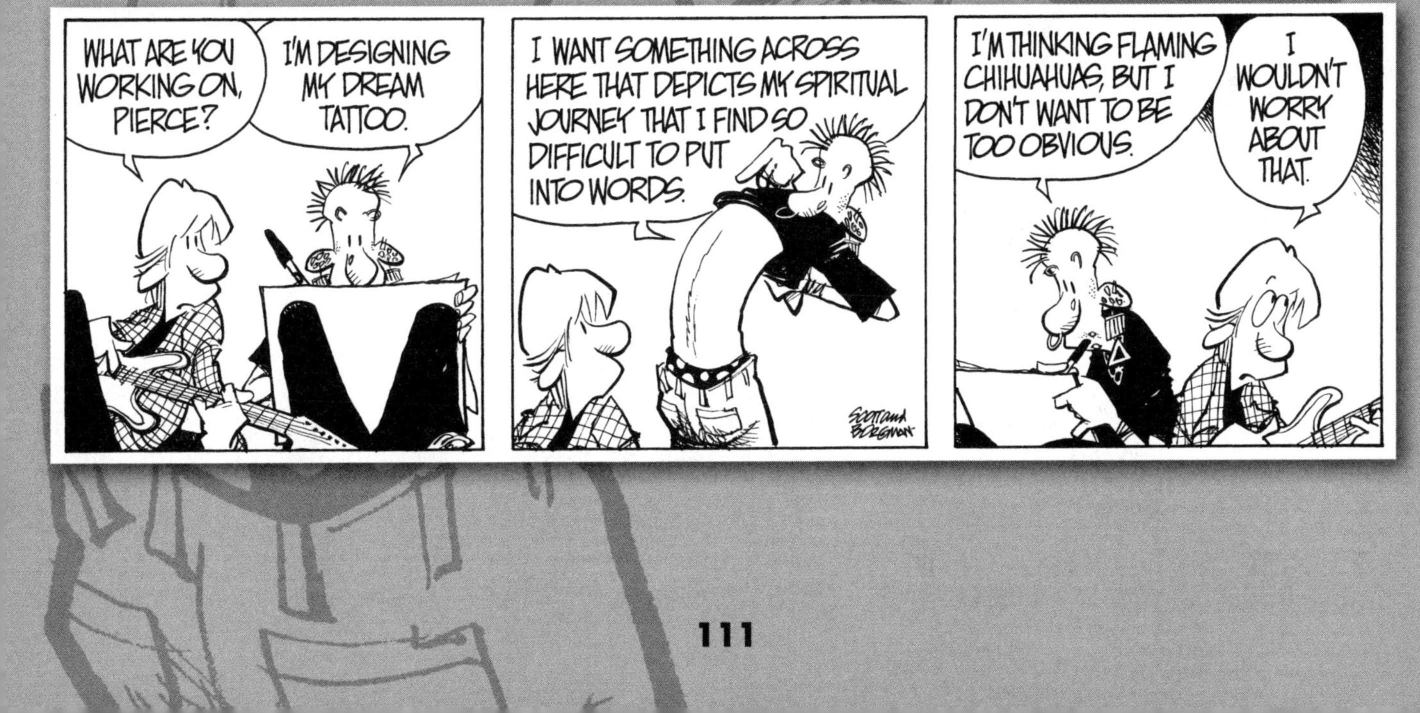
WHAT ARE YOU WORKING ON, PIERCE?
I'M DESIGNING MY DREAM TATTOO.
I WANT SOMETHING ACROSS HERE THAT DEPICTS MY SPIRITUAL JOURNEY THAT I FIND SO DIFFICULT TO PUT INTO WORDS.
I'M THINKING FLAMING CHIHUAHUAS, BUT I DON'T WANT TO BE TOO OBVIOUS.
I WOULDN'T WORRY ABOUT THAT.

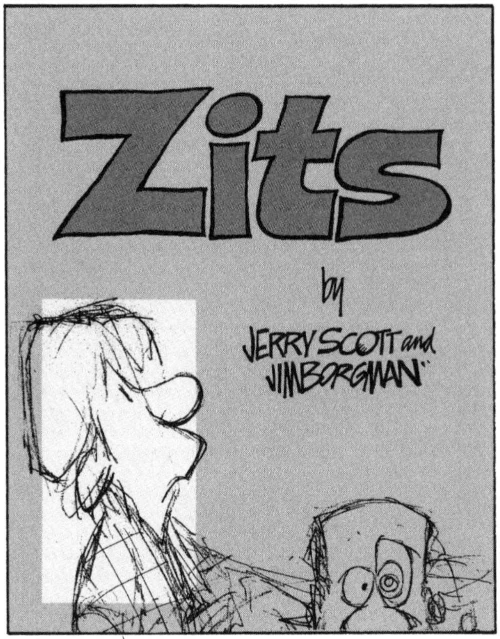
Zits
by
JERRY SCOTT and
JIM BORGMAN

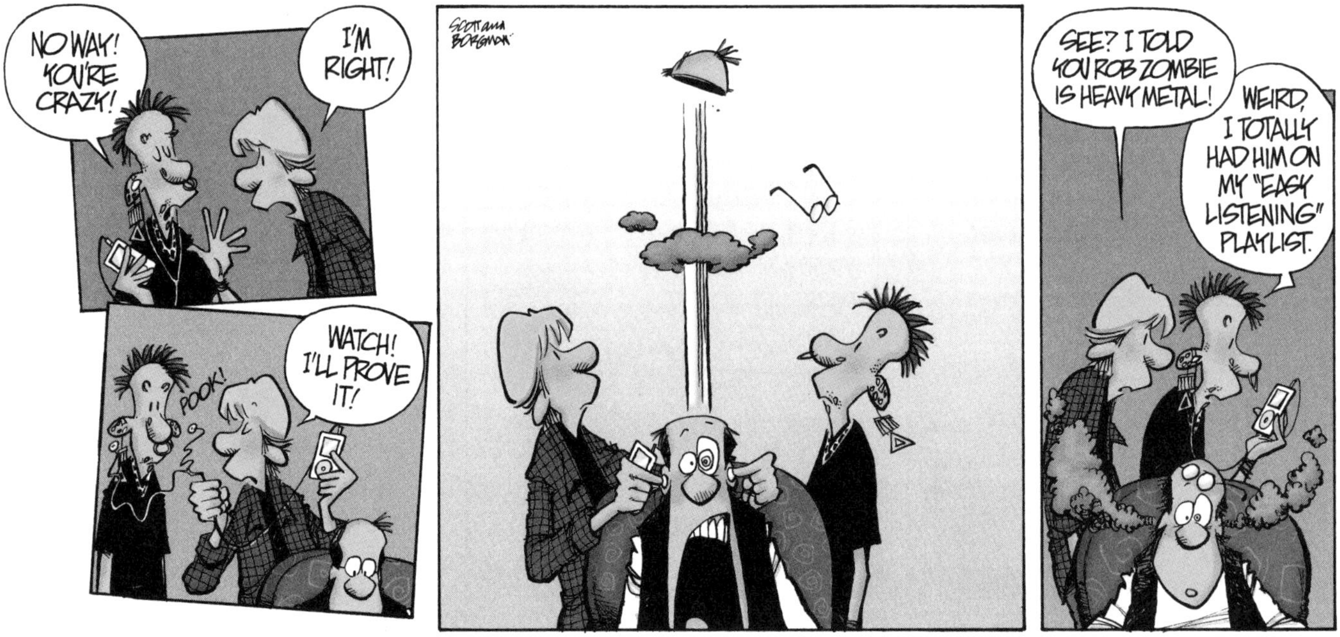
NO WAY! YOU'RE CRAZY!
I'M RIGHT!
POOK!
WATCH! I'LL PROVE IT!
SEE? I TOLD YOU ROB ZOMBIE IS HEAVY METAL!
WEIRD, I TOTALLY HAD HIM ON MY "EASY LISTENING" PLAYLIST.

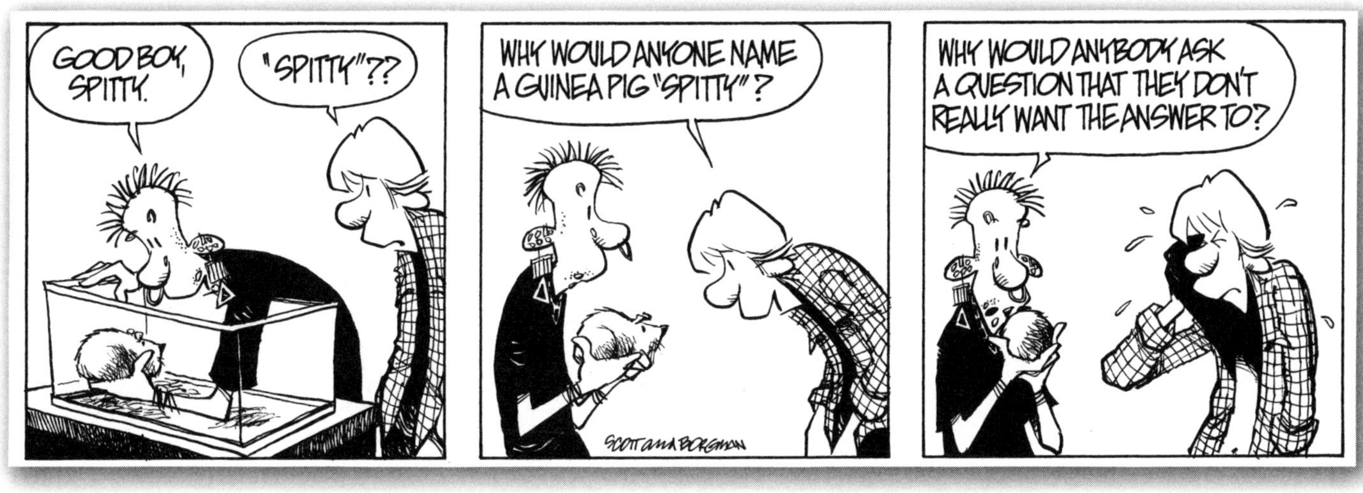
GOOD BOY, SPITTY.
"SPITTY"??
WHY WOULD ANYONE NAME A GUINEA PIG "SPITTY"?
SCOTT and BORGMAN
WHY WOULD ANYBODY ASK A QUESTION THAT THEY DON'T REALLY WANT THE ANSWER TO?

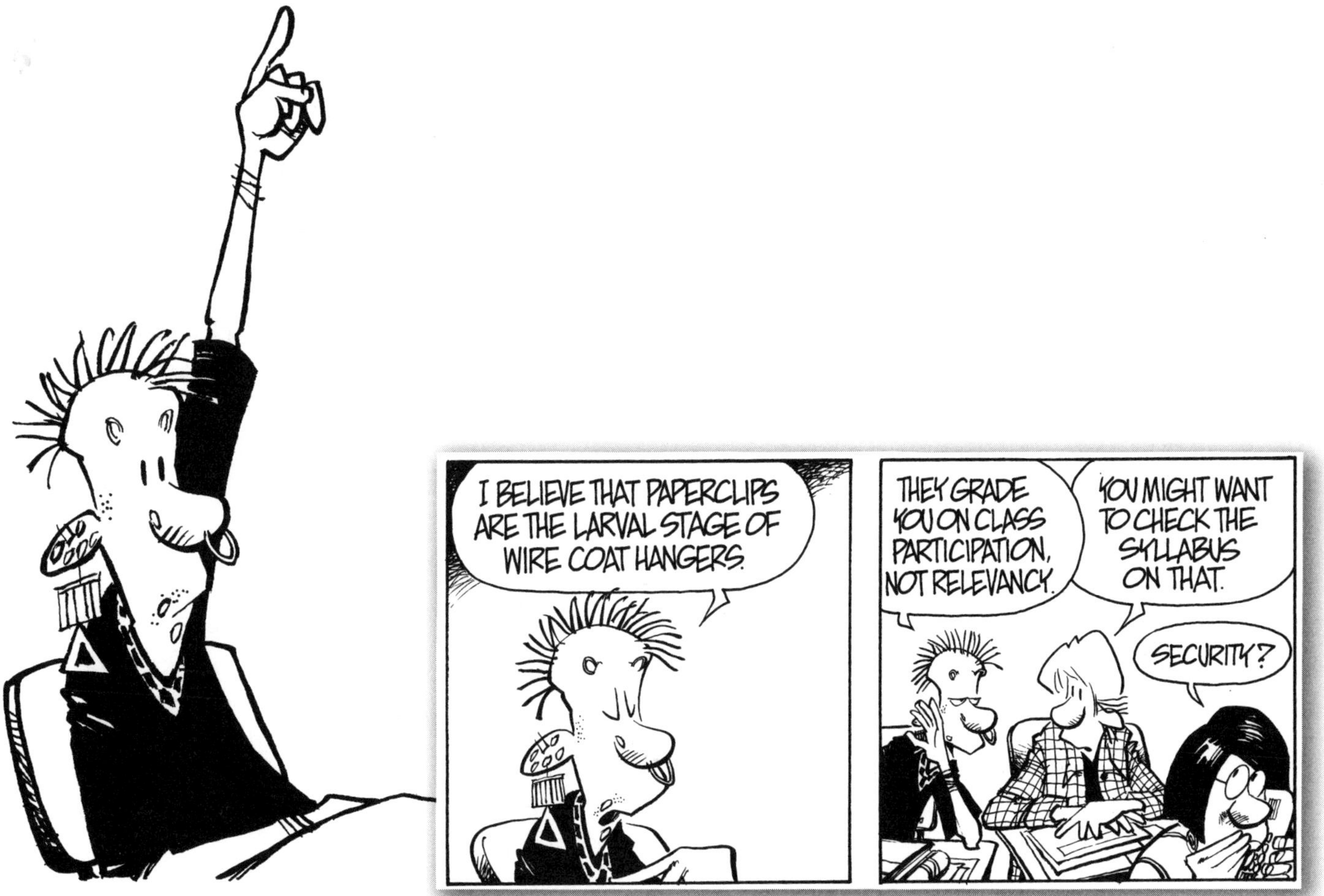
I BELIEVE THAT PAPERCLIPS ARE THE LARVAL STAGE OF WIRE COAT HANGERS.
THEY GRADE YOU ON CLASS PARTICIPATION, NOT RELEVANCY.
YOU MIGHT WANT TO CHECK THE SYLLABUS ON THAT.
SECURITY?

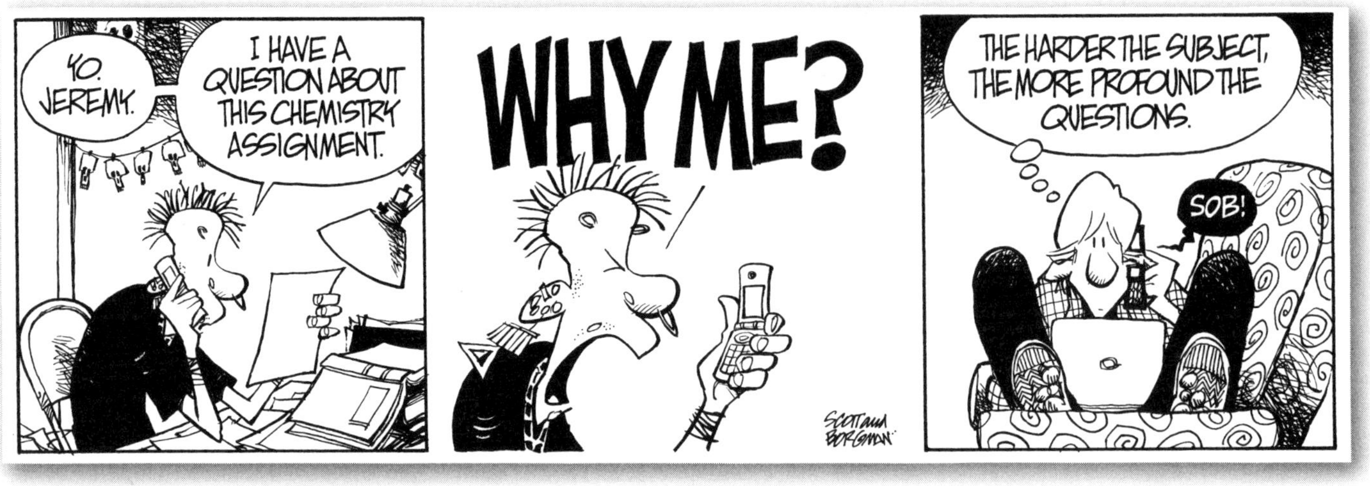
YO. JEREMY.
I HAVE A QUESTION ABOUT THIS CHEMISTRY ASSIGNMENT.
WHY ME?
THE HARDER THE SUBJECT, THE MORE PROFOUND THE QUESTIONS.
SOB!

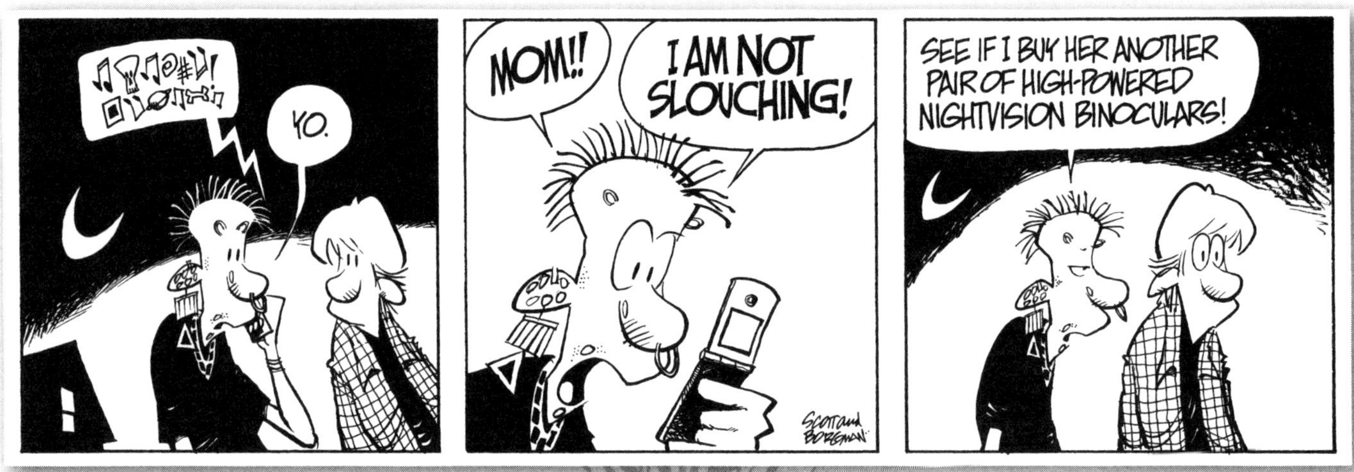
YO.
MOM!!
I AM NOT SLOUCHING!
SEE IF I BUY HER ANOTHER PAIR OF HIGH-POWERED NIGHTVISION BINOCULARS!

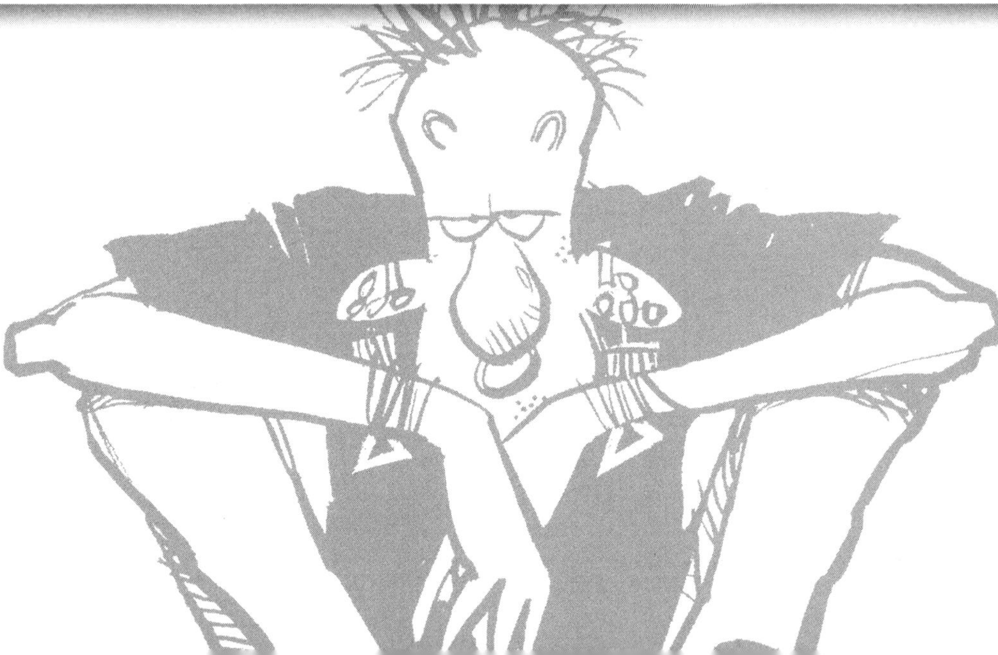

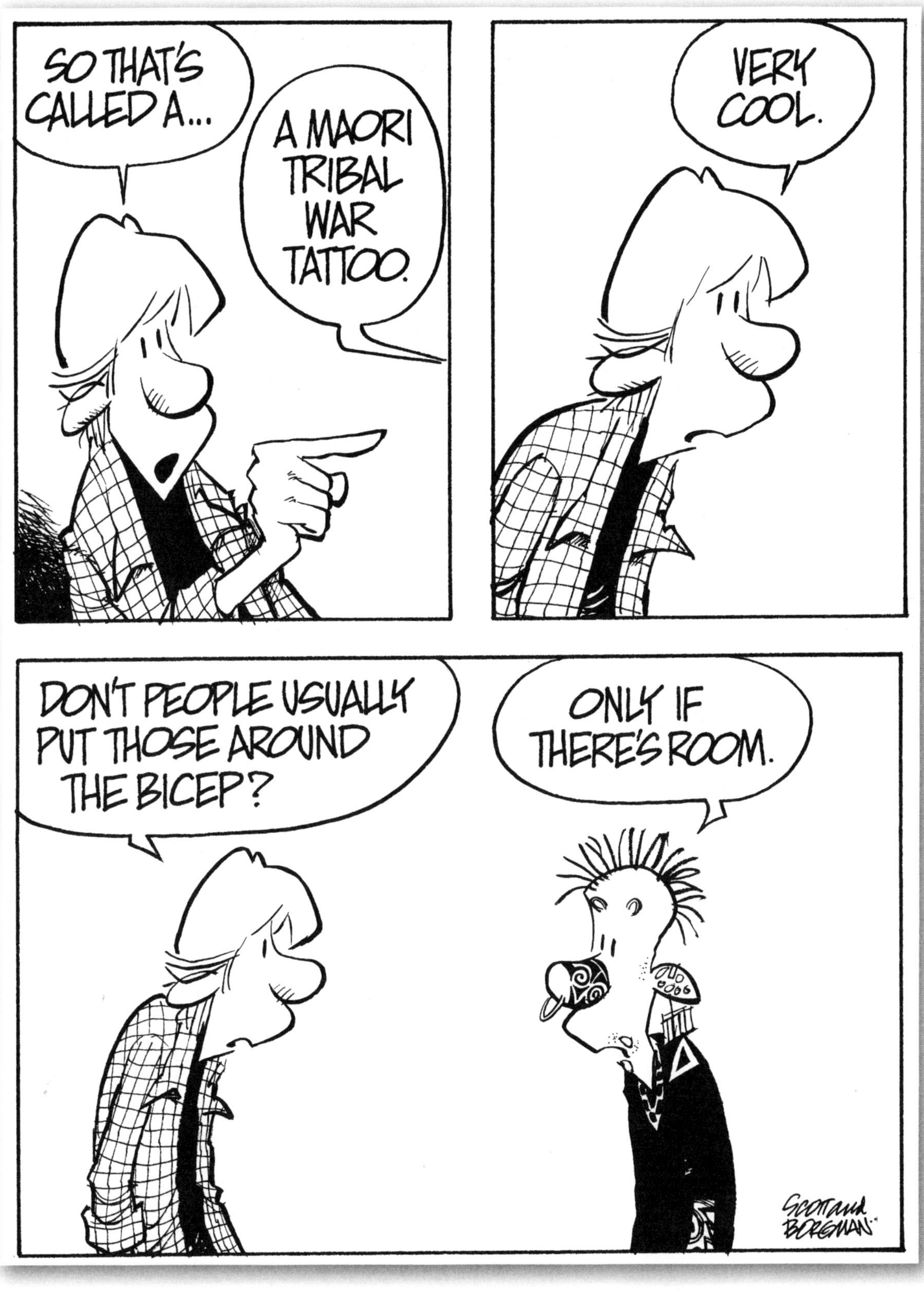
SO THAT'S CALLED A...
A MAORI TRIBAL WAR TATTOO.
VERY COOL.
DON'T PEOPLE USUALLY PUT THOSE AROUND THE BICEP?
ONLY IF THERE'S ROOM.
SCOTT AND BORGMAN

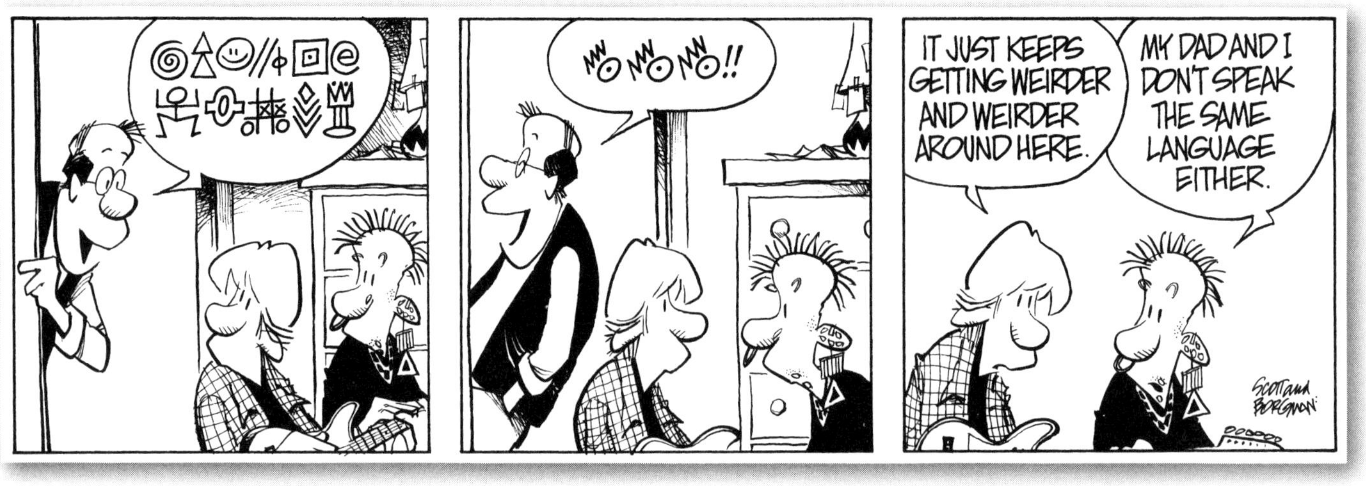
NO NO NO!!
IT JUST KEEPS GETTING WEIRDER AND WEIRDER AROUND HERE.
MY DAD AND I DON'T SPEAK THE SAME LANGUAGE EITHER.
SCOTT and BORGMAN

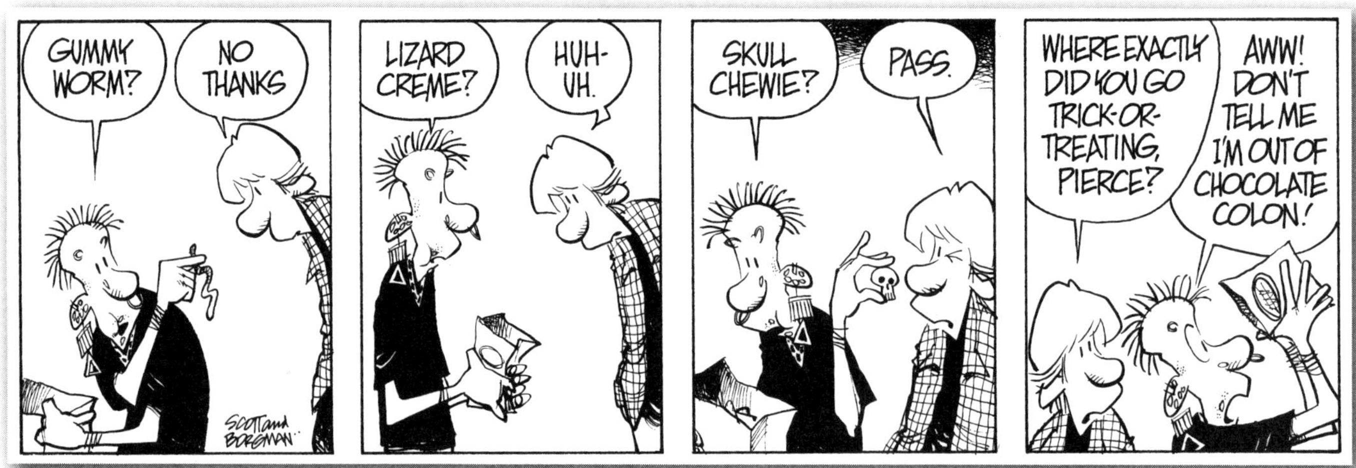
GUMMY WORM?
NO THANKS
SCOTT and BORGMAN
LIZARD CREME?
HUH-UH.
SKULL CHEWIE?
PASS.
WHERE EXACTLY DID YOU GO TRICK-OR-TREATING, PIERCE?
AWW! DON'T TELL ME I'M OUT OF CHOCOLATE COLON!

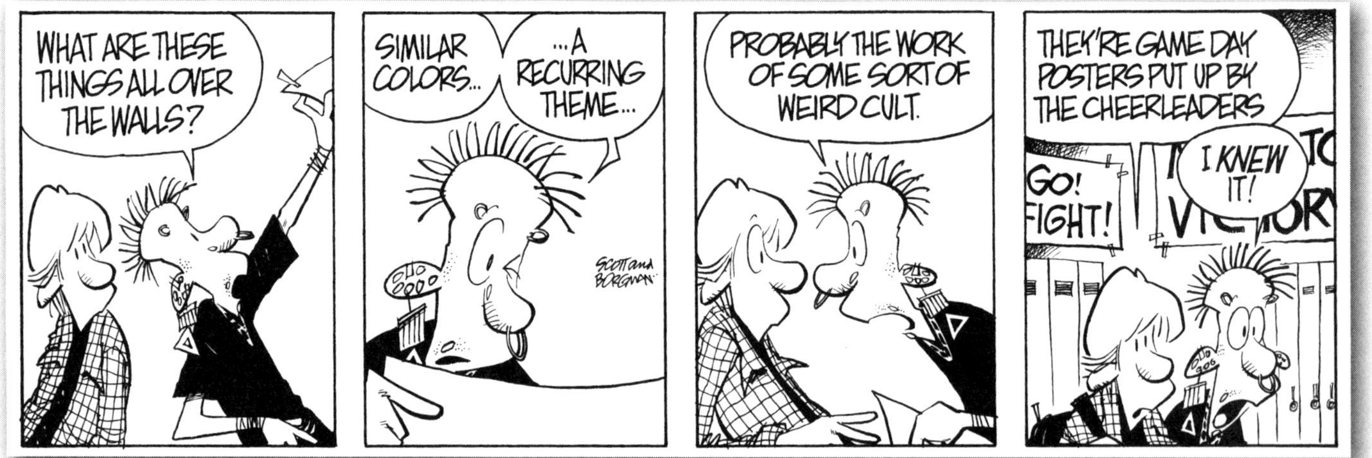
WHAT ARE THESE THINGS ALL OVER THE WALLS?
SIMILAR COLORS...
...A RECURRING THEME...
SCOTT and BORGMAN
PROBABLY THE WORK OF SOME SORT OF WEIRD CULT.
THEY'RE GAME DAY POSTERS PUT UP BY THE CHEERLEADERS
GO! FIGHT!
I KNEW IT!

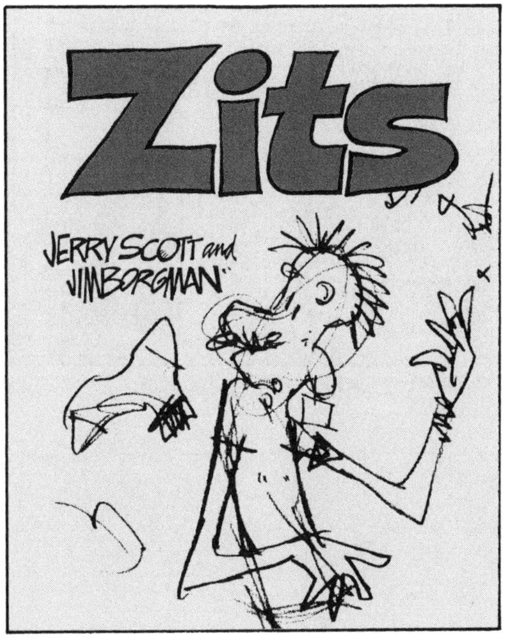
Zits
JERRY SCOTT and JIM BORGMAN

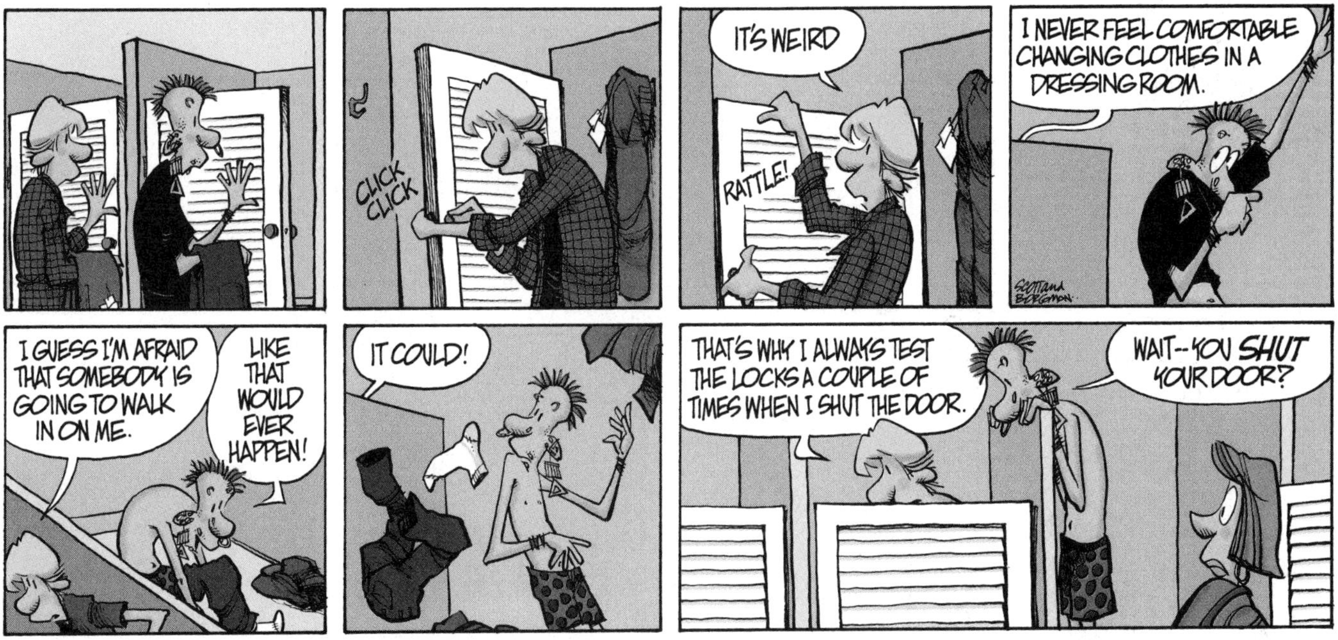
CLICK CLICK
IT'S WEIRD
RATTLE!
I NEVER FEEL COMFORTABLE CHANGING CLOTHES IN A DRESSING ROOM.
SCOTT and BORGMAN
I GUESS I'M AFRAID THAT SOMEBODY IS GOING TO WALK IN ON ME.
LIKE THAT WOULD EVER HAPPEN!
IT COULD!
THAT'S WHY I ALWAYS TEST THE LOCKS A COUPLE OF TIMES WHEN I SHUT THE DOOR.
WAIT-- YOU SHUT YOUR DOOR?

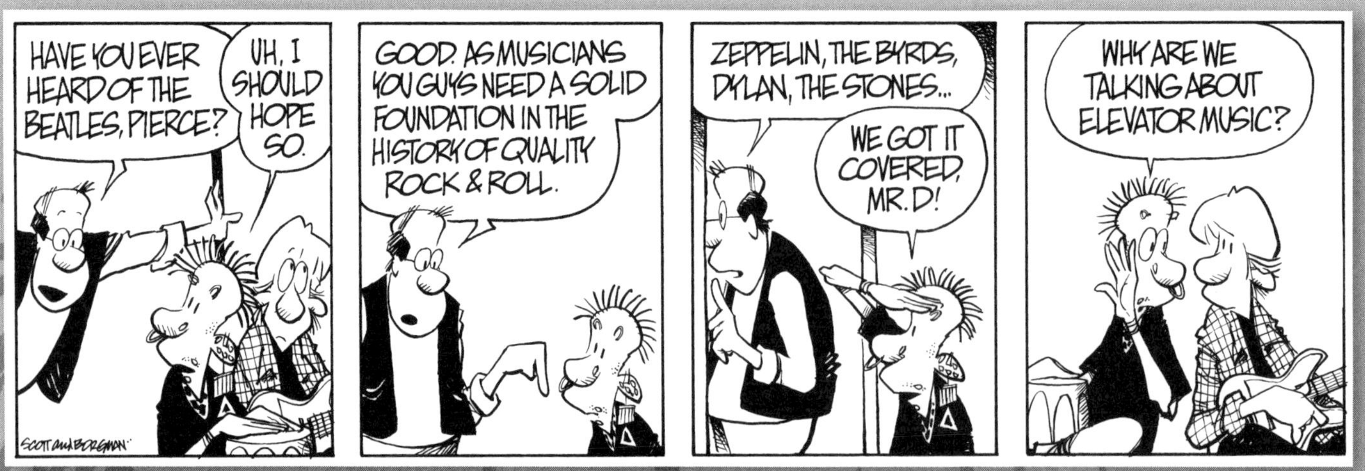
HAVE YOU EVER HEARD OF THE BEATLES, PIERCE?
UH, I SHOULD HOPE SO.
GOOD. AS MUSICIANS YOU GUYS NEED A SOLID FOUNDATION IN THE HISTORY OF QUALITY ROCK & ROLL.
ZEPPELIN, THE BYRDS, DYLAN, THE STONES...
WE GOT IT COVERED, MR. D!
WHY ARE WE TALKING ABOUT ELEVATOR MUSIC?
SCOTT and BORGMAN

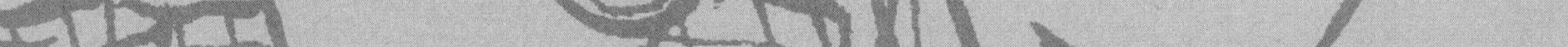
PIERCE! CAN I BORROW A PENCIL?
YUH.
HELP YOURSELPH.
I DIDN'T KNOW YOU WERE INTO FUNCTIONAL ORNAMENTATION.
IT'S A GREENER LIFESTYLE.
SCOTT and BORGMAN

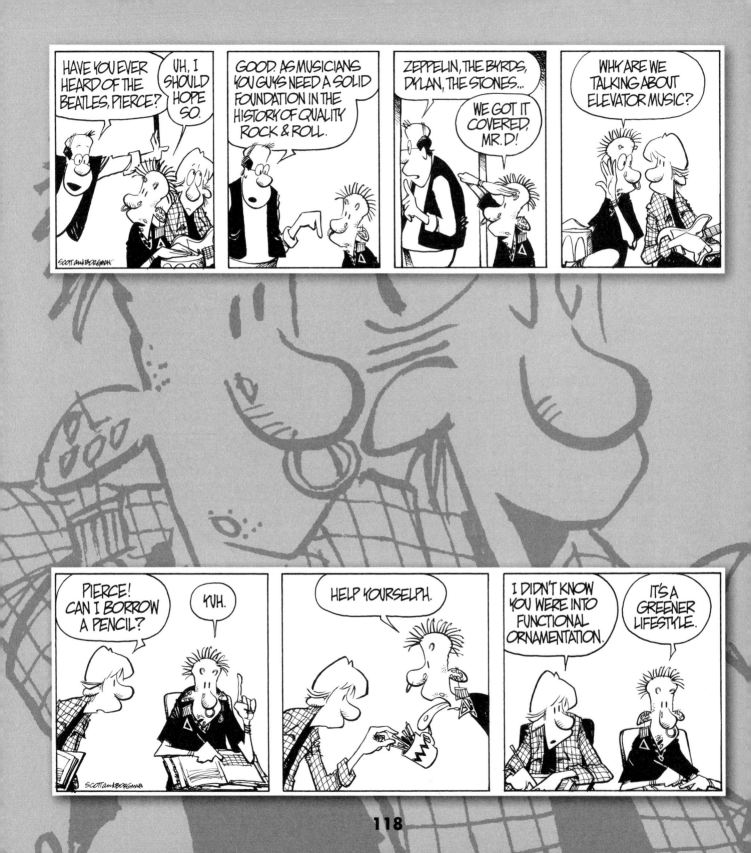

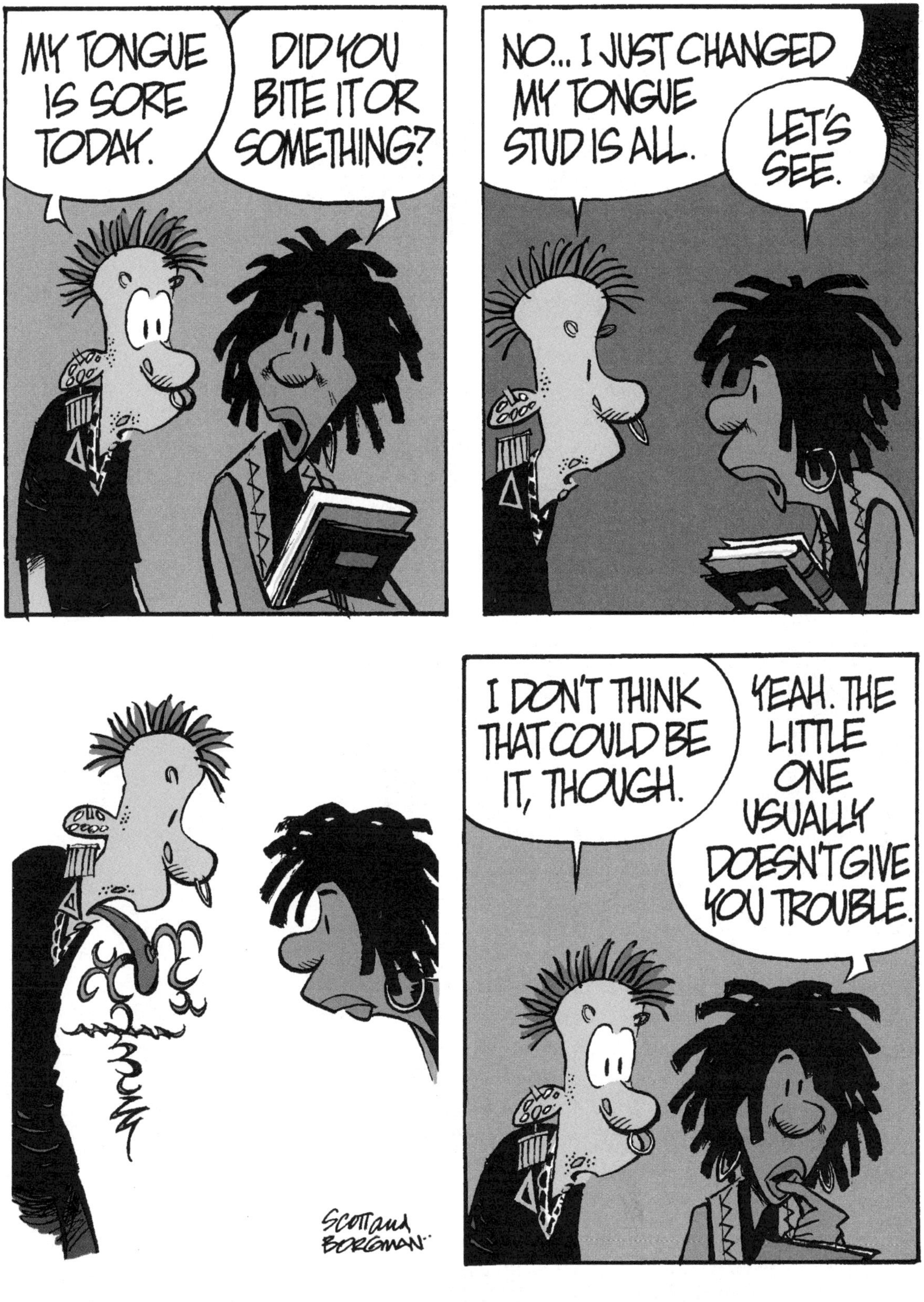
MY TONGUE IS SORE TODAY.
DID YOU BITE IT OR SOMETHING?
NO... I JUST CHANGED MY TONGUE STUD IS ALL.
LET'S SEE.
I DON'T THINK THAT COULD BE IT, THOUGH.
YEAH. THE LITTLE ONE USUALLY DOESN'T GIVE YOU TROUBLE.
SCOTT and BORGMAN

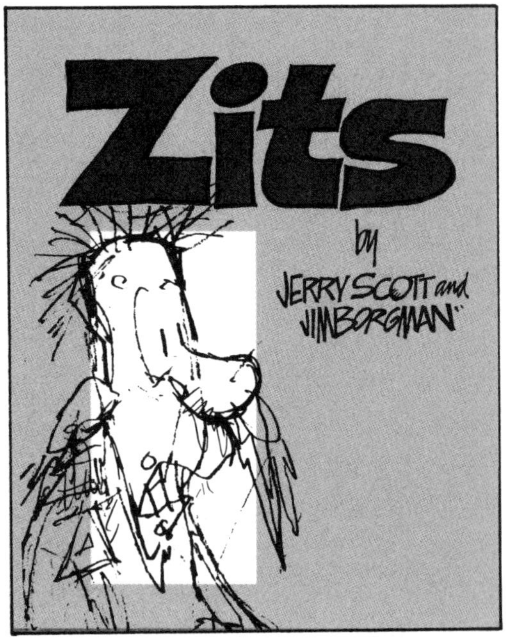
Zits
by
JERRY SCOTT and
JIM BORGMAN

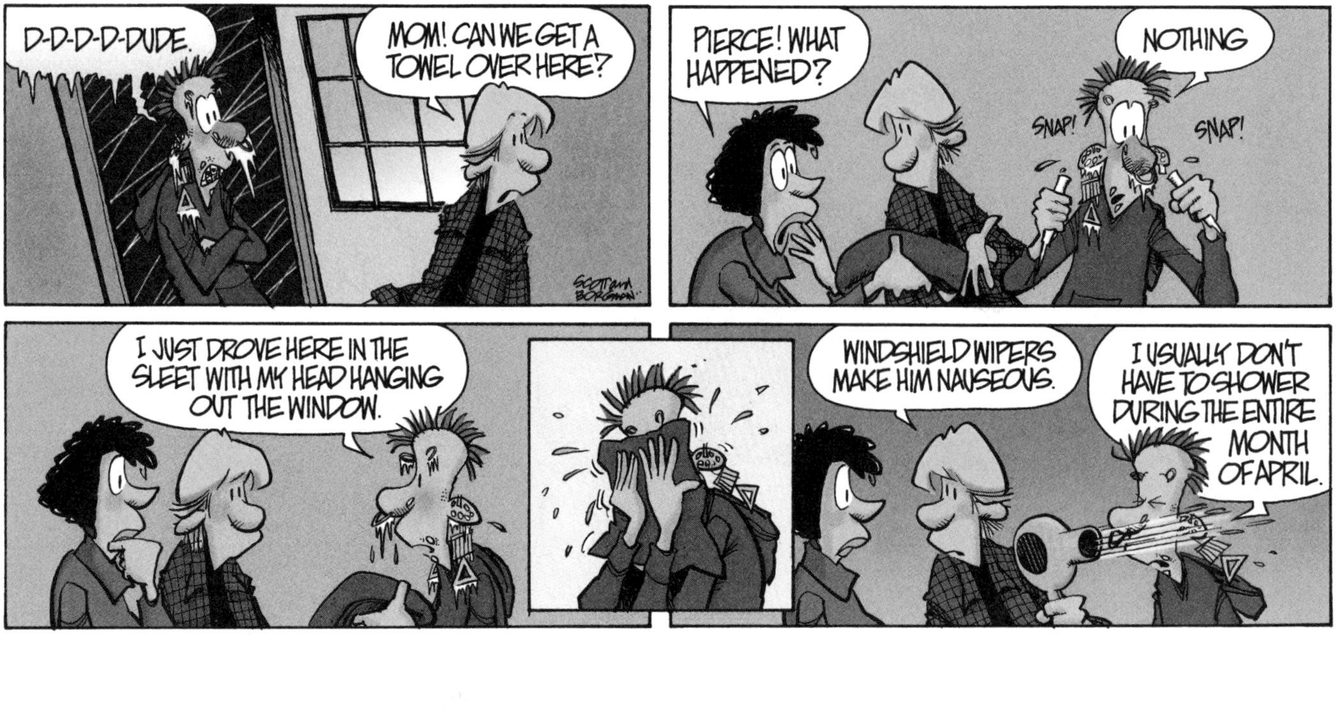
D-D-D-D-DUDE.
MOM! CAN WE GET A TOWEL OVER HERE?
PIERCE! WHAT HAPPENED?
NOTHING
SNAP!
SNAP!
I JUST DROVE HERE IN THE SLEET WITH MY HEAD HANGING OUT THE WINDOW.
WINDSHIELD WIPERS MAKE HIM NAUSEOUS.
I USUALLY DON'T HAVE TO SHOWER DURING THE ENTIRE MONTH OF APRIL.

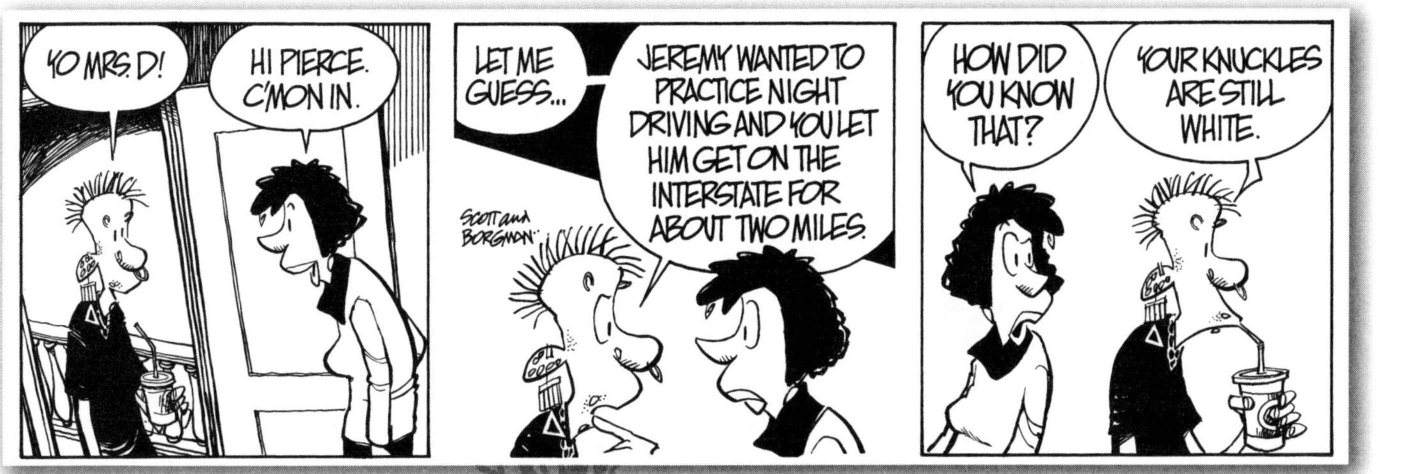
YO MRS. D!
HI PIERCE. C'MON IN.
LET ME GUESS...
JEREMY WANTED TO PRACTICE NIGHT DRIVING AND YOU LET HIM GET ON THE INTERSTATE FOR ABOUT TWO MILES.
SCOTT AND BORGMAN
HOW DID YOU KNOW THAT?
YOUR KNUCKLES ARE STILL WHITE.

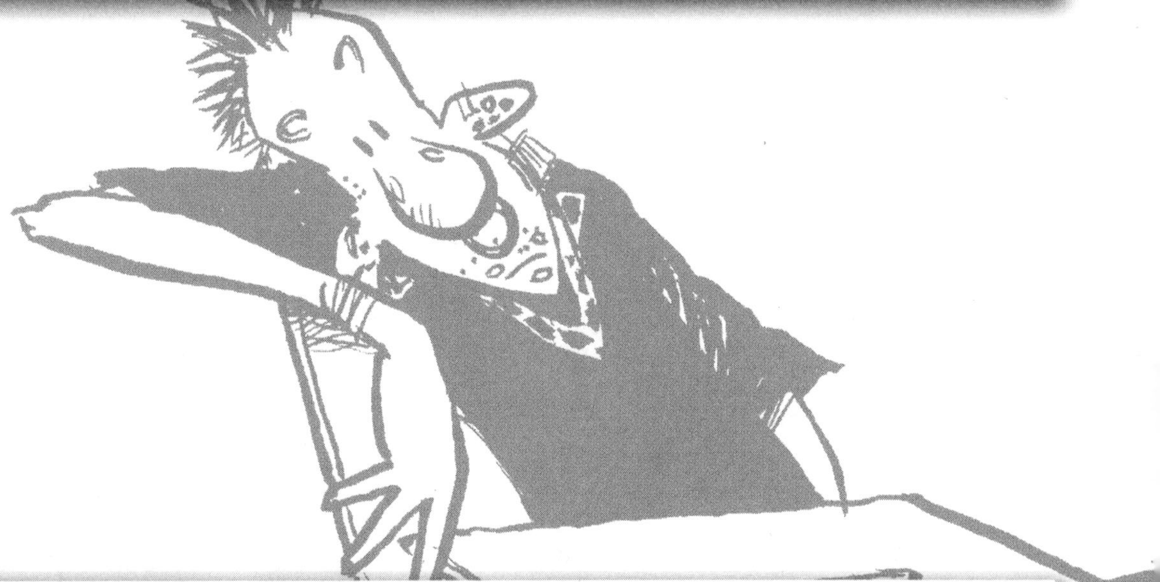

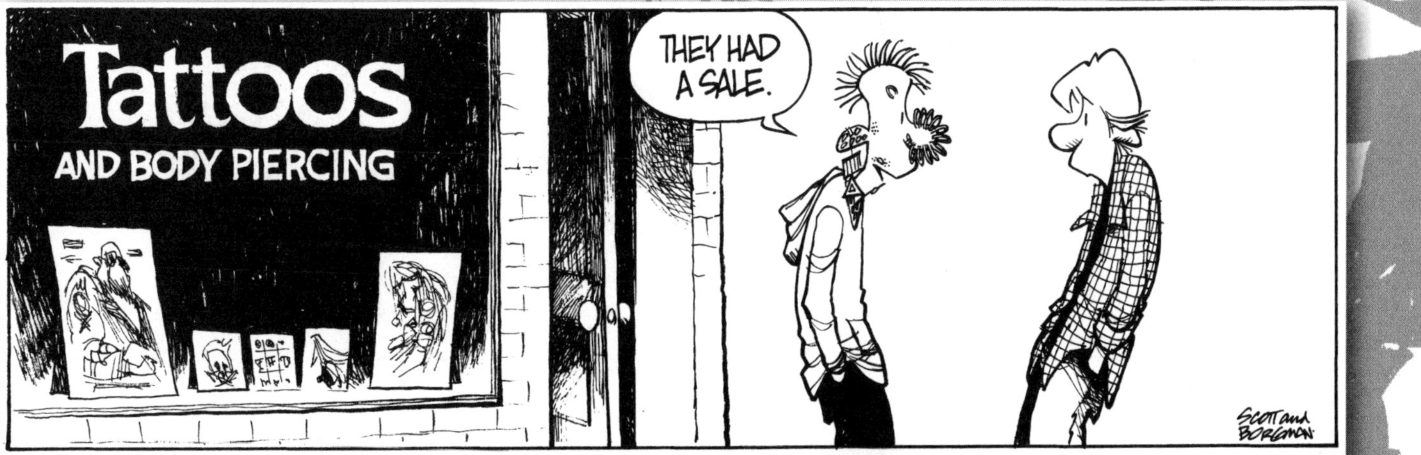
Tattoos
AND BODY PIERCING
THEY HAD A SALE.
SCOTT AND BORGMAN

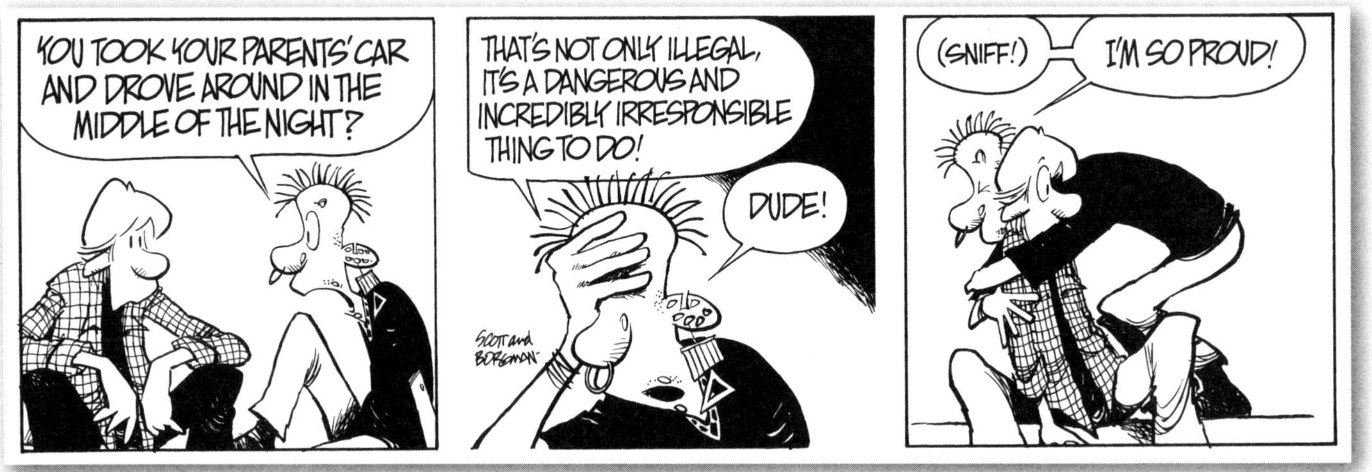
YOU TOOK YOUR PARENTS' CAR AND DROVE AROUND IN THE MIDDLE OF THE NIGHT?
THAT'S NOT ONLY ILLEGAL, IT'S A DANGEROUS AND INCREDIBLY IRRESPONSIBLE THING TO DO!
DUDE!
SCOTT and BORGMAN
(SNIFF!)
I'M SO PROUD!

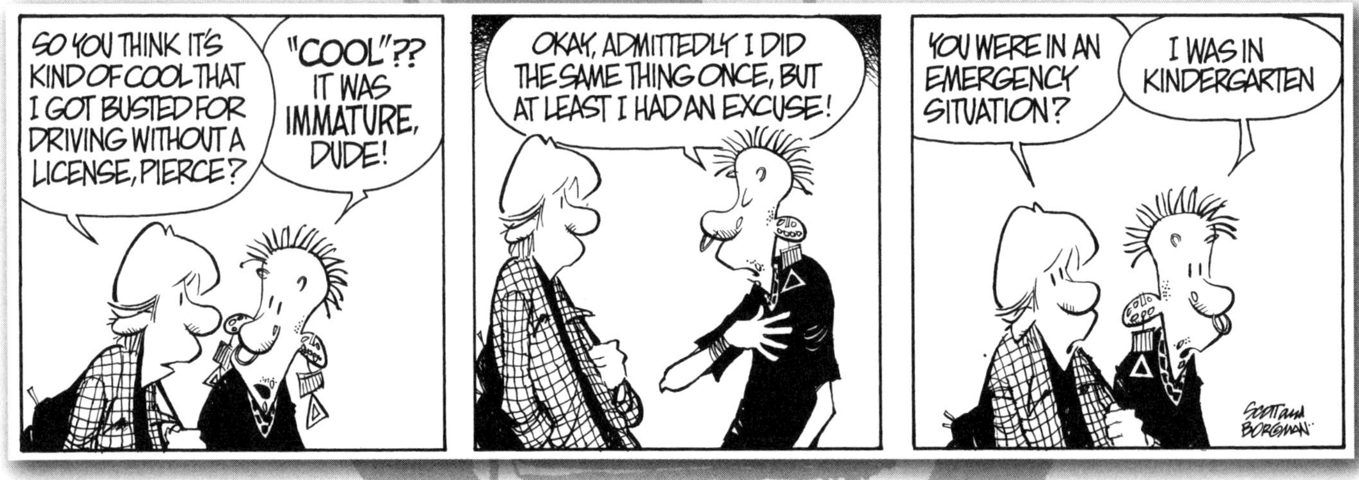
SO YOU THINK IT'S KIND OF COOL THAT I GOT BUSTED FOR DRIVING WITHOUT A LICENSE, PIERCE?
"COOL"?? IT WAS IMMATURE, DUDE!
OKAY, ADMITTEDLY I DID THE SAME THING ONCE, BUT AT LEAST I HAD AN EXCUSE!
YOU WERE IN AN EMERGENCY SITUATION?
I WAS IN KINDERGARTEN
SCOTT and BORGMAN

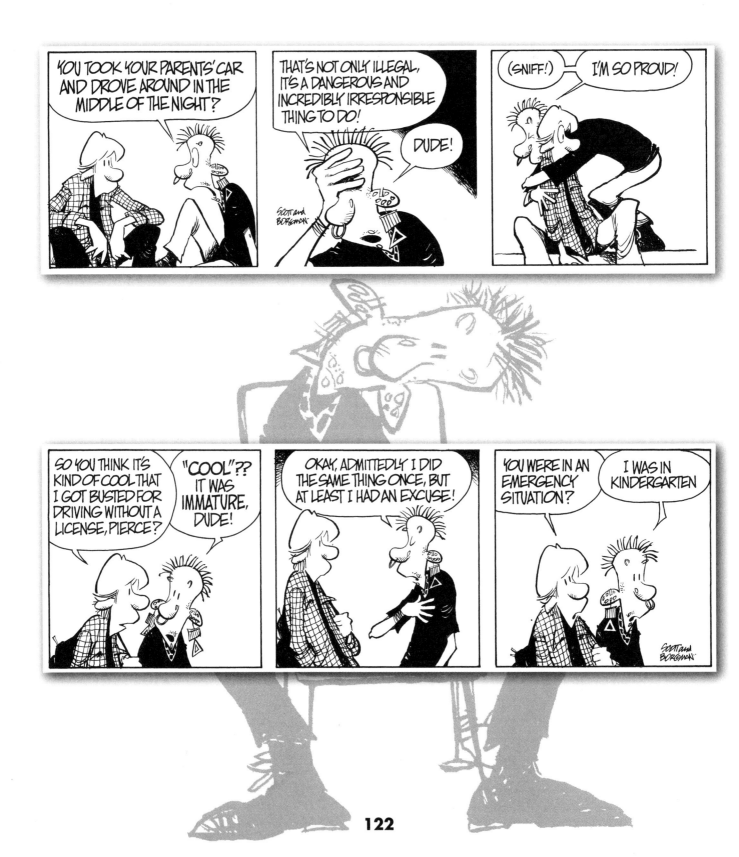

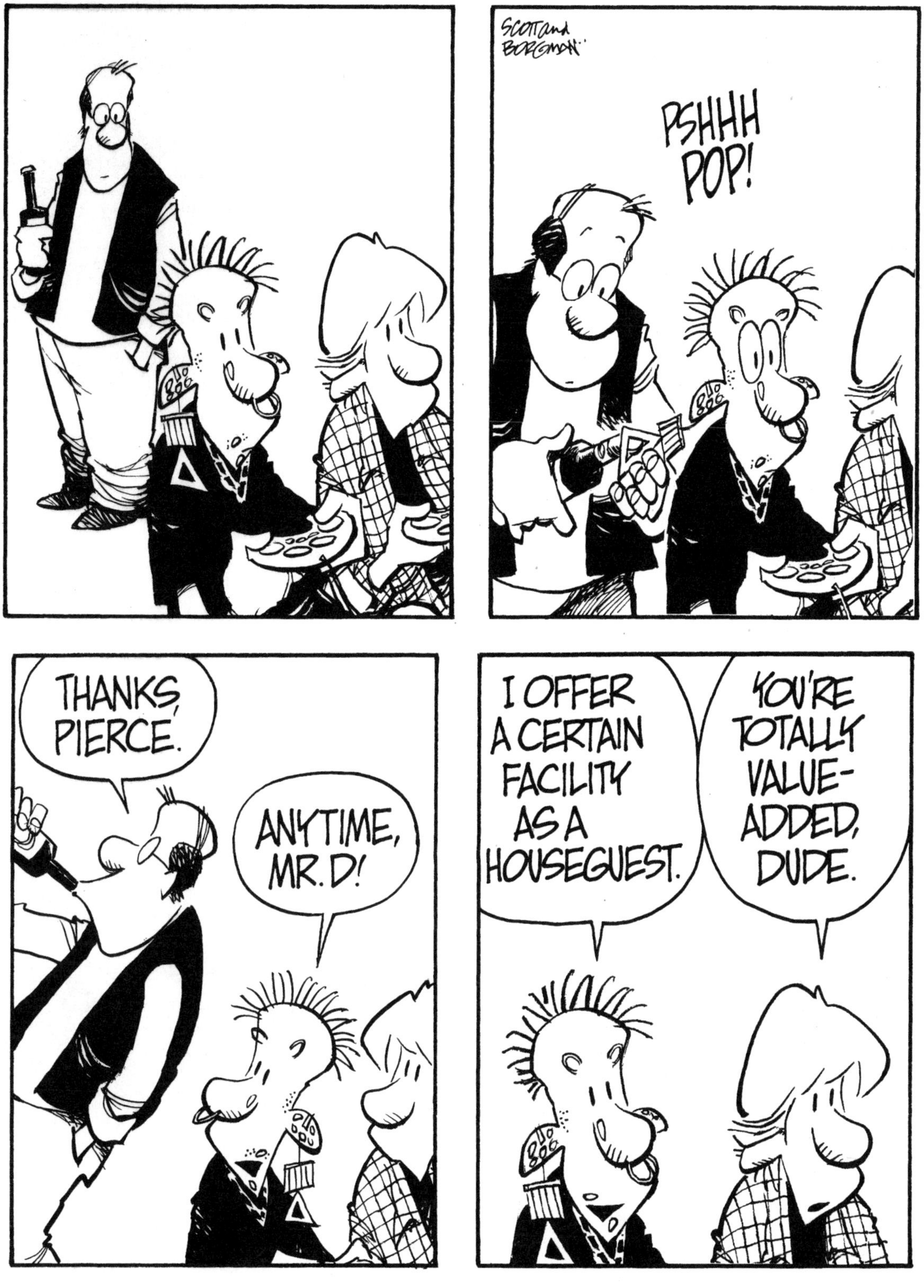
SCOTT and BORGMAN
PSHHH POP!
THANKS, PIERCE.
ANYTIME, MR. D!
I OFFER A CERTAIN FACILITY AS A HOUSEGUEST.
YOU'RE TOTALLY VALUE-ADDED, DUDE.

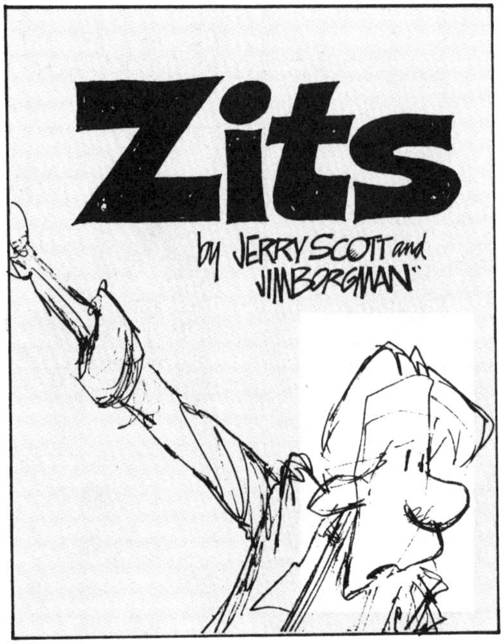
Zits
by JERRY SCOTT and
JIM BORGMAN

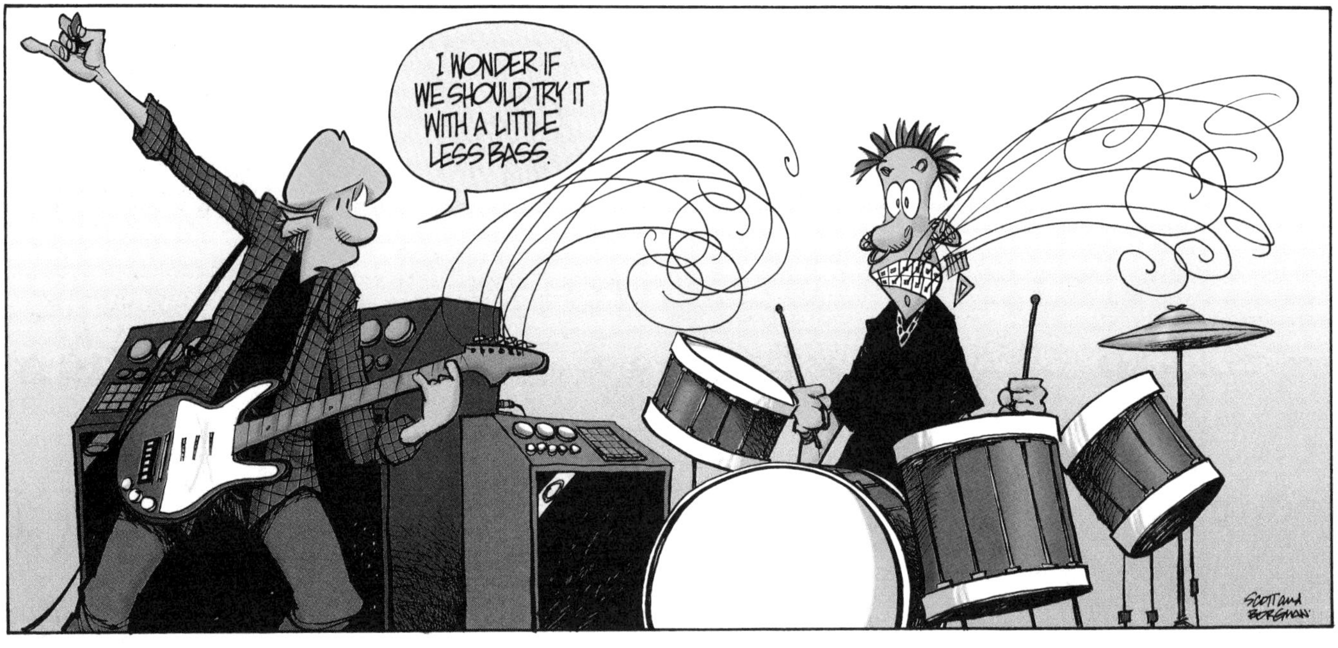
I WONDER IF WE SHOULD TRY IT WITH A LITTLE LESS BASS.
SCOTT and BORGMAN

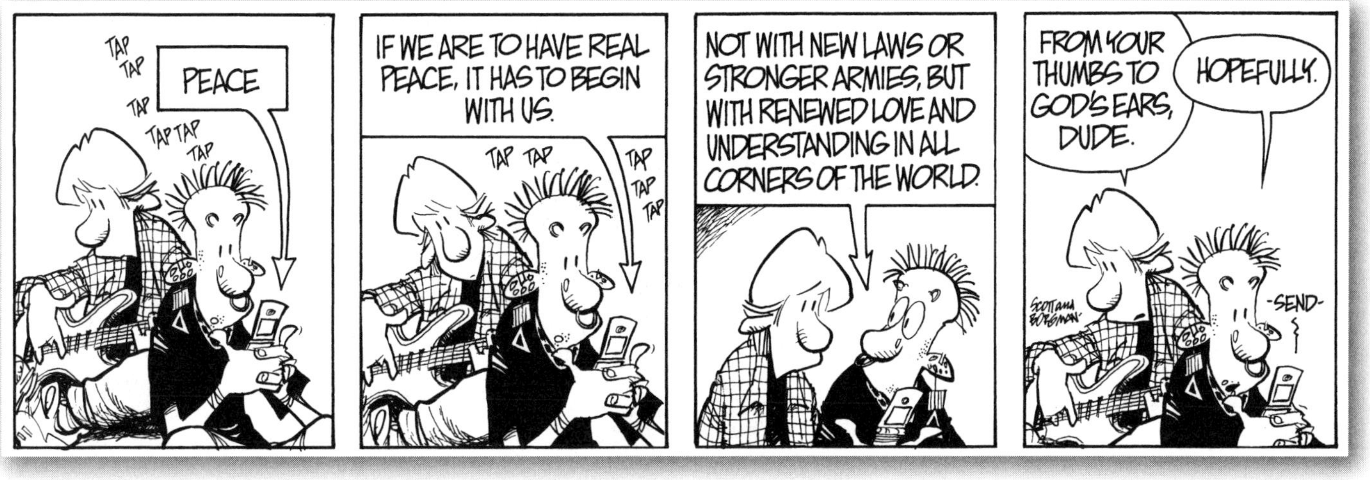
TAP TAP
PEACE
TAP
TAP TAP
TAP
IF WE ARE TO HAVE REAL PEACE, IT HAS TO BEGIN WITH US.
TAP TAP
TAP TAP TAP
NOT WITH NEW LAWS OR STRONGER ARMIES, BUT WITH RENEWED LOVE AND UNDERSTANDING IN ALL CORNERS OF THE WORLD.
FROM YOUR THUMBS TO GOD'S EARS, DUDE.
HOPEFULLY.
-SEND-
SCOTT and BORGMAN

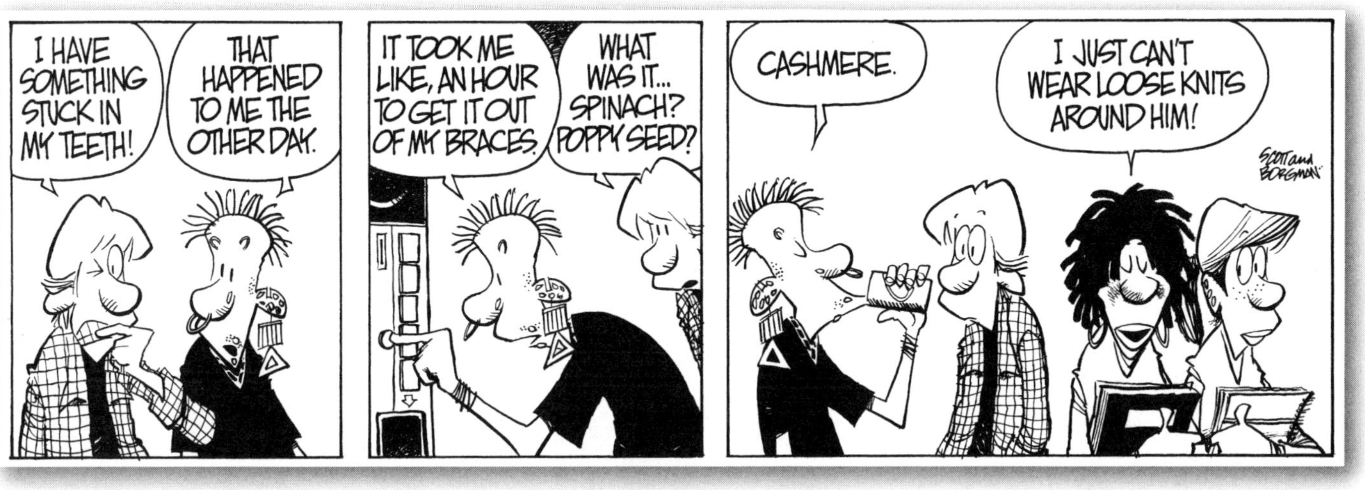
I HAVE SOMETHING STUCK IN MY TEETH!
THAT HAPPENED TO ME THE OTHER DAY.
IT TOOK ME LIKE, AN HOUR TO GET IT OUT OF MY BRACES.
WHAT WAS IT... SPINACH? POPPY SEED?
CASHMERE.
I JUST CAN'T WEAR LOOSE KNITS AROUND HIM!
SCOTT and BORGMAN

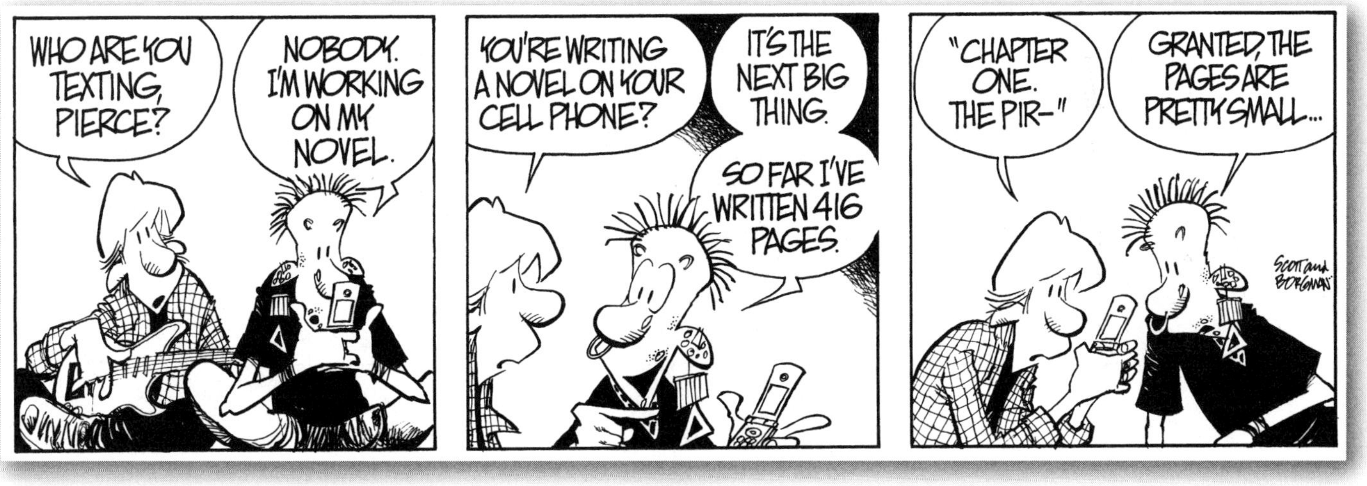
WHO ARE YOU TEXTING, PIERCE?
NOBODY. I'M WORKING ON MY NOVEL.
YOU'RE WRITING A NOVEL ON YOUR CELL PHONE?
IT'S THE NEXT BIG THING.
SO FAR I'VE WRITTEN 416 PAGES.
"CHAPTER ONE. THE PIR-"
GRANTED, THE PAGES ARE PRETTY SMALL...
SCOTT and BORGMAN

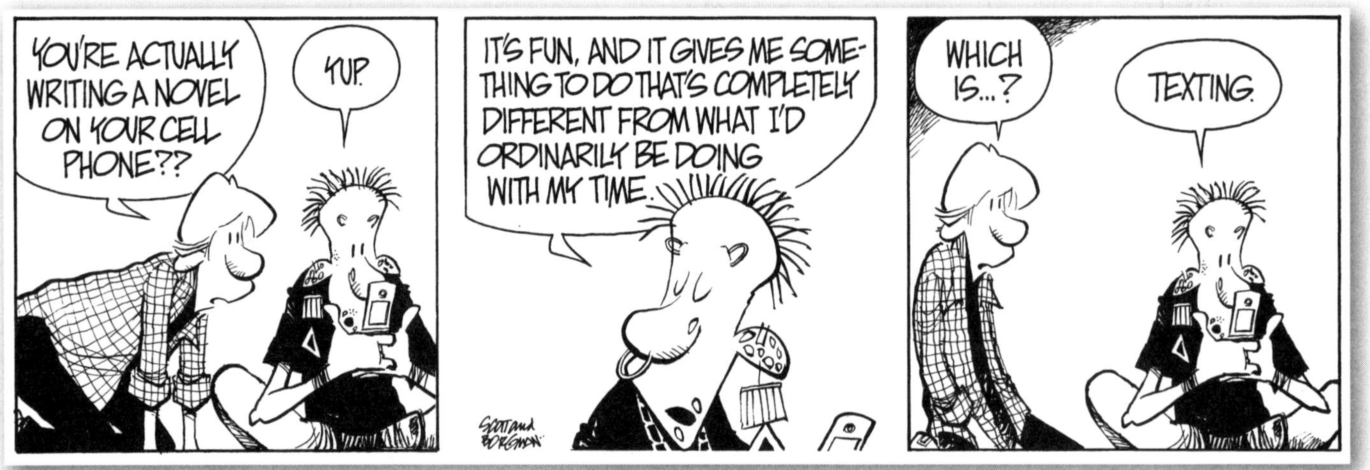
YOU'RE ACTUALLY WRITING A NOVEL ON YOUR CELL PHONE??
YUP.
IT'S FUN, AND IT GIVES ME SOMETHING TO DO THAT'S COMPLETELY DIFFERENT FROM WHAT I'D ORDINARILY BE DOING WITH MY TIME.
SCOTT AND BORGMAN
WHICH IS...?
TEXTING.

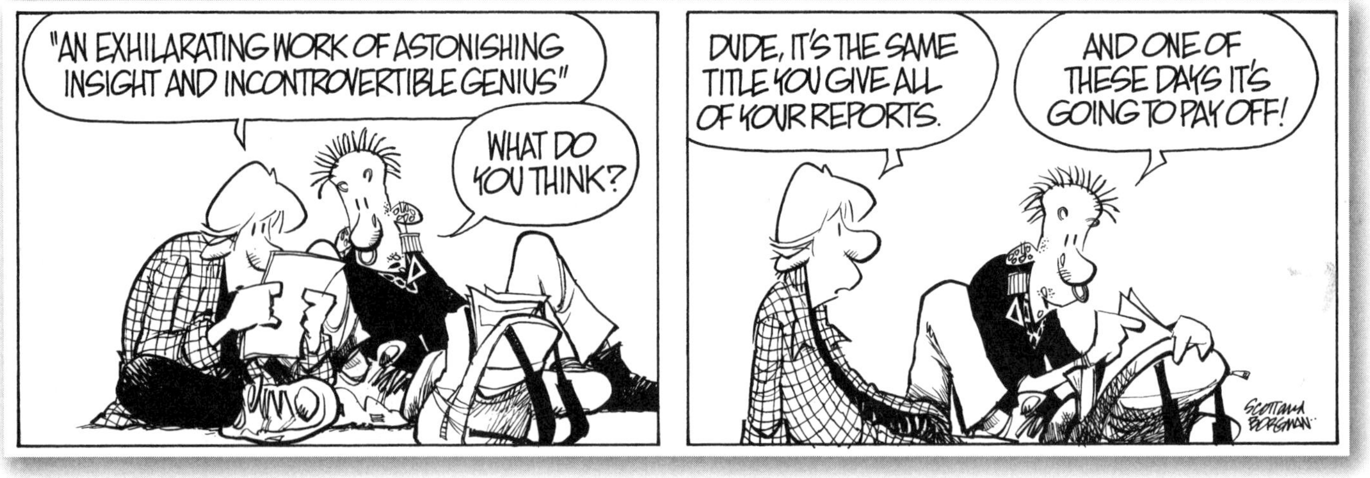
"AN EXHILARATING WORK OF ASTONISHING INSIGHT AND INCONTROVERTIBLE GENIUS"
WHAT DO YOU THINK?
DUDE, IT'S THE SAME TITLE YOU GIVE ALL OF YOUR REPORTS.
AND ONE OF THESE DAYS IT'S GOING TO PAY OFF!
SCOTT AND BORGMAN

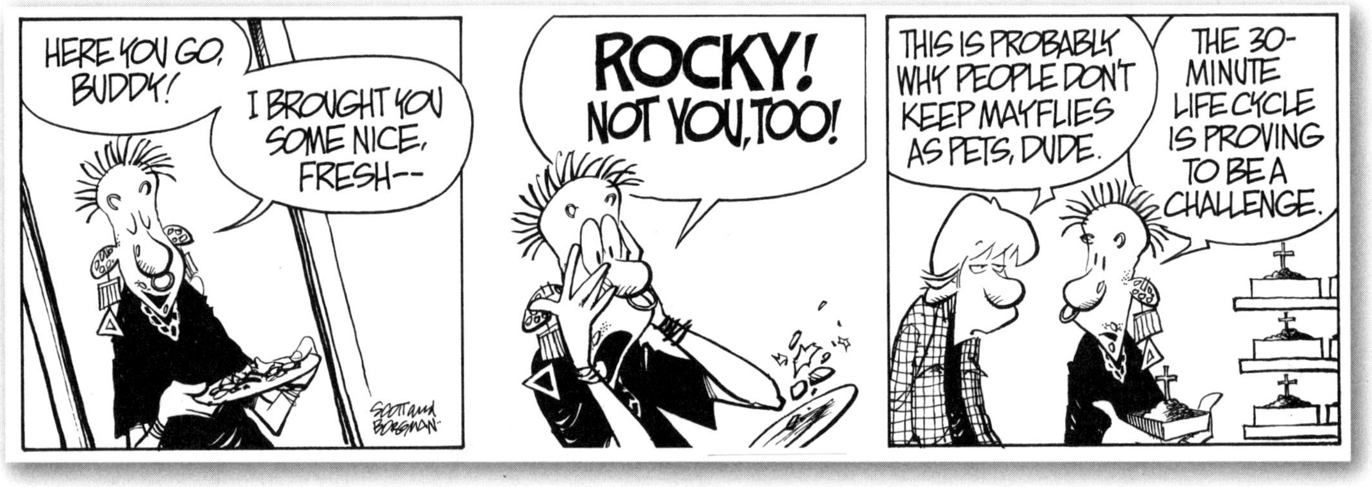
HERE YOU GO, BUDDY!
I BROUGHT YOU SOME NICE, FRESH--
SCOTT AND BORGMAN
ROCKY! NOT YOU, TOO!
THIS IS PROBABLY WHY PEOPLE DON'T KEEP MAYFLIES AS PETS, DUDE.
THE 30-MINUTE LIFE CYCLE IS PROVING TO BE A CHALLENGE.

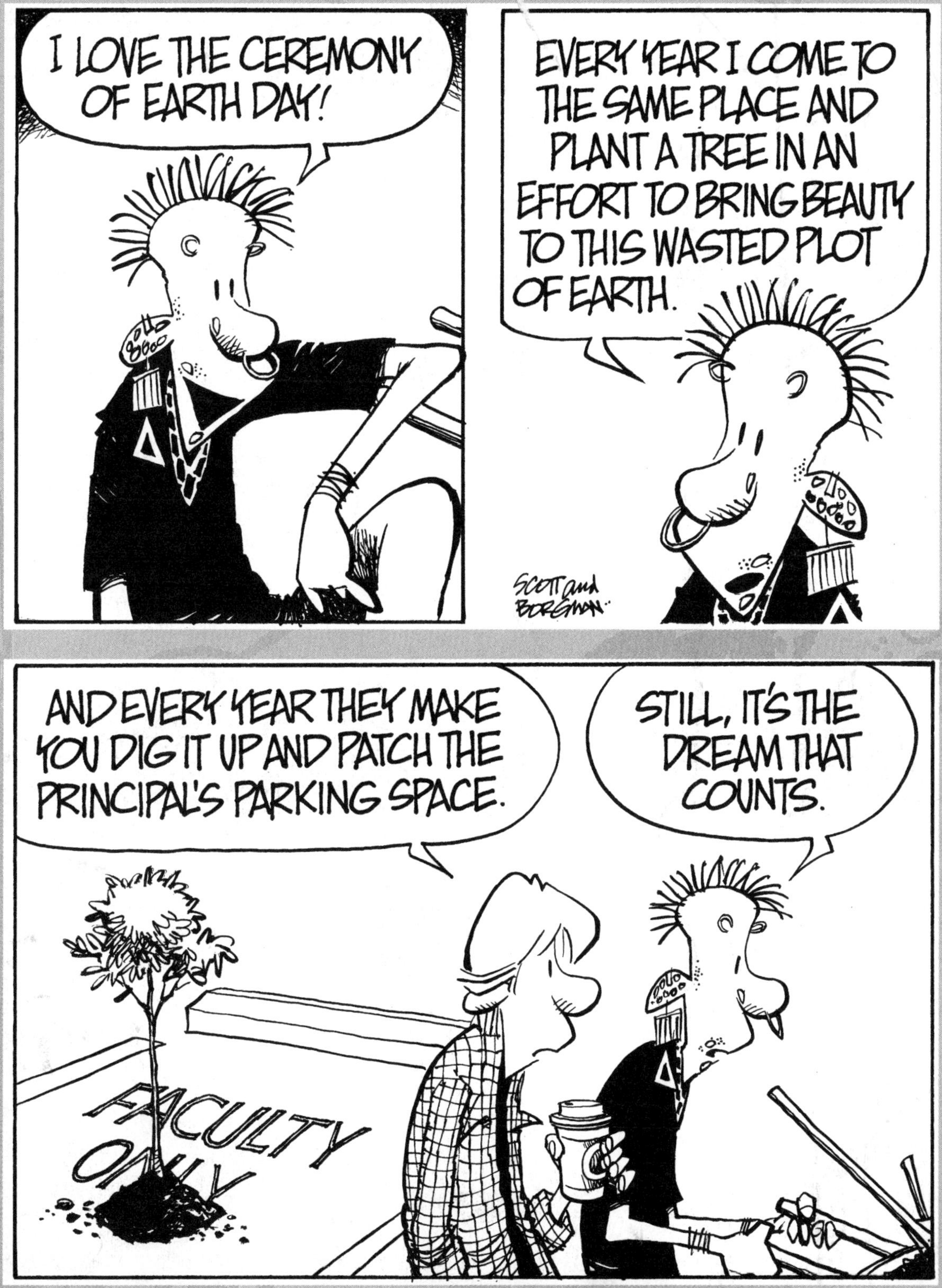
I LOVE THE CEREMONY OF EARTH DAY!
EVERY YEAR I COME TO THE SAME PLACE AND PLANT A TREE IN AN EFFORT TO BRING BEAUTY TO THIS WASTED PLOT OF EARTH.
SCOTT and BORGMAN
AND EVERY YEAR THEY MAKE YOU DIG IT UP AND PATCH THE PRINCIPAL'S PARKING SPACE.
STILL, IT'S THE DREAM THAT COUNTS.
FACULTY ONLY

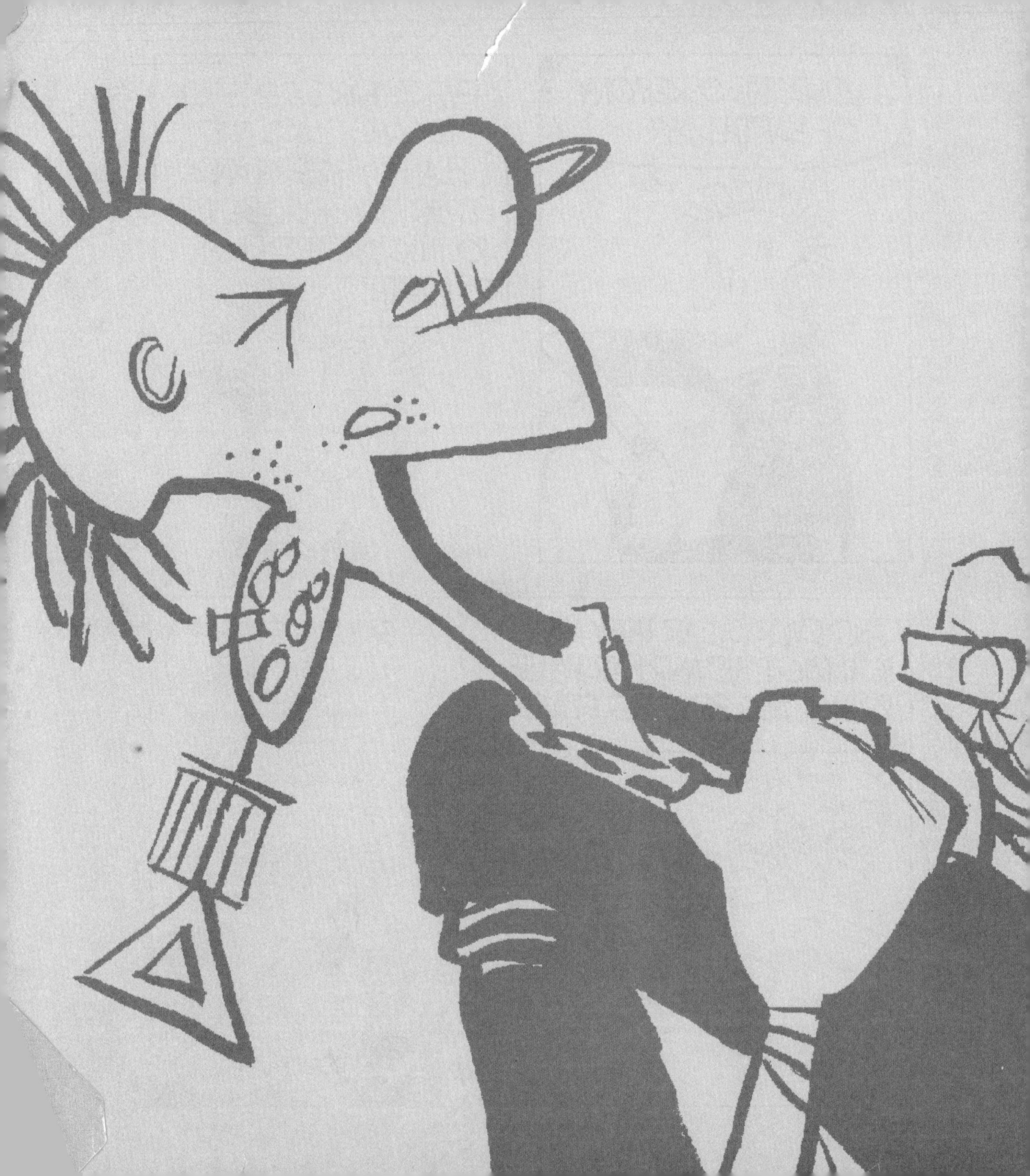